TRANSITIONAL JUSTICE AND DEVELOPMENT

This volume is the third in the *Advancing Transitional Justice Series,* a joint project of the International Center for Transitional Justice and the Social Science Research Council. Other volumes include:

Alexander Mayer-Rieckh and Pablo de Greiff, eds., *Justice as Prevention: Vetting Public Employees in Transitional Societies*

Ruth Rubio-Marín, ed., *What Happened to the Women? Gender and Reparations for Human Rights Violations*

ADVANCING TRANSITIONAL JUSTICE SERIES

TRANSITIONAL JUSTICE AND DEVELOPMENT

Making Connections

EDITED BY PABLO DE GREIFF AND ROGER DUTHIE,
INTERNATIONAL CENTER FOR TRANSITIONAL JUSTICE

SOCIAL SCIENCE RESEARCH COUNCIL • NEW YORK • 2009

INTERNATIONAL CENTER FOR TRANSITIONAL JUSTICE

The International Center for Transitional Justice (ICTJ) assists countries pursuing account-ability for past mass atrocity or human rights abuse. The Center works in societies emerging from repressive rule or armed conflict, as well as in established democracies where historical injustices or systemic abuse remain unresolved.

In order to promote justice, peace, and reconciliation, government officials and nongov-ernmental advocates are likely to consider a variety of transitional justice approaches includ-ing both judicial and nonjudicial responses to human rights crimes. The ICTJ assists in the development of integrated, comprehensive, and localized approaches to transitional justice comprising five key elements: prosecuting perpetrators, documenting and acknowledging violations through nonjudicial means such as truth commissions, reforming abusive institu-tions, providing reparations to victims, and facilitating reconciliation processes.

The field of transitional justice is varied and covers a range of disciplines, including law, public policy, forensics, economics, history, psychology, and the arts. The ICTJ works to develop a rich understanding of the field as a whole, and to identify issues that merit more in-depth research and analysis. Collaborating with colleagues in transitional societies and often commissioning outside studies, the Center targets its research to address the complex issues confronting policymakers and activists. Identifying and addressing the most important gaps in scholarship, it provides the benefit of comparative analysis to its staff and to practitioners worldwide.

SOCIAL SCIENCE RESEARCH COUNCIL

The Social Science Research Council (SSRC) leads innovation, builds interdisciplinary and international networks, and focuses research on important public issues. Independent and not-for-profit, the SSRC is guided by the belief that justice, prosperity, and democracy all require better understanding of complex social, cultural, economic, and political processes. The SSRC works with practitioners, policymakers, and academic researchers in all the social sciences, related professions, and the humanities and natural sciences. With partners around the world, the Council mobilizes existing knowledge for new problems, links research to practice and policy, strengthens individual and institutional capacities for learning, and enhances public access to information. The SSRC brings necessary knowledge to public action. A new publications initiative, represented here in this co-publication with the ICTJ, complements and enhances the SSRC's mission to disseminate necessary knowledge in innovative ways.

Published by the Social Science Research Council
Printed in the United States of America

Editorial production by the International Center
for Transitional Justice

Designed by Julie Fry

Cover photograph by Per-Anders Pettersson (Getty)

Library of Congress Cataloging-in-Publication Data

Transitional justice and development : making
    connections / edited by Pablo de Greiff and
    Roger Duthie.
    p.   cm.
ISBN 0-9790772-9-6
1. Transitional justice. 2. Economic development—
    Political aspects. 3. Developing countries—
    Politics and government. 4. Developing
    countries—Economic conditions. I. De Greiff,
    Pablo. II. Duthie, Roger. III. Social Science
    Research Council (U.S.)

JC571.T699 2009
338.0—dc22   2009018685

Contents

Contributors

Tony Addison is executive director of the Brooks World Poverty Institute (BWPI) at the University of Manchester, associate director of the Chronic Poverty Research Centre (CPRC), and professor of development studies, University of Manchester. He was previously deputy director of the United Nations University's World Institute for Development Economics Research (UNU-WIDER) in Helsinki. He has also held positions at the University of Warwick, the School of Oriental and African Studies (London University), and the Overseas Development Institute (ODI, London). He began his career as an ODI fellow in Tanzania, and is a graduate of the University of East Anglia and Birkbeck College, London University. His books include *From Conflict to Recovery in Africa* (Oxford University Press, 2003), *Making Peace Work: The Challenges of Economic and Social Reconstruction* (Palgrave Macmillan, 2008), and *Poverty Dynamics: A Cross-Disciplinary Perspective* (Oxford University Press, forthcoming). He was a lead author for *The Chronic Poverty Report 2008–09: Escaping Poverty Traps.*

Rolando Ames Cobián is a professor in the Department of Social Sciences and coordinator of Political Science and Government in the School of Social Sciences at the Universidad Católica del Perú. He has been dean of the School of Social Sciences on two occasions. Currently he is coordinating a research project on the promotion of democracy in Andean countries for the International Institute of Democracy and Electoral Assistance (IDEA). He was a Senator of the Republic from 1985 to 1990, and chaired the Congressional Committee in charge of investigating the massacre of prison inmates in 1986. From 2001 to 2003, he served as one of the twelve commissioners on Peru's Truth and Reconciliation Commission. He also served as a board member for the International Movement of Catholic Intellectuals. His areas of research are democracy in Latin America and social movements in relation to violence and political culture.

Pablo de Greiff is the director of research at the International Center for Transitional Justice (ICTJ) in New York. Born in Colombia, he graduated from Yale University (B.A.) and from Northwestern University (Ph.D.). Before joining the ICTJ he was associate professor (with tenure) in the Philosophy Department at the State University of New York at Buffalo, where he taught ethics and political theory. He was Laurance S. Rockefeller Fellow at the Center for Human Values, Princeton University, and held a concurrent fellowship from the National Endowment for the Humanities. De Greiff has published extensively on transitions to democracy, democratic theory, and the relationship between morality, politics, and law. He is the editor of nine books, including Jürgen Habermas's *The Inclusion of the Other* (MIT Press, 1998), and, in areas related to transitional justice, *Global Justice and Transnational Politics* (MIT Press, 2002) and *The Handbook of Reparations* (Oxford, 2006), among others. He authored the UN Office of the High Commissioner for Human Rights' (OHCHR) *Rule-of-Law Tools for Post-Conflict States: Reparations Programmes* (OHCHR, 2008).

Roger Duthie is a research associate at the International Center for Transitional Justice in New York, where his work has focused on transitional justice and development; disarmament, demobilization, and reintegration (DDR); and vetting. His publications include "Toward a Development-Sensitive Approach to Transitional Justice," *International Journal of Transitional Justice* 2, no. 3 (2008). He previously worked as a researcher, writer, and editor at KPMG; at the Carnegie Council on Ethics and International Affairs; and at Oxford University Press. He has an M.A. in international relations from Yale University and a B.A. in history with a concentration in international relations from Cornell University.

Emily E. Harwell is an independent consultant with nearly two decades' experience researching issues of resource conflict, ethnic identity, human rights, and postconflict peacebuilding in Indonesia, East Timor, Colombia, Paraguay, the United States, and Canada. She earned her Ph.D. in environmental anthropology at the Yale University School of Forestry and Environmental Studies, and her B.Sc. in ecology from the University of the South. She has published research on resource property and conflicts, natural resource extraction issues and human rights, ethnic violence, rural underdevelopment and international resource extraction markets, truth and reconciliation commissions, postconflict reintegration of ex-combatants, and resource management reform. She has consulted for Human Rights Watch, the International Crisis Group, the Center for International Forestry Research, the Center for International Environmental Law, the UNDP, and the International Center for Transitional Justice, and has taught environmental politics and anthropology of development at Yale University, George Mason University, and Middlebury College.

Chris Huggins is a researcher specializing in the relationships between land rights, violent conflict, and postconflict development, particularly in Africa. He has worked in Eastern and Central Africa since 1998 for several major nongovernmental organizations, most recently as Rwanda researcher for Human Rights Watch. He is currently working as a freelance consultant. He was coeditor of *From the Ground Up: Land Rights, Conflict and Peace in Sub-Saharan Africa* (ACTS Press / ISS, 2005), and has recently contributed book chapters on indigenous land rights in Rwanda (for a forthcoming publication by Forest Peoples Programme), and on land in refugee and IDP return in the Great Lakes Region (for a forthcoming publication by the Humanitarian Policy Group of the Overseas Development Institute), and is currently cowriting a textbook/anthology on housing, land, and property rights in postconflict contexts.

Philippe Le Billon is associate professor at the University of British Columbia (UBC) with the Department of Geography and the Liu Institute for Global Issues. Before joining UBC, he was a research associate with the Overseas Development Institute (ODI) and the International Institute for Strategic Studies (IISS), having previously worked on humanitarian and resource management issues in Angola, Cambodia, Sierra Leone, and the former Yugoslavia. His research interests include the political economy of war and reconstruction, geographies of violence, governance of extractive sectors, and corruption. His publications include *Fuelling War: Natural Resources and Armed Conflict*, Adelphi Paper 373 (London: Routledge / IISS, 2005).

Marcus Lenzen is a conflict programme specialist with the United Nations Development Programme's (UNDP) Bureau for Crisis Prevention and Recovery (BCPR). He has worked on a range of issues related to conflict prevention and recovery and has served for several years as the bureau's focal point for transitional justice. He is currently cochairing a task force that is taking stock of and upgrading the UNDP's approach to conflict-sensitive development. Since joining the UNDP in 2004, Lenzen has worked on assessments and program development support to a wide range of UNDP country offices on conflict and armed violence prevention, transitional justice, community security, and social cohesion. Countries he has worked on include Afghanistan, Timor-Leste, Liberia, Niger, Tanzania, Guatemala, El Salvador, Bosnia-Herzegovina, Serbia, and Croatia. Prior to joining the UNDP, he worked on transitional justice and conflict transformation with the German Development Service in Peru and Guatemala, where he advised human rights organizations working with the Peruvian Truth and Reconciliation Commission. A political scientist and development specialist, he holds master's degrees from the London School of Economics and Political Science and the University of Münster, Germany.

Alexander Mayer-Rieckh is an expert in postconflict public sector reform. From 2003 to 2008, he was director of the Security System Reform Program at the International Center for Transitional Justice. Mayer-Rieckh worked for the United Nations in Geneva, Rwanda, Ethiopia and Eritrea, and East Timor; he was also the chief of the Human Rights Office of the UN Mission in Bosnia and Herzegovina. In 2003, he was the recipient of a fellowship at the Center for Civil and Human Rights, University of Notre Dame Law School, where he conducted research on vetting of public employees in transitional contexts. His publications include "The United Nations and East Timor: From Self-Determination to State-Building," *International Peacekeeping* 12, no.1 (Spring 2005) (coauthored with Ian Martin), and *Justice as Prevention: Vetting Public Employees in Transitional Societies* (New York: Social Science Research Council, 2007) (coedited with Pablo de Greiff). Mr. Mayer-Rieckh obtained his B.A. in philosophy at the Hochschule für Philosophie in Munich, his M.Div. at the Weston School of Theology in Cambridge, Massachusetts, and his Masters in Law at the Universities of Vienna and Salzburg.

Muna B. Ndulo is professor of law and director of the Institute for African Development at Cornell University. He is an authority on African legal systems, human rights, constitutions, election monitoring, international development, and legal aspects of foreign investments in developing countries. After receiving his LL.B. from the University of Zambia and LL.M. from Harvard Law School, Dr. Ndulo was public prosecutor for the Zambian Ministry of Legal Affairs. He was dean of the University of Zambia School of Law, and from 1986 to 1996 served the United Nations Commission for International Trade Law. From 1992 to 1994 he was political adviser to the UN Mission in South Africa. He joined Cornell Law School's faculty in 1996, and has continued to advise UN Missions in East Timor and Kosovo. He teaches international organizations and human rights institutions, the legal aspects of foreign investment in developing countries, and the common law and African legal systems. His publications include *Security, Reconstruction and Reconciliation: When the Wars End* (ed.) (University of London Press, 2007), and *Democratic Reform in Africa: Taking Stock of Its Impact on Governance and Poverty Alleviation* (James Currey Publisher and Ohio University Press, 2006).

Katharine Orlovsky is a legal officer for the Women's Initiatives for Gender Justice, an international human rights organization advocating for gender-inclusive justice and working toward an effective and independent International Criminal Court. She has previously worked or consulted for a number of international NGOs, including the International Center for Transitional Justice, where she organized workshops in Phnom Penh on the legacy of the Extraordinary Chambers in the Courts of Cambodia; the Legal Section of the Hague Office of the Coalition for the International Criminal Court; the International Justice Program at Human Rights Watch in the Brussels Office, where she contributed to the report *Courting History: The Landmark International Criminal Court's First Years*; and the International Justice Project at the International Secretariat of Amnesty International. She has an LL.M. from the School of Oriental and African Studies, University of London, a J.D. from the University of California Hastings College of the Law, and a B.A. from Columbia University.

Félix Reátegui is a sociologist and coordinator of the Research Unit of the Institute of Democracy and Human Rights of the Pontificia Universidad Católica del Perú, where he is also professor of sociological theory and of political sociology in the Department of Social Sciences. He worked in the Truth and Reconciliation Commission of Peru (2001–2003) as technical coordinator of the Final Report Unit. Since 2004, he has been a consultant with the International Center for Transitional Justice on projects related to truth-seeking and memory, mainly in Colombia.

Naomi Roht-Arriaza is a professor of law at the University of California, Hastings College of Law in San Francisco. She teaches international human rights, law and development law, and torts. She graduated from Boalt Hall in 1990, and clerked for Judge James Browning of the Ninth Circuit Court of Appeals. She was the first Steven Riesenfeld Fellow in International Law at Boalt. Roht-Arriaza is the author of *The Pinochet Effect: Transnational Justice in the Age of Human Rights* (University of Pennsylvania Press, 2004), the editor of *Impunity and Human Rights in International Law and Practice* (Oxford University Press, 1995), and coeditor of *Transitional Justice in the Twenty-First Century: Beyond Truth vs. Justice* (Cambridge University Press, 2005), as well as numerous law review articles and book chapters on transitional justice and reparations. She was involved with the Victims' Rights Caucus and was an NGO delegate to the 1998 Rome Conference on the International Criminal Court. She serves on the advisory boards of a number of human rights–related groups.

Acknowledgments

This book is the result of the collaboration and support of numerous institutions and individuals, and we are happy to acknowledge and give thanks to all involved. We would like in particular to express our deep gratitude to the German Federal Ministry for Economic Cooperation and Development (BMZ), which provided the funding for this research project and hosted two important project meetings; the Swiss Federal Department of Foreign Affairs (FDFA), which provided the funding and organizational support for a productive meeting of authors; and the Working Group on Development and Peace (FriEnt) for its valuable collaboration and support of the project.

Special thanks go to the members of the project's advisory group of experts: Mô Bleeker, Tilman Brück, David Crocker, Bernd Gruschinski, Marcus Lenzen, Henning Plate, M. G. Quibria, Sylvia Servaes, Elin Skaar, George Wachira, and Natascha Zupan; to the contributors to the volume; to those who participated in the project's research and/or meetings, including Gary Belkin, Mark Drumbl, Julia Paulson, and Jonathan Sisson; and to Undine Kayser-Whande, for reviewing and providing valuable comments on most of the project papers. At the International Center for Transitional Justice (ICTJ), our gratitude is owed to the institution as a whole, but in particular to Paige Arthur, Lizzie Goodfriend, Ana Patel, and Debbie Sharnak, and interns Maya Karwande and Leah Malone.

Pablo de Greiff and Roger Duthie
New York, April 2009

Introduction

Roger Duthie

Two decades into its existence as a field, transitional justice is at a stage where fundamental questions are being asked about it—about its meaning, the type of justice it involves, its objectives, its precise measures and activities, how it works, its impact, its appropriateness in certain contexts, its boundaries, and its relationship to other fields. More than fifty years after its emergence, such questions have long been asked about the much broader field of development. This book examines the relationship between the field of transitional justice and the field of development. As one of the first efforts to address this relationship, it surely opens up many issues that will require further thought, experience, and research, but it does seek to significantly advance the emerging discussion of the topic. Importantly, by addressing the intersection of the two fields, the book responds to some of the difficult questions listed above from the perspectives of both transitional justice and development.

Transitional Justice and Development presents the results of a two-year research project conducted by the International Center for Transitional Justice (ICTJ) in cooperation with its partners the German Federal Ministry for Economic Cooperation and Development (BMZ), the Swiss Federal Department of Foreign Affairs (FDFA), and the Working Group on Development and Peace (FriEnt). The contributors to the volume include diverse experts and practitioners in transitional justice, international development, development economics, sociology, political science, institutional reform, law, natural resources, and land. The project brought into dialogue those who often work alongside each other in transitional and developing societies, but not always together in providing a coherent response to the interconnected concerns of development and justice. Hopefully this dialogue will continue. Hopefully it will contribute to a more coherent response. I begin here with a brief discussion of definitions and motivation for the project, as well as a brief overview of the chapters to follow.

DEFINITIONS

The project operated without expecting or forcing consensus among participants as to definitions. Nevertheless, the range of conceptions used does exhibit commonalities. So, despite differences, by "transitional justice" people in the project refer to measures to redress massive human rights abuses, which typically include criminal prosecutions, truth-telling, reparations, and certain kinds of institutional reform. But the list of measures varies, as does the relative importance of each and, particularly, the point of implementing them. Defining the range of "development" is much harder, among other factors because there is no set of measures that lead to an overlap among practitioners. But, nevertheless, the term is used typically to refer to processes whose most general aim is to improve the socioeconomic conditions of people. During its long history, the field has sprawled, and now it is seen to include in its purview not just measures to improve economic growth and distribution, but also measures that are seen to be related to the social, institutional, and political factors that could impinge on economic well-being. The participants in this project largely share the tendency to adopt expanded, comprehensive conceptions of development, but that does not mean they converge on a particular one.

Different conceptions of development end up being examined, including, for example, "human development," espoused by the United Nations Development Programme (UNDP) and closely related to Amartya Sen's approach based on capabilities—that is, the choice and opportunity that people have to exercise their reasoned agency.[1] Human development includes but is not limited to economic development. Participants also refer to the "rights-based approach to development," which, as explained by Peter Uvin, differs from other approaches to development in that it is "about helping people realize claims to rights, not providing them with charity," and in that it involves "the realization that the process by which development aims are pursued should itself respect and fulfill human rights."[2] As is discussed throughout this book, human development and the rights-based approach to development are useful for articulating links between transitional justice and development because the focus on capabilities, human rights claims, and processes that respect human rights allow us to examine not just direct links but also the ways in which the objectives of the two fields converge.

MOTIVATION

There are important reasons for thinking about the ways in which transitional justice and development may relate to each other. The majority of armed conflicts today occur in countries at low levels of development. Poverty, inequality, and underdevelopment may not in themselves cause armed conflict and human rights abuses, but they can be contributing or enabling factors.[3] Moreover, armed conflict and authoritarianism, and the humanitarian disasters and massive human rights abuses that often accompany them, can have an immensely negative and long-lasting impact on development.[4] As a result, transitional justice is often pursued in a context of severely underdeveloped economic and social institutions, widespread scarcity of resources, and myriad competing needs. At the same time, justice initiatives come with a number of costs, and so decision-makers in transitional societies face dilemmas about where to allocate available resources. In this context, it makes a great deal of sense to think about the relationship between transitional justice and development.[5]

There is, indeed, growing attention to the issue. To begin with, a number of voices—within the general field of human rights and of transitional justice in particular—have called for transitional justice measures to engage not just violations of civil and political rights, but also economic, social, and cultural rights, and economic crimes, understood generally to be important from a development perspective. The former UN High Commissioner for Human Rights, Louise Arbour, for example, has argued for integrating economic, social, and cultural rights into the transitional justice framework, thereby making "the gigantic leap that would allow justice, in its full sense, to make the contribution that it should to societies in transition."[6] In 2008, the *International Journal of Transitional Justice* devoted a special issue to the topic of transitional justice and development, in which a number of contributors argued for the expansion of the purview of transitional justice to include development issues. Zinaida Miller, for example, examines the potential costs for transitional societies if transitional justice institutions continue to neglect the economic roots and consequences of conflict, the absence of socioeconomic redistribution, and government development plans. The divorce of development strategies from transitional justice, she argues, "allows a myth to be formed that the origins of conflict are political or ethnic rather than economic or resource based. It suggests that inequality is a question of time or development rather than the entrenched ideology of elites, as well as that the need to memorialize the past does not require the narration of past economic oppression." Ruben Carranza, in the same issue, contends that an impunity gap results when transitional justice measures ignore accountability for large-scale corruption and economic crimes, and that "addressing poverty and social inequality must be regarded as among the strategic goals of any transitional justice undertaking."[7] Others have echoed these arguments, particularly concerning truth commissions.[8]

Transitional justice, it has also been pointed out, may impact development in some ways even if it maintains a focus on violations of civil and political rights, without explicitly addressing development issues or seeking development outcomes. Jane Alexander, for example, suggests that transitional justice can have a positive impact on development through direct effect and by helping to create the conditions that may facilitate development. First, through such measures as individual and collective reparations, property restitution, rehabilitation, and reintegrating victims and perpetrators, transitional justice measures may alleviate marginalization, exclusion, and vulnerability by bringing people and groups into the economy, recognizing and empowering them as citizens, and perhaps generating economic activity. Second, four key conditions—political and social stability; safety, security, and access to justice; conflict prevention; and social and economic justice—that can foster development may be facilitated by transitional justice objectives, such as addressing grievances, reconciling groups, and restoring trust in institutions.[9] At the same time, however, concern has been expressed that transitional justice measures may in fact have a negative impact on development by, for instance, diverting resources away from it.[10]

Others have suggested that transitional justice practitioners adopt or learn from certain development strategies, including their associated benefits and challenges. A "participatory approach" is one example that many in the transitional justice field have looked toward. "If a key task today is to consider what principles might underpin a 'bottom-up,' participatory approach to transitional justice," write Patricia Lundy and Mark McGovern, "there are many lessons to be learnt from how such strategies towards development emerged, what key concepts have underwritten this process, and some of the problems and issues that have arisen with their implementation."[11] The key concepts of this approach—participation, empowerment, and community-based processes—are all relevant to transitional justice, but so too are the potential risks: romanticization and co-option, which involve the imposition of external agendas and the denial of power dynamics within civil society.[12] Etelle Higonnet makes the same point with regard to prosecution efforts. "Post-atrocity legal structures," she argues, "must incorporate elements of local justice and culture or, at the very least, be sensitive to realities and norms on the ground. A useful parallel to draw here is the near universal consensus in development philosophy that local involvement is critical to sustainable long-term development."[13]

The ways in which development may facilitate or be a precondition for the pursuit of transitional justice have also been highlighted. Development, for example, may make more resources and capacity available to invest in justice efforts. A country's level of development does not predict or determine the extent to which it will pursue transitional justice, but it can act as both a precondition for and a constraint on the pursuit of justice. In other words, poorer countries may be less able to afford justice than richer ones, and countries with weaker institutions may be less capable of implementing justice measures than those with stronger ones. Such constraints are often exacerbated by the damaging effects of the conflict itself. As Jon Elster puts it, one "factor that may explain low levels of retribution as well as reparation is the scarcity of money and qualified personnel often found in periods of transition."[14] Tonya Putnam has argued that most transitional justice "presupposes the existence of an entire set of functioning institutions to investigate, prosecute, and punish individuals who commit human rights violations. In societies emerging from civil wars, such institutions are normally weak or nonexistent, if indeed they existed beforehand."[15] Indeed, one empirical study shows that the economic health of a country may in fact affect the decision to pursue transitional justice.[16]

In this way, development cooperation, such as that which supports security and justice institutions, may indirectly facilitate transitional justice. At the same time, development cooperation, in the form of funding and technical assistance, can be directed toward transitional justice measures themselves. Indeed, one recent study shows that 5 percent of development aid to Rwanda and Guatemala between 1995 and 2005 was in the form of assistance to transitional justice initiatives (although more than half of this went to security sector reform [SSR] broadly defined).[17] At a 2007 conference on donor strategies for transitional justice, organized by the ICTJ and the UK Department for International Development (DFID), participants concluded that donors make "many contributions to the field of transitional justice," the most important being in the areas of "capacity building, strengthening of international law, integrating local actors into internationally supported institutions, and increasing the understanding of the impact of transitional justice."[18]

Finally, there are those who propose that transitional justice and development have the potential to reinforce each other in pursuit of shared long-term goals—goals that involve transforming society. If one or the other type of initiative is absent, these shared objectives may be undermined. If reconciliation of individuals, groups, and society is among the goals of transitional justice measures, for example, Alex Boraine suggests that "reconciliation without economic justice is cheap and spurious."[19] Similarly, Rama Mani argues that effective peacebuilding efforts must incorporate three dimensions of justice—legal, rectificatory, and distributive—which, she says, reinforce each other. She points to South Africa and Rwanda as examples of countries in which justice will remain incomplete in the eyes of citizens until the socioeconomic inequalities that were a factor in those conflicts are redressed.[20] In 2007, at the major conference "Building a Future on Peace and Justice" in Nuremberg, a FriEnt-organized workshop explored "how development work and transitional justice mechanisms can mutually reinforce the process of overcoming socioeconomic as well as political inequalities and contribute to sustainable peace and justice."[21] The "transformative" potential of both transitional justice and post-conflict development work is emphasized by experts in both fields.[22]

THE RESEARCH

Discussions about some of the general but very important questions concerning the relationship between the two fields were, then, beginning to emerge, although still in a fragmented and piecemeal way. This project was initially intended to provide an occasion for thinking about these issues in a systematic way, and to move the discussion forward in significant ways along different dimensions. The project sought to collect and organize information (facts, data) about past experience; to identify approaches and strategies that ought to be taken in the future; to explore the potential for greater coordination and mutual reinforcement between the fields; to identify and to warn of potential tensions and risks; and to articulate the convergence of objectives—using such concepts as trust, recognition, the rule of law, governance, reconciliation, prevention, vulnerability, equality, security, transformation, social reintegration, and citizenship—and how this helps to provide guidance and to shape policy. These are among the issues addressed by the essays in this volume.

The first three chapters of the book explore the links between transitional justice and development at a conceptual level, each taking a different starting point—namely, transitional justice, development, and political economy. In many ways these chapters are meant to be read together. In chapter one, Pablo de Greiff provides a broad conceptual framework for thinking about how transitional justice and development relate to each other. He begins by articulating the reasons why massive human rights violations may be thought to matter from a development perspective, and then explores ways in which transitional justice measures may contribute to development efforts both directly and indirectly. The main focus of his chapter is on the indirect links, the ways in which transitional justice measures contribute to development. According to de Greiff, transitional justice measures are norm affirming, and as such provide recognition to victims, promote civic trust, and make a contribution to the democratic rule of law. In these ways, they help redress some of the obstacles to development left by massive human rights abuses in their wake, obstacles that include, precisely, "adverse terms of recognition," weak bonds of trust, and fragile or nonexistent regimes of rights. Framing the same argument in terms of a concept that has become crucial for development work, de Greiff argues that perhaps the most significant contribution transitional justice can make to development is to strengthen the norms that underlie participatory citizenship. Transitional justice, then, can contribute to development if seen as an instrument of social integration.

This is followed by chapter two, in which Marcus Lenzen also makes the case for why dealing with past abuses is important for development actors in pursuit of development goals, but building his argument from the particular perspectives of the peacebuilding arena and the rights-based approach to development. Development has an important role to play, he contends, in fostering institutions that are able to take on justice issues seriously and sustainably. In the third chapter, Tony Addison examines the political economy of transitions from authoritarianism. In particular, he looks at the economic legacies of authoritarianism—unproductive expenditures, undisciplined rent seeking, and macroeconomic destabilization—and their implications for democratization and transitional justice. He also identifies potential synergies between transitional justice and development in terms of resources, priorities, social protection, and integration in the global economy.

The next set of papers examines the links between particular transitional justice measures and development. In chapter four, Rolando Ames Cobián and Félix Reátegui argue that transitional justice and development have their own respective spheres of action, and that the most significant convergence between them is not in immediate tasks but in their ultimate shared objective of facilitating systemic social transformation. Truth commissions, they contend, as highly public and political actors in periods of transition, can, through their discourse and action, draw attention to the need for a long-term process of change, and mobilize support behind it.

In chapter five, Naomi Roht-Arriaza and Katharine Orlovsky articulate both the convergence of reparations and development in the area of social reintegration and the many potential synergies between reparations programs and capabilities-based, bottom-up development efforts. Reparations cannot and should not replace development, the authors argue, but they can be designed and implemented in such a way as to increase trust and rights possession among victims, thereby reinforcing long-term relations between the state and its citizens.

Chapters six and seven address two types of institutional reform that relate in important ways to both transitional justice and development. First, Alexander Mayer-Rieckh and Roger Duthie argue that SSR and transitional justice can be understood to complement each other in ways that have received little attention so far, and that bringing in a substantive and direct focus on past abuses can make a useful contribution both at the conceptual and at the practical level to the development approach to SSR. Development-focused SSR is a critical tool in the prevention of the recurrence of widespread and serious abuses—an important objective of transitional justice—and it is a directly enabling factor for certain transitional justice measures. At the same time, a justice-sensitive approach may have the potential to enhance the developmental impact of SSR by improving the legitimacy of security institutions and promoting the inclusion of citizens. In the following chapter, Muna Ndulo and Roger Duthie examine the links between judicial reform, development, and transitional justice measures, particularly criminal prosecutions. There is potential, they suggest, for these three interrelated notions to be mutually reinforcing, and that practitioners working in the different areas can learn from each other as they face similar challenges in terms of capacity and resources, political contexts, participatory processes, legitimacy of institutions, and overall coherence.

The final two chapters explore the ways in which transitional justice and development can connect with each other through a focus on specific development-related issues. In chapter eight, Emily Harwell and Philippe Le Billon discuss the role that natural resources play in armed conflict and authoritarianism, and argue for addressing the multidimensional concept of vulnerability as it relates to natural resources as a common aim of both transitional justice and development. They propose a modest expansion of the transitional justice mandate to engage natural resource issues, and, more broadly, specific steps to build both an externally coherent response to natural resources among transitional justice and development actors and an internally coherent response from the development community. In chapter nine, Chris Huggins provides a detailed look at how land relates to both development and conflict, particularly in times of transition and with regard to massive human rights abuses. Drawing on the experiences of specific countries, he suggests several ways in which transitional justice measures may be incorporated into a broader and more effective program of land tenure reform in transitional societies, taking note also of the risks involved in doing so.

The results of this research provide ample grounds for thinking that it is important for transitional justice and development practitioners and scholars alike to improve their dialogue and to explore ways of maximizing the synergies between the two fields, without necessarily eroding all boundaries between them. Certainly, there is a lot of room for improvement at every level, for thus far the fields, academically and in practice, have proceeded largely isolated from one another. These papers provide initial testimony of the potential of increased communication.

NOTES

1   See Amartya Sen, *Development as Freedom* (New York: Knopf, 1999). The United Nations Development Programme (UNDP) defines human development as "a process of enlarging people's choices. The most critical ones are to lead a long and healthy life, to be educated, and to enjoy a decent standard of living. Additional choices include political freedom, guaranteed human rights and self-respect." United Nations Development Programme (UNDP), *Human Development Report* (New York: UNDP, 1990), 10.

2   Peter Uvin, *Human Rights and Development* (Bloomfield, CT: Kumarian Press, 2004), 175–76.

3   See, e.g., Cynthia J. Arnson and I. William Zartman, eds., *Rethinking the Economics of War: The Intersection of Need, Creed, and Greed* (Baltimore: The Johns Hopkins University Press, 2005); Karen Ballentine and Jake Sherman, eds., *The Political Economy of Armed Conflict: Beyond Greed and Grievance* (Boulder: Lynne Rienner, 2003); and Wayne Nafziger, Frances Stewart, and Raimo Väyrynen, eds., *War, Hunger, and Displacement: The Origins of Humanitarian Emergencies* (Oxford: Oxford University Press, 2000).

4   See, e.g., Paul Collier et al., *Breaking the Conflict Trap: Civil War and Development Policy* (Washington, DC: World Bank, 2003).

5   Roger Duthie, "Toward a Development-Sensitive Approach to Transitional Justice," *International Journal of Transitional Justice* 2, no. 3 (2008): 292–309.

6   Louise Arbour, "Economic and Social Justice for Societies in Transition" (Second Annual Transitional Justice Lecture hosted by the Center for Human Rights and Global Justice at New York University School of Law and by the ICTJ, October 25, 2006).

7   Zinaida Miller, "Effects of Invisibility: In Search of the 'Economic' in Transitional Justice," *International Journal of Transitional Justice* 2, no. 3 (2008): 267–68; and Ruben Carranza, "Plunder and Pain: Should Transitional Justice Engage with Corruption and Economic Crimes?" *International Journal of Transitional Justice* 2, no. 3 (2008): 329.

8   See, e.g., Jane Alexander, "A Scoping Study of Transitional Justice and Poverty Reduction: Final Report," prepared for the UK Department for International Development (DFID), January 2003; James Cockayne, "Operation Helpem Fren: Solomon Islands, Transitional Justice, and the Silence of Contemporary Legal Pathologies on Questions of Distributive Justice," Center for Human Rights and Global Justice Working Paper, Transitional Justice Series, No. 3, 2004, NYU School of Law; and on truth commissions, in particular, James L. Cavallaro and Sebastian Albuja, "The Lost Agenda: Economic Crimes and Truth Commissions in Latin America and Beyond," in *Transitional Justice from Below: Grassroots Activism and the Struggle for Change*, ed. Kieran McEvoy and Lorna McGregor (Oxford: Hart Publishing, 2008).

9   Alexander, "A Scoping Study," 3, 49–53.

10   See, for instance, Peter J. Boettke and Christopher J. Coyne, "The Political Economy of Forgiveness: The Necessity of Post-Atrocity Reconciliation," *Society* 44, no. 2 (2007): 53–59; and Helena Cobban, "Helena Cobban Replies," Letters, *Foreign Policy* (May/June 2006): 8–10.

11   Patricia Lundy and Mark McGovern, "The Role of Community in Transitional Justice," in *Transitional Justice from Below*, 108.

12   Ibid., 110–12. Lundy and McGovern point to the Ardoyne Commemoration Project in Belfast, Northern Ireland, and the Recovery of Memory's (REMHI) Nunca Mas initiative in Guatemala as examples of transitional justice efforts influenced by participatory theory as it emerged from the field of development.

13   Etelle R. Higonnet, "Restructuring Hybrid Courts: Local Empowerment and National Criminal Justice Reform," *Arizona Journal of International and Comparative Law* 23, no. 2 (2006): 360. See also Dustin N. Sharp, "Prosecutions, Development, and Justice: The Trial of Hissein Habré," *Harvard Human Rights Journal* 16 (2003): 147–78.

14   Jon Elster, "Introduction," in Jon Elster, ed., *Retribution and Reparation in the Transition to Democracy* (Cambridge: Cambridge University Press, 2006), 10. Pablo de Greiff makes the point in relation to massive reparations programs in "Reparations and Development," in *Transitional Justice and Human Security*, ed. Alex Boraine and Sue Valentine (Cape Town: International Center for Transitional Justice, 2006).

15   Tonya Putnam, "Human Rights and Sustainable Peace," in *Ending Civil Wars: The Implementation of Peace Agreements,* ed. Stephen John Stedman, Donald Rothchild, and Elizabeth Cousens (Boulder: Lynne Rienner Publishers, 2002), 248. See also Maryam Kamali, "Accountability for Human Rights Violations: A Comparison of Transitional Justice in East Germany and South Africa," *Columbia Journal of Transnational Law* 40 (2001): 89–141; and Jack Snyder and Leslie Vinjamuri, "Trials and Errors: Principle and Pragmatism in Strategies of International Justice," *International Security* 28, no. 3 (Winter 2003/2004): 5–44.

16   Tricia Olsen, Leigh Payne, and Andrew Reiter, "At What Cost? A Political Economy Approach to Transitional Justice" (paper prepared for the Midwest Political Science Association Conference, Chicago, IL, April 14, 2007).

17   Ingrid Samset, Stina Petersen, and Vibeke Wang, "Foreign Aid to Transitional Justice: The Cases of Rwanda and Guatemala, 1995–2005," in Kai Ambos, Judith Large, and Marieke Wierda, eds., *Building a Future on Peace and Justice: Studies on Transitional Justice, Peace and Development* (Heidelberg: Springer, 2009).

18   International Center for Transitional Justice (ICTJ) and the UK Department for International Development (DFID), "Donor Strategies for Transitional Justice: Taking Stock and Moving Forward," conference report, October 15–16, 2007.

19   Alex Boraine, *A Country Unmasked* (Oxford: Oxford University Press, 2000), 357.

20   Rama Mani, *Beyond Retribution: Seeking Justice in the Shadows of War* (Cambridge: Polity / Blackwell, 2002).

21   Susanne Reiff, Sylvia Servaes, and Natascha Zupan, "Development and Legitimacy in Transitional Justice" (report from workshops co-organized by the Working Group on Development and Peace at the conference "Building a Future on Peace and Justice," Nuremberg, June 25–27, 2007). For the papers presented at the conference, see *Building a Future on Peace and Justice.*

22   Ruth Rubio-Marín and Pablo de Greiff, "Women and Reparations," *International Journal of Transitional Justice* 1 (2007): 318–37; Gerd Junne and Willemijn Verkoren, "The Challenge of Postconflict Development," in *Postconflict Development: Meeting the Challenges,* ed. Gerd Junne and Willemijn Verkoren (Boulder: Lynne Rienner, 2004); and Martina Fischer, Hans J. Gießmann, and Beatrix Schmelzle, eds., *Berghof Handbook for Conflict Transformation,* online resource published by the Berghof Research Center for Constructive Conflict Management, www.berghof-handbook.net/.

CHAPTER 1

Articulating the Links Between Transitional Justice and Development: Justice and Social Integration

Pablo de Greiff[1]

E. M. Forster begins his novel *Howards End*—a novel which itself raises interesting questions about social relations under conditions of inequality—with an epigraph that has been an important source of guidance for my work on justice in general, and which has proven particularly useful in thinking about the present chapter. That epigraph reads, simply:

"Only connect…"

In this chapter, I try to make explicit some links between transitional justice and development, two sprawling fields characterized by fuzzy conceptual borders and by both internal and external dissent. Taking seriously the idea of connecting, however, also means preserving the integrity of the things that are being connected. Forster says "only connect" rather than "only conflate." Thus, while I am interested in establishing links between transitional justice and development, I am also interested in drawing certain boundaries around each—not just for reasons of clarity, but in the belief that effective synergies depend on sensible divisions of labor.

The interest in the relationship between transitional justice and development can be explained in many ways: a good number of transitional societies face immense developmental challenges, and a good number of developing countries face abiding "justice deficits" concerning massive human rights abuses in their pasts. The number of countries that face these challenges increases if, following recent trends, one extends the domain of application of "transitional justice" from its original context—namely, societies emerging from authoritarianism—to societies emerging from conflict.[2] The latter, particularly, but not exclusively, are frequently beset by poverty, huge inequalities, weak institutions, broken physical infrastructure, poor governance, high levels of insecurity, and low levels of social capital, among other problems of the sort that are nowadays part of the development brief. Postconflict countries also face the typical legacy of massive rights abuses, including large numbers of victims, direct and indirect—people who have been displaced and marginalized, people who have been handicapped, widowed, and orphaned, people who have strong claims to justice, who with good reason feel aggrieved and resentful—all of which calls into question the currency of basic norms and the effectiveness of the system of law and its ability to respond not just to victims' claims but to the claims to justice of the population at large, which in turn feeds into some of the developmental problems mentioned above.

Given this, and aside from the fact that it is not unreasonable to think that unless people's overall living conditions improve in the aftermath of political transitions the implementation of transitional justice measures will over time become a series of relatively inconsequential "events," several questions motivate an interest in the relationship between transitional justice and development. Did developmental deficits contribute to the generation of conflict or of the sort of systematic human rights violations that transitional justice measures seek to redress? And if this is the case, would justice as well as prudence not require making up for these deficits? Even if there are some contexts in which this argument about root causes overstates the role of developmental deficits in the generation of violence, massive human rights violations frequently leave such deficits in their wake: massive and systematic violations may cause poverty, deepen inequality, weaken institutions, destroy infrastructure, impoverish governance, increase insecurity, deplete social capital, and so on, and if this is the case, again, it would seem that both justice and prudence would call for thinking about the relationship between transitional justice and development.[3] So, just as there are reasons for transitional justice promoters to take an interest in development, there are reasons for development promoters to take an interest in transitional justice.

This is not all, however. While justice practitioners celebrate the increasing entrenchment of justice norms and practices both at the domestic and the international levels, they must also face tough questions about the costs of implementing justice initiatives, particularly in contexts characterized by chronic scarcity. What justifies, for example, spending more than a billion dollars for the International Criminal Tribunal for Rwanda (ICTR) for the prosecution of, at most, fifty-five individuals for participating in the genocide, when the total domestic justice sector budget for the relevant years is well below a fifth of that amount?[4] Self-reflection about justice measures should also lead to questions about the developmental preconditions of the implementation of such measures: trials require operative courts; reparations programs require, among other things, resources to distribute; even the mildest form

of institutional reform, vetting, requires institutions strong enough to withstand having personnel removed. It is not clear that these preconditions obtain
everywhere that massive human rights violations have taken place. Where
they do not, there are important questions about how much effort—and how
many resources—transitional societies should spend on "dealing with the
past" before operative institutions, which among other things guarantee the
satisfaction of immediate and urgent needs of the population, including security, are in place. Perhaps a strategy that is more mindful of these developmental preconditions of justice would be more amenable to a "sequencing" that is
sensitive, in the long run, to both justice and development concerns.

Questions about the relationship between transitional justice and development arise if one approaches the issue starting with an interest in development as well. A variety of currents in the field of development are converging
on and lending support to the idea that economies grow not just by "getting
prices right"—that is, by setting efficient market systems, but that markets
themselves, not to speak about their growth, rest on a whole host of dispositions, practices, norms, and institutions that, among other things, ground
the incentives to participate actively in the market in the first place. Among
this thick web of dispositions, practices, and institutions, the rule of law has
a special place. The analyses of development that take as their starting point
such notions as social capital, social exclusion, and institutionalist economics, among others, lend support to this idea. If this is correct, then in contexts
in which massive human rights abuses have taken place, questions of justice
become unavoidable even for development promoters with an economistic outlook—let alone for others with more expansive conceptions of development—for trying to set up normative systems that respect the rule of law
is never akin to establishing a *Novus Ordo.*" There is no such thing as a new
beginning, for, among other reasons, victims and nonvictims will coexist in
whatever new order is established, and victims, in particular, will rightly claim
that equity calls for their differentiated treatment. There is little reason to
assume that they will be willing, from the outset, to set aside the memories of
what they were subjected to and participate in the new order as if the slate had
been wiped clean. Victims will need to be persuaded to do that, which usually
requires satisfying their normative expectations calling for the effective recognition of what happened to them. Moreover, since the effects of systematic
human rights violations ripple beyond direct victims, it will be important, and
not just for victims, to see serious efforts to reestablish the force of norms and
the strength and reliability of institutions. This is precisely one of the tasks of

transitional justice, and therefore development promoters may find a reason to be interested in the contribution that transitional justice measures can make to development work.

My aim in this chapter, fortunately, does not consist in resolving some of the large, underlying questions, such as the causal role of underdevelopment in the generation of human rights violations. Instead of focusing on these motivating considerations, I assume that it has become important to think about the potential links between transitional justice and development, and that what needs to be done is to clarify the way these two fields relate to one another, starting at the conceptual level. It goes without saying that there are many ways of articulating the potential links between two fields as expansive as the two in question here. This chapter does not aspire to be either exhaustive or definitive, and it self-consciously deals more with conceptions of transitional justice and development than with specific programs.

The chapter is organized as follows. In section I, I look for direct links between transitional justice and development (understood largely in terms of economic growth). In subsequent sections, I change tacks, both to broaden the understanding of development and to examine links with transitional justice that, although more "indirect," seem to me to be much more promising. Before engaging this exercise, however, in section II I provide an analysis of the conditions that transitional justice measures seek to respond to. This analysis, which turns on the notion of norm breaking and norm affirmation, makes the links with development easier to see. In the remaining sections, I build on this account to explain why the sort of violations that are the object of concern for transitional justice matter also from a development perspective, borrowing from the development literature to make the case. In section III, I argue that the notion of social capital helps to demonstrate the relevance of past massive rights violations to development work. In section IV, I sketch the contours of an expanded conception of development using the notion of human development as an example, and then try to show how massive norm breakdowns can be thought to hinder development thus understood. Finally, in section V, I present two versions of an argument that articulates what transitional justice can contribute to development. One version, articulated in terms that are familiar to transitional justice practitioners, spins around the norm-affirming role of transitional justice, and the difference that this might make in terms of recognition, trust, and political participation, issues that emerged as significant in the interactions with the development literature in sections II through IV. The other version of the argument is articulated in terms that might be more familiar to development practitioners, and hinges on the contribution that transitional justice might make to strengthening a robust regime of inclusive, participatory citizenship. Transitional justice, I argue, can thus be conceived of as a set of interventions that promote social integration, and it is in this capacity that it overlaps with and may serve the interests of development. Citizenship, as I argue, stands both in an instrumental and a constitutive relationship with justice and with development. The web of relationships, then, is thick, indeed.

One final general caveat is called for before proceeding. It is important to think about the relationship between transitional justice and development in both directions. Taking the last formulation of the argument I offer, one way of putting the point is the following: One reason why it makes sense for development agents, stereotypically oriented to the future, to concern themselves with efforts to deal with the legacies of massive human rights abuses is that doing so is necessary for full citizenship ("full" both in the sense of "robust" and in the sense of "for all"). By the same token, the reason why transitional justice promoters, cartoonishly portrayed as being worried mainly with the past, must concern themselves with development is that their aspiration to give force to a rights-based regime, a citizenship regime, is not only a matter of abstract rights but of securing the material and social conditions for the exercise of those rights and capabilities. For many reasons, including expertise, this chapter is written taking transitional justice as a starting point, and asking how it can contribute to development processes.[5] But I emphatically signal, from the start, that the very possibility of implementing transitional justice measures depends on the satisfaction of developmental preconditions to which transitional justice promoters have not always been sufficiently attuned.

I. "DIRECT LINKS"

In this section, I start the effort to clarify the links between transitional justice and development, taking as a starting point a very rough understanding of each term. "Transitional justice" ostensively refers to the implementation of criminal justice, truth-telling, reparations, and institutional reforms, particularly of the security sector. "Development," in a similarly coarse way of understanding the term, refers to questions of economic growth, and perhaps distribution, broadly speaking.[6] The simplest way of thinking about the relationship between the two fields consists of trying to draw the developmental preconditions and consequences of the implementation of transitional justice measures, and vice versa. Given that there has been little systematic thinking or research done specifically on this relationship,[7] what follows does not summarize previous results, sketch best practices, or make empirical predictions. It is offered, rather, as an approach to possible links that need to be researched, both conceptually and empirically, in more detail than I can do here—something the remaining chapters in this volume start doing. For reasons of space, I concentrate in this section on the potential developmental effects of transitional justice measures. I have tried to think about both proximate and distant effects, and instead of taking current transitional justice practices as set in stone, I have tried to think about whether those effects can be enhanced by modifying those practices. A final prefatory note is that I start this analysis by adopting a loosely economistic conception of development, one that takes development to relate to economic growth and distribution.[8] Although this understanding of development (for good reasons) no longer has any track among development practitioners, I adopt it here initially in the belief that if on this basis one can construct a plausible argument to spark interest in the linkages between transitional justice and development, the case can only be stronger and easier to make with respect to more expansive conceptions of development.

I.1. JUDICIAL CASES AND DEVELOPMENT

There are different ways of thinking about potential developmental effects of transitional prosecutions, even those that concentrate on the violation of a fairly traditional list of civil and political rights:

- In the course of trying criminal cases, with or without correlated civil cases, economic resources amassed by perpetrators are in theory subject to recovery, and in theory usable for reparations and other reconstruction purposes.
- In the course of investigating human rights abuses for purposes of criminal prosecutions, other forms of criminality, some of them having important economic consequences, are often disclosed. Ironically, these disclosures sometimes have even more severe delegitimizing effects on perpetrators than the original investigations for politically motivated human rights abuses, as the "Riggs Bank" disclosures against Pinochet illustrate.[9]

More indirectly, the potential developmental effects of transitional judicial cases include:

- Trying cases in the aftermath of authoritarianism or conflict discloses information about the economic practices of the regime responsible for massive human rights violations, information that in most cases pertains directly (but not only) to those who stand accused. Massive abuse is generally systemic, which has two implications: it involves organization; and, in turn, it consumes resources, often both involving and generating illegal economic activities. In the face of more severe human rights violations, property crimes tend to receive little attention, despite the fact that they are part and parcel of the experience of abuse for many people. They were certainly pervasive in the German Holocaust, Argentina, the former Yugoslavia, Morocco, and Timor-Leste. Authoritarian and conflict regimes also often get involved in economic activities that constitute serious if not illegal market distortions, including money laundering, aggressive rent seeking and abuse of natural resources, monopoly formation, and crony licensing agreements.[10] Even if these behaviors are neither prosecuted nor become the independent object of investigation, information about them collected as part of criminal investigations may have some deterrent effect, or may make a contribution to transparency, which is, arguably, a contribution to development.

· Trying cases for human rights violations, it has been said, strengthens the rule of law. To the extent that the rule of law is a precondition of development, prosecutions may have beneficial, if indirect, effects on development.

All of the above rests on surmises about the impact on development that the well-known, narrowly focused transitional judicial procedures may have. These (theoretical) effects may be enhanced, again, *at least in theory*, if "transitional judicial procedures" as a practice were not taken as given and the scope of prosecutorial policies were broadened.[11] In other words, the impact may be enhanced if investigations and prosecutions were to focus directly, and not incidentally, on "economic crimes";[12] and if the class of perpetrators was enlarged to include both those who *enabled* human rights violations by, among other things, making their perpetration economically feasible by sustaining the structures without which systemic crimes would not have been possible, and those who knowingly *benefitted* from those violations.

I.2. TRUTH-TELLING AND DEVELOPMENT

The case for the potential developmental impact of transitional truth-telling strategies is very similar to the one just sketched for judicial procedures.[13] It can be thought to be stronger, however, for truth-telling instances generally enjoy a broader mandate, one that explicitly calls upon them to investigate the structural conditions that made massive human rights violations possible. In particular, truth commissions have made significant recommendations concerning judicial systems and the strengthening of the rule of law,[14] which, again, is strongly linked with development. Even the Chilean Truth and Reconciliation Commission, which was limited to investigating crimes leading to death, made far-reaching recommendations concerning the judicial system. The Guatemalan, Peruvian, and South African commissions went even further, including in their reports broad-ranging analyses of the general socioeconomic structures within which violations took place. Furthermore, truth commissions are not hampered in this task by procedural and evidentiary rules that limit the admissibility of evidence to that which is directly relevant to the behavior of those who stand accused. Having said this, the developmental (and other) impact of truth-telling exercises is limited by the inevitable gap between insight and transformation; understanding the dynamics leading to violations may be a necessary but not a sufficient condition for changing those dynamics, as illustrated by the many unimplemented recommendations of truth commissions. Without repeating the arguments that could be made *mutatis mutandi* for the developmental impact of truth-telling, one could contend that:

- In the course of investigating massive human rights violations, truth commissions disclose information that is relevant to other forms of criminality, including those that have a direct developmental dimension.
- In the course of investigating human rights violations, and because of the investigatory leeway mentioned, truth commissions can recommend the removal of personnel and the restructuring of institutions that may act as developmental blockages.
- Truth commissions gather information about victimization that may be crucial for purposes of economic reintegration; this is true both of categories of persons and of geographical areas that were the particular targets of violence, and which therefore need special programs if they are to be effectively reintegrated into national economies. To illustrate the point: the commission in Guatemala emphasized how state policy led to the victimization and deepened marginalization of indigenous communities already living in precarious conditions;[15] similarly, the Peruvian commission examined the differential impact of violence both state-sponsored and perpetrated by Shining Path on the Andean and Amazonian communities;[16] and Morocco's commis-

sion acted similarly in focusing on the way in which areas that had illegal detention centers were deliberately deprived of infrastructure and other forms of investment.[17]

Again, if one does not take previous truth-telling exercises as precedent in terms of setting limits, these (theoretical) effects could (in theory) be enhanced. This is what underlies the calls for broadening the mandate of truth commissions to allow them to investigate economic crimes, including corruption, the exploitation of "conflict resources," and so on.[18]

1.3. REPARATIONS AND DEVELOPMENT

Because reparations involve the direct distribution to victims of a set of goods, including economic transfers, those who are interested in the developmental impact of transitional justice initiatives have placed particular stock in this measure.[19]

- Monetary compensation to individuals for human rights violations may be thought to boost the economic capacity of the beneficiaries, which in turn may be thought to provide a developmental boost. This can arguably be augmented if the benefits are crafted in ways that are "developmentally sensitive," by, for example, distributing not just cash but shares in microfinance institutions.[20]
- Since "reparations" under international law includes "restitution,"[21] restitutory practices, particularly those that seek to clarify and entrench property or use rights, serve development ends by means of concrete instruments, such as titles.
- The trend in large-scale reparations programs is in the direction of greater "complexity"—that is, toward the distribution of measures that go beyond monetary compensation, such as provisions for health and education.[22] Both of these are themselves factors of development. But discussions about the provision of health and educational services as reparations can also disclose gaps in existing institutions and provide an incentive for improving them, and not necessarily just for the direct victims.
- There is also an emerging trend in reparations rhetoric (if not in practice) toward "collective" or "community" reparations. The Guatemalan commission made recommendations to this effect, as did the Peruvian and the Moroccan commissions, both of which are slowly starting their implementation. That questions linger about whether such

measures can be sufficiently differentiated from development programs speaks to their theoretical developmental impact.[23]

As with other transitional justice measures, the impact of reparations could (in
theory) be thought to be enhanced if we are willing to countenance innovations
to current practices (beyond those mentioned). The simplest way of doing so
would be to increase the categories of violations for which reparations benefits
are offered, to include, for instance, certain types of economic crimes.[24]

I.4. INSTITUTIONAL REFORM AND DEVELOPMENT

- At least in part because, generally speaking, vetting procedures are
  administrative rather than criminal in nature, they can make use of
  relaxed evidentiary and procedural rules that may make them more
  efficient than criminal trials as forms of redress for certain types of
  abuses.[25] These may include typically hard-to-prove economic crimes,
  such as illicit enrichment, money laundering, and so on. Vetting procedures can use as criterion of screening and exclusion a concept of
  "integrity" with farther reach than the usual human rights criteria
  used by the other redress measures, thus making it possible, in theory,
  to screen for economic abuses.[26]
- But it is largely on account of an expected "peace dividend" that comes
  about from institutional reform under the umbrella of security sector
  reform (SSR) that this sort of measure awakens enthusiasm among
  those interested in the development potential of transitional justice.
  The savings, both direct and indirect, of shutting down, for example,
  security agencies involved in massive human rights violations—savings from reduced security-related expenditures, from efficiencies that
  result from increased security, and so on—the argument goes, could
  be put to better use in the area of development.[27]

I.5. CAVEATS

I have concentrated so far on possible developmental consequences of the
implementation of transitional justice measures that it would not be unreasonable to expect, all other things being equal, and at a high level of generality. In
practice, however, rarely are all other things equal, and there is a big difference
between what is plausible (in the thin sense of either not being contradictory
or flowing from general premises) and what is probable (in the thicker sense of

being reasonably expected when all relevant factors are taken into account). I would like, then, to present a list of caveats that explain why, for all the plausibility of such links between transitional justice and development, I still think we can do better.

The three main problems with articulating the links between transitional justice and development in terms of the direct developmental impact (understood economistically) of transitional justice measures can be put in the following terms:

- *Significance.* It is likely that the *economic* impact of the implementation of these measures is either too small or too difficult to monitor or measure. The impact of transitional trials on growth or distribution, for example, is likely to be minimal or non-traceable. Although leaders of regimes responsible for massive human rights violations are often wealthy (almost always as a result of illegal economic activities), the recovery record both of national and of international courts is generally dismal. The more indirect contribution of such trials—for example, by strengthening the rule of law—is virtually impossible to trace (not only because, as with other transitional justice initiatives, isolating their independent contribution is impossible, but also because it is not clear what element of a trial—a complex and protracted procedure—one is supposed to trace: the indictment, proceedings, sentences, their actual fulfillment?).[28] The *economic* impact of truth-telling exercises is even harder to estimate, given the huge gap between insight and transformation. There are reasons to believe that this is so even regarding the two transitional justice measures that are most promising in terms of development (understood in this manner), reparations and institutional reform. The budgets of reparations programs, with very few exceptions, are simply too small to make much of a difference in terms of either growth or distribution.[29] They are usually nothing more than a fraction of the budget of even rudimentary welfare services. As for the "peace dividend" of SSR, in most cases this simply does not come to pass, especially in the short run. Even rapid reductions of forces generate large expenses, for personnel are usually not simply released—for good reasons, including the fear that they will become "spoilers." It is doubtful, then, that the best case for linking transitional justice and development can be made in terms of a direct impact on growth or distribution.

• *Overload*. It may be said that the observations above simply emphasize the need to transform transitional justice practices so as to improve their development impact, most importantly by broadening their mandate to include violations of social and economic rights, or at least economic crimes. There are countervailing considerations, however, that must be kept in mind.[30] The claim that criminal prosecutions can be as effective in addressing economic crimes as in addressing serious human rights violations may rest on a mistaken understanding of what it takes to prosecute successfully two quite different categories of crimes. The issue is not simply one of different prosecutorial techniques, with everything that that involves, including evidence, witness cooperation, and so on. There is an overarching structural limitation that must be kept firmly in mind, and which almost certainly will lead to very different outcomes in each case: both national and international law on economic crimes is much less developed than national and international law applicable to mass atrocities.[31]

Truth commissions may not have the size, capacity, resources, right set of investigative skills, appropriate methodologies, or time to thoroughly conduct a broader investigation into economic crimes.[32] Including such crimes in the mandate of a commission may risk expanding the mandate "so broadly that it may be impossible to reasonably complete its task."[33] The increased complexity of the mandate may overburden commissions, which usually find it challenging to complete their tasks within their allotted life spans, and, most important, a significant expansion of thematic areas of focus will likely lead to watered-down reports, to analyses that operate only at a broad level of generality, and to recommendations that seem "utopian" in the sense of being all-encompassing *and* not containing feasible prescriptions to get from "here to there."

Similarly, providing reparations to victims of economic and social rights violations during conflict or under authoritarianism would simply be beyond the capacity of reparations programs, which are typically chronically underfunded. Expanding the scope of beneficiaries will likely entail the dilution of benefits to the point that *no one* is satisfied by them. Moreover, because reparations entail an acknowledgment of responsibility and an effort to target victims particularly for special treatment (meant *as* redress), reparations are not the same thing as development programs or initiatives to correct structural inequalities.[34]

- *Efficacy.* At least in part for the reasons just mentioned, it is not clear that transitional justice instruments should be considered efficient instruments for the pursuit of developmental aims. In fact, trying to maximize the satisfaction of developmental aims (understood at this stage of the chapter mainly in terms of economic growth and distribution) may threaten the ability of such measures to satisfy their characteristic aim — namely, the redress of massive human rights violations. This is so not just because a broadened mandate may dilute resources and competencies, but for two additional reasons. First, in addition to the fact that the normative framework for prosecuting and otherwise redressing practices leading to maldistribution, underdevelopment, and economic crimes is much weaker than the legal framework for prosecuting and otherwise redressing human rights violations, the former practices are also both more culturally entrenched and more widespread, and therefore much harder to redress. Second, it would be irresponsible to ignore the risk that political opposition to transitional justice measures might increase significantly if their mandate is broadened to include economic issues. To illustrate: if expanding the scope of transitional justice means that broader, entrenched, and powerful economic elites (who may have gained or strengthened their position during and because of the favor of predecessor regimes) instead of supporting the transition not only oppose it, but block it, then it may be prudent to postpone dealing with them to more favorable times.[35]

None of the above denies that there are connections between transitional justice and distributive justice measures that need to be explored, synergies to be maximized, and conflicts to be avoided. Nor is it intended to deny that transitional justice measures should be designed and implemented in a way that enables their developmental potential, however large or small that might be.[36] But there is one main lesson I derive from the considerations above: the best way of articulating the relationship between transitional justice and development is unlikely to fall out of observations about the *direct economic* consequences of the implementation of transitional justice measures. In the next section, then, I change tack and carry out the analysis in terms of a richer understanding of both development and transitional justice, and this, I argue, allows us to bring into relief more clearly the reasons why transitional justice is relevant to development, and vice versa.

II. TRANSITIONAL JUSTICE, NORM BREAKING, AND NORM AFFIRMATION

Here I focus on two legacies of atrocities that make addressing these violations particularly relevant in a discussion of the relationship between transitional justice and development.[37] First, those who experience serious human rights violations are often left with a deep and abiding sense of fear and uncertainty. Second, this effect is not limited to those who have suffered the violations bodily; it applies to significantly larger groups. These "spillover effects" and the reasons that underlie them help show the importance, from a development perspective, of addressing past massive violations—almost independently of how development might be conceived.

As to the first point, various scholars, from diverse disciplines, have provided accounts of the consequences of suffering severe human rights violations. The "phenomenology of victimhood" is dense and complex, but it overwhelmingly gravitates toward the conclusion that the pain and suffering endured in the violation itself is merely the beginning of sequelae that frequently include a deep sense of uncertainty and a debilitating and in some cases incapacitating sense of fear.[38] The reason lies in the fact that serious human rights violations shatter normative expectations fundamental to our sense of agency in the world. The expectations that get broken whenever human rights are violated are not just whimsical ones; they are based on general norms—that is, they are expectations whose satisfaction we reasonably feel *entitled* to. These norm-based expectations are the manifestation of the basic structure, the ground or framework, of our agency. They are expectations about, for example, what constitutes legitimate treatment of others and at the hands of others, about situations in which it is "normal" to expect the assistance of others, about the state being the guarantor, rather than the violator, of fundamental rights, and so on. The very basic, fundamental nature of these expectations explains the pervasive fear that their defeat generates: victims experience a deep sense of normative disorientation (How could *this* have happened? If this happened, then *anything* can happen), of solitude (How could *anyone* do this to me, and, crucially, how come *no one* prevented it?), and of resentment (This should have *never* happened, I was entitled to better treatment).[39]

In the context of this chapter, it is even more important to note that it is not just ("direct") victims who are affected by violations; in the end, it is significantly larger groups as well.[40] Ultimately, this is not only a function of bonds of concern or even of relations of dependence, but also a function of the nature of the norms that are shattered when human rights are violated—namely, the general norms that give rise to the expectations that undergird basic agency and social competence. In contexts of massive human rights abuses, nonvictims often have the sense that after what happened to the victims, no one can be safe, no one can really know what to expect. The end result is a generalized weakening of agency, not just the agency of victims. It is not uncommon for victims of massive abuse to lead substantially more reclusive lives than they led before the violations, to withdraw from public spaces, to disengage from social networks, and particularly to refrain from making claims to authorities and formal institutions. This is also true for nonvictims.[41]

These effects have been borne out in a variety of cases. For example, Jaime Malamud-Goti characterizes the effects of the years of terror in Argentina in terms of "avoidance strategies" adopted by the population:

> people abandoned, first, their political activities; second, they abandoned their political beliefs. They reduced associational activities and denied any evidence that inhumane practices were being carried out. Members of groups that were political targets of state terror cultivated deliberate ignorance about what was going on. People adopted selfish strategies of survival.[42]

This is, in fact, an intended consequence of the exercise of "disarticulating power," since it makes coordinated response to the exercise of power virtually impossible.[43]

Accounting for some of the legacies of massive human rights violations in this way helps advance the argument for the relationship between transitional justice and development for two important reasons. First, by providing an explanation of how the effects of serious human rights violations ripple from direct victims to much broader constituencies, the account clarifies that justice is not a matter of interest to victims alone, and in that way it helps us to see the overlap in constituencies between justice and development measures. To the extent that the violation of fundamental rights is at the same time the breach of general norms, *everyone* is affected by it. The norms that are supposed to regulate—to "norm" (*normen*)—our interactions are shown to have little or no force with each violation. Focusing on the diminished agency not just of victims but of entire communities that comes in the wake of massive violations of human rights helps us to see the developmental relevance of transitional justice measures. Transitional justice measures, by dealing directly with the legacies of those violations, might protect possibilities of agency—and not for victims only.

Second, and more important, the account clarifies that the overlap between transitional justice and development should not be considered merely in terms of coinciding constituencies, but that it ultimately involves a factor that is critical to any understanding of development—namely, the very possibility of social coordination. If this account of the legacies of atrocities is correct, the point to stress is not merely that showing that basic norms have no force does not merely affect those who experience the violations themselves, and not even that the norms are so basic as to diminish the victims' very agency, their possibility of initiating action in the world. For development purposes, it may be more compelling to stress that the violations thereby diminish the possibility of having people *act together*.

III. MASS ATROCITY, AGENCY, AND SOCIAL COORDINATION; THE DEPLETION OF SOCIAL CAPITAL

In order to illustrate and to make more plausible these last two claims, I borrow from the development literature first. Different currents in development work illuminate "mechanisms" that explain how different social conditions affect people's possibilities for agency.[44] These currents dovetail with work in other disciplines that describe how adverse social conditions diminish expectations, the phenomenon of "adaptive preferences." The World Bank, for example, in its 2006 *World Development Report* takes the position that poverty leads to diminished expectations, which, in turn, has a negative impact on development.[45] Philosophers and social scientists have long argued that people shift their preferences in light of considerations of feasibility rather than suffer permanently defeated expectations,[46] and that this leveling of expectations among the disadvantaged operates even in economically prosperous countries, particularly among those affected by structural, "horizontal inequalities."[47]

Leaving aside the motivations that individuals may have for reducing their expectations, the following is a particular account of how this process takes place. Arjun Appadurai frames the argument in terms of how deep poverty stunts "the capacity to aspire." This capacity is not simply a matter of individual needs, wants, preferences, and plans, not simply the individual ability to "wish," but is also related to social experiences and norms. People aspire to realize particular aims—say, attain a particular professional and economic status— only within contexts in which those wishes, and, most important, all the more concrete and particular choices that lead to those aims, make sense. This capacity, according to Appadurai, is not evenly distributed in any society:

> the better off you are (in terms of power, dignity, and material resources), the more likely you are to be conscious of the links between the more

and less immediate objects of aspiration. Because the better off, by defi-nition, have a more complex experience of the relation between a wide range of ends and means, because they have a bigger stock of available experiences of the relationship between aspirations and outcomes, because they are in a better position to explore and harvest diverse expe-riences of exploration and trial, because of their many opportunities to link material goods and immediate opportunities to more general and generic possibilities and options [sic].[48]

Social experiences and norms have a huge effect in shaping people's capac-ity to aspire, which, in the case of the poor, Appadurai argues, leads to what he calls "adverse terms of recognition." The poor operate under conditions in which they are encouraged to "subscribe to norms whose social effect is to fur-ther diminish their dignity, exacerbate their inequality, and deepen their lack of access to material goods and services."[49]

This account of diminished agency, then, can be put in terms that track the norm-based account of the effects of atrocities offered in section II, above. The mechanism is arguably the same in both cases. Both poverty and victimization weaken the capacity to aspire, diminish people's expectations. Over time, their readiness to initiate action and particularly to *raise claims* against others, espe-cially against state institutions—something that lies at the core of the notion of individuals as bearers of rights—is weakened as well. In this way, "adverse terms of recognition" become generalized.

An argument that is familiar in the domain of development, then, illus-trates an argument about the effects of massive human rights violations. But there is more. Recall that this claim was part of the effort to motivate an inter-est in the legacies of atrocities from a development perspective by arguing that these legacies have "spillover effects," that massive human rights violations do not affect victims alone. One way to see this is precisely by noticing that the occurrence of unredressed systematic human rights violations speaks of the weakness of general norms. Again, while there is no reason to assume that the price of weak, general norms is equally distributed—the well off can "buy" protection through other means while the disadvantaged are forced in "Faus-tian bargains" with disastrous consequences for their well-being[50]—the point is that the diminished agency produced by massive violations, the weakness of protections that such violations manifest, generates "costs" for everyone, the well off included, and that this has an impact on development.[51]

From a development perspective, as mentioned before, it may be that the urgency of dealing with the legacies of atrocities will be even more compelling if stress is laid not so much on diminished agency as on the obstacles those legacies generate for coordinated social action, the second claim made above. One of the factors that facilitate action coordination is civic trust, the "twin" of social capital, to use the term most familiar in development.[52] The sense of trust in question here is not the thick trust that characterizes relations between intimates, but neither is it reducible to a mere expectation of regularity or predictability.[53] Trust, as an alternative to monitoring and the appeals to sanctions, involves shared normative expectations: I trust someone not merely when I experience confidence in the regularity of his or her behavior—I can be highly confident that in grossly corrupt systems officials will predictably try to extort me, but that, of course, does not mean I trust them—but rather, when I am convinced that among that person's reasons for actions is a commitment to values, norms, and principles that we share. In dealing with strangers and with institutions in complex and highly differentiated societies, the relevant values, norms, and principles are abstract and general. So, we trust an institution when we act on the assumption that the institution's constituent norms are shared by those who run and participate in the institution.

Accounts of the developmental impact of civic trust have centered on its effects on transaction costs and on rates of investment. At the most general level, the former argument turns on the idea that in the absence of trust, parties to economic exchanges face unattractive alternatives indeed: they can try to rely on complex formal contracts that attempt to anticipate *all* contingencies. Aside from the fact that it is impossible to anticipate all contingencies, this would render contracts inflexible, which in itself increases costs. These arrangements also require, *ex ante*, difficult negotiations and intensive monitoring for the duration of the agreement, both of which are expensive. Finally, *ex post*, redeeming differences on the basis of intricate contracts obviously makes for complex litigation and therefore expensive enforcement.[54] What ends up happening in low-trust environments is that participants try to cope with these costs through exchanges in informal networks, among people who know one another, which is also, in itself, a costly alternative. It is akin to a reduction in market size, and the abiding uncertainties reduce the availability of credit, put a premium on capital, and force producers to avoid customizing items and to reduce the magnitude of orders they are willing to accept. At the limit, as an end result of the aggregation of constraints, it leads to a deflationary, downward adjustment of expectations about what is feasible to achieve, which was dealt with above.

That trust between people is correlated with growth, and even with increased equity, there seems to be no doubt any longer. Large cross-country studies indicate that increases in levels of trust between people are associated with increases in growth both in gross domestic product (GDP) and investments, and that inequality is associated with lower trust levels.[55]

Just as important as trust between individuals, but closer to our main concern, is trust at the macropolitical level—that is, as a characteristic not just of relations between persons, firms, and civil society organizations but also of their relations with the institutions of the state. Once again, and perhaps less surprising, empirical research seems to confirm that there are correlations between levels of trust in institutions and economic performance: countries with strong institutions, institutions that among other things protect civil and political rights, have higher levels of trust, and it is precisely these countries that turn out to perform best economically, again, in terms of rates of growth and investment.[56] Several cross-national studies using a variety of indicators show strong correlations between respect for civil and political rights and economic growth, and show conversely that violence and political instability are negatively related to growth rates and investment. Stephen Knack, for instance, argues that a review of the relevant studies leads to the conclusion that "a consensus has developed on the importance of government social capital for economic performance: a similar consensus is rapidly developing on civil social capital." While this may be an intuitively obvious result, as the literature acknowledges, explanations for the ways in which trust at the macropolitical level impacts development are not nearly as worked out as they are for its impact at the microeconomic level.[57] One may surmise, however, that some of the same factors are at work. Again, on the understanding that trust refers to norm conformity, environments in which there are high levels of trust in state institutions are indicative of norm-abiding institutions, which diminish risks, increase predictability, and therefore facilitate economic growth.

If this is the case, the sort of mistrust, both between citizens and primarily between citizens and state institutions, left in the wake of massive human rights violations should be a cause of concern from a development perspective. Again, Malamud-Goti's account of the effects of Argentina's dirty war is illustrative:

> [t]he lack of trust that people felt was another cause of the avoidance strategies: people avoided sensitive issues unless they were certain of the loyalty of the audience. Careless disclosures were as dangerous as deliberate reports. Vast portions of society sequestered themselves in their own family circle, restricting non-kin relationships to old friends. This tactic proved to be extremely isolating.... For parents, fear of

strangers and the constant effort to keep their children away from politics and trouble fostered family authoritarianism: children's activities were monitored. "Macro-authoritarianism" thus turned into micro-authoritarianism. This process of mental closure could be detected in the increasing nationalism, xenophobia, and tribalist exaltation of the family and fatherland.[58]

Malamud-Goti is not thinking about the developmental consequences of the breakdown of trust he describes. But one does not need to agree with the details of the social capital literature to acknowledge that unaddressed massive human rights violations make social coordination more difficult, that this has developmental consequences, and therefore to consider seriously whether the type of redress offered by transitional justice measures can, indeed, make a contribution to development.[59]

IV. HUMAN DEVELOPMENT

It is time to shed the economistic slant on development that has largely informed the chapter up to this point. This will presumably make it easier to see the links with transitional justice. Without question, the best-known expanded conception of development in contemporary discussions is the notion of "human development."[60] One of the underlying motivations for introducing the concept was, precisely, to overcome the tendency to think about development in purely economic or utilitarian terms, and to reconnect with an older tradition—going back to Aristotle—that thought about the general purpose of economics in terms of increasing human well-being.[61] Some of the problems with an economistic reduction of development include the following. First, measures of wealth, income, and growth (for example, GNP, GNP per capita) say little about their distribution within societies. More important, there are factors that affect human well-being that do not correlate easily with wealth, income, and growth—as important as the latter may be. These are not merely "incidental" factors for well-being; they include education and health care, life expectancy, opportunities for political participation, and the presence or absence of various forms of inequality, factors around which there are significant differences in countries at the same level of wealth, income, and growth.[62] Measuring human development in terms of the availability of resources fares better, but does not resolve all problems, for as Amartya Sen has argued, resources do not automatically lead to well-being given the great variations between individuals in their needs and in their possibility of con-verting resources into well-being.[63] Thus, for example, even classes of individ-uals, say, the chronically disadvantaged or women, in societies that have tradi-tionally discriminated against them in the educational sphere (as well), will not be able to convert a given set of educational opportunities into the same level of well-being as the (usually male) more advantaged, who are well settled into educational and career paths.[64]

So, what is development on the "human development" approach? Accord-ing to the United Nations Development Programme (UNDP): "Human devel-opment is a process of enlarging people's choices."[65] Sen's work, which has played a foundational role for the concept of human development, is worth quoting more extensively:

> Development can be seen…as a process of expanding the real freedoms that people enjoy. Focusing on human freedoms contrasts with narrower views of development, such as identifying development with the growth of gross national product, or with the rise in personal incomes, or with industrialization, or with technological advance, or with social modern-ization. Growth of GNP or of individual incomes can, of course, be very important as *means* to expanding the freedoms enjoyed by the members of the society. But freedoms depend also on other determinants, such as social and economic arrangements…as well as political and civil rights.… If freedom is what development advances, then there is a major argument for concentrating on that overarching objective, rather than on some particular means, or some specially chosen list of instruments. Viewing development in terms of expanding substantive freedoms directs atten-tion to the ends that make development important, rather than merely to some of the means that, inter alia, play a prominent part in the process.[66]

Now, one does not get a full impression of how far-reaching this conceptual expansion of the notion of development really is from the UNDP's definition alone, nor from the index developed to measure it. Not surprisingly, given the scarcity of cross-country information on some relevant issues, but perhaps also due to the difficulties that a UN agency would have in stressing certain conceptions of freedom (particularly those related to political participation), the UNDP has articulated human development mainly in terms of longevity (using expected lifetime as an indicator), "knowledge" (using literacy as an indicator), and "a decent living standard" (using a variant of purchasing-power-adjusted GDP estimates).[67]

Martha Nussbaum's and Sen's work provide a better indication of the scope of human development. The point of their "capabilities approach" is to get us to think about development in terms of the real possibilities people have to "do or be certain things deemed valuable."[68] Nussbaum proposes a methodology and also a resulting list of ten complex general capabilities.[69] Sen has refused to produce such a list, concentrating rather on the formulation of the reasons why freedom in general is important both in itself and instrumentally for development, and on the articulation of links between five types of freedoms: political freedoms, economic facilities, social opportunities, transparency guarantees, and protective security.[70] Both Nussbaum and Sen insist, and this is the point I want to stress here, that what is distinctive about the capabilities approach to development is the conviction that "choice is not pure spontaneity, flourishing independently of material and social conditions,"[71] that the aim of development is the (enormous) task of securing the material and social conditions that enable the exercise of such capabilities, the enjoyment of freedom, understood in the broadest sense.

As suggested before, the broader one's understanding of development, the greater its conceptual overlap with transitional justice. Clearly, massive atrocities constitute an affront and lead to the diminution of these capabilities, a point to which I will return. But, not the least because transitional justice can be thought of as a multifaceted set of responses to human rights violations, in order to sharpen the relationship between transitional justice and development, it would help to review, briefly, how the relationship between human development and human rights has been conceptualized.[72]

In the year 2000, that is, ten years after issuing its first *Human Development Report*, the UNDP decided to examine the relationship between human rights and development directly, a worthy endeavor for a development agency that, after all, is part of the same institution charged with shepherding international human rights agreements and norms. Having spent a great deal of energy by that point on the notion of human development, it faced a dual challenge—namely, to try to show that human development is a distinctive notion (for otherwise, what would it add to human rights discourse?), but, at the same time, that it is at least "compatible" with human rights (for otherwise, among other consequences, the UN would lose coherence regarding, arguably, its two most important functions).

At the broadest level, it is argued that "[h]uman rights and development share a common vision and a common purpose—to secure the freedom, well-being and dignity of all people everywhere."[73] Of course, this is merely where the challenge starts. Articulating precisely the distinct contributions of each concept, as well as their interrelationship, is much more difficult. I do not attempt a comprehensive review here, but merely offer the following sketch. The UNDP seems to settle on an account according to which there is a sort of functional complementarity (and an attendant division of labor) between the notions of development and human rights, captured by the pairing of development with "enhancement," on the one hand, and human rights with "claims," on the other. Let me illustrate. According to the report,

> If human development focuses on the enhancement of the capabilities and freedoms that the members of a community enjoy, human rights represent the claims that individuals have on the conduct of individual and collective agents and on the design of human arrangements to facilitate or secure these capabilities and freedoms.[74]

Unpacking this account, the report argues that development contributes to human rights modes of *"qualitative and quantitative analyses,"* which "help to give concreteness to human rights analysis," clarify the policy trade-offs involved in efforts to balance commitments to different types of rights, remind human rights promoters of "causally important institutional and operational variables," and, finally, add a dynamic perspective that "can help to deepen the understanding and broaden the usefulness of the human rights approach."[75]

Although the differences between the contributions are not always apparent, none of this seems wrong to me. The account is, however, surprising in that it turns development, basically, into an analytical tool. Contrast this with the role the report assigns to human rights. Far from being considered mere analytical tools, human rights are thought to determine the course of social development—at least in the sense of "channeling" it. Adopting the understanding of rights as justified claims, the report argues that rights, in the first place, determine the duties of others (both individuals and institutions), and it places special emphasis on official, state duties. Rights also determine development in the sense that they establish limits to what can be done to individuals in the pursuit of social goals. Finally, the report argues, rights play a crucial role in systematizing and institutionalizing obligations.[76]

Again, in their own terms, none of these claims (that is, that rights are justified claims, that they can act as side constraints, and that they help to institutionalize obligations) is wrong. But I would like to make two points about this particular articulation of the relationship between development and human rights. From the standpoint of the interests of this chapter—clarifying the possible links between transitional justice and development—this account helps in one way but is not particularly helpful in another.

First, the positive point. The report's emphasis on the understanding of rights as justified claims, as mechanisms to assign duties, and therefore as the basis of judgments about accountability, culpability, and responsibility, and as the grounds on which remedies can be established,[77] is clearly a helpful starting point for thinking about how transitional justice and development intersect with one another. One can say that making rights fundamental to development and emphasizing these functions of rights would provide support for an argument to the effect that transitional justice tools—as accountability measures, as complex remedies for human rights violations—make a contribution to development, especially to the extent that human rights are understood as central to development. I certainly pursue this argument below.[78]

As for the second point: Perhaps inevitably, given the role of human rights in the UN—as a sort of justificatory "bedrock," but one whose grounds are themselves better left unexamined, on pains of generating dissent—development is in some ways subordinated to human rights by the UNDP's account. In the end, force resides in rights, and development is conceived of as a "laudable goal":

> To have a particular right is to have a claim on other people or institutions that they should help or collaborate in ensuring access to some freedom. *This insistence on a claim on others takes us beyond the idea of human development.* Of course, in the human development perspective, social progress of the valued kind is taken to be a very good thing, and this should encourage anyone who can help to do something to preserve and promote it. But the normative connection between laudable goals and reasons for action does not yield specific duties on the part of other individuals, collectivities or social institutions to bring about human development—or to guarantee the achievement of any specified level of human development, or of its components.[79]

Now, we should acknowledge that sorting out the relationship between development (understood expansively) and human rights is genuinely complicated for a fundamental, general reason: the more expansive the understanding of development, the more it is likely to include goods the provision of which may not be the subject of particular rights, or the satisfaction of which may not be liable to any neat distribution of duties. In this sense, the mere introduction of the general vocabulary of rights into the sphere of development may not only fail to resolve practical issues but resolves conceptual issues only provided that an agreement about something being a matter of right has already been reached. When Nussbaum, for example, argues that the concept of human rights is useful in discussions of development since it helps us draw normative conclusions from the fact of basic capabilities—the crucial normative conclusion being that people have justified claims to specific forms of treatment[80]—and similarly, when the UNDP argues that human rights link "the human development approach to the idea that others have duties to facilitate and enhance human development,"[81] this does not happen in virtue of the general conception of human rights alone. The mere introduction of the general conception of human rights as justified claims does not turn a central human capability—say, the ability to play—into a right. There is a gap between capabilities and the distribution of claims concerning them that cannot be closed simply with a general conception of rights.[82]

I close this section, then, by returning to the core idea behind expanding the conception of development, and asking, as I have done in previous sections, how not just atrocities but *unaddressed* atrocities might be thought to affect development. Atrocities and the legacies of unaddressed atrocities arguably undermine most of the basic capabilities in Nussbaum's version of a capability account of development—that is, most of those capacities that make a life human. These include longevity (life), bodily health, and bodily integrity, all of which are diminished in obvious ways by systematic abuses; the exercise of emotions (which according to her require "not having one's emotional development blighted by fear and anxiety"[83]); the ability to use practical reason (stunted by atrocities to the extent that their legacies lead to, among other things, great distortions in one's sense of control over one's own life plans); the capacity to engage in forms of affiliation that are free from humiliation and that exemplify respect, including equal worth; the ability to play (in the sense of being able to laugh and enjoy recreational activities); and the ability to have basic control over one's political and material environment—all of which are diminished or undermined in the wake of abuses.[84] These effects, as is well known, can be transgenerational,[85] and, as I argued in section II, ripple out from victims to nonvictims. Thus, if development is understood in terms of basic capabilities, as it is by Nussbaum, unaddressed atrocities impede development.

Leaving aside particular accounts of capabilities, or even a particular account of human development, in expanding the notion of development to include such things as civil and political rights (as well as their material and social preconditions)—as we saw in briefly reviewing the UNDP's efforts in this direction—one of the challenges will always be to clarify the relationship between these rights and development (a task not entirely different from the justification of such expansion). There are various alternatives, which are not necessarily mutually exclusive.[86] One could say that civil and political rights protect goods and interests that are inherently valuable, and therefore that any defensible formulation of development will ultimately have to move from a purely economic understanding to one that encompasses these rights. Why these goods are intrinsically valuable can be spelled out in different ways, but one would be to say that the very exercise of rational agency would suffer a deprivation if people are not allowed their rational capacities in order to choose, precisely, how to organize themselves politically. There are other explanations. In any case, what this strategy involves, ultimately, is saying that for a society to be developed *means* in part securing civil and political rights.

The expansion of development to include civil and political rights can also be defended instrumentally, in various ways.[87] For instance, it can be argued that civil and political rights serve developmental purposes, either by promoting growth—as some of the literature on democracy and economics does[88]—or by promoting equity (which in turn will promote growth)—as the World Bank suggests in its 2006 report[89]—or, even more indirectly, but no less importantly, by promoting good governance (which in turn is seen as instrumental to equity and growth)—as is argued by a good number of international organizations and development agencies.[90] Finally, one could also hold the view that civil and political rights are instruments of development not so much because they induce growth but because they play an important preventive role, a position made famous by Sen and Jean Drèze, who argue that no substantial famine has occurred in a democratic country, no matter how poor.[91] Civil and political rights, then, minimally, protect development already achieved against famine and other crises.

There is an additional way of articulating the possible relationship between civil and political rights, on the one hand, and development, on the other, which, both because it straddles the two previous strategies—the "constitutive" and the "instrumental"—and because it is as distinct as underexplored, merits separate mention. On this account, rights to political participation contribute to the definition of people's needs and of acceptable ways of satisfying these needs, and, to this extent, they contribute to the construction of the very concept of development.[92]

However one accounts for the expansion of the concept of development, it is arguable that if one espouses such expansion, one would have to acknowledge that atrocities and their unaddressed legacies have a negative impact on development thus understood. This is seen most clearly if one thinks that rights are constituent measures of development; rights are not simply promissory notes, prospective guarantees, but also triggers of remedies in case they are violated. To the extent that there are groups of citizens whose fundamental rights were systematically violated and no redress has been forthcoming, one of the constituent features of development would have not been satisfied. And, going back to the analysis of normative breakdown in section II, the point is not so much that the constituent features would not have been satisfied for *some* (the victims), but that to the extent that the norms that are broken are basic norms, not just in the breach but in their unredressed breach, they are not satisfied for *anyone*. To some extent, the same can be said with respect to constructive accounts of the relationship between rights and development; the sort of massive breakdown of norms that is characteristic of contexts in which massive human rights violations take place is liable to leave in its wake weak civil societies and poor levels of political participation. This might slant discussions about social needs and about feasible ways of satisfying them, and in this sense development would be hampered. Finally, on instrumentalist accounts of the relationship between rights and development, it is likely that unaddressed massive violations will get in the way of the particular mechanism that is supposed to serve developmental purposes, via some of the processes examined in sections II through IV, above.

V. THE "INDIRECT LINKS" BETWEEN TRANSITIONAL JUSTICE AND DEVELOPMENT: TRANSITIONAL JUSTICE AS A MECHANISM OF SOCIAL INTEGRATION

If the argument presented up to this point is correct, then there are reasons to be concerned, from a development perspective, about the unaddressed legacies of massive human rights violations, almost independent of how narrowly economistic or how expansive one's understanding of development might be. In the first section of the chapter, I presented some of the ways in which transitional justice measures may be thought to serve development interests directly. In this final section, I explore more indirect ways in which transitional justice might contribute to development. By "indirect links," I do not mean flukes, unpredictable effects. Indeed, the effects that I concentrate on are as predictable (or unpredictable) as the effects of any other large-scale social intervention. They are "indirect" in the sense that, at least up to now, transitional justice interventions have not been designed with an eye to their developmental potential, nor have these interventions been integrated into development strategies. In the end, it is likely that these "indirect" contributions will be the most significant—one more reason to think about the potential synergies with care.

I present two versions of what at the core is the very same argument, one formulated in terms that are more familiar to transitional justice practitioners, and the other in terms that might be more familiar to development practitioners. In summary, the first argument can be framed in terms of what it is transitional justice measures seek to achieve. Among other aims, they seek to provide recognition to victims, promote civic trust, and strengthen the democratic rule of law.[93] How do they achieve these goals (to the extent they do)? In virtue of their norm-affirming potential. This is what makes them adequate responses to the breakdown of fundamental norms characteristic of contexts in which massive abuses take place, described in section II.[94] Why does this matter to development? Because "adverse terms of recognition," lack of trust, and a weak or inoperative democratic rule of law were identified as obstacles to development in the analysis provided in sections II through IV. Helping to overcome these obstacles can, therefore, make a difference to development efforts.

The second version of the same argument can be framed in terms of the notion of *citizenship* (including robust participatory rights); transitional justice measures can be seen from this perspective as mechanisms of social integration, as efforts to strengthen a regime of citizenship rights. This type of regime has become an object of concern to development practitioners as well, either because this type of citizenship is considered to be constitutive of development, or an instrument of development, or a means of articulating, of constructing, what development means.

V.1. THE ENDS OF TRANSITIONAL JUSTICE

So, to the first version of the argument. Elsewhere I have presented a systematic, normative conception of transitional justice, so I will not rehearse the position in detail here. Briefly, the main idea is that the various parts of a comprehensive transitional justice policy are tied together by the fact that the different measures can be thought to promote certain goals. The ultimate goal of transitional justice is, of course, to promote justice in the sense, for example, of contributing to "giving everyone his or her due," or to strengthening the link between effort and success, or whatever one's general understanding of justice might be. The problem is that this is too abstract to be of real help. I have long argued, however, in a reconstructive spirit—and independently of development considerations—that transitional justice measures can be seen as measures that promote recognition, civic trust, and the democratic rule of law, and that to the extent they contribute to the attainment of these goals—which certainly they cannot achieve *on their own*—they do so in virtue of their norm-affirming character.[95]

The goals attributed to these measures seem to conveniently match developmental blockages identified in earlier parts of this chapter. The conception, however, was articulated independently of development considerations. What makes this a systematic conception is, precisely, that it does not attribute aims that, as desirable as they might be, may nevertheless be random. What makes it reasonable to claim that recognition, trust, and the democratic rule of law are goals of transitional justice measures is not only that these ends relate conceptually to one another but, more important, that they are closely related with justice. In fact, they can be understood as dimensions or as both preconditions and consequences of the effort to give concrete expression *through law-based systems* to the necessarily more abstract notion of justice: a system of justice (a legal one, at least), meaning a system of effective and legitimate *rights*, is unimaginable without minimal levels of recognition, trust, and political participation. At the same time, systems of justice of this sort also stimulate and strengthen recognition, trust, and political participation. The goals, then, are closely tied to justice. Here I argue that they may also matter to development.

A. RECOGNITION

Each transitional justice measure can be said to pursue immediate goals of its own. At one remove of abstraction, however, it can be said that all transitional justice measures seek to provide recognition to victims.[96] The sort of recognition at issue is actually a complex one. To begin with, it refers to something akin to granting victims moral standing as individual human beings. At the limit, and at its most basic, this requires acknowledging that they can be harmed by certain actions. Almost without fail, one of the first demands of victims is, precisely, to obtain recognition of the fact that they have been harmed, and intentionally so.

But this is only one dimension of the sort of recognition that transitional justice measures arguably provide to victims. Indeed, from my perspective, it is not the victims' great capacity to endure *suffering* that needs to be primarily acknowledged. Even the first dimension of recognition has been described in terms not of sheer suffering, but of *harms*, a normatively thicker notion.[97] Ultimately, what is critical for a transition, and what transitional justice measures arguably aim to do, is to provide to victims a sense of recognition not only *as victims*, but as *rights bearers*.

The way in which transitional justice measures can do this is the following: criminal justice can be interpreted as an attempt to provide *recognition* to victims by denying the implicit claim of superiority made by criminals through their behavior. This is done through a sentence, a punishment, which is meant to reaffirm the importance of norms that grant equal rights to all.[98] Truth-telling provides recognition in ways that are perfectly familiar, and which are still probably best articulated by the old difference proposed by Thomas Nagel between knowledge and acknowledgment, when he argued that although truth commissions rarely disclose facts that were previously unknown, they still make an indispensable contribution in acknowledging these facts.[99] In light of the difficulties and deficiencies that normally accompany prosecutions, as well as the potential charge that truth-telling is "cheap talk," reparations buttress efforts aimed at recognition not only by demonstrating a sufficiently serious commitment so as to invest resources but, more important, if the program is well crafted, by giving beneficiaries the sense that the state has taken their interests to heart. Finally, institutional reform, with vetting as a starting point, in excluding official employees who abused their positions of authority, is guided by the ideal of guaranteeing the conditions under which citizens can relate to one another and to the authorities as equals. Summarizing, then, each transitional justice measure may be said to have an immediate aim or aims of its own. At a higher level of abstraction, however, all of them can be thought to pursue the goal of providing recognition to victims as individuals and as victims, but also, and primarily, as bearers of rights.

B. CIVIC TRUST

Another aim that arguably the various transitional justice measures seek to attain is the promotion of civic trust. Given space limitations I must be brief, and rather than argue for a particular way of understanding civic trust, I only stipulate the way in which I am using the term.[100] Trusting an institution, the case that is particularly relevant for us, amounts to assuming that its constitutive rules, values, and norms are shared by its members or participants and are regarded by them as binding.

How do transitional justice measures promote this sense of civic trust? Prosecutions can be thought to promote civic trust by reaffirming the relevance of the norms that perpetrators violated, norms that precisely turn natural persons into rights bearers. Judicial institutions, particularly in contexts in which they have traditionally been essentially instruments of power, show their trustworthiness if they can establish that no one is above the law. An institutionalized effort to confront the past through truth-telling exercises might be seen by those who were formerly on the receiving end of violence as a good faith effort to come clean, to understand long-term patterns of socialization, and, in this sense, to initiate a new political project around norms and values that this time around are truly shared.[101] Reparations can foster civic trust by demonstrating the seriousness with which institutions now take the violation of their rights, a seriousness that is manifested, to put it bluntly, by the fact that "money talks"—and so do symbolic reparations measures—that even under conditions of scarcity and competition for resources, the state responds to the obligation to fund programs that benefit those who were formerly not only marginalized but abused.[102] Finally, vetting can induce trust, and not just by "re-peopling" institutions with new faces, but by thereby demonstrating a commitment to systemic norms governing employee hiring and retention, disciplinary oversight, prevention of cronyism, and so on.[103]

C. DEMOCRATIC RULE OF LAW

Transitional societies not only claim to commit themselves to the rule of law but also claim that the implementation of transitional justice measures is both an expression of that commitment and a means to strengthen the rule of law. This claim can, and has been, fleshed out in different ways,[104] but the general point is that the various transitional justice measures contribute to strengthening the rule of law as follows: criminal trials that offer sound procedural guarantees and that do not exempt from the reach of justice those who wield power illustrate nicely the generality of law; truth-telling exercises that contribute to understanding the many ways in which legal systems failed to protect the rights of citizens provide the basis on which, *a contrario*, legal systems can behave in the future; reparations programs that try to redress the violation of rights serve to exemplify, even if it is *ex post facto*, the commitment to the notion that legal norms matter; and, finally, institutional reform measures, even those that screen out those who abused their positions, help to make rule of law systems operative, prospectively at least.

The point I am interested in making here is that the claim that transitional justice has as one of its goals the promotion of the rule of law has to be understood in its full richness. When transitional justice promoters argue that the measures they defend strengthen the rule of law they do not mean merely that the implementation of these measures will provide a boost to independent courts, where decisions are reasoned and taken on the basis of law (as important as these ideas are); courts that satisfy these minimal conditions have been part of pre-transitional regimes (for example, in Chile and South Africa) and have in fact either contributed to or failed in preventing the violations that transitional justice measures are meant to redress. Indeed, transitional justice promoters mean more with their commitment to the rule of law than a commitment to a formalist understanding of the rule of law would suggest; by the "rule of law" they do not refer only to the constraints on the exercise of power by means of laws that are "general, promulgated, not retroactive, clear, consistent, [and that impose obligations that are] not impossible to perform."[105] Indeed, a purely formal understanding of the rule of law according to which the rule of law is satisfied if formal criteria for the exercise of power, such as thin forms of impartiality, are adopted (for example, by treating similar cases alike) is compatible not with all but with many forms of arbitrariness, as long as these are regularly and predictably patterned.

Surely, this is not what the defenders of transitional justice mean when they say that they are committed to the rule of law. They use the concept of the rule of law as a standard to criticize regimes that have violated human rights, even if they have done so—indeed, particularly if they have done so—in regular and predictable ways with the support of law and legal operators. Transitional justice measures are supposed to act as markers of significant political transformation. They are supposed to both manifest and strengthen a more robust understanding of what a legitimate regime of law means, and this involves taking seriously the idea that legitimacy depends on not just formal characteristics of law, but also characteristics of the very process of *making* laws and on the substance of the laws thus produced.

In this sense, the commitment to the rule of law that underlies transitional justice is one that points in the direction of democracy. A rule is recognized as a legal *norm* not only in virtue of attending to facts pertaining to the rules themselves (for example, the fact that the rule has formal properties such that is has the capacity to guide behavior), but in virtue of the fact that those subject to it, after taking a normative, evaluative attitude, endow the rule with the authority to "norm" (*normen*) their behavior. Under conditions of modernity, this authority is a function of what I call "the dynamics of inclusion and ownership" behind lawmaking;[106] the authority of law depends, ultimately, upon its legitimacy, something that a law gains precisely in virtue of the fact that we can consider it to be *our* rule (ownership), one that we give to ourselves—via recognized procedures—where the "ourselves" keeps growing (inclusion).

Just as in the attribution to transitional justice of the goals of providing recognition and promoting civic trust, I want to emphasize that in claiming that transitional justice has as one of its "final goals" the promotion of democracy, the argument is not merely that democracy is a desirable goal, but that it is closely connected with justice. The democratic rule of law is both a precondition and a consequence of justice; the possibilities of achieving justice overall and of attaining its full effects usually depend on the possibility of establishing democratic participatory practices. At the same time, these practices and rights are enabled by giving everyone grounds for thinking of themselves as fairly treated by the institutions under which they live.

To round off this first version of the argument about the possible contribution of transitional justice to development, I want to highlight the special role of norms in this account. The effects of massive human rights violations and of leaving their legacies unaddressed, articulated in section II in terms of norm breakdown, is now matched by an account of transitional justice according to which transitional justice measures seek the reestablishment of the force of fundamental norms, and, in virtue of this norm-affirming potential, contribute to overcoming not just obstacles to the achievement of justice but, if the accounts in later sections is correct, obstacles to development as well.

V.2. CITIZENSHIP AND SOCIAL INTEGRATION

The second version of this same argument I frame in terms that are closer to debates in the field of development—namely, in terms of an inclusive conception of *citizenship*. The claim is that transitional justice measures can be thought of as mechanisms of social integration. Of course, this is not to say that transitional justice measures can solve problems of exclusion and marginalization or that they can repair social cleavages *on their own*.[107] There is no question that this requires the implementation of various types of policies, including familiar development programs, thus emphasizing the need to think about the possible *programmatic* links between transitional justice and development.

Ultimately, since these are two versions of the same core argument, this follows a path that should now be familiar. Although it is not common to understand the rule of law in this manner, it is not far-fetched to regard the requirements that the ideal imposes as those that are necessary for the inclusion of others as equal citizens in a common political community. Thus, for example, the requirement of generality simply provides reasons for others to be part of a common political project, for they would understandably be reluctant to join in if they felt at risk of being singled out for discriminatory treatment. The requirements of promulgation and publicity simply confirm our status as fellow members of the project, by insisting that if we are in this together, the least that can be expected is that common norms should be made known. And so on for the different formal dimensions of the rule of law.

Following this interpretive angle, which takes the rule of law as a social integration mechanism, makes it easier to see why the ideal of the rule of law to which transitional justice defenders commit themselves entails a commitment to inclusive and participatory citizenship, one of the fundamental concerns of development agencies.[108] If the legitimacy of laws depends on the possibility of those subject to them being able to call them meaningfully "their own," then the safest way of guaranteeing that this will be the case is by offering them the possibility in participating in functional ways in the formulation of these laws. The way this takes place in modern, complex, and differentiated societies is by the construction of a regime of rights that turn natural into legal persons, endowing them with a special status — that is, the status of *citizens*. On this argument, however, citizens are not simple passive recipients of, say, civil rights "foisted" on them by the authorities. The argument is that citizens can enjoy as *rights* — and not merely as dispensations from those who hold power — the protections that are meant to be provided by the traditional liberal civil rights enshrined in laws that satisfy the formal conditions of the ideal of the rule of law only if, at the same time, they can enjoy rights to political participation. The different requirements of the rule of law, including the requirement that citizens should have participatory rights, express efforts to secure the conditions under which it would make sense for them to participate in a common political project.

The core idea, then, is that transitional justice measures can be thought of as efforts to enable the activity and participation of citizens who were previously excluded and marginalized. These efforts turn on the possibility of giving force to general procedures and norms. In this sense, transitional justice can be thought of as a tool of social integration. This process not just of turning victims into citizens but thereby of strengthening inclusive citizenship — something that I hasten to reiterate cannot be achieved by transitional justice on its own — may, in the end, be the most significant contribution transitional justice can make to development.

CONCLUSION

I hope that some of the foregoing arguments help motivate giving greater attention to the possible interactions between transitional justice and development, and to the articulation of the conceptual relationship between the two fields. And yet, I hope that the arguments do not lead to conflating them. One way of thinking about both the proximity and the distinctness of the two fields appeals (momentarily) to the classical distinction between corrective and distributive justice. Justice, the argument would say, understood in a broad sense, precisely the sense that deep social transformation calls for, has both corrective and distributive dimensions. Transitional justice is functionally designed to address issues in the sphere of corrective justice, and development can also deal with issues in the "distributive" side of justice. This is not an argument to leave the traditional isolation between the two fields untouched, however, and in this sense the distinctions between corrective and distributive will not be taken to be watersheds. Just as transitional justice is interested not merely in correcting isolated, "token" abuses, but also in correcting systematic violations, which obviously requires systemic reform, development should not be thought to be interested merely in distributing already existing material goods and possibilities, but must take seriously how existing goods and possibilities came about. This is precisely what leads to the overlap between them; the "correction" of past abuses ultimately has an impact on prospective life chances. At the same time, however, the "distribution" of life chances must heed not just end points but starting points as well. Both "corrective" justice and "distributive" justice are necessary, and in some ways they implicate and reinforce one another. The challenge, then, is to find ways of observing the injunction to connect, without giving in to the temptation to conflate.

NOTES

1   My gratitude to Debbie Sharnak for unfailing research assistance and to Roger Duthie for research and useful comments on earlier versions of this chapter. The chapter does not necessarily represent ICTJ's position.

2   In my mind, this is not an unproblematic extension, and it deserves much more thought than it has received. The extension rests on an analogy between post-authoritarian and postconflict contexts, and as all analogies, this one rests on making salient relationships of similarity and leaving aside differences. This may be all right for some purposes, but certainly not for all. This will be the subject of an upcoming research project at the International Center for Transitional Justice (ICTJ).

3   See the chapter by Tony Addison, "The Political Economy of the Transition from Authoritarianism," in this volume.

4   Since its creation in November 1994, the International Criminal Tribunal for Rwanda (ICTR) has had budgets totaling more than US$1.1 billion. Its budget for 2008–2009 is $280,386,800 (see 69.94.11.53/default.htm). The 2008 budget for Rwanda's Ministry of Justice (which includes the supreme court, gacaca, and the ministry of justice) is $14.7 million (see www.rwandagateway.org/article.php3?id_article=7218). See also Ingrid Samset, Stina Petersen, and Vibeke Wang, "Foreign Aid to Transitional Justice: The Cases of Rwanda and Guatemala, 1995–2005," in *Building a Future on Peace and Justice: Studies on Transitional Justice, Peace and Development: The Nuremberg Declaration on Peace and Justice*, ed. Kai Ambos, Judith Large, and Marieke Wierda (Heidelberg: Springer, 2009).

5   It is meant to be read alongside Marcus Lenzen's chapter in this volume, "Roads Less Traveled? Conceptual Pathways (and Stumbling Blocks) for Development and Transitional Justice," which examines some of these issues from a perspective more informed by development practice.

6   Development was indeed understood in terms of economic growth for a good part of the 1950s and 1960s. The concern with issues of distribution in the specific sense of equity is a relatively late one. See Erik Thorbeke, "The Evolution of the Development Doctrine, 1950–2005," in *Advancing Development*, ed. George Mavrotas and Anthony Shorrocks (Houndmills: Palgrave, 2007).

7   See *International Journal for Transitional Justice* 2, no. 3 (2008), a special issue on transitional justice and development. There is also a great deal of work on related issues—e.g., on the relationship between development and human rights, some of which is referred to by Lenzen in his chapter in this volume. See also Philip Alston and Mary Robinson, eds., *Human Rights and Development* (Oxford: Oxford University Press, 2005). On the relationship between democracy and development, see, e.g., Amartya Sen's impressive body of work and work stimulated by it, some of which I cover in section IV.

8   Starting in section III, this economistic bias will be shed in favor of expanded conceptions of development.

9   See, e.g., Terence O'Hara and Kathleen Day, "Riggs Bank Hid Assets of Pinochet, Report Says," *Washington Post*, July 15, 2004, A01.

10   See Addison's chapter in this volume.

11   Of course, this will likely carry costs, which should also be taken into account. I begin to do this section in 1.5.

12   See Emily E. Harwell and Philippe Le Billon, "Natural Connections: Linking Transitional Justice and Development Through a Focus on Natural Resources," and Chris Huggins, "Linking Broad Constellations of Ideas: Transitional Justice, Land Tenure Reform, and Development," in this volume.

13   See Rolando Ames Cobián and Félix Reátegui, "Toward Systemic Social Transformation: Truth Commissions and Development," in this volume.

14   See Pablo de Greiff, "Truth-Telling and the Rule of Law," in *Telling the Truths: Truth Telling and Peace Building in Post-Conflict Societies*, ed. Tristan Anne Borer (Notre Dame, IN: University of Notre Dame Press, 2006).

15   Comisión de Esclarecimiento Histórico, *Guatemala Memoria del Silencio* (UNOPS: June 1999).

16   See, e.g., Comisión de la Verdad y Reconciliación, *Informe Final de la Comisión de la Verdad y Reconciliación*, vol. 1 (Lima, 2004). See also Claudia Paz y Paz Bailey, "Guatemala: Gender and Reparations for Human Rights Violations," and Julie Guillerot, "Linking Gender and Reparations in Peru: A Failed Opportunity," in *What Happened to the Women? Gender and Reparations for Human Rights Violations*, ed. Ruth Rubio-Marín (New York: Social Science Research Council, 2006); and Ruth Rubio-Marín, Claudia Paz y Paz Bailey, and Julie Guillerot, "Indigenous Peoples and Claims for Reparation: Tentative Steps in Peru and Guatemala" (unpublished ms., ICTJ, 2008).

17   See the summary of the commission's final report: Authority on Equity and Reconciliation, *Summary of the Final Report* (Rabat: Authority on Equity and Reconciliation, 2007).

18   Again, the decision to broaden the mandate of truth commissions in this fashion would not be cost-free, either, a point I also postpone until section 1.5.

19   See Naomi Roht-Arriaza and Katharine Orlovsky, "A Complementary Relationship: Reparations and Development," in this volume.

20   See Hans Dieter Seibel and Andrea Armstrong, "Reparations and Microfinance Schemes," in *The Handbook of Reparations* (hereafter *The Handbook*), ed. Pablo de Greiff (Oxford: Oxford University Press, 2006).

21   See, e.g., Basic Principles and Guidelines on the Right to a Remedy and Reparation for Victims of Gross Violations of International Human Rights Law and Serious Violations of International Humanitarian Law, Resolution 60/147 of 16 December 2005, Annex, para. 19ff.

22 See Pablo de Greiff, "Introduction: Repairing the Past," in *The Handbook*.

23 Despite the importance of establishing links between reparations and development programs, they ought not to be confused with one another; strictly speaking, these are different programs, entail different types of acknowledgment of responsibility, normally serve different constituencies, and ought to distribute slightly different types of goods, and for different reasons. I elaborate this argument in Pablo de Greiff, "Justice and Reparations," in *The Handbook*.

24 And just as with respect to the possibility of similarly enhancing the impact on development of the other transitional justice measures, these choices concerning reparations will also present difficulties, some of which are examined in section 1.5.

25 See Alexander Mayer-Rieckh, "On Preventing Abuse: Vetting and Other Transitional Reforms," and Federico Andreu-Guzmán, "Due Process and Vetting," in *Justice as Prevention: Vetting Public Employees in Transitional Societies*, ed. Alexander Mayer-Rieckh and Pablo de Greiff (New York: Social Science Research Council, 2007).

26 On integrity in vetting procedures, see Mayer-Rieckh, "On Preventing Abuse."

27 On this general issue, see Alexander Mayer-Rieckh and Roger Duthie, "Enhancing Justice and Development Through Justice-Sensitive Security Sector Reform," in this volume.

28 In the Argentinean case, for example, the trials of nine Junta leaders ended in December 1985 with three of them being absolved and the remaining six being sentenced to prison terms ranging from four and a half years to life sentences. In 1989, those convicted benefited from President Carlos Menem's pardons (although, as it turns out, this was not the end of their confrontation with the criminal justice system, which reinitiated cases against some of them years later). So, what, precisely, should one attribute a developmental potential to in a case such as this? The literature on Argentina's experience with prosecutions and other transitional justice measures is extensive. See, e.g., Alexandra Barahona de Brito, "Truth, Justice, Memory, and Democratization in the Southern Cone," in *The Politics of Memory*, ed. Alexandra Barahona de Brito, C. Gonzalez-Enriquez, and P. Aguilar (Oxford: Oxford University Press, 2001).

29 Even when the budgets are large in terms of the total sums distributed (such as that of Argentina, estimated at more than a billion U.S. dollars—there are no known official tallies), that does not necessarily mean that they make a significant difference at the macro level. Of course, this does not mean that individual beneficiaries are not better off because of the programs. But even here, the economic difference the programs make must be put in perspective; even the most "munificent" reparations programs rarely distribute sums that approach the victims' lifetime earnings. For the Argentinean case, see María José Guembe, "Economic Reparations for Grave Human Rights Violations: The Argentine Experience," in *The Handbook*, and for the concept of "munificence" in reparations, see de Greiff, "Introduction," in *The Handbook*. Disarmament, demobilization,

and reintegration (DDR) programs, which generally have significantly larger budgets than reparations programs, have not been shown to have measurable growth or distributive consequences, despite what their defenders like to claim. Claims about the developmental import of DDR programs have seeped into the otherwise realistic and comprehensive Integrated Disarmament, Demobilization and Reintegration Standards (IDDRS); see United Nations Inter-Agency Working Group (IAWG) on DDR, *Integrated Disarmament, Demobilization and Reintegration Standards* (New York: UN Department of Peacekeeping Operations, 2006), sect. 2.10. See Pablo de Greiff, "DDR and Reparations: Establishing Links Between Peace and Justice Instruments," in *Building a Future on Peace and Justice*. For discussions about the economic consequences of DDR programs, I thank Marcelo Febre at the World Bank.

30   The following borrows from an ICTJ document, "Transitional Justice and Economic Crimes," prepared by Roger Duthie with my collaboration in March 2008.

31   There is, indeed, in this disparate degree of development, an element that goes beyond mere historical contingency; criticisms of the leniency with which "white-collar" crime is treated in virtually all jurisdictions are no longer new. See, e.g., John Hagan and Patricia Parker, "White-Collar Crime and Punishment: The Class Structure and Legal Sanctioning of Securities Violations," *American Sociological Review* 50, no. 3 (June 1985): 302–16.

32   Priscilla Hayner and Lydiah Bosire, "Should Truth Commissions Address Economic Crimes? Considering the Case of Kenya," ICTJ Memorandum submitted to the Kenya Task Force on the Establishment of a Truth, Justice and Reconciliation Commission, March 26, 2003.

33   UN Office of the High Commissioner for Human Rights (OHCHR), *Rule-of-Law Tools for Post-Conflict States: Truth Commissions* (New York and Geneva: United Nations, 2006), 9.

34   De Greiff, "Introduction," in *The Handbook*; and Lisa Magarrell, "Reparations for Massive or Widespread Human Rights Violations: Sorting Out Claims for Reparations and the Struggle for Social Justice," *Windsor Yearbook of Access to Justice* 22 (2003): 85–98.

35   Cases in which powerful economic elites who owed some of their power to long authoritarian rule, but who over time became disaffected by the regime and therefore agents of transition, are not at all unknown. This tendency increases in periods in which economic elites become interested in processes of integrating national economies into international markets. The cases of Spain and El Salvador are revealing in this respect. Whether these elites would have maintained their support for the transitions if they had become the target of transitional justice measures is not too hard to tell.

36   This would have an impact, e.g., on whether to emphasize repairing material losses in a reparations program over other types of violations (doing so has regressive consequences), on the selection of violations to be repaired, and on the possibility of prioritizing some victims for purposes of the temporal distribution of reparations benefits

on the basis of their special vulnerability. See Ruth Rubio Marín and Pablo de Greiff, "Women and Reparations," *International Journal for Transitional Justice* 1, no. 3 (2006): 318–37, esp. 328–30.

37 The account that follows owes a lot to Margaret Walker's work, although she does not frame it in relationship to development issues. See Margaret Walker, *Moral Repair* (Cambridge: Cambridge University Press, 2006); and Pablo de Greiff, "The Role of Apologies in National Reconciliation Processes: On Making Trustworthy Institutions Trusted," in *The Age of Apology: Facing Up to the Past*, ed. Mark Gibney et al. (Philadelphia: University of Pennsylvania Press, 2008).

38 See Walker, *Moral Repair*; Elaine Scarry, *The Body in Pain* (Oxford: Oxford University Press, 1987); and Lawrence Weschler, *A Miracle, A Universe* (Chicago: University of Chicago Press, 1998).

39 "Resentment" here is not the name for just any negative affective reaction, but rather, as characterized by Walker, for a specific type of anger, one that attributes responsibility for the defeat, or the threat of defeat, of *normative expectations*. See her "Damages to Trust" in Walker, *Moral Repair*.

40 For an illuminating discussion of the notion of "victim" in the context of reparations programs, see Ruth Rubio-Marín, Clara Sandoval, and Catalina Díaz, "Repairing Family Members: Gross Human Rights Violations and Communities of Harm," in *The Gender of Reparations*, ed. Ruth Rubio-Marín (Cambridge: Cambridge University Press, forthcoming).

41 The spreading out of the effects of human rights violations from direct victims to others can be magnified when the violence has an identity dimension.

42 Jaime Malamud-Goti, *Game Without End* (Norman: University of Oklahoma Press, 1996), 120. There is nothing peculiar about the Argentinean case in this respect. The same phenomenon recurs again and again wherever massive human rights violations take place. Research into the sort of social fragmentation that comes about under extreme circumstances was intense in the postwar era. Martin Niemöller's famous explanation of how the Holocaust was possible gives expression to the same phenomenon: "First they came for the Communists but I was not a Communist so I did not speak out. Then they came for the Socialists and the Trade Unionists but I was not one of them, so I did not speak out. Then they came for the Jews but I was not Jewish so I did not speak out. And when they came for me, there was no one left to speak out for me." Karl Jaspers's notion of "metaphysical guilt" has at its nucleus, precisely, the breakdown of social bonds. See Karl Jaspers, *The Question of German Guilt*, E. B. Aston, trans., 2nd ed. (New York: Fordham University Press, 2001). For an insightful analysis of Jaspers's position, see also David Luban, "Intervention and Civilization: Some Unhappy Lessons of the Kosovo War," in *Global Justice and Transnational Politics*, ed. Pablo de Greiff and Ciaran Cronin (Cambridge, MA: MIT Press, 2002).

43   As Hannah Arendt put it, "[t]otalitarian government, like all tyrannies, certainly could not exist without destroying the public realm of life, that is, without destroying, by isolating men, their political capacities…." Hannah Arendt, *The Origins of Totalitarianism*, 2nd ed. (New York: Meridian Books, 1958), 475. Chaps. 3 and 4 of Malamud-Goti, *Game Without End*, provide a rich account of what he calls "disarticulating power," which is relevant to anyone interested in the developmental consequences of massive human rights violations (although development is not the focus of his attention).

44   On the notion of "social mechanisms," see, e.g., Peter Hedström and Richard Swedberg, "Social Mechanisms," *Acta Sociologica* 39 (1996): 281–308.

45   World Bank, *World Development Report 2006: Equity and Development* (Washington, DC: World Bank, 2006), chap. 2, esp. 48ff.

46   See, e.g., Robert Goodin, "Laundering Preferences," in *Foundations of Social Choice Theory*, ed. Jon Elster and Aanund Hylland (Cambridge: Cambridge University Press, 1986); and Cass Sunstein, "Democracy and Shifting Preferences," in *The Good Polity: Normative Analysis of the State*, ed. Allan Hamlin and Phillip Pettit (Oxford: Polity Press, 1989).

47   See, e.g., Jay Macleod, *Ain't No Makin' It* (Boulder: Westview Press, 1995). For the notion of horizontal inequalities, see Frances Stewart, ed., *Horizontal Inequalities and Conflict: Understanding Group Violence in Multiethnic Societies* (Basingstoke: Palgrave, 2008).

48   Arjun Appadurai, "The Capacity to Aspire: Culture and the Terms of Recognition," in *Culture and Public Action*, ed. Vijayendra Rao and Michael Walton (Stanford: Stanford University Press, 2004), 68. See also Amartya Sen, "How Does Culture Matter?" in the same collection.

49   Appadurai, "The Capacity to Aspire," 66.

50   See Geoffrey Wood, "Staying Secure, Staying Poor: The 'Faustian Bargain,'" *World Development* 31 (2003): 455–71.

51   I use scare quotes around costs to emphasize that these costs are not merely economic. The point is that weak general norms and diminished agency affect not merely victims but larger groups in various ways.

52   Alejandro Portes and Patricia Landolt call trust the "twin" of social capital in "The Downside of Social Capital," *American Prospect* 26 (1996): 18–21.

53   Partha Dasgupta thinks of trust in terms of mere regularity, a conception of trust that unfortunately figures prominently in the social capital literature, even though in that setting it is particularly unhelpful. See Partha Dasgupta, "Trust as a Commodity," in *Trust: Making and Breaking Cooperative Relations*, ed. Diego Gambetta (Oxford: Blackwell, 1988). For a more detailed elaboration of the norm-based conception of trust I use here, see, e.g., de Greiff, "The Role of Apologies."

54   Compare, e.g., Francis Fukuyama, "Social Capital, Civil Society and Development," *Third World Quarterly* 22 (2001): 7–20; and Gaute Torsvik, "Social Capital and Economic Development: A Plea for the Mechanisms," *Rationality and Society* 12 (2000): 451–76.

55 See, e.g., Stephen Knack and Philip Keefer, "Does Social Capital Have an Economic Payoff? A Cross-Country Investigation," *Quarterly Journal of Economics* 112, no. 4 (1997): 1251–88; Paul J. Zak and Stephen Knack, "Trust and Growth," *Economic Journal* 111 (2001): 295–321; and Stephen Knack, "Social Capital, Growth, and Poverty: A Survey of Cross-Country Evidence," in *The Role of Social Capital in Development: An Empirical Assessment*, ed. Christiaan Grootaert and Thierry van Bastelaer (Cambridge: Cambridge University Press, 2002).

56 Knack, "Social Capital, Growth, and Poverty," 73. See also Philip Keefer and Stephen Knack, "Why Don't Poor Countries Catch Up? A Cross-National Test of an Institutional Explanation," *Economic Inquiry* 35 (1997): 590–602. Deepa Narayan, in a World Bank paper, summarizes the results of one relevant study as follows: "[the authors] examined the relationship between the level of per capita GDP in 1960 and 1985 as well as the average growth of per capita GDP and an exhaustive list of political and social indicators. They found that higher levels of GDP were associated with greater civil and political rights. This included protection of human rights, tolerance for diversity and compromise in conflict. They also found that higher levels of GDP were associated with lower levels of political instability and higher levels of efficiency in public institutions, as measured by the efficiency of the judiciary and civil service bureaucracy and lower corruption [sic]." Deepa Narayan, "Bonds and Bridges: Social Capital and Poverty," Poverty Group, World Bank (n.d.), 20. She is summarizing the findings in Johannes Fedderke and Robert Klitgaard, "Economic Growth and Social Indicators: An Exploratory Analysis," *Economic Development and Cultural Change* 46 (1998): 455–89.

57 Knack, "Social Capital, Growth, and Poverty," 55.

58 Malamud-Goti, *Game Without End*, 114 (footnote omitted).

59 This argument may encounter two objections, which I can only meet here briefly. First, it may be objected that people do not make their judgments about the trustworthiness of institutions *in toto*, but sector by sector. This is less likely, however, in contexts in which institutions engage in massive and systematic human rights abuses. This is due both to the severity and systematicity of the abuses, and (relatedly) because these are contexts in which separations of powers and institutional differentiation and autonomy have frequently broken down. Second, it may be objected that this argument implies that economic activity automatically diminishes with the onset of human rights violations, which empirically may or may not be the case, particularly in the short run. This objection, however, oversimplifies the complicated relationship between politics (broadly conceived) and economic activity. The argument is that trust is one (of many) enabling conditions of social coordination, and therefore weak bonds of trust (or narrow, intragroup bonds — what in the social capital literature is called "bonding," rather than broad, intergroup, or "bridging" social capital) do not, as in a uni-causal mechanism, impede growth. Obviously, reality is more complicated than that. This second

objection may also lead to ignoring that over time abusive regimes frequently engage in forms of economic behavior that include rampant cronyism and corruption, leading to unproductive expenditures, undisciplined rent seeking, and macroeconomic destabilization, as Tony Addison in his chapter in this volume argues authoritarian regimes often do. On bridging and bonding social capital, see, e.g., Alejandro Portes, "Social Capital: Its Origins and Applications in Modern Sociology," *Annual Review of Sociology* 22 (1998): 1–24; Portes and Landolt, "The Downside of Social Capital"; Margaret Levi, "Social and Unsocial Capital," *Politics and Society* 24 (1996): 24–55; and Theda Skocpol, "Unraveling from Above," *American Prospect* 25 (1996): 20–25.

60   UNDP's *Human Development Reports* have been the primary vehicle for the dissemination of this concept of development.

61   As the *Human Development Report 1990* puts the point, "[t]echnical considerations of the means to achieve human development—and the use of statistical aggregates to measure national income and its growth—have at times obscured the fact that the primary objective of development is to benefit people." UNDP, *Human Development Report 1990* (hereafter *HDR 1990*) (New York: Oxford University Press, 1990), 9.

62   See, e.g., *HDR 1990*, chap. 1.

63   See, e.g., Amartya Sen, "Well-Being, Agency, and Freedom," *Journal of Philosophy* 82 (1985): 169–221; and Amartya Sen, "Capability and Well-Being," in *The Quality of Life*, ed. Martha Nussbaum and Amartya Sen (Oxford: Clarendon Press, 1993).

64   This, and the problem of "adaptive preferences" encountered before, among other reasons, explains why a utilitarian perspective on development, one that takes the basic criterion to be "preference satisfaction," which calls for asking people for their level of well-being, is unsatisfactory as well. See, e.g., Amartya Sen, *Development as Freedom* (Oxford: Oxford University Press, 2001), 58–63. See also Martha Nussbaum's very useful "Capabilities and Human Rights," in *Global Justice and Transnational Politics*.

65   *HDR 1990*, 1.

66   Sen, *Development as Freedom*, 3. For a useful account of Sen's and Nussbaum's capability approach, see David Crocker, "Functioning and Capability: The Foundations of Sen's and Nussbaum's Development Ethic," *Political Theory* 20 (1992): 584–612.

67   See *HDR 1990*, 13. The report does insist that analyses of human development "must not ignore" political freedom, personal security, interpersonal relations, the physical environment, and "the more qualitative dimensions of human life," but that these aspects "largely escape measurement now" (ibid.). UNDP's *Human Development Report 2000: Human Rights and Human Development* (hereafter *HDR 2000*) (New York: Oxford University Press, 2000) is actually quite emphatic on the importance of political rights, and specifically of *democratic* political rights for development. In its foreword, Mark Malloch Brown, UNDP Administrator at the time, calling the report "unapologetically independent and provocative," summarizes its main thrust as follows: "[the report] clearly

underlines the fact that human rights are not, as has sometimes been argued, a reward of development. Rather, they are critical to achieving it. Only with *political freedoms*—the right for all men and women to participate equally in society—can people genuinely take advantage of economic freedoms" (*HDR 2000*, iii [emphasis added]). The body of the report does make a strong pitch for taking seriously the rights-protecting functions of democracy (see esp. chap. 3, "Inclusive Democracy Secures Rights") and reviews some of the indices that others have developed to, among other things, track progress in democracy and the rule of law (see chap. 5, "Using Indicators for Human Rights Accountability"). The human development index remains unchanged, however.

68   Nussbaum, "Capabilities and Human Rights," 119.

69   These include: life; bodily health; bodily integrity; senses imagination, and thought; emotions; practical reason; affiliation (friendship and respect); being able to live in relation to the world of nature; play; and control over one's political and material environment. See Nussbaum, "Capabilities and Human Rights," 129–30.

70   Sen, *Development as Freedom*, 38–41.

71   Nussbaum, "Capabilities and Human Rights," 134.

72   Lenzen's chapter in this volume examines the related question of the links between transitional justice and the rights-based approach to development.

73   *HDR 2000*, 1.

74   Ibid., 20.

75   Ibid., 23–24.

76   Ibid., 20–21.

77   See ibid., 21.

78   Since my purpose here is not so much to provide a review of HDR but to consider ways of thinking about development and its relationship with transitional justice, I leave the following commentary for a footnote, but not without emphasizing its importance. Oddly, the report does not pursue the argument that its own conception of rights invites about the contribution of transitional justice measures to development, despite the fact that its chapter on democracy and human rights has a section on the legacies of authoritarian regimes (see *HDR 2000*, 61–63, and the table on truth commissions, 72). This section, surprisingly, treats truth commissions (alone among transitional redress mechanisms) as one of three ways of "convert[ing] militarist or fascist states into democracies" (alongside the external imposition of democratic institutions—as in Germany and Japan after World War II—and an internal consensus on democracy that decides "not to rake up a difficult past in human rights"—as in Spain). Worse, questioning the usefulness of even this part of transitional justice "when there is a consensus in society about the direction of transition, and no perceived threat of a reversal," the section concludes that countries "fear[ing] the resurgence of authoritarian forces may well consider the

utility of a truth and reconciliation commission to put such forces on the defensive" (*HDR 2000*, 61–62). This both overestimates the capacities of a (single) transitional justice measure, truth commissions, and underestimates its functions (which go well beyond putting authoritarian forces on the defensive). As I will argue, a comprehensive transitional justice policy can make more significant contributions to development.

79   *HDR 2000*, 21 (emphasis added).

80   Compare Nussbaum, "Capabilities and Human Rights," 138–39. Her position is ultimately complicated, for she shares the interest in rights of liberal political philosophy, but she is also an Aristotelian, who therefore thinks that an account of capabilities *justifies* the account of rights. See, e.g., her "Non-Relative Virtues," in *The Quality of Life*, and her "Aristotelian Social Democracy," in *Liberalism and the Good*, ed. Richard Douglass, Gerald Mara, and Henry Richardson (New York: Routledge, 1990).

81   *HDR 2000*, 21.

82   To state the obvious, I am not arguing *against* the conception of rights, but against thinking that a general understanding of rights settles questions about whether we have rights to particular goods in the fashion described above.

83   Nussbaum, "Capabilities and Human Rights," 129.

84   Compare the list of basic capabilities in Nussbaum, "Capabilities and Human Rights," 129–30.

85   See, e.g., Yael Danieli, ed., *International Handbook of Multigenerational Legacies of Trauma* (New York: Springer, 2007).

86   Sen's work obviously influences the presentation that follows of the different strategies underlying an expansion of the notion of development. His own account of development as freedom is distinctive not the least in linking all of them. The challenges involved in expanding the notion of development to include civil and political rights, however, are general, and therefore I will not frame the arguments in terms of how he responds to them. For Sen's own account of how these links work, see *Development as Freedom*, esp. Introduction, chaps. 1–3, and 6.

87   How rich the catalogue of civil and political rights that forms part of an expanded conception of development might be is a separate question, also subject to intense debate. Among institutionalist economists, for example, there is agreement that the rights usually associated with the rule of law plus a stable regime of property rights are crucial (instrumentally) for development. There are intense debates, however, about whether to interpret the rule of law so as to include rights to political participation.

88   The literature on this topic is large. See, e.g., Robert J. Barro, "Democracy and Growth," *Journal of Economic Growth* 1, no. 1 (March 1996): 1–27; and Dani Rodrik and Romain Wacziarg, "Do Democratic Transitions Produce Bad Economic Outcomes?" *American Economic Review* 95, no. 2 (2005): 50–55.

89   *World Development Report 2006.*

90   The World Bank's work on good governance may be seen in this light, but so can, e.g., the UK Department for International Development's (DFID) work on accountability and good governance.

91   Jean Drèze and Amartya Sen, *Hunger and Public Action* (Oxford: Clarendon Press, 1989). See Sen, *Development and Freedom*, chap. 7.

92   See Sen, *Development and Freedom*, chap. 6.

93   Each measure can be thought to pursue some immediate goals of its own; collectively, all the measures can be thought to pursue at least one more causally distant goal than the three mentioned above — namely, to further reconciliation. I present in detail the case for attributing these particular goals to transitional justice measures in "Theorizing Transitional Justice," in *Transitional Justice*, ed. Melissa Williams and Rosemary Nagy, Nomos XLX (forthcoming).

94   I say "adequate" responses not in the sense of "sufficient," for there is no transitional justice policy that has led to the prosecution of each and every perpetrator of human rights violations (let alone to their punishment in proportion to the gravity of the harms they caused); that has implemented a truth-seeking strategy leading to the disclosure of the fate of each and every victim, or to an absolutely thorough disclosure of the structures that made the violations possible; that has led to the establishment of a reparations program making each and every victim whole (providing them with benefits proportional to the harm they suffered); or that, particularly in the short run, has led to the reform of each and every institution that was either involved in or made possible the violations in question. I mean "adequate" in the sense of "proper" or "fitting," in the sense that massive norm breakdown is redressed by means that seek the restoration or the establishment of the force of the norms that were systematically breached.

95   See de Greiff, "Theorizing Transitional Justice," for the steps of the argument and for references to earlier pieces. In my opinion, it is also important to distinguish between these goals in terms of causal proximity and (degrees of in-)sufficiency. But I cannot address this point here.

96   On the notion of recognition, see, among others, Axel Honneth, *The Struggle for Recognition: The Moral Grammar of Social Conflicts* (Cambridge, MA: MIT Press, 1995); and Axel Honneth and Nancy Fraser, *Redistribution or Recognition: A Political-Philosophical Exchange* (New York: Verso, 2003).

97   Joel Feinberg, e.g., argues that there are two different ways of understanding "harms": (1) harm as a setback to interests, and (2) harm as a wrong to another person. Only the latter is relevant to the law. See his *The Moral Limits of the Criminal Law*, vol. 1, *Harm to Others* (Oxford: Oxford University Press, 1987), 31–36.

98   See Jean Hampton, "The Moral Education Theory of Punishment," *Philosophy and Public Affairs* (1981): 209–38.

99   Thomas Nagel argues that there is "a difference between knowledge and acknowledgment. It is what happens and can only happen to knowledge when it becomes officially sanctioned, when it is made part of the public cognitive scene." Quoted in Lawrence Weschler, "Afterword," in *State Crimes: Punishment or Pardon*, Aspen Institute Report, Washington, DC, 1989, 93.

100   In "Theorizing Transitional Justice," I examine the notion of civic trust in some detail.

101   See de Greiff, "Truth-Telling and the Rule of Law."

102   See de Greiff, "Justice and Reparations."

103   See Pablo de Greiff, "Vetting and Transitional Justice," in *Justice as Prevention*.

104   In "Truth-telling and the Rule of Law," I canvass some of the ways in which truth-telling, in particular, may be thought to promote the rule of law.

105   This is Judith Shklar's summary of the familiar requirements of the rule of law, in Judith Shklar, "Political Theory and the Rule of Law," reprinted in her *Political Thought and Political Thinkers* (Princeton: Princeton University Press, 1998), 33.

106   See de Greiff, "Truth-Telling and the Rule of Law."

107   Indeed, whether the measures contribute at all to social integration in any given case is an empirical issue that depends on many factors. It is also important to keep in mind the many ways in which the implementation of the measures can actually undermine social integration; actual or perceived biases in the selection of cases to prosecute or in the determination of the periods to be covered by a truth commission investigation, in the types of violations to be investigated or that will be the subject of reparations, or in the offices to subject to vetting exercises, will obviously hamper the capacity of transitional justice measures to contribute to social integration.

108   The development literature on this issue is huge. The following are samples. See, e.g., Andrea Cornwall, *Beneficiary, Consumer, Citizen: Perspectives on Participation for Poverty Reduction*, Swedish International Development Cooperation Agency (SIDA) Studies no. 2 (Stockholm: SIDA, 2000). See the emphasis on participation in UN Department of Economic and Social Affairs (UNDESA), "Participatory Dialogue: Towards a Stable, Safe, and Just Society for All," ST/ESA/310, the 2007 report from UNDESA on the notion of social integration.

CHAPTER 2

Roads Less Traveled?
Conceptual Pathways (and Stumbling Blocks) for Development and Transitional Justice

Marcus Lenzen[1]

Pero es bello amar al mundo
Con los ojos
De los que no han nacido
todavía.
—Otto Rene Castillo[2]

Development theory and practice to date has not engaged extensively with transitional justice, a field of the human rights sphere that has received growing attention under that label over the past decade. My aim in this chapter is to explore tentative pathways to conceive of how development and transitional justice practices connect—from a development practitioner's point of view. It is my hope that these pathways may serve other practitioners to reflect further on linkages as they encounter one another in different arenas. The guiding questions I address here are: (1) Why should development actors be concerned with transitional justice? (2) Which concepts may help thinking about linkages (and limitations or contradictions)? (3) What could transitional justice learn from development practice (and vice versa)? and (4) Which dilemmas (or stumbling blocks) arise that require further scrutiny?

The challenge is to know what we are comparing. "Development" and "transitional justice" can be understood as discourses, as communities of practice, as conceptual fields.[3] Neither one has a singularly agreed upon definition. Both are contested territories with diverging bodies of (at least emerging) theory, policy, and practice.[4] What they have in common is that they are both process-oriented fields in the sense that they are concerned with change toward improving human lives and societies. At a minimum, it is argued in both fields that to achieve said positive change, a mix of measures is needed that depends on given and envisioned conditions and capabilities. From this point onward, the debate endures as to what the most suitable mix of measures is, what the best sequencing may be, what the best approaches are, what exactly the desired outcome of these processes should be, and who gets to have a say in determining all this.

To find—and often negotiate—answers to these questions, a "practitioner" needs to understand what the issue is, both conceptually and in real terms; what the stakes are, and who the stakeholders are; and what the objectives are, and the means and conditions necessary to achieve them. He or she would ask which policies, approaches, tools, and mechanisms exist to help achieve the objective, what evidence there is for more or less successful ones, and what the constraints and risks may be when trying to implement a given process or mechanism. A development practitioner confronted with the challenge of implementing or interacting with a transitional justice measure may first draw on his or her own conceptual and practical "tool box." But how applicable are development tools and approaches to the implementation of transitional justice measures? Should a development actor assume that a transitional justice "issue" or process could be addressed like other development issues, with a similar set of tools and approaches?

To give my answer to the last question right away: no, they should not. This does not mean that development practice has nothing to offer to further transitional justice, but we need to better understand what it does have to offer exactly, and to what extent. Discussing and comparing concepts and theories of transitional justice and development are important to further our understanding. They help influence policies, and policies shape practice. A wide range of development actors are involved in this practice, from donors to multilateral, bilateral, national, and nongovernmental agencies, down to program or project managers at the country level as well as the "beneficiaries" of development projects.

Many of the countries dealing with transitional justice issues are less-developed countries where a plethora of these development actors are operating. Conversely, many development actors find themselves in countries with (recent or more distant) histories of massive human rights violations, which those countries may or may not be trying to deal with. Even if we leave questions of mandate and the comparative advantage of development actors aside for the moment, in practice development actors come into direct contact with transitional justice concerns and processes by the mere fact that they are present and active as service providers in a given country.[5] Donors are requested (or proactively decide) to invest Official Development Assistance (ODA)[6] in support of transitional measures; development agencies with offices and facilities on the ground are asked to help administer aid to transitional justice institutions, and to help build their capacities—if for no other reason than simply because "they can"—in other words, because they have the financial and technical delivery mechanisms in place required for disbursing development aid relatively quickly, and relatively reliably.

The fact that a given actor is able to administer development aid *efficiently*, however, does not suffice to ensure that development aid is spent *effectively* on transitional justice. Development actors need to be concerned with the effectiveness of aid, not in the least for accountability reasons—both to donors and to beneficiaries. Yet, how is development aid to be considered effective when it comes to dealing with the past? What are suitable result and impact indicators? In fact, before even getting to the details of delivering aid and implementing projects—the daily bread of many development actors—what about the bigger question that I left aside above: Should development actors be concerned with transitional justice in the first place? Is it part of their mandate? Do they have a comparative advantage? Last but not least, are they sufficiently equipped with the requisite conceptual understanding as well as practical approaches to help address transitional justice matters?

I am not able to answer all of these questions here. In fact, the point of this chapter is to underline why it is important for development actors to address these questions more thoroughly, given that they have become increasingly involved in directly supporting transitional justice processes, or at least have been increasingly operating in contexts where transitional justice dynamics have evolved. This has happened by and large without an overall policy framework for development assistance in this area.[7]

Over the past few years, some development donors and agencies have begun to grapple with this issue, at least tentatively, but they are only slowly coming to grips with what transitional justice means to them, and what their roles should be. There has been an increasing number of workshops and meetings hosted by development actors, but often also by foreign offices, on the matter of dealing with the legacy of mass atrocities and human rights violations. It has not emerged as a headline topic in development policy papers and practice notes, but it does find mention.[8] Practical experience is more advanced than policy in this regard, although too little of it has been systematically captured. I think it is time to take stock of that experience in order to inform policy through practice.

My argument, however, goes further than a call to account for practical experience. For one, transitional justice—or the range of processes and institutions through which a society seeks to come to terms with a past of massive human rights violations—can be of *instrumental* value to larger development goals in post-authoritarian and postconflict societies. If we accept that transitional justice is concerned with how to restore trust and confidence between the state and its citizens, and among citizens, then development actors involved in processes of state building and strengthening (democratic) governance institutions have a reason to be interested in and seek to understand transitional justice.[9]

Second, I argue that, in order to avoid doing harm, development actors operating in contexts where significant parts of the population have been affected by and participated in massive human rights violations need to be conscious of the issues with which transitional justice is concerned. This I mean in a dual sense. On one hand, when involved in directly supporting transitional justice measures, development actors need to understand both the *normative* human rights dimensions at stake and the *intrinsic* worth of transitional justice processes for the victims and survivors.[10] For example, development actors need to know how to avoid confusing reparations measures with development services.[11] On the other hand, even when not directly involved in supporting transitional justice processes, development actors should at a minimum be aware of the legacies of human rights violations and their impact on people's lives and their perceptions, no matter what development initiative they are engaged in. There are, for instance, development agencies that have hired predominantly national staff from one particular ethnic group in countries marked by ethnically tainted conflicts. However inadvertent this may (or may not) have been, what is the message that such a recruitment practice is sending? How aware is the development actor about the impact on public perception?[12]

Third, I argue that development actors have important perspectives and experience to contribute to transitional justice efforts, especially from a practical point of view. Development actors should have a good notion of the developmental condition of a country in question.[13] They should be able to contribute a good sense of the kind of institutions and processes that are feasible in light of existing national capacities and conditions. And, by engaging seriously with transitional justice actors, development actors should be able to proactively avoid overloading transitional justice measures with heavy developmental expectations. In other words, they should help to ensure that people's needs and expectations with regard to transitional justice are not conflated with socioeconomic development aspirations. For, as Pablo de Greiff concludes in his chapter in this volume, "the best way of articulating the relationship between transitional justice and development . . . is unlikely to fall out of observations about the *economic* consequences of the implementation of transitional justice measures."

I elaborate on these arguments, in the next step, by exploring linkages between the concepts of transitional justice and development, and in particular by looking at some of the arenas of theory and practice where the two meet and overlap. Notably, these are the arenas of "peacebuilding" (and the related one of "state building") and "human rights–based approaches to development." Against these conceptual discussions, I then sketch both opportunities for mutual learning, and limitations and challenges. This chapter raises more questions than it answers, but I hope it can help point the way toward the right approach to finding the answers.

DEVELOPMENT, TRANSITIONAL JUSTICE, AND PEACEBUILDING

There has been an increasing recognition in academic and policy forums that development has a role to play to help build sustainable peace, essentially a long-term process. Earlier (academic) explorations focused on the question of the kind of development that would foster more peaceful socioeconomic and political structures. Following the end of the Cold War, development and peace research do not seem to have engaged much with one another. Both fields, however, focused increasingly on the causes and consequences of civil war, and on how development initiatives in postconflict countries needed to pay more attention to how to keep them from falling into a "conflict trap."[14]

Although transitional justice's conceptual origins as a field have to be understood in the context of democratic transitions,[15] it has become increasingly articulated as one of the measures to help build peace in societies emerging from the devastations of war.[16] This is in part a reflection of the types of war the world has witnessed since the end of the Cold War—that is, an increased number of civil wars marked by brutal and massive human rights violations, war crimes, and crimes against humanity. In response, over the course of the 1990s, the UN transformed a more limited notion of "peacekeeping" to a much more involved notion of "peacebuilding."[17] At the same time, justice and accountability were increasingly accepted as an integral part of peacebuilding in postconflict societies. Thus, the UN itself became the "conduit for the application of international norms and standards of accountability" in many transitional societies.[18] This was expressed very clearly in a report of the UN secretary-general to the Security Council on *The Rule of Law and Transitional*

Justice in Conflict and Post-Conflict Societies,[19] still the defining high-level docu-ment on these concepts for the UN.

At a policy level, development has come to be concerned with capaci-ties and conditions for peace because without peace, development gains are eroded, under threat, or impossible to achieve with equity for society at large. Similarly, the development community had to come to terms with the fact that its interventions can do harm and fuel violent conflict if it remains ignorant of conflict dynamics extant in every society.[20] At a practice level, develop-ment actors therefore have been seeking to adapt their approaches to be more conflict-sensitive, and have had to ask themselves about the kind of capacities, institutions, and processes they should seek to strengthen and support through their available tools and mechanisms in order to foster conditions for sustain-able peace—and development. Importantly, from a development perspective, peacebuilding should not be conceived of only as a postconflict agenda; it also needs to deal with the capacities for dealing peacefully with conflict. Develop-ment actors ostensibly have an important contribution to make because they tend to be present in a country before, during, and (long) after a violent conflict occurs—albeit with very different levels of presence and maneuverability.

Transitional justice can be thought to be an essential building block for peacebuilding because if a society leaves the legacies of mass atrocities and abuse unaddressed, or deals with them insufficiently, sustainable peaceful coex-istence may remain elusive.[21] As the UN secretary-general put the point: "Our experience in the past decade has demonstrated clearly that the consolidation of peace in the immediate postconflict period, as well as the maintenance of peace in the long term, cannot be achieved unless the population is confident that redress for grievances can be obtained through legitimate structures for the peaceful settlement of disputes and the fair administration of justice."[22] De Greiff articulates the underlying reasons appealing to the breakdown of trust and adverse terms of recognition left in the wake of mass atrocities.[23]

Ultimately, "dealing with the past" has to be understood as a long-term process of societal change. This connects with the notion of the "final" aims of transitional justice discussed by de Greiff: reconciliation and democracy (based on certain norms and the rule of law).[24] Dealing with the past is about chang-ing mind-sets with regard to oneself and the other—the two (or more) parts that have been in conflict with one another, have sought to control, subject, or dominate the other, and in the process have dehumanized, discriminated, persecuted, tortured, and sought to destroy the other (and/or escape or defend oneself in the face of such acts). The change in mind-sets is presumably a req-uisite if such harm is not to recur. Changing mind-sets necessitates not only the ability to relate to the other, and to trust in peaceful intentions, but also to (re)build confidence in the institutions that have not been able or willing to prevent the violence and abuse in the first place. These institutions—defined as sets of norms and values—have to be upheld, guaranteed, and promoted by the state. When a state has abused its power, lost its power, or never developed the power to provide for the security and peace of all its citizens, then it will have no—or lost all—confidence from its citizens.

After a violent conflict or a period marked by massive human rights violations, it is thus even more important to change or develop the capacity of state (and societal) institutions to foster conditions for peaceful coexistence for all citizens. In order to be able to do so, such institutions must have the confidence of citizens and be accountable, equitable, equally accessible for all, and able to manage societal conflict peacefully.

Here we are, then, at a convergence point of development and transitional justice in the peacebuilding arena: both are concerned to some extent with contributing to the development of institutions and their capacities to ensure the conditions for peaceful coexistence. This means being concerned with the renewal of civic trust and confidence between the state and citizens—which is ultimately about the renewal of the social contract. Both fields therefore stand to benefit from an increased conceptual dialogue with regard to the necessary conditions and processes required for sustainable peacebuilding. Such a dialogue may also help inform the (re)emerging debate on "state building," which is presently receiving increasing attention in the international development community. Since that debate is concerned with how to make fragile states more *resilient* and *responsive*—and how to renew the social contract in postconflict peacebuilding situations—our discussion here should be able to provide insights concerning some of the necessary elements to renew civic trust.[25]

STRUCTURAL (DEVELOPMENTAL) CONDITIONS
FOR SUSTAINABLE PEACE AND TRANSITIONAL JUSTICE

When discussing peacebuilding and development challenges from a practice point of view, there is always a risk of focusing too much on the kind of processes that the international aid machinery tends to put in place or support. These tend to be "projectizable" and "operationalizable," relatively time-bound measures whose sequencing can be debated and context-dependent, but often follow similar patterns (immediate humanitarian aid; disarming, disbanding, and reintegrating armed groups; destroying mines; organizing democratic elections; strengthening administrative and service provision capacities of central and local government institutions; (re)training security forces; setting up a truth commission, and so on).

A discussion of conceptual linkages between development and transitional justice, however, needs to go further. Development should be concerned with the structural conditions of inequality and poverty, which are often intricately linked to the histories of violence that peacebuilding tries to overcome, and that transitional justice tries to "deal with." Given the long-term nature of the kind of societal change discussed above, and the long-term nature of changing structural conditions of inequality, poverty, and violence, it is worthwhile to look for even deeper conceptual linkages.

Indeed, one could argue that there is a "missing link" between peacebuilding efforts and efforts dedicated to restoring justice. Some favor a more holistic and integrated approach, one that looks beyond a justice that deals only with the consequences of conflict (war crimes, crimes against humanity), and that embraces multiple dimensions of justice (legal, rectificatory, distributive) that also address the symptoms and root causes of conflict.[26] De Greiff (in this volume) reminds us that although distributive and corrective justice implicate and reinforce one another, there are risks that go with forgetting that transitional justice measures are primarily functionally designed to address issues in the sphere of corrective justice. I agree that, both conceptually and programmatically, it is important to understand the potential for complementarity, but also to retain the respective integrity of the two fields.

Addressing symptoms and causes of conflict in turn requires thinking about structural conditions of peace. In practical terms, the question is about the kind of factors and indicators we choose in order to analyze and to understand the structural conditions of peace and of conflict. The choice of these factors and indicators is in turn influenced by the concepts and theories (of change) that influence policy and practice. My point is that it would be useful to explore further: (1) how well such structural conditions are being analyzed and understood in development (and peacebuilding) practice; (2) which factors are typically being used; and specifically (3) to what extent dealing with the past can be conceived of as a variable to further measure the relationship between peace, development, and (the recurrence of) violence.[27]

INSIGHTS FROM HUMAN RIGHTS IN DEVELOPMENT PRACTICE

Transitional justice is to a large degree a field within the wider sphere of human rights. Until recently, the global human rights project and the development enterprise had "lived in splendid isolation" from one another.[28] I argue that some of the challenges as well as linkages between transitional justice and development can be understood from the history of (non-)engagement between the development and human rights communities. As the relationship between human rights and development has been increasingly scrutinized in recent years, there are some useful conceptual entry points emerging that can help inform our thinking about development and transitional justice. However, just as the debate on the interface between development and human rights is far from conclusive, there is still a lot of unchartered territory with regard to implications for transitional justice. Most of the work on human rights and development has paid little or no explicit attention to dealing with past human rights abuses.

Since the 1990s, human rights language and discourse has been increasingly incorporated into statements, policies, and frameworks of the development community. Yet it remains a question of debate whether human rights rhetoric in development has remained window dressing, or whether the discursive shift is eventually trickling down to a change in policy and, more significantly, in practice.

By consequence, development initiatives can claim that the services they provide contribute to the realization of human rights somehow by default. Critics point out how such a service-based approach dressed in human rights language dodges addressing the structural inequalities that make poverty endemic and fails to address the real tensions between economic development (for whom?) and human rights. A true human rights–based approach would lead to a different kind of development because it means talking very directly about the relationship between a state and its citizens—about long-term guarantees, particularly for the most "vulnerable" and marginalized in society. This is very similar to points raised in the previous section concerning structural conditions for peace.[29]

To structure the following discussion, I find it helpful to follow the analytical and practice-oriented approach Peter Uvin takes in his analysis of human rights and development.[30] While he does not give much specific consideration to elements of transitional justice, I try to do so. To summarize some of his most salient points:

A) Development and human rights have had separate intellectual histories and worlds of practice, which have only recently begun to interact more with one another.

B) Development and human rights communities both have had to struggle with certain challenges and criticisms—notably the charge of

Eurocentrism and/or neocolonialism—that are comparable and offer scope for mutual learning.

c) Development practice has sought to integrate human rights elements through political conditionality, positive support, and the human rights–based approach to development.

Points a and b I discuss briefly. Point c offers analytical categories that lend themselves to a more detailed discussion.

On point a, the intellectual history of development is much shorter than the history of human rights. Yet resources and attention dedicated to the development enterprise since it came into full bloom in the 1960s—the watershed for decolonization—have massively surpassed those available for the human rights agenda. Uvin estimates that "by the mid 1990s, development had become a $50 billion a year business, whereas the entire human rights community lived on much less than 1 percent of that amount."[31] The international community had been able to make development a "technical" (and thus presumably but falsely "apolitical") enterprise focused largely on economic growth and basic needs, with a significant operational infrastructure in both the capitals of the center and those of the periphery of the developing world, both at bilateral and multilateral levels. The international human rights project, on the other hand, with a strong concern for exposing and protecting against abuses of power (predominantly of the state), did not galvanize the international community in an operational way. It is thus mostly development actors who have far-flung operational infrastructures on the ground, with which they engage in implementing programs and projects. It is mostly through this infrastructure that the international community channels its aid.

On point b, human rights practitioners can learn from the methods that development practitioners have created over the past decades to make "development" (projects, programs, policies) nationally or locally owned, and to develop national capacities. From a practice point of view, a development practitioner would argue that this is the only way "to do" sustainable development.[32] From a discourse point of view, it can be said that this is how (international) development actors have sought to avoid being charged with interventionism based on "Western" priorities, values, and approaches. Human rights scholars, on the other hand, "much more than development specialists, have done sophisticated intellectual work to think through the issues of culture and universality, intervention and ownership, yet, they have done little in practice."[33]

Regarding point c, it is worth discussing each analytical category—political conditionality, positive support, and the human rights–based approach to development—in terms of its implications for transitional justice.

POLITICAL CONDITIONALITY

Should development aid to a postconflict or post-authoritarian state be made conditional on its addressing past human rights violations? The answer to this question depends on one's analysis of the effectiveness and the ethics of conditionality. Some authors have voiced concern over resuming ODA disbursement too quickly, or too much, for fear that state actors would be inclined to ignore the plight of victims of violence with little incentive (or disincentive, see below) to pay more attention.[34] There is little empirical research available, however, that would allow us to understand better the extent to which international aid and other actions actually influence a state's decisions vis-à-vis adopting transitional justice measures to a greater or smaller degree.[35]

We can glean some insights from the discussion on conditionality of development aid based on human rights and democratic performance. These two criteria have become prominent in policy debates since the end of the Cold War among scholars, activists, and politicians alike. International and bilateral organizations have adopted policies that include some measure of conditionality with actual impacts on aid disbursements. The focus has perhaps been more on democracy than on human rights, although there is some evidence for the latter as well.

Conditionality faces many difficulties that have led a majority of scholars, and even some major development organizations, such as the International Monetary Fund (IMF), to conclude that the strategy is all too often ineffective at best, and counterproductive at worst: (1) conditionality is unethical, for example, because it hits the poorest and weakest hardest, and because it is not applied fairly and equally among different countries; (2) it is inefficient because donors never fully agree, and loopholes are left that render it useless; (3) it only deals with symptoms, not with causes, and therefore does not produce the desired results; (4) conditionality is counterproductive because it undermines domestic accountability.[36]

Development actors have therefore sought to improve conditionality: by fine-tuning conventional policies; by being more selective and basing conditionality on actual performance rather than promises; and by introducing "process conditionality"[37] schemes that have, in fact, become the principal frameworks for negotiating the goals of development cooperation between donors and the recipient country. These are notably the Poverty Reduction Strategy Papers (PRSPs) developed by the World Bank, and similar frameworks, such as the UN Development Assistance Frameworks (UNDAF). Ostensibly, the condition for aid is following the process of designing these frameworks by means of a "partnership" approach between the international donor community and the recipient state. They should be based on broad consultations and discussions in the country and on strong notions of ownership and capacity development. The advantages and shortcomings of these frameworks cannot be discussed here; suffice it to say that cases can be made for both. They do offer at least a potential entry point for human rights–based approaches, *if* both the process and the substance of PRSPs were to incorporate rights-based frameworks and indicators to measure progress.

Donors and other development actors need to think more about what minimum behavior they expect from a recipient government in a postconflict situation. Uvin has talked of "principled behavior" on how aid can be used to create incentives and disincentives for peace. He distinguishes this from conditionality in the conventional sense and tries to imbue it with a sense of a moral bottom line, irrespective of the potential policy gains or changes.[38] At a bare minimum, this entails acts of violence against citizens of donor countries and the overthrow of legitimately elected governments. A more comprehensive bottom line should include acts of massive human rights violations against civilians. If this is considered for countries sliding into violent conflict, then how does it resurface when the violent conflict is over and the time and space for reckoning with the violations has come?[39]

POSITIVE SUPPORT

Positive support is a pathway that goes beyond the shorter-term goals of the politics of conditionality. The questions asked here are: What conditions and capacities are needed to achieve specific human rights outcomes, and what support is needed to create these conditions and to develop these capacities? The answers and initiatives implied here are almost by default of a medium- to long-term nature. Both this time spectrum and the capacity development dimension are, of course, close to home for development actors.

Indeed, "positive support" to human rights outcomes has grown significantly in the attention of international development assistance since the 1990s. Over a little more than a decade, aid portfolios grew to about 10 percent of overall aid flows into positive support to democracy, human rights, and governance—from next to nothing around 1990. The proportion was even higher in the case of postconflict countries, where the (re)building of governance and justice institutions was seen as an important foundation for sustainable peace. Yet, while *human rights organizations* have advocated for improvements in human rights practice, judicial reform, investigation of past abuses, and other elements of democratization both vis-à-vis national governments and international aid agencies, they have been much less involved in project implementation and technical assistance on the ground. That role has been taken on much more by *development organizations*.[40]

We can use Uvin's "incentives and disincentives for peace"[41] as a model for categorizing how ODA can be employed also for development and transitional justice purposes. Incentives seek to use aid to strengthen positive dynamics for peace (elsewhere, one would speak of "drivers") (points a–c below); disincentives seek to use aid to change the dynamics conducive to violence ("spoilers") (point d). These incentives and disincentives include:

A) Influencing actors' behaviors
B) Modifying actors' capacities
C) Changing relations between actors
D) Changing the social and economic environment in which conflict and peace dynamics take place

I would argue that there are more "modern" development actors that are quite aware of the rather explicit political nature of these kinds of intervention that require political savvy, sensitivity to conflict, and a certain mandate in order to be carried out with some legitimacy, such as that of the UN. Traditionally, it may be true that many development actors have seen their interventions as apolitical—not only by conviction, but also by necessity because of sovereignty issues. While I do think that there have always been development actors who were quite aware that development is inherently a political process, I am also aware that to this day there are those who prefer to be blind to this dimension and focus on the technical aspects of their assistance, who very explicitly say, "development is not political," or, "development aid should stay clear of (national) politics and get on with the fight against poverty."[42]

With regard to positive support—or development assistance—to transitional justice per se, there is still little systematic empirical research and knowledge available to date concerning the priorities and choices of donors, and the dynamics of foreign aid to transitional justice. The few existing pieces of work have made some attempts at quantitative analysis to be able to "take stock" of transitional justice aid to particular countries, but they have not analyzed the impact of such aid, public perceptions of the beneficiaries, or the policy patterns of donors. There is therefore scope and need for more research, particularly of a comparative nature.[43]

THE HUMAN RIGHTS–BASED APPROACH TO DEVELOPMENT

While a right to development has been proclaimed to exist (by the UN Commission on Human Rights in 1977), it has not made a tangible difference in development and human rights practice, according to most analyses.[44] By contrast, the human rights–based approach (HRBA) to development has sparked much more debate and practice efforts among policy-makers, practitioners, and academics of both communities. Notwithstanding many efforts to "mainstream" this approach, progress has not been without resistance. It has been slow and stands in competition with other mainstreaming agendas—from gender equality to environmental sustainability to conflict sensitivity. Especially in their multitude and multiplicity, these mainstreaming agendas are perceived by many development practitioners as a hindrance, a policy-led rhetoric that ultimately adds little to the practice on the ground, to the achievement of results in poverty reduction.[45]

Proponents of the HRBA argue that it is a higher level of thinking about human rights and development. It is about an *integration* of the two practices, rather than *complementarity* or *instrumentality*.[46] The HRBA tells us to think differently about both the *end* and the *process* of development. Those who are supposed to benefit the most from development in terms of ending poverty— that is, the poor—are not to be conceived of as beneficiaries, recipients, or "target groups" of development and aid (aid as charity, as an ultimately disempowering service delivery). Rather, they are to be conceived of as rights bearers and claimants. In a similar vein, Amartya Sen talks of constitutive (the end) and instrumental (the means) purposes of development, which are closely interconnected.[47]

In view of the "mediate" aims of transitional justice, the notion of rights bearers also informs the aim of recognition. As de Greiff puts it (in this volume): "Ultimately, what is critical for a transition, and what transitional justice measures arguably aim to do, is to provide to victims a sense of recognition not only as *victims*, but as *rights bearers*." Any actors involved in supporting transitional justice measures, but particularly development actors informed by and familiar with rights-based approaches, should consequently seek to shape their programs in a way that accounts for this understanding of the beneficiaries, rather than seeing them as "passive victims."[48]

We can thus see how the language of the rights-based approach is also relevant for and applied by transitional justice. Consequently, one could presume that development actors engaging with the HRBA may find and understand linkages with transitional justice. Nonetheless, there are some caveats.

I am not implying that transitional justice and the HRBA can somehow be directly equated. The link is established through the lens that the HRBA offers, asking us to perceive "beneficiaries" of development in a different manner, as rights bearers. The same lens recognizes victims of rights violations as rights bearers.

In practice, HRBA-related policies and tools do not make much explicit reference to the dimension of how to deal with the legacy of human rights violations. Let us consider, for example, the HRBA in the UN system. The cornerstone document for it is the "Common Understanding on the Human Rights–Based Approach to Development Co-operation," adopted in 2003 by the UN Development Group. The Common Understanding was reached based on the recognition that UN planning frameworks needed coherent approaches to be effective on the ground. It has since been complemented by certain "plans of action" and guidelines covering specific areas — yet none of them deal with transitional justice, or how to program in contexts where massive human rights violations have occurred.[49] The closest is a concept paper on "National Systems of Human Rights Protection," which contains one brief section on "redress for human rights violations" as one of several basic elements for national systems of human rights protection.[50]

CHALLENGES AND LIMITATIONS FOR DEVELOPMENT AND TRANSITIONAL JUSTICE

In light of the conceptual discussion, there are a number of challenges and limitations that we can consider.

ADEQUACY OF DEVELOPMENT TOOLS AND APPROACHES FOR TRANSITIONAL JUSTICE

As discussed above, some prefer to see development as technical assistance provided at the request of a government, without political interference. It is certainly true that, without the agreement of a host government, development actors cannot run massive projects, no matter what they are for. In a situation where a government is less interested in pursuing a transitional justice agenda, then, can and should development actors try to use aid as incentives and disincentives to "nudge" that government in a certain direction? Do development actors have the political savvy to convince them, let alone the mandate to engage in these matters? Leaving conditionality (force) aside, good policy advice needs to be based on both moral (the right thing to do) and empirical (this is the most likely approach to get a certain result) arguments. Rights language may be available to make a moral argument in favor of transitional justice measures, but to what extent do development actors, who are often those with the closest (albeit not always easy or harmonious) relationships to national governments, able and willing to use it?[51]

Second, what are the instruments at a development actor's disposal to provide (technical) assistance for transitional justice? To start with, they tend to be in project format (at best, a more comprehensive program) — vehicles with a limited budget created to deliver tangible, preferably measurable results, with a rather short-term, foreseeable duration. In that sense, development actors — by virtue of having an established presence on the ground and the mechanisms to implement projects — may be a conduit for "delivering" certain transitional justice "projects," such as supporting the implementation of a truth commission, or delivering training on international criminal law to national judges. But does the ability to deliver projects suffice to make them a good conduit?

Surely, transitional justice tries to address violations whose causes are often deeply entrenched in a nation's system of political power and inequality, and in highly unequal perceptions of "the other" in a society. Moreover, we are not dealing with a change formula along the lines of "1 + 1 = 2." It is difficult to predict the result of a given measure (or input, in project-speak) because the social context is not static, but "emergent" and hybrid.[52] It is a fallacy to think that short-term projects of "technical assistance" can bring about a change in these structures and conditions. Much longer-term visions and actions would be required to come to terms with the past.[53] On one hand, development actors — whose institutions usually do have a fairly long-term staying power — could be well situated to tackle some of these challenges by truly embracing this "comparative advantage" they like to tote. On the other hand, development practice reality is different. The staff on the ground change too frequently for longer-term continuity, and many projects do depend on individuals' commitment to and interpretation of a certain approach. Translating a pilot project into a truly institutional commitment and approach that is carried through in the long run, regardless of changing project staff, is a significant challenge.

Third, are "normal" development project modalities well suited to support such political and, at the end of the day, deeply emotional processes? How could existing modalities be adjusted, adapted, or changed altogether to be more conducive to support these kinds of processes? Do development agencies have access to enough adequately trained professionals to design and run such projects? Do they ask the right questions? Do they realize that for their partners, this is about much more than the successful completion of a technical project that duly delivered its finances and results and corresponding reports?

Indeed, as one critic points out, only short shrift is given to the extent to which development agencies' mandates and capacities actually make them able actors to lead on human rights issues. Even in more nuanced takes, the demand is that development agencies should go through far-reaching changes and adopt significantly different frameworks of analysis that may not at all be easily brought into line with their usual mandated concerns.[54]

PRIORITIZATION OF RESOURCE ALLOCATION AND POLITICS OF ODA

The HRBA argues that effective poverty eradication requires all of the above dimensions to be addressed, not just economic needs, such as income generation. Conversely, addressing rights without changing living conditions also falls short. One of Sen's major arguments in his *Development as Freedom* is very similar.

In a postconflict context, when the needs and actors are many, transitional justice—like other areas of concern—is often faced with the question: How can we justify investing millions of dollars into these measures and processes when millions of people continue to live below the poverty line? The dichotomy here is one that the question of guaranteeing political and civil rights vis-à-vis reducing poverty also often poses. Do development actors (national and international) have to make a choice between the two? They do have to make many choices in terms of priority setting, but is this juxtaposition not a false dichotomy? Sen answers yes, it is false because one has to see political freedoms and economic needs as interconnected: (1) political and civil rights *directly* impact on human living (for example, social and political participation); (2) they are *instrumental* in allowing people to give voice to their claims in political decision-making processes; and (3) they are *constructive* in conceptualizing needs (including, but not limited to, economic needs in a social context).[55]

Transitional justice processes often (albeit not always) take place in moments when a comparatively high amount of ODA funds are available. Global media attention may be high—but only for a short time. Sometimes this is not the case at all. Either way, the paradox of disproportionately higher levels of ODA being made available in postconflict recovery and peacebuilding settings, as opposed to for the purposes of preventing or stopping violent conflict and massive human rights violations in the first place, also affects transitional justice. It would be worthwhile to explore aid to transitional justice mechanisms compared to that which was invested into human rights protection and conflict prevention measures. Transitional justice measures, from a "projectizable" perspective, are easier to "invest" in, as they appear to be more time-bound, and deliver measurable results (reports, convictions, and so on). A transition period is often one in which the full extent of atrocities becomes fully visible, access and space for action is easier, and people in rich countries are mobilized to make donations by the images of suffering they see. The development and peacebuilding machineries may find themselves with more willing counterparts, and/or with a UN Security Council mandate.

RETURNS ON INVESTMENT? EVIDENCE-BASED PROGRAMMING AND TRANSITIONAL JUSTICE

The empirical basis in support of transitional justice as being conducive to peace and therefore, ultimately, development (especially when defined as "freedom") is still weak. This poses again several challenges. How to convince a government (both the donor and the recipient, for that matter) that it should invest in such measures — and that it should do so over a long period of time? How does a development agency providing technical assistance to a particular measure know whether it is having the desired success (and can therefore justify a continuation of a new project phase, and so on)?[56]

Answers to these questions tend to fall, broadly speaking and not limited to transitional justice support, into two camps: (1) Much more literature is available that documents failures, painting a very negative picture of the shortcomings and even the detrimental effects of development aid and its instruments on national processes of social change and indigenous capacity development;[57] and (2) the general acceptance of this being an imperfect system, but also the absence of real alternatives that would be better, wherefore one has to strive to make the system work better.

POLITICAL RISKS AND CONFLICT SENSITIVITY

Supporting transitional justice processes poses a certain risk. Tricky questions are being raised; awful things are being brought into the harsh daylight. The outcomes are not always positive, they do not lead to reconciliation in a linear way — certainly not in the lifetime of a normal (development) project. On the contrary, there is always a risk of more conflict being generated by rocking the foundations of power structures that still persist, notwithstanding peace agreements, regime changes, and democratic transitions. Many development actors are rather risk-averse because they do not want to endanger their maneuverability in other sectors; because they do not want to compromise whatever political clout or standing their institution may have in that country; or because specific people simply do not want to lose their jobs (for example, by being declared persona non grata by the host government).

This point is to a large degree about an issue that has been much debated since the origins of transitional justice—namely, whether one can (and sometimes has to) balance claims for justice with claims for "peace" in the sense of stability and appeasement of certain influential stakeholders. It is much debated within the field of transitional justice, and certainly offers many points of friction with other actors, such as those from the development field, who may see stability as a priority and certain measures of justice at the wrong time as a hindrance.[58] By now, there are of course some international standards codified by the UN regarding aspects of the impermissibility of impunity and obligations of reparations. Once again, the question is to what extent a development actor in a certain position of influence vis-à-vis certain state actors understands these, and is willing and able to draw on them.

ACCOUNTABILITY AND CONFIDENCE BUILDING

Once we conceive of citizens as claimants and rights holders, as the HRBA would have it, then accountability of those institutions that bear the duty to uphold the rights moves into the spotlight. So do the methods of holding those who violate rights accountable. In many developing contexts, and even more so in conflict and postconflict contexts, there are few institutions that are or have been fully accountable to their citizens. The rule of law, especially one where everyone is equal before the law, has broken down during the conflict, and may never have been extant before, either. Transitional justice is, of course, concerned with holding those who have committed violations accountable, especially for the gravest violations.

Development should therefore be very much concerned with helping to strengthen institutions that can be held accountable, and the methods through which rights holders can bring their claims to bear. This requires a focus on strengthening institutions that ensure the rule of law, but also those that allow for a realization of human rights beyond the formal legal system. As Uvin contends:

All organizations that seek to adopt a rights-based approach to development should focus their work on dramatically improving the rule of law at the level of daily life. It is worth nothing to have laws and policies—even if these laws and policies conform to human rights standards—if they are not implemented, if certain groups are excluded from them, if the relevant facts are not known to most people, if channels of redress do not function, if laws are systematically circumvented, or if money, guns, and political influence always tend to get the better of them.[59]

People need the rule of law to be able to organize and act for social change. At the same time, the rule of law requires functioning institutions capable of delivering it, and that have the confidence of the people.[60] This is an area where human rights (and transitional justice) and development actors should be able to work well together, to complement one another: The human rights actors by focusing on the legal frameworks, the judiciary, and other formal human rights mechanisms; the development actors by bringing their experience and networks to bear with regard to participatory methods, the facilitation of dialogue and consultations, the mobilization and organization of groups, information sharing, and so on.

CAPACITY DEVELOPMENT AND NATIONAL OWNERSHIP

Capacity development and national ownership are two of the fundamental principles of a developmental approach (in theory). An HRBA would have development actors change their practice by emphasizing different types of capacities to be developed; by choosing different or additional partners to collaborate with, both to develop their capacities and in terms of the type of "service providers" they choose as "implementing partners"; and by perhaps shifting their priorities with regard to the institutions they focus on (more).

With regard to transitional justice, this means developing a better understanding of the type of capacities needed to sustain related processes; adjusting or developing respective tools; and changing the kind of partnerships often formed. The HRBA calls for longer-term and more programmatic partnerships that go beyond a mere project and service-delivery nature. This call is nothing new in and of itself—the inadequacies of the mainstream development cooperation mechanism have been discussed and criticized for quite some time.

Participatory development approaches and the HRBA have in common that they promote development as a process that needs to explicitly and proactively include all citizens, and therefore pay particular attention to enabling those who are typically excluded and marginalized from decision-making processes. These citizens need to be given voice (although this language implies that someone is a giver, and another a recipient—in itself an unequal power relationship). Again, this is nothing new for development practice, but it does not hurt to highlight and to explore how the experience and tools of participatory approaches can be employed when trying to support transitional justice processes and measures that are locally owned.[61]

Capacity development and national ownership principles are notorious for a number of challenges that especially large development agencies still struggle with. The systems and procedures of these agencies usually require a certain mirror capacity from their partners to comply with financial and operational rules and regulations. This is a conditionality of a different kind: if you cannot produce the kind of proposals I need, and the subsequent financial and progress reports, then I cannot enter into a partnership with you. This can apply to both governmental and nongovernmental actors, but it is more pronounced among the latter, and also more crucial when and if development actors seek to support capacities of local organizations, let alone individuals, who are ostensibly rights holders and claimants but who are far from the level of organization required to access the external (financial) aid.

At the same time, capacity development for transitional justice, for claimants concerned with dealing with human rights violations, poses risks for those who provide the assistance. Capacity development here is not just about the technical capacity to drill a well or run a health clinic (and even here, it is a fallacy to assume these processes are apolitical). It is about social and political skills and capacities that are difficult to monitor both for immediate results (How do I know that my capacity development program strengthened NGO X in a way to be better at fostering reconciliation?), and for mediate impact (What happens when an organization that benefited from my human rights and transitional justice training program acts in a way that upsets local or national elites, let alone the government on whose "partnership" I depend in order to be able to stay in the country?).

HISTORICAL RESPONSIBILITY, COMPLICITY, AND NEGLIGENCE

There is a moral (if not a legal) dilemma for the development community when it comes to transitional justice. Often, many of the major development actors will have been operational in countries during periods of human rights abuses. They may have turned "a blind eye" to the actions of an autocratic regime in order to be able to carry out some of their "technical" work, or neglected to see the writing on the wall. Donor countries may have directly supported a violent regime. In this sense, a (developing) country's effort to deal with the past cannot be regarded as concerning only national actors.

In some cases, then, development institutions may have to ask themselves what their role has been while the human rights violations under scrutiny were going on. This may bring up some very uncomfortable issues, but it may be morally (and possibly legally) necessary, and it would certainly add another dimension to the question of how development actors are linked with transitional justice matters.[62]

At the risk of stretching the conceptual confines of what transitional justice has largely come to be understood as, there is a longer historical context to consider, one that goes beyond the actions and responsibilities of development actors in post–Cold War conflicts. After all, many donor countries are former colonial powers. Colonial history influenced the shape and state of many developing nations significantly, even if not exclusively. Dealing with the past of colonialism may mean something quite different from current transitional justice evocations, but I believe that Paige Arthur is right in pointing out that they should not be ignored just because the conceptual history of transitional justice did not include notions of postcolonial justice claims.[63]

SUSTAINABILITY AND RESPONSIBILITY (TO REMEMBER) FOR FUTURE GENERATIONS

All of the above faces some of the known challenges that participatory approaches should be familiar with. Development cast as an intervention by both national and international actors can be as participatory as it wants, but it can rarely ever reach every single citizen, and choices have to be made about who gets to participate, in what kinds of a process, and whose voice gets heard above the others. Participatory approaches may lead to the design of mechanisms, processes, and benefits more in tune with the preferences and needs of those most affected by the violations of the past, and the ongoing deprivation of freedoms. To my mind, transitional justice—or dealing with the past—is, however, about more than the needs of the current generation, of the survivors. The current generation also has to take a responsibility for those who follow.

Different authors and initiatives have sought to explore and describe conceptual synergies between human development and sustainability (the use of resources for development and poverty reduction now that does not compromise the well-being of future generations).[64] If we cast sustainability not only in terms of environment and economic viability but also in terms of sustainable peaceful coexistence for future generations, then there is a legitimate concern about what a generation in the present owes to future generations if they are also to have a right to a life in dignity and peace. Present generations may therefore have a moral responsibility to ensure those who follow will remember. From a development (forward-looking) perspective, then, the question becomes whether or not (or to what degree) transitional justice processes and measures contribute to ensuring sustainable human development, viewed as a right and responsibility for generations present and future. Indeed, it seems that much, if not all, hinges on what transitional justice can contribute to changing perceptions and dimensions of human interaction and coexistence.

CONCLUDING REMARKS

In this chapter, I have explored different pathways between development and transitional justice and tried to establish potential linkages as well as limitations of their encounters. It appears to me that both the peacebuilding arena and rights-based approaches bring to the fore reasons that underline both such linkages and limitations. They are roads that both development and transitional justice actors are to some extent familiar with. There seems to be scope both to travel a bit closer together on these roads and to deepen the dialogue, for there are many unanswered questions. Like de Greiff, I see scope for more complementarity without losing sight of the fact that development and transitional justice do not have all goals in common. On the contrary, sometimes their goals can even be seen to be at odds with one another—at least as far as the question of timing and sequencing of certain measures over others is concerned.

I think one can best establish useful linkages that would help inform practice by talking about concrete, shared goals, and the ways in which to best achieve these. Peacebuilding entails a range of goals, and for some of them it would be most beneficial to combine the approaches and practices of the different fields. This is certainly the case for efforts to reestablish civic trust, as de Greiff has also found.[65] Another related example is (re)conciliation. Importantly, to my mind, neither civic trust nor reconciliation can be conceived of as a static end state. Even if one manages to measure changes (and establish what exactly contributes to improvements), they will need to be maintained in the long term. This is why I am convinced that development has a role to play here that needs to be much better articulated. It is not only about the longer-term development aid commitments that may be required for some of the measures necessary to achieve these goals; it is also about the fostering of national institutions that are able to take these issues on seriously and sustainably.

Cast in this light, it is also necessary to understand transitional justice not only as shorter-term measures of "justice in transition contexts." Rather, it needs to be understood also in terms of longer-term measures and capacities required to deal with the past so that present and future generations may never be subjected to the same atrocities again (hence the quotation at the beginning of the chapter).

In sum, these reflections put greater emphasis on the *instrumental* value of transitional justice measures than on their *intrinsic* worth. While I do not want to discard the latter, I believe that the former offers more entry points when it comes to exploring linkages between transitional justice and development.

NOTES

1 While all responsibility for the contents of this chapter is, of course, mine, I would like to express my gratitude to Pablo de Greiff and Roger Duthie for their critical support, guidance, and patience. Their comments on drafts at different stages of the chapter helped improve it considerably. My thanks also go to Pontus Ohrstedt for being a constructive listener at an early conceptual stage, and to Patrick van Weerelt and Julia Kercher for pointing me in useful directions on the human rights–based approach to development. Lastly, all views expressed in this chapter are personal and do not necessarily reflect those of the United Nations Development Programme (UNDP).

2 "But it is beautiful to love the world through the eyes of those who have not yet been born" (author's translation), a stanza taken from Castillo's poem *Frente al balance, mañana*.

3 For a lucid, insightful, and comprehensive account of the origins of "transitional justice" as a "field," see Paige Arthur, "How 'Transitions' Reshaped Human Rights: A Conceptual History of Transitional Justice," *Human Rights Quarterly* (forthcoming, 2009). She describes the "field" as "an international web of individuals and institutions, whose internal coherence is held together by common concepts, practical aims, and distinctive claims for legitimacy."

4 It is beyond the scope and point of this chapter to discuss the many definitions and debates around "development." Suffice it to say here that this is a field with a tremendous body of literature tackling multiple dimensions of development, from theories of economic growth to social and political dimensions, sustainability, effectiveness of development aid, and more. Some of these theories I draw on later in the chapter, such as Amartya Sen's theory of development as freedom. See Amartya Sen, *Development as Freedom* (Oxford: Oxford University Press, 1999). For an example of the heavily contested orthodoxies of economic development, see Ha-Joon Chang and Ilene Grabel's

dissection of neoliberal "myths" in Ha-Joon Chang and Ilene Grabel, *Reclaiming Development: An Alternative Economic Policy Manual* (London and New York: Zed Books, 2003), and Chang's important critical history of institutional and economic development strategies in Ha-Joon Chang, *Kicking Away the Ladder: Development Strategy in Historical Perspective* (London: Anthem Press, 2002). My thanks go to James Putzel and Julia Kercher for introducing me to Chang's work. Still relevant is also Colin Leys, *The Rise and Fall of Development Theory* (Nairobi, Bloomington, Indianapolis, Oxford: EAEP / Indiana University Press / James Currey, 1996).

5   Arguably, large multilateral and bilateral development actors often have a much closer proximity and relationship with national governments than do human rights actors. This means that they can help influence national decision-making processes from a privileged vantage point, depending on the context. The question, then, is whether a development actor cares to or has the know-how to address transitional justice issues with national partners, at what level of priority, and with what rationale.

6   The Organisation for Economic Co-operation and Development (OECD) defines ODA as: "Flows of official financing administered with the promotion of the economic development and welfare of developing countries as the main objective, and which are concessional in character with a grant element of at least 25 percent (using a fixed 10 percent rate of discount). By convention, ODA flows comprise contributions of donor government agencies, at all levels, to developing countries ('bilateral ODA') and to multilateral institutions. ODA receipts comprise disbursements by bilateral donors and multilateral institutions. Lending by export credit agencies—with the pure purpose of export promotion—is excluded." OECD Glossary of Statistical Terms, stats.oecd.org/glossary/detail.asp?ID=6043.

7   A seminar cohosted by the UK Department for International Development (DFID) and the International Center for Transitional Justice (ICTJ) in 2007 recognized this very issue and tried to start addressing the gap of lacking donor strategies toward transitional justice. See ICTJ/DFID, "Donor Strategies for Transitional Justice: Taking Stock and Moving Forward," conference report, October 15–16, 2007.

8   DFID was among the first big bilateral agencies to commission a comprehensive scoping study on the potential impact of transitional justice measures on poverty reduction and the attainment of the Millennium Development Goals (MDGs). See Jane Alexander, "A Scoping Study of Transitional Justice and Poverty Reduction: Final Report," DFID, 2003. Transitional justice is also referred to in several recent policy practice papers, one of which remarks how "high-level rule of law accountability" was still relatively new to DFID. See DFID, "Justice and Accountability," DFID Practice Paper, May 2008, 14; see also the following footnote on DFID, "Governance, Development, and Democratic Politics: DFID's Work in Building More Effective States," Policy Paper, 2007. DFID's 2008 Annual Report mentions that the UK government was committed to dealing with

the legacy of human rights violations, but only gives short shrift to specific funding examples in different parts of the report. Switzerland began exploring policy options for dealing with the past around the same time. See Mo Bleeker and Jonathan Sisson, eds., "Dealing with the Past: Critical Issues, Lessons Learned, and Challenges for Future Swiss Policy," Koff Working Paper Series (Bern: Swiss Peace Foundation [swisspeace], 2004). The Swiss Federal Department of Foreign Affairs (FDFA) has since supported a series of workshops and conferences to facilitate platforms of discussion on the utility of dealing with the past and transitional justice for peace, human rights, the rule of law, and democracy. See, e.g., FDFA, "Dealing with the Past and Transitional Justice: Creating Conditions for Peace, Human Rights and the Rule of Law," and FDFA, "El legado de la verdad: Impacto de la justicia transicional en la construcción de la democracia en América Latina," in Dealing with the Past—Series, ed. Mo Bleeker (Bern: FDFA, 2007). That the topic galvanizes the interest of a range of development agencies to some extent can be seen, e.g., in the fact that a 2007 FDFA- and ICTJ-organized conference in Bogota on the impact of transitional justice on democratization in Latin America could be held under the joint auspices of the United Nations Development Programme (UNDP), the Swedish International Development Agency (SIDA), the Spanish Agency for International Cooperation (AECI), and the main German bilateral development agency, Gesellschaft für Technische Zusammenarbeit (GTZ), in addition to several embassies (FDFA, "El legado de la verdad"). Germany is another example where both development (e.g., GTZ and Friedrich Ebert Stiftung [FES], "From Dealing with the Past to Future Cooperation: Regional and Global Challenges of Reconciliation, General Report," GTZ/FES, 2005) and foreign affairs branches have been seeking how to best engage with the topic. The German government (under the leadership of the Foreign Office) together with the governments of Finland and Jordan organized (in partnership with a number of specialized nongovernmental organizations) a particularly large and high-level conference, "Building a Future on Peace and Justice," in 2007 (www.peace-justice-conference.info). That conference was perhaps the most ambitious of its kind to date regarding its outcome. It produced the "Nuremberg Declaration on Peace and Justice," which aimed at providing recommendations on how to deal with potential tensions between justice and peace, which included one on "promoting development." It was transmitted as an annex in a joint letter to the secretary-general of the United Nations in the context of the 62nd General Assembly session pursuant to the "comprehensive review of the whole question of peacekeeping operations in all their aspects" ("Letter Dated 13 June 2008 From the Permanent Representatives of Finland, Germany and Jordan to the United Nations Addressed to the Secretary-General," United Nations General Assembly [2008]). To gauge its impact and to better understand international consensus and policy formation in this area requires further research that I cannot provide here. Other bilateral and multilateral actors that have engaged in supporting transitional justice measures include

Belgium, Canada, the European Commission (EC), the Netherlands, the Organization of American States (OAS), and the United States Agency for International Development (USAID). See, e.g., Ingrid Samset, Stina Petersen, and Vibeke Wang, "Foreign Aid to Transitional Justice: The Cases of Rwanda and Guatemala, 1995–2005," in Kai Ambos, Judith Large, and Marieke Wierda, eds., *Building a Future on Peace and Justice: Studies on Transitional Justice, Peace and Development* (Heidelberg: Springer, 2009).

9   A DFID policy paper highlights different transitional justice measures (explicitly and implicitly) as important for peaceful dispute resolution, reconciliation, and a "better understanding of the recent past" (DFID, "Governance," 25). It does not, however, discuss in more detail what the underlying challenges are, and what the linkage to development is—other than the general policy conviction that good governance is crucial for (socioeconomic) development; that it matters for addressing causes of violent conflict (for which exclusion is often a factor, and which the poor usually suffer the most from), and for supporting institutions that manage disputes peacefully (ibid., 23–26). The World Bank is another development actor that has asked itself, albeit tentatively, whether the specific transitional justice measure of a truth commission can be instrumental, or at least informative, for its work on governance, postconflict reconstruction, and the legal, gender, and social dimensions of conflict. A specific study it commissioned reveals how there is potential, but no straightforward answer, in light of the Bank's mandate. See World Bank, "Gender, Justice, and Truth Commissions," Washington, DC: World Bank, 2006, esp. 24–28.

10 On the important difference between the "instrumental value" and the "intrinsic worth" of human rights in development, see Philip Alston, "Ships Passing in the Night: The Current State of the Human Rights and Development Debate Seen through the Lens of the Millennium Development Goals," *Human Rights Quarterly* 27 (2005): 755–829, esp. 793.

11 See Naomi Roht-Arriaza and Katharine Orlovsky, "A Complementary Relationship: Reparations and Development," in this volume.

12 The general point of this argument was also underlined in the above-mentioned "Nuremberg Declaration on Peace and Justice." It includes "promoting development" as one of its recommendations, and while the content of this recommendation remains rather thin, it does call on national and international development actors to "be sensitive in dealing with the past when designing post-conflict development strategies and take into account relevant recommendations of accountability mechanisms" (para. 3.4).

13 See Pablo de Greiff, "Articulating the Links Between Transitional Justice and Development," in this volume, on questions relating to the "developmental preconditions" for transitional justice, both in terms of institutional capacity and resource availability. The latter alludes to the general point that severe underdevelopment and resource scarcity put constraints on the implementation of transitional justice measures. The challenge of "coming to terms with large-scale past abuses" in a context marked by "myriad deficits"

was underlined prominently in a seminal review of UN experience by the secretary-general. See UN Security Council, *The Rule of Law and Transitional Justice in Conflict and Post-conflict Societies, Report of the Secretary-General*, S/2004/616, August 23, 2004, para. 3.

14 The much-debated Paul Collier et al., *Breaking the Conflict Trap: Civil War and Development Policy* (Washington, DC: World Bank and Oxford University Press, 2003). More recently, Paul Collier, *The Bottom Billion: Why the Poorest Countries are Failing and What Can Be Done About It* (Oxford: Oxford University Press, 2008). See also Jon Barnett, "Peace and Development: Towards a New Synthesis," *Journal of Peace Research* 45 (2008): 75–89; and Frances Stewart and Arnim Langer, "Horizontal Inequalities: Explaining Persistence and Change," CRISE Working Paper No. 39 (2007). For a critical account of how "development" became increasingly "radicalized" by its taking on of conflict and security agendas, see Mark Duffield, *Global Governance and the New Wars: The Merging of Development and Security* (London and New York: Zed Books, 2001).

15 See, e.g., Neil Kritz, ed., *Transitional Justice: How Emerging Democracies Reckon with Former Regimes*, vol. I (Washington, DC: United States Institute for Peace Press, 1995).

16 As de Greiff also points out in this volume, this is not an "unproblematic extension." While it can be objectively observed that transitional justice elements have been incorporated into the peacebuilding architecture, it may indeed be warranted to explore further how the notion of transitional justice has migrated from democratic transition to postconflict peacebuilding, and what the consequences are. Arthur's work ("How 'Transitions' Reshaped Human Rights," forthcoming, 2009) on the conceptual history of transitional justice is extremely informative in this regard. It would be most interesting to build on her findings and use a similar approach in analyzing transitional justice's conceptual evolution in the postconflict peacebuilding arena.

17 The key UN document heralding this change was Secretary-General Boutros Boutros-Ghali's 1992 report to the Security Council, *An Agenda for Peace: Preventive Diplomacy, Peacemaking and Peace-keeping*, A/47/277-S/24111, June 17, 1992. Here he defined "postconflict peace-building" as "action to identify and support structures which will tend to strengthen and solidify peace in order to avoid a relapse into conflict" (para. 21). For a brief overview and discussion, see Elizabeth M. Cousens, "Introduction," in *Peacebuilding as Politics: Cultivating Peace in Fragile Societies*, ed. Elizabeth M. Cousens, Chetan Kumar, and Karin Wermester (Boulder: Lynne Rienner Publishers, 2001).

18 Eric Newman, " 'Transitional Justice': The Impact of Transnational Norms and the UN," *International Peacekeeping* 9 (2002): 31.

19 UN Security Council, *The Rule of Law and Transitional Justice*. It is noteworthy that the lead UN agency on matters of transitional justice, the Office of the High Commissioner on Human Rights (OHCHR), developed its series of (to date, seven) tools on how to support different transitional justice measures with a view toward the UN's role in peace operations, i.e., in postconflict rather than in post-authoritarianism contexts. See OHCHR,

Rule-of-Law Tools for Post-Conflict States (Geneva: OHCHR, 2006–08), available at www.ohchr.org/EN/PublicationsResources/Pages/SpecialIssues.aspx.

20 See, e.g., Mary Anderson, *Do No Harm: Supporting Local Capacities for Peace through Aid* (Cambridge, MA: Development for Collaborative Action, 1996). The genocide in Rwanda was one of the most disastrous events of the 1990s to inform this shift among development actors. For one of the most insightful studies of how the "development enterprise" reacted or failed to react to the conflict dynamics in Rwanda, see Peter Uvin, *Aiding Violence: The Development Enterprise in Rwanda* (West Hartford, CT: Kumarian Press, 1998).

21 On the "necessity of reconciliation," for instance, see David Bloomfield, Teresa Barnes, and Luc Huyse, eds., *Reconciliation after Violent Conflict: A Handbook* (Stockholm: International IDEA, 2003), 14ff.

22 UN Security Council, *Rule of Law and Transitional Justice*, para. 2.

23 See de Greiff, "Articulating the Links," in this volume; and Pablo de Greiff, "Theorizing Transitional Justice," in *Transitional Justice*, ed. Melissa Williams and Rosemary Nagy, Nomos XLX (forthcoming).

24 De Greiff, "Theorizing Transitional Justice."

25 See, e.g., OECD DAC, "Concepts and Dilemmas of State Building in Fragile Situations: From Fragility to Resilience," OECD DAC Discussion Paper, OECD, 2008; and Alan Whaites, "States in Development: Understanding State-Building," DFID Working Paper, 2008.

26 Rama Mani, *Beyond Retribution: Seeking Justice in the Shadows of War* (Cambridge: Polity Press, 2002).

27 Poignantly, a recent study of how well the international development community had advanced with using conflict early-warning analysis and response into their programming quipped that despite some progress, the international community was still not in a position to prevent another Rwandan genocide. The study does not, however, discuss dealing with the past as a variable in early-warning systems. David Nyheim, *Can Violence, War and State Collapse Be Prevented? The Future of Operational Conflict Early Warning and Response Systems* (Paris: OECD, 2009).

28 Peter Uvin, *Human Rights and Development* (West Hartford, CT: Kumarian Press, 2004), 1.

29 Alston's detailed analysis of the relationship between the Millennium Development Goals (MDGs) and human rights is a case in point (Alston, "Ships Passing in the Night," 778–84), while also illustrating the influence of the "development as freedom" theory discussed above. While the MDGs themselves make no explicit reference to human rights, the underlying policy agreement, the Millennium Declaration, does. "We will spare no effort to promote democracy and strengthen the rule of law, as well as respect for all internationally recognized human rights" (Millennium Declaration 2000, 24). And "freedom" is one of the fundamental values here, defined as, "Men and women have the right to live their lives and raise their children in dignity, free from hunger and the fear

of violence, oppression or injustice. Democratic and participatory governance based on the will of the people best assures these rights" (ibid., 6). Notwithstanding these proclamations, Alston concludes that, in practice, monitoring and implementation strategies of the MDGs are by and large not placed within a human rights framework. See also Uvin, *Human Rights and Development*, 51ff.

30   Uvin, *Human Rights and Development*.

31   Ibid., 13.

32   UNDP, "Capacity Development Practice Note," UNDP, New York, May 2008; and OECD DAC, *The Challenge of Capacity Development: Working Towards Good Practice* (Paris: OECD, 2006).

33   Uvin, *Human Rights and Development*, 19.

34   Jon Elster, ed., *Retribution and Reparation in the Transition to Democracy* (Cambridge: Cambridge University Press, 2006).

35   One such empirical effort has been undertaken by Tricia Olsen, Leigh Payne, and Andrew Reiter, "At What Cost? A Political Economy Approach to Transitional Justice" (paper prepared for the Midwest Political Science Association Conference, Chicago, IL, April 14, 2007), applying a political economy approach to transitional justice. Their results, based on testing the statistical significance of a variety of variables, such as foreign direct investment or gross domestic product (GDP), on a country's adoption of transitional justice measures are inconclusive. They point out the necessity of more research in this regard. In sum, based on data on more than ninety countries that transitioned to democracy between 1974 and 2003, they found that countries with healthier economies were more likely to adopt transitional justice measures. Economically integrated countries were, however, contrary to their hypothesis, less likely to adopt transitional justice measures. I owe thanks to Roger Duthie for making me aware of this piece of research.

36   Compare Uvin, *Human Rights and Development*, 59–69. Some of these points are made even more complicated by the emergence of new donors that do not necessarily "play by the rules" of the Western-dominated development aid establishment, such as China. See Martyn Davies et al., "How China Delivers Development Assistance to Africa," Centre for Chinese Studies, University of Stellenbosch, 2008; and Moisés Naím, "Rogue Aid," *Foreign Policy* (March/April, 2007), 95–96.

37   David Booth, "Overview of PRSP Processes and Monitoring," in *PRSP Institutionalisation Study: Final Report* (London: Overseas Development Institute [ODI], 2003).

38   Peter Uvin, "The Influence of Aid in Situations of Violent Conflict" (paper prepared for the OECD DAC Informal Task Force on Conflict, Peace and Development Co-Operation, Paris, September 1999).

39   A World Bank study muses almost in passing that donors could use conditionalities for loans and grants to make governments implement recommendations of truth

commissions. The vagaries of such an approach are, however, not discussed further. See World Bank, "Gender, Justice, and Truth Commissions," 24.

40 See Uvin, *Human Rights and Development*, 85–88, for an overview of this growth process among different major development agencies.

41 Uvin, "The Influence of Aid."

42 For an illustration of just how much a development agency such as the World Bank may deliberate the ins and outs of its mandate and role vis-à-vis transitional justice, see a discussion of the possible relationships between the World Bank and truth commissions in World Bank, "Gender, Justice, and Truth Commissions," esp. 25ff.

43 See Samset et al., "Maintaining the Process?" This study was notably commissioned by the German Ministry for Economic Cooperation and Development (BMZ) in an effort to address some of the above-mentioned gaps. It is an interesting approach to get a sense of the scope of aid to transitional justice, but it leaves many questions open. See also the discussion of shortcomings and challenges of impact evaluation in ICTJ/DFID, "Donor Strategies," 6–8.

44 Alston, "Ships Passing in the Night," 755–829, esp. 799.

45 See Paul Gready and Jonathan Ensor, eds., *Reinventing Development? Translating Rights-Based Approaches from Theory into Practice* (London and New York: Zed Books, 2005).

46 Uvin, *Human Rights and Development*, 122–66.

47 Sen, *Development as Freedom*, 36ff.

48 In fact, development actors should be sufficiently familiar with the underlying notion, as there are many similarities with the (by now old) concept of participatory development. See, e.g., Robert Chambers, *Rural Development: Putting the Last First* (Harlow: Longman, 1983); and Robert Chambers, *Whose Reality Counts? Putting the First Last* (Warwickshire: IT Publications, 1997). When you ask "the poor," it becomes clear that poverty from their perspective is about more than the lack of income. It is about exclusion, inequality, social inferiority, powerlessness, lack of freedoms and capabilities. But let us be careful: "the poor" are not a homogenous group anywhere, nor are they passive human beings suffering always what the structures around them hold in store. There will be those who have knowledge and experience with coping and improving their immediate conditions, and may very well have practiced "everyday forms of resistance" in the face of oppression by elites. See James C. Scott, *Weapons of the Weak: Everyday Forms of Peasant Resistance* (New Haven: Yale University Press, 1986).

49 There are, of course, the above-mentioned OHCHR *Rule-of-Law Tools* that provide some guidance on how to directly support specific transitional justice measures. However, they are of a more normative character, as opposed to specific programming tools, and they are not listed in the same place as the HRBA-related tools and guides, meaning they may well have a different audience (at least in the way they are presently presented and disseminated).

50 UN Development Group, "National Systems of Human Rights Protection," May 2005, www.undg.org/archive_docs/7964-Concept_Paper_on_National_Protection_System. doc, point 14a. See the UN Development Group Web site for a list of policy and guidance on the HRBA to development programming, www.undg.org/?p=221. The normative and policy history that gave rise to the Common Understanding was summarized in the same document: The UN Charter founds the UN on peace, justice, freedom, and human rights. The Universal Declaration on Human Rights proclaimed human rights as the foundation for the other three. The Vienna Declaration, several decades on, reaffirmed all of the above, and stated that democracy, development, and respect for human rights were interdependent and mutually reinforcing. In 1997, the secretary-general launched his UN Program of Reform, which called on all UN agencies to mainstream the normative foundations of the UN (human rights) into their policies and programs within their respective mandates. Many UN agencies proceeded to do so, but each with its own interpretation of how this was to be operationalized. This arguably did not help consistent approaches, and hence the Common Understanding was reached.

51 At the level of the UN, there are efforts under way to equip Resident Coordinators (who nowadays wear the multiple hats of responsibility for coordinating the UN's actions in a given country in both the development [including governance] and humanitarian fields) with human rights advisors. It is not inconceivable that these advisors could have some knowledge of or training on dealing with past human rights abuses. The OHCHR's *Rule-of-Law Tools* offer at least a potential library of norm-setting "textbooks" in this regard. The challenge here is to roll out such curricula on a massive scale, to keep staff up-to-date, and to properly induce new staff—no easy feat given the high staff turnover or short-term contract modalities with which many UN agencies operate.

52 Christopher Colvin, "Purity and Planning: Shared Logics of Transitional Justice and Development," *International Journal of Transitional Justice* 2 (2008): 412–25.

53 When looking at the conceptual origins of transitional justice, a similar "fallacy," to my mind, can be observed. Transitional justice in the discussions of democratic transitions was conceived of as short-term measures intrinsically linked with the ongoing political change processes, not as ways to come to terms with the past. See Arthur, "How 'Transitions' Reshaped Human Rights."

54 Alston, "Ships Passing in the Night," 755–829, esp. 802–07.

55 Sen, *Development as Freedom*, 147–48.

56 This is a persistent donor concern. See the discussion in ICTJ/DFID, "Donor Strategies," 6–8.

57 There is much to be read in this regard about aid to civil society and NGOs, to states and government institutions, to democratization writ large, and the failures to reach the poorest of the poor. See, e.g., Uvin, *Human Rights and Development*, 95–112; Peter Bauer, *The Development Frontier: Essays in Applied Economics* (Hempstead: Harvester Wheatsheaf,

1991); and Alex de Waal, *Famine Crimes: Politics and the Disaster Relief Industry in Africa* (London: African Rights and The International African Institute, 1997).

58 See the discussion in Arthur, "How 'Transitions' Reshaped Human Rights," of the debate within the transitional justice field, as well as Diane Orentlicher, "Settling Accounts: The Duty to Prosecute Human Rights Violations of a Prior Regime," *Yale Law Journal* 100 (2001): 2537–615, on the "duty to prosecute human rights violations of a previous regime," and Louis Joinet, *Question of the Impunity of Perpetrators of Human Rights Violations (Civil and Political), Revised Final Report*, E/CN.4/Sub.2/1997/20/Rev.1, October 2, 1997. See also Priscilla Hayner, *Unspeakable Truths: Facing the Challenges of Truth Commissions* (New York and London: Routledge, 2002), 183–205, for a discussion of when it may be more appropriate to "leave the past alone," rather than insisting on a truth-telling measure at a given moment in time.

59 Uvin, *Human Rights and Development*, 155.

60 UN Security Council, *The Rule of Law and Transitional Justice*; and UNDP, "Capacity Development."

61 Christopher Colvin, "Civil Society and Reconciliation in Southern Africa," *Development in Practice* 17 (2007): 322–37.

62 Some truth commissions, such as those of Peru and Guatemala, have at least to some extent examined the role of external actors in directly or indirectly supporting a rights-violating regime. This may not extend to development actors per se, but given the complexity of "development actors," there may well be some fine lines. I am currently not aware of work that has looked comparatively at the treatment of international (development) agencies in truth commissions or war crime trials, but it may be insightful to do so, both to see what has been captured and what has been omitted.

63 Arthur, "How 'Transitions' Reshaped Human Rights."

64 P. B. Anand and Des Gasper, "Conceptual Framework and Overview, Special Issue on Human Security, Well-being and Sustainability: Rights, Responsibilities, and Priorities," *Journal of International Development* 19 (2007): 449–56, argue that the "informational space" that links these three approaches are freedoms, rights, responsibilities, values, and deliberative processes. They point out how such a framework invites such questions as "whose rights, whose responsibilities, and whose priorities should matter" (452).

65 De Greiff, "Articulating the Links," in this volume.

CHAPTER 3

The Political Economy of the Transition from Authoritarianism

Tony Addison[1]

The last two decades have seen many societies attempt the move from authoritarianism to democracy. Some of these transitions have been successful, while others remain tentative, and some have been reversed with either a relapse into full dictatorship or with the trappings of democracy used to cloak semi-authoritarianism. Some transitions have involved ending long and bloody civil wars, while others have been made with few lives lost. In some societies, long civil wars continue after periodic, but failed, attempts at peace and are spreading themselves across borders to become larger regional conflicts.

Transition is a highly complex phenomenon. One dimension is transitional justice, defined as "efforts during postconflict and post-authoritarian transitions to address the legacies of massive atrocities and human rights abuses."[2] Violence is often used to create distributive injustice (the expropriation of land from indigenous people, for example) and to perpetuate it (including the exploitative economic relations that underpin high social inequality). The fiscal cost of the military and security apparatus left by authoritarianism can be a significant burden to new democracies, and the economic involvement of the military and other powerful elites left over from authoritarianism can continue to impose a heavy economic price well beyond the end of authoritarian rule. If authoritarianism created a distorted economy and high inequality, democrats may find this difficult to change. Democracy's prospects will then be endangered since expectations of social justice will be high but frustrated. Consequently, transition is unlikely to succeed unless its economic dimensions are adequately addressed.

This chapter explores the political economy of the transition from authoritarianism. The following section outlines the goals for transitional societies and the complementarities (and tensions) that can exist between goals. Particular emphasis is placed on the relationship between transitional justice and distributive justice. The third section discusses the political economy of different types of authoritarian regimes, noting how economic success (more often found in East Asia than Latin America) tends to reduce the need for rulers to resort to state violence to secure their power, and therefore the scale of the subsequent task for transitional justice. The next section focuses on the behaviors that persist after the end of authoritarianism and that are associated with unproductive expenditures, undisciplined rent seeking, and macroeconomic destabilization. These distort economies and make democratization and transitional justice more difficult.

The fifth section makes some recommendations, focusing on resources, priorities, social protection, and integration in the global economy. It identifies synergies between justice and development, including "quick wins" that build confidence, thereby helping to secure an end to authoritarianism. Creating a system of social protection is recommended as a way to reverse long-standing and interrelated injustices, and social protection is becoming important in consolidating Latin America's democratization. But to succeed these measures need to be embedded in a supportive policy framework, including trade arrangements that benefit the developing world, as well as vigorous international measures to tackle corruption (especially in mineral-rich countries). The final section concludes that successful political transitions — of which transitional justice is a part — are founded on successful economic development. Good intentions, however, are insufficient; implementation is critical.

OBJECTIVES IN THE TRANSITION FROM AUTHORITARIANISM

Transitional societies face a multiplicity of goals. There are at least five:[3]

Transitional Justice — bringing to account perpetrators of human rights abuses and recognizing victims through criminal prosecution, truth-telling, reparations, and institutional reform.

Distributive Justice — at minimum, the elimination of absolute poverty. Societies may also set themselves the broader goal of reducing inequality.

Prosperity — raising society's level of output and income ("economic growth"), the scale of the task depending on the economic impact of authoritarianism and/or conflict.

Participation — most often seen as democratization, or the return to democracy after authoritarian politics.

Peace — ending large-scale violence and low-intensity violence, depending on the origins of the conflict and the way it evolved.

The definition of "development" has evolved over time: initially it focused very much on raising prosperity, narrowly defined as gross domestic product (GDP) per capita. Eventually absolute poverty reduction was added as a goal, as well as inequality reduction. The notion of inequality has also broadened to include gender equality and group ("horizontal") equality. These goals have been wrapped together under the term "distributive justice," with societies varying in the value they attach to each (thus, European societies traditionally give more weight to reducing income inequality than does U.S. society). Participation and peace are also increasingly cited as development goals.

Although conceptually separate, these five goals are very much linked—"everything connects," as Pablo de Greiff emphasizes in the overview chapter for this volume. Both distributive and corrective justice influence the prospects for peace; the former because grievances can ignite conflict, the latter because a peace deal may require the correction of past injustice. The likelihood of peace is also determined by the scale and nature of participation—for example, whether the political process accommodates all interests. Prosperity makes it easier to achieve the other goals by generating more resources and reducing the need to make difficult trade-offs between goals.

What of the relationship between transitional justice and development? When viewed as a technocratic endeavor, development is about getting the "right" policies and institutions in place to build up, over time, society's stocks of human and physical capital—thereby delivering rising prosperity accompanied by absolute poverty reduction. This perspective is orientated to the future, with little thought to the past—in particular understanding why it is that many people start with so few assets, or live in areas that make livelihoods difficult. But present circumstances may be the product of a past in which communities were subject to violence, the dispossession of their assets, and forced displacement from lands that were valuable to powerful colonizers. Indeed, all these forces may still be at work, ensuring that poverty is transmitted across generations. This is captured in the notion of *chronic* poverty: your parents (and their parents) were poor, you are poor, and it is likely that your children—and their children—will be poor.[4]

Chronic poverty cannot be understood without a sense of history. The plight of indigenous people provides an example. Historically they have been marginalized and, at worst, enslaved or exterminated. The inequities of the past structure their lives in the present and, without social action, their futures. Many, perhaps most, are in absolute poverty (although their sense of dignity may lead them to reject the "poverty label" as demeaning).[5] Recognizing the injustice of their historic marginalization is necessary if society is ever to perceive them as "full citizens." Addressing their present poverty is necessary for them to be able to exercise their rights, and exercising those rights is part of the social action necessary to end their poverty—thereby enabling them to become citizens in the full meaning of the word.[6]

In dealing with the past or, more strongly, in *righting past injustice*, transitional justice speaks to a conception of development rooted in social transformation, not just technocratic endeavor. In speaking of *full* citizenship, transitional justice reinforces the idea that the poor have agency, that they are not passive actors whom the development process "acts upon" but people who can engage in "good struggles" to end their oppression and poverty.[7]

"BOUNDED" JUSTICE

So much for the goals. What of the *means*? Transitional justice, particularly criminal prosecution, can be expensive. The annual cost of administering international justice was US\$240 million in 2006.[8] At the International Criminal Tribunal for Rwanda (ICTR), more than US\$1 billion has been spent prosecuting fifty-five people involved in the genocide.[9] Holding war crimes trials in Liberia will require resources beyond the means of the hard-pressed national judicial system.[10] When perpetrators reduce prosperity they make it more difficult to bring them to justice later—especially when the result is civil war. The typical civil war in a poor country costs US\$64.2 billion, including the value of both the lost output and the lost human capital.[11] This destruction of prosperity (including core state institutions) and human life (including core skills, especially in the justice system itself) impedes the subsequent pursuit of justice for human rights abuses.

Moreover, the number of absolutely poor people increases when prosperity is undermined, thereby intensifying the acute ethical dilemma that societies eventually face in allocating resources between transitional and distributive justice (a tension evident in Rwanda). Switching resources to transitional justice may bring killers to account, but at the cost of less absolute poverty reduction. Switching resources to distributive justice reduces child deaths, but may leave killers to roam freely. Poor societies are in a dilemma, one at its worst in those impoverished by civil war. The dilemma is less acute when considering less expensive transitional justice measures, such as truth commissions, but the general point still holds: transitional justice requires resources that are in short supply in developing country contexts.

In summary, the political will to engage with justice, be it transitional or distributive, is crucial; but once the political decision is made, the resources available to the task can limit progress in poor societies unless the international community is generous.[12] Without that help, justice often becomes proportionate to per capita income (that is, to a country's level of "economic development"). In that sense, justice is "bounded." This should be morally unacceptable. Hence, the rationale for international assistance to help reduce the ethical dilemmas that necessarily arise when limited domestic resources set tight boundaries to justice. I return to this role for the international community later on.

THE ECONOMIC RECORD OF AUTHORITARIANISM

Authoritarian regimes pursue a very wide range of economic strategies. These economic choices are driven by personal gain, ideology, and nationalism—the motives depending on the type of authoritarianism. Economic strategy may vary from market liberalism to state planning, and while authoritarianism has sometimes delivered economic success, economic failure is more common. This economic legacy will continue into a democratic transition, and the economic structure created under authoritarianism will influence the prospects for consolidating democracy. If authoritarianism delivered economic growth and diversification, then democrats will not be sidetracked by economic crisis or, in the worst case, the need to recover from civil war. If authoritarianism created a distorted economy and high inequality, democrats may find this difficult to change. Democracy's prospects will then be endangered since expectations of social justice will be high but frustrated. Moreover, patterns of behavior harmful to economic development may be embedded in authoritarianism's institutional legacy. These include rampant cronyism and corruption.

In short, authoritarian regimes are often accompanied by a set of *practices* that have pernicious consequences for development. These practices have received insufficient attention in the transitional justice literature and have almost never been addressed directly by transitional justice measures. Some of these practices will be examined in the next section, but this section is concerned with questions of economic policy under authoritarianism, to illustrate the point that authoritarian regimes do not necessarily share the same policy orientation and that the economic record of authoritarian regimes is not uniform; that record contains both successes and failures. The success of economic policy affects the perceptions and actions of authoritarian rule, which in turn can have an impact on the sorts of issues transitional justice deals with; economic prosperity has made some authoritarian regimes popular—at least temporarily—therefore diminishing their "need" to use violence to keep themselves in power.

East Asia is lauded for its fast development, the takeoff occurring under authoritarianism. Thus, it took the United Kingdom fifty-four years to become a middle-income country, while it took South Korea and Taiwan only ten years from the mid-1960s.[13] State technocrats worked closely with business in each.[14] In South Korea and Taiwan, bureaucratic authoritarians built strong economies from weak ones, amidst the legacy of war. The Kuomintang (KMT) government ended Taiwan's hyperinflation (associated with China's civil war) and South Korea recovered and grew from a GDP per capita that was below Ghana's in the 1950s.[15]

Korea's military regime (1961–1987) suppressed the opposition, sometimes violently (notably in the 1980 Gwangju uprising), but it could not contain the social forces unleashed by rising prosperity. A growing middle class, organized working class, and student body strengthened the pro-democracy movement.[16] The death under torture of Park Jong-chul, a student activist, triggered the June 1987 pro-democracy demonstrations leading to transition—and the election in 1992 of the first civilian president in thirty years.[17] Rising prosperity performed a similar role in Taiwan, with the Democratic Progressive Party (DPP)—essentially a party of young middle-class professionals—emerging in the late 1970s to challenge the ruling KMT.[18] The DPP was eventually legalized and in the 2000 elections it ended the KMT's long monopoly on power.

Rising prosperity under authoritarianism built support for these regimes in their early years. The Korean state disciplined rent seeking so that the rents generated by state controls were channeled into productive uses to diversify the economy and deliver high growth.[19] Korea's *chaebol* reaped the benefits of the increasing economies of scale that come from exporting and from a protected position in domestic markets. Both South Korea and Taiwan undertook early and comprehensive land reform, which increased the egalitarian impact of subsequent growth and added to the popular support enjoyed by the regimes. A rapid shift of labor from agriculture and strong employment growth followed success in labor-intensive manufacturing, with inequality and absolute poverty falling sharply.[20]

The behaviors developed under authoritarianism yielded success. However, in South Korea, disenchantment with the increasingly corrupt nature of relations between the ruling party and the *chaebol* contributed to support for democratic transition in the late 1980s. The 1997–1998 Asian financial crisis exposed the weaknesses in Korea's *chaebol*, which had by then become bloated oligopolies. This set the stage for their subsequent reform and accelerated anticorruption efforts. Yet while Korea had to go through a painful economic adjustment, the core of its economic model remained intact.

In contrast to South Korea and Taiwan, Argentina and Brazil illustrate economic failure under authoritarianism. Argentina's economy was in worse shape by the end of the military dictatorship (1976–1983) than at the beginning. The military rationalized its takeover as necessary to restore economic prudence. In the event, the regime committed a series of policy blunders, notably overvaluation of the currency. This encouraged both the private and public sectors to rapidly accumulate external debt.[21] By 1985, Argentina was once again on the verge of hyperinflation. The military itself became an obstacle to the neoliberal reform agenda pushed by the technocrats around the minister of finance, José Alfredo Martínez de Hoz. The minister of planning, General Ramón Díaz, favored a corporatist model, and military officers took a stake in state-owned monopolies and resisted their privatization. This contrasts with Chile, where neoliberal technocrats persuaded Augusto Pinochet to overrule opposition by the military to privatization.[22]

As the Argentinean economy went into crisis, the excesses of the military increased. The military looted the personal property, and in some cases took the children, of those it imprisoned, tortured, and killed. Property became the main motive in selecting many of the victims.[23] Yet as atrocious as these actions were, it is arguable that the military regime's economic fallout had greater human effect—given the number of people impoverished by the recession and hyperinflation. Poverty jumped and inequality deepened under Argentina's military dictatorship.[24] Through a prohibition on union activity and control over wage setting, the military government ensured that organized labor, rather than capital, bore the brunt of the crisis; real wages fell sharply from 1976 to 1983, especially as the economy went into deep recession after 1982.[25] Low-income households suffered the largest drop in income between 1974 and 1987, and many of the well-educated middle class were also pushed into poverty. In Buenos Aires, the proportion of households below the poverty line rose from 7.6 percent in 1980 to 28.5 percent by 1990, as post-military governments struggled to stabilize the economy.[26]

The scale of human rights abuses committed during Brazil's military-backed governments (1964–1985) was smaller than in Argentina and Chile. This, together with periods of high growth, has left a more favorable impression of Brazil's period of authoritarian rule. But a careful examination shows that from the perspective of prosperity, the military regime of 1964–1985 was largely a failure, as it went from boom to bust. With regard to distributive justice, it was a complete failure.

Following the 1964 coup d'état, the repression of organized labor favored capital accumulation. The resulting slowdown in wages supported the stabilization effort of 1964–1966 and reduced inflation.[27] Growth was strong from 1965 to 1974 (the era of Brazil's so-called growth miracle), giving the military confidence to hold relatively free congressional elections in 1974. However, voters turned against its party, the National Renewal Alliance Party [*Aliança Renovadora Nacional*] (ARENA). In response, and to shore up its political base, the regime reversed the earlier wage squeeze, borrowing abroad to offset the deflationary impact of the first and second oil shocks. To expand patronage, the state's role in production and distribution was increased. In the state of Minas Gerais, the number of government agencies tripled and public employment doubled.[28]

As in Argentina, the result was an unsustainable external debt position and macroeconomic turmoil in the 1980s, with a severe compression in consumption; recovery only began in the 1990s.[29] The private sector had welcomed the 1964 coup d'état, but it became increasingly disillusioned as the state intervened in the economy, which crowded out private investment, and as external borrowing became unsustainable. This loss of support was an important factor in initiating the return to democracy.[30]

Judged by the standard of distributive justice, the military's social project was an unmitigated failure. The government of General Castelo Branco, the first president after the coup d'état, attached priority to agrarian reform. But the regime repressed many social movements fighting for distributive justice, alleging (often spurious) links to communism or a threat to "social order." Among the 10,000 to 50,000 arrested (and often tortured) following the 1964 coup were trade unionists, peasant leaders, and workers in charities, such as the Catholic Church's *Movimento de Educação de Base*.[31]

In the 1970s, the government attempted to shore up its support by extending state corporatism into the rural areas, creating "official" unions of smallholders and the landless, a rural welfare program (PRORURAL), and a large-scale expansion of rural credit. But its efforts were fundamentally contradictory, as its own elite power base blocked progress, especially in the very poor northeast region. By the end of military rule, the infant mortality rate (IMR) in the poorest areas of the northeast was an astonishing 200 per 1,000 births, compared to a country average of 60 per 1,000.[32] As Riordan Roett argues, "the political elites that supported the government between 1964–1985 were principally from the region: they were the most fervent defenders of the status quo."[33] As a result, by the end of military rule (1985) inequality was higher than at its start (1964); as one study concludes: "The benefits from growth in the 1960s went disproportionately to the rich, and the costs of the 1980s stagnation fell disproportionately on the poor."[34]

Brazil's military has continued to back elite rural interests against progressive social movements, especially as far as indigenous peoples are concerned. It continued to act in an authoritarian manner in Amazônia after the return to democracy, supporting settlers and powerful landed interests against the indigenous population.[35] In August 2008, the head of the army's Amazônia command publicly attacked the federal government's indigenous policy, again backing the settlers.

In summary, success in delivering prosperity and distributive justice provided a measure of popular support for bureaucratic authoritarianism in South Korea and Taiwan, thereby reducing the "need" to resort to state violence (with the mobilization of nationalism against external threat also bolstering these regimes). Thus, while both these Asian countries had to deal with an authoritarian legacy of human rights abuses, transitional justice was much less of an issue than in Latin America—where most authoritarian regimes failed to deliver either the prosperity or distributive justice necessary to broaden their support. Without the support that prosperity brings, dictators in these countries came to rely on state violence to retain power, resulting in large-scale human rights abuses.

THE ECONOMIC LEGACY OF AUTHORITARIANISM

Authoritarian regimes frequently leave in their wake a series of negative legacies that up to this point have not received sufficient attention in the literature on transitions, and even less by transitional justice measures. These legacies include *unproductive expenditures*—expenditures that have a high opportunity cost for development, in particular spending on a repressive state apparatus (intelligence services, the military, paramilitaries, and so on). These expenditures are often accompanied by *undisciplined rent seeking*, whereby the state fails to ensure that the economic rents generated by its controls are used for the national development project—and these behaviors then become embedded in ways that are harmful to economic development under democracy. In the worst cases, both unproductive spending and rent seeking result in *macroeconomic destabilization*—characterized by capital flight, excessive debt accumulation, and macroeconomic crisis. I consider each in turn, as well as some of their implications for development and transitional justice.

UNPRODUCTIVE EXPENDITURES

The "fiscal space" is arguably the most important battleground in the political economy of transition. How public money is allocated and spent, and

who pays the taxes, are truer indicators of priorities than any political statement — for fiscal outcomes reflect the underlying balance of political power.
Authoritarian actors can continue to shape the fiscal space for many years
after democratic transition.

The military can be especially powerful and vocal, absorbing large amounts
of public money well beyond authoritarianism's end, a concern in Argentina,
Brazil, and Chile, countries in which the military and civilian politicians negotiated the handover in "pacted transitions."[36] The militaries tried to retain their
prerogatives and "reserve powers" after democratic transition.[37] Argentina's
military was far less successful than Chile's in ensuring a favorable post-transition outcome for itself, partly because economic failure left it with a weak
hand.[38]

In contrast to Argentina, Chile's military secured its financial base. Chile's
1958 Ley del Cobre Reservado ("copper law") allocated 10 percent of the copper earnings of the state-run Corporación del Cobre (Codelco) to the military.
Pinochet changed the law in 1987, applying it to 10 percent of total Codelco
export earnings, including gold. This arrangement is estimated to fund between
20 and 30 percent of the armed forces budget, particularly arms imports.
Chile's privatization program under the military was the region's most comprehensive, but Codelco was excluded and Pinochet appointed active military
officers to head the company and thereby facilitate its cooperation.[39]

The Chilean military secured for itself a number of other privileges during
its rule. The military pension system was excluded from the privatization of
social security, undertaken in the 1980s.[40] It remains a generously funded pensions system in a country where social security is still not comprehensive. The
military also demanded (and achieved) a number of economic conditions in
negotiations with civilians following the 1988 plebiscite.[41] It demanded that the
status of the central bank as an autonomous state organ (enshrined in the 1980
constitution) be retained.[42] This might be regarded as relatively unobjection-
able (greater independence for central banks became conventional wisdom in
1990s economic policy-making), but the military's requirement that it choose
the central bank's president was decidedly unconventional. The military also
insisted that the conduct of the privatizations undertaken toward the end of
the regime should not be investigated.

The Organic Constitutional Law on the Armed Forces (Law 18,948, February 1990) guaranteed the military a specific minimum budget. This elevated the
copper law to constitutional rank, and removed the ability of Congress to use
the annual budget to control the military.[43] The copper law has been a continuing source of tension. Opposition from the right in Congress thwarted reform

in 1992.[44] In the early 1990s, the copper price fell, but military expenditure was protected, the rest of the public budget in effect absorbing the adjustment — to the detriment of the social programs of the new democratic administration.

The government has chipped away at the military's budget: it fell from 5 percent of GDP in 1988 to 3.6 percent in 2006.[45] This has accompanied political reforms to reduce the military's participation in political decisions. The 2005 constitutional reforms abolished unelected senators and downgraded the status of the National Security Council. Nevertheless, the recent commodity boom gave the military a massive windfall, via the copper law, that it duly spent.[46] While Chile is well below Brazil, the region's largest spender on defense (US$3.8 billion and US$13.2 billion, respectively), it is Latin America's biggest spender on a per capita basis.[47]

Chile has avoided the economic problems associated with resource wealth.[48] Nevertheless, Codelco's role in funding the military has distorted the company's investment policies to the detriment of its financial performance, and inhibited Codelco's role in economic development.[49] Moreover, although Chile's economy has diversified, the scale of military spending — in a country that has not fought a war since the War of the Pacific (1879–1883) — is a major constraint on growth. The money spent on imported military hardware could have funded a better education system, with all its associated social and economic benefits, a point made by student demonstrators in 2006; their placards highlighted the boom in copper prices and the shortfall in education.[50]

Chile illustrates the close link between natural resource revenues and military expenditure, in this case through copper. In Indonesia, the link is through oil and rice. Whereas Chile's military secured for itself an institutional arrangement embedded in law — and therefore amenable to eventual democratic restraint, albeit not easily — Indonesia's military has managed to draw resources from the economy in increasingly opaque ways, many of which continued beyond the end of the Suharto regime. Indonesia demonstrates the pernicious effect of behaviors carried over from military dictatorship, behaviors that civilian politicians have had greater difficulty in controlling.

UNDISCIPLINED RENT SEEKING

Rent seeking is often described as wholly unproductive, constituting a waste of a society's resources. What really matters, however, is the *use* to which the rents are put. Under authoritarianism in South Korea and Taiwan, the economic rents generated by state controls were mostly channeled into productive use, thereby diversifying and growing the economy. Their states disciplined rent seeking to ensure that rents served the national project of economic development (although eventually cronyism came to the fore, but not before both countries had achieved developed-country status).

Unlike those resource-poor countries, Indonesia enjoys the advantage of natural resource rents derived from hydrocarbons, timber, and minerals. Indonesia was once seen as a successful manager of the development effects of oil. In the 1970s, these revenues were invested in the rural economy, contributing to its success in generating growth and poverty reduction. This contrasted sharply with experiences elsewhere in the world, for example, in Nigeria, where both civilian and military regimes mismanaged oil revenues in the 1970s and 1980s, thereby undermining the non-oil economy.[51]

Behind Indonesia's story of technocratic success, however, is another, far darker one of kleptocracy in which resource rents funded the military together with the presidential family, resulting, eventually, in a financial meltdown. Suharto and his family stole US$441 million between 1978 and 1998, but this (government) estimate is almost certainly too low. Transparency International calculates that the family took as much as US$35 billion over the thirty-two years of Suharto's rule, more than either Ferdinand Marcos (up to $10 billion) or Mobutu Sese Seko ($5 billion).[52]

Indonesia's military is small in relation to the country's population, but it has had a disproportionate impact on the economy. Suharto set out a dual-function (dwi-fungsi) role for the army, with a sociopolitical role in addition to its security function.[53] Shortly after the 1965 coup d'état, Suharto created the state oil company Pertamina, headed by one of his generals, to fund the military generously and ensure its loyalty. Opaque procedures were created to do this. Pertamina also borrowed heavily, benefiting from the Organization of Petroleum Exporting Countries (OPEC) price increases of the 1970s. Its revenues subsequently amounted to one-sixth of Indonesia's GDP, and its international debt eventually exceeded that of the government itself.[54]

The state food distribution system, Badan Urusan Logistik (Bulog), created in 1966, exemplified dwi-fungsi. Bulog had its roots in military procurement (dating back to the Dutch colonial system), and was central to restoring food security after the hyperinflation of the 1960s.[55] It was successful in stabilizing the real price of rice, a key expenditure for the poor, for more than twenty years.[56] To do this, Bulog controlled import licenses for rice and other food staples, which were allocated to the military—with military officers taking positions in Bulog—and to Suharto's family and supporters, generating them large fortunes from the economic rents.[57]

During Indonesia's 1998 financial crisis, Bulog was unable to contain the impact of the rupiah's devaluation on food prices. The doubling of rice prices after so many years of stability was a major shock, especially for poor consumers, such as the rural landless, who experienced a 24 percent fall in real incomes as a result.[58] GDP dropped by 15 percent and poverty doubled from 11 to 22 percent, forcing a humiliated Suharto into the hands of the International Monetary Fund (IMF).

The IMF and the World Bank insisted on Bulog's reform to reduce its rent seeking and cronyism, which was by then rampant. It was reorganized into a public corporation in 2003,[59] but this has had limited impact. After Suharto's fall, Bulog developed close relations with his successors, including President Abdurrahman Wahid (being implicated in his downfall in 2001) and the family of President Megawati Sukarnoputri.[60] It continues to receive generous fiscal subsidies, and the associated corruption goes unchallenged, with Bulog seeking to extend its control over food imports again.[61] The relationship with the military's leadership remains close, with senior military figures being implicated in successive corruption scandals. Bulog has been used to procure military equipment, including a 2004 deal bartering rice for Russian jet fighters worth US$192 million. In summary, Bulog's modus operandi has proved largely impervious to the democratic transition.

The military's human rights abuses in Indonesia's outlying provinces, including Aceh, East Timor (now Timor-Leste), and West Papua, are well documented.[62] They were driven not only by the need to secure Jakarta's political control over these territories (most brutally in the invasion of East Timor), but also by the military's economic interests. Budgeted expenditures on defense—which show defense spending to be 1.3 percent of GDP in 2006—have never given a true indication of the military's burden on the economy.[63] Indeed, Suharto kept budgeted expenditures low in order to give the appearance that development headed the list of budgetary priorities.[64]

In Indonesia, the military partly self-finances itself via "military-owned enterprises, informal alliances with private entrepreneurs to whom the military often provides services, mafia-like criminal activity, and corruption."[65] Although there are no accurate estimates, it is generally accepted that only 25 to 30 percent of military expenditures are covered by the national budget. Under a 2004 law, the military is required to withdraw from all economic activity, but action has been slow. The military can be expected to offer considerable resistance, since any challenge to its economic interests threatens the personal wealth of senior commanders, together with the institution's power base and social standing. The global economic slowdown will reduce the fiscal space available to accommodate military spending, and will encourage the military to keep much of its activity off the budget.

In summary, Indonesia illustrates the link between security sector reform (SSR, central to transitional justice)[66] and fiscal space. Effective civilian oversight of the military is impossible while it continues to fund part of its operations from sources outside the government budget. This semiautonomy from the budgetary process limits the ability of civilians to demand accountability and to curtail the military's human rights abuses. It also provides a basis for unproductive rent seeking and corruption. The military's engagement with the economy raises transaction costs for legitimate businesses (through the payment of protection money) and contributes to Indonesia's dramatic environmental degradation, especially deforestation (which has made Indonesia the world's second largest emitter of carbon).

MACROECONOMIC DESTABILIZATION

In Argentina and Brazil, the military justified its actions as necessary to restore prosperity—but impoverishment ensued, as discussed earlier. Both countries illustrate the difficulties that post-authoritarian governments face in stabilizing the economy, restoring growth, and reducing poverty. Argentina's recession lasted long after the military left power, and indeed it deepened over the 1980s as the macroeconomic impact of the earlier debt accumulation took effect. Because economic policy-making lost all credibility under the military regime, Argentina entered a macroeconomic straitjacket—the convertibility law—which eventually created a crisis of its own; 1999–2002 saw, once again, debt default and a severe recession.[67] Brazil's economy has done better, but went through a series of tough reforms after the return to democracy. Indonesia's regime had greater earlier success, but succumbed to the 1998 Asian financial crisis, which exposed the murky financial world that went alongside the rent seeking and patronage created during the thirty-two years of Suharto's rule. As in Argentina, the new government in Indonesia found it exceptionally difficult to restore policy credibility, and the economy was unstable for a number of years, with high costs for the poor.

Nigeria is another example of how behaviors created under dictatorship have carried through to the democratic transition, thereby impeding the achievement of macroeconomic stability and development. Nigeria has oscillated between civilian and military rule since independence; between 1966 and 1999 there were only four years of civilian government. The military cited corruption and economic mismanagement to justify its takeovers—and then engaged in similar behavior. Macroeconomic mismanagement led to an excessive foreign debt burden and to deepening poverty, spectacularly so under the last military ruler, General Sani Abacha (1993–1998).[68]

Abacha looted the state finances, and having burdened the country with odious debt he then engaged in scams around debt repayments. One involved the notorious Ajaokuta steel plant, built by Russian contractors.[69] A debt of US$2.5 billion was accumulated on the project, which was purchased for US$500 million in 1996 by a company operating as a front for the Abacha family. The Nigerian treasury then repaid the debt—for the whole US$2.5 billion.

In 2007, power was transferred from one civilian regime to another, for the first time in Nigeria's history. President Umaru Yar'Adua promised to continue the anticorruption drive, but in 2008 the head of the Economic and Financial Crimes Commission (EFCC) was removed. At the time, the EFCC was prosecuting a number of former state governors closely linked to the ruling party, including a former governor of the oil-rich Delta province who financed President Yar'Adua's campaign. Little has been done to improve the management of oil revenues, and the 2008 collapse in oil prices is now straining the public finances. This is reducing the government's ability to balance competing regional interests and to keep the lid on conflict in the Niger Delta, where political patrons use the many unemployed youth to extort funds from the state as well as the foreign oil companies. Macroeconomic destabilization is therefore likely and the attendant social fallout will threaten the democratic consolidation. The interweaving of oil money, party politics, and corruption remains deeply rooted in Nigeria, seemingly impervious to the transition from dictatorship to democracy.

Kenya has displayed a similar resilience in corruption, and the close link between corruption and party politics, after its democratic transition in 2002 from the autocracy of Daniel Arap Moi (who became president in 1978), and his predecessor, Kenya's first president, Jomo Kenyatta.[70] State-business relationships (and the associated corruption) have not been developmental in the same way as those in East Asia, and Kenya failed to create a "Weberian bureaucracy" during authoritarianism. From the 1990s onward, aid donors threatened to suspend aid unless Moi's government reformed.[71]

The political economy of Kenya's democratization initially looked favorable, but the benefits of high commodity prices masked an economy held back by an ineffective state that has been incapable of addressing distributive injustice. The violence and serious human rights abuses following the December 2007 elections are being addressed through an electoral violence tribunal, but little has been done to reduce the horizontal inequalities underlying ethnic animosity.[72] The crisis delivered a massive macroeconomic shock, which has undermined recent economic growth. As in Nigeria, the corruption that became embedded under autocracy remains resilient in Kenya; some US$1 billion has been stolen since democratization in 2002, and, as in Nigeria, efforts to vigorously challenge corruption have been thwarted; John Githongo, the country's anticorruption czar (appointed by President Mwai Kibaki upon his election in 2002) eventually fled the country.[73] Despite the high hopes of donors, multiparty politics has in many ways intensified the use of the state for patronage.

The hyperinflation and collapse in living standards under Robert Mugabe in Zimbabwe will leave an immense burden for any incoming democratic government. Indeed, the necessary macroeconomic stabilization measures could worsen the lot of the poor, as they did in post-dictatorship Argentina in the 1980s. Mugabe constructed a narrative around distributive justice—in particular the country's very unequal distribution of land (itself a product of the colonial era and the Ian Smith regime)—which was used to expropriate white farmers and transfer their land to Mugabe's cronies. The instruments of distributive justice, in particular famine relief, have been used to perpetuate that rule in increasingly sham elections: voting for the Zimbabwe African National Union-Patriotic Front (ZANU-PF) is often a requirement to receive food aid, a powerful tool for manipulating the popular vote in a country as drought-prone as Zimbabwe.[74]

Transitional justice will necessarily require support from a new agenda for distributive justice in Zimbabwe—not only in adding the crime of impoverishment to human rights abuses (cholera has probably now killed more Zimbabweans than direct state violence), but also in quickly addressing the very high levels of inequality that now characterize the country. Unless macroeconomic stabilization can be achieved in ways that renew prosperity, however, the prospects for either form of justice remain dismal. And the insertion of Mugabe's allies, including the military, into the economic fabric of the country (in particular through their appropriation of previously white-owned farms) threatens to leave the country on a trajectory similar to that of Nigeria or Indonesia, once Mugabe and his immediate circle exit the stage; that is: a continuation, in new forms, of unproductive spending (particularly on the military) and undisciplined rent seeking with the associated macroeconomic instability.

In short, these examples—to which could be added many more—illustrate the pernicious practices that all too often accompany authoritarianism, and which need to be taken account of in the principles and practices of transitional justice. While authoritarian regimes do not have a monopoly over unproductive expenditures, rent seeking, and macroeconomic destabilization, these are common legacies of authoritarianism. Crucially, the short time horizon of most authoritarian regimes implies a greater willingness to resort to pernicious economic behaviors than under well-functioning democracies. These perverse incentives are at their worst in many of the poorer countries, especially in Africa (and especially those with mineral wealth), where years of instability and war too often encourage political actors to maximize their loot during their expected short time in power. By fostering corruption, weakening the rule of law, and diminishing the possibility of effective accountability and oversight (especially of the security apparatus), these authoritarian practices add to the difficulties of democracy—if it can be established. By distorting economies, they slow (or undermine) the rate of economic growth, thereby adding to poverty; distributive injustice is further aggravated by the diversion of state finances away from pro-poor and development expenditures. Weak states are generally the result, further adding to the difficulties of subsequent attempts to deal with human rights abuses (Liberia is a case in point).

Serious human rights abuses and, in the worst cases, genocide are rightly the center of attention for the transitional justice community. But to these crimes must be added the negative economic impact of authoritarianism, together with its attendant social fallout: the increased child mortality, the lower life expectancy, and the greater prevalence of chronic poverty. Poverty kills people as surely as a machete or a bullet, and therefore the increased poverty (and other forms of distributive injustice) that accompany most experiences of authoritarianism should be incorporated into the charges laid before perpetrators, the mandates of truth commissions, and the target of SSR. Not to do so is to ignore a major (social) crime, and to encourage demagogues in the belief that they will never be accountable for actions that undermine national prosperity.

RECOMMENDATIONS

RESOURCES

Justice requires resources: financial, human, and institutional. In poor transitional societies—especially those recovering from civil war—resources can become stretched too thinly, so that no goal is achieved satisfactorily. Domestic tax revenues are typically low, as authoritarianism and conflict usually reduce the economy's size and thus the tax base.[75] Moreover, powerful elites may block reforms to raise revenues. In Guatemala, the peace agreement specified an increase in social spending to 5 percent of GDP to provide basic services to indigenous groups and to reduce the grievances that fed thirty-six years of civil war. As part of the agreement, tax reforms were promised to raise the tax-to-GDP ratio to 12 percent of GDP; however, the elite, which controls the legislature, blocked the revenue-raising measures.[76] This failure has contributed to macroeconomic problems, as the fiscal deficit has been financed through external debt accumulation. Transitional arrangements need to focus on how domestic resources can be raised, and how to create binding commitments to do so.

While it is true that poor societies have few financial resources on average (as evidenced in their low per capita income), a sizeable number possess significant natural resource wealth. This is truly immense in some cases, for example, Angola, Equatorial Guinea, and Nigeria, three countries with authoritarian histories. Sometimes this may be outside the control of the government, and in rebel hands, in which case it needs to be brought back into the public domain. The revenues can then be used for state building and to meet the needs of transitional justice; this remains a major imperative in the Democratic Republic of Congo (DRC).[77] In other instances, resource revenues may be in state hands, but not used for the public good (for example, Equatorial Guinea). If revenues can be reallocated to the public good (the aim of such initiatives as the Extractive Industries Transparency Initiative [EITI]), then more resources become available to pursue transitional justice. The main resource constraint then becomes institutional (and new institutions take time to build) and human (the skills necessary to pursue transitional justice), rather than financial.

Security sector reform should assess how much the military absorbs of resource revenues. This link is often used to justify classifying information on resource revenues as a state secret (in Angola, Equatorial Guinea, and most of the Middle East, for example). Transparency is needed in the public accounts to effectively deal with the issue of the military's overdependence on natural resource revenues and the resulting opportunity costs for development. But given the resistance (and power) of entrenched interests, this is likely to be a long haul; EITI is only a start, one that needs to be followed through at the global level.

The "resource envelope" of a transitional government is the sum of domestic revenues plus official aid for the government, together with foreign direct investment and portfolio flows for the private sector. Domestic revenues will take time to recover, especially when new institutions to mobilize revenue have to be created (a new customs and excise service, for example).[78] Private capital flows also typically take time to recover, since investors are usually wary. Official aid will therefore account for a great deal of the external financial inflow in the early years, and a great deal of the finance for the budget—typically most of the public investment budget and often more than half of the recurrent budget in postconflict countries (in Rwanda, for example).

A limited resource envelope provides the international community with an opportunity to link transitional justice with its support to economic recovery and then longer-term development. Project aid to assist the rehabilitation and resettlement of the victims of human rights abuses and genocide together with assistance to disarmament, demobilization, and reintegration (DDR) are crucial, and much has been learned over the last two decades about the best means. As the situation stabilizes, it is desirable to move an increasing share of aid toward budget support, but progress depends on: (1) rebuilding and reforming the state institutions dealing with the public finances so that they are able to properly use (and account for) the budgetary aid; and (2) ensuring that political leaders show commitment to taking transitional justice measures.

Regarding the first of these issues, it is generally agreed that not enough priority was given to the state-building dimension in earlier years, especially in postconflict reconstruction during the 1990s. The result was a wide spread of donor projects, each donor operating with its own procedures, often independently of the state itself. Mozambique in the immediate postwar years is one example. The so-called sector-wide approach, in which donors sign on to a common strategy to deliver aid, has improved matters somewhat. But poor donor coordination remains a problem in Afghanistan, where a plethora of donor projects implemented by expensive UN agencies and nongovernmental organizations (NGOs) divert attention and resources away from the urgent need to build the Afghan state itself, especially in its capacity to manage public finance.[79]

Regarding the second issue, there is a strong case for linking aid to transitional justice measures at the outset, so as to remove from power—and potentially to deliver into custody for trial—perpetrators of human rights abuses (the exception is humanitarian aid, delivered to the suffering population while the authoritarian regime continues). Aid from the Organisation for Economic Co-operation and Development's Development Assistance Committee (OECD DAC) members is currently being withheld from Zimbabwe in an effort to end the Mugabe regime, and a link between aid flows and progress in transitional justice is likely once democracy is established. Once significant aid inflows have begun, and donors have made an investment in the necessary country operation, however, they may be reluctant to suspend or slow disbursements.

If they let progress on transitional justice stall in the early years, they might not press the issue in later years. Moreover, donors may not present a united front, some being less willing than others to give priority to justice, especially when they have significant commercial or geopolitical interests at stake in the recipient country (this was the case in postwar Cambodia).

Official debt relief will be an important part of official aid, and where the debt is "odious" a rapid write-off is desirable. Critical too is the repatriation of public money looted by the previous incumbents (a major issue in Nigeria, where some [modest] success has been achieved). We still lack, however, the instruments to effectively address the problem of looted capital. Europe's financial authorities dallied for years in tracking down the estimated US$3 billion stolen by Abacha. In 2005, Swiss banks were forced by the country's supreme court to return US$505 million of funds looted by the Abacha family.[80] This was then allocated to poverty reduction, an important step in convincing the population that the repatriated funds would be used for distributive justice and not squandered again.

SETTING PRIORITIES

Fundamentally, we must look for synergies—ways in which justice and development can reinforce each other—a point made by de Greiff.[81] These synergies are likely to vary across countries, depending on institutions, histories, and available resources. Successful strategies will therefore need to be closely crafted to the circumstances of individual countries. But I can nevertheless make some general recommendations.

Removing from power those guilty of human rights abuses, together with other "spoilers," is vital, but insufficient, for successful transitions. Quick wins to cut into distributive injustice are also essential, especially when it has an ethnic, religious, or spatial dimension that makes socioeconomic inequality a source of conflict.[82] Many transitions take place against a backdrop of economic failure, as discussed earlier. The expectations of the populace are therefore often low, and cynicism may well abound (including among politicians and civil servants). New administrations need to generate credibility, and quickly. Politicians make plenty of promises, especially around the time of peace deals, but delivering tangible and real gains is paramount. If this can be achieved, and living standards start to grow, then the populace has some stake in the new political order; and demagogues will find it harder to recruit followers when the young have new livelihoods. This imperative needs much greater attention in transitional agendas.

Given the multiplicity of needs, it is tempting to promise to do everything. Then the danger is that a weak implementation capacity is spread too thinly, so that little if any tangible benefit results. Aid donors and NGOs, with their own interests, tend to add to this effect when everyone wants to fund their own niche (and in their own way), as noted above. Sri Lanka is an example of a country that has failed to deliver an economic "dividend" (in its case to end a long-running and brutal civil war), resulting in even more cynicism about the prospects for ever securing peace.[83]

A better strategy is to focus on some highly visible core areas where there is a reasonable chance of success: health is one such area—a strategy that delivers basic health care, especially to children, is a signal of the seriousness of the state's intent, especially to deal with previously marginalized areas, which are often the centers of rebellion and secession.[84] Just after independence, Namibia managed to deliver primary health care quickly to bring down infant mortality and morbidity in its poorer northern regions. Such a strategy of focus can be likened to the military strategy of "win-hold-win": that is, select a key sector, achieve rapid improvements ("win"), sustain those improvements ("hold"), and then draw upon the experience and lessons and resulting confidence to take action in other priority areas ("win").[85]

SOCIAL PROTECTION

Social protection offers a way of moving from the imperatives of the short run to a more sustained and longer-term approach in post-authoritarian societies. Social protection consists of a wide variety of measures, the most important being contingent cash transfers.[86] In Brazil and Mexico, low-income households who send their children to school are provided with cash transfers, thereby reducing their need for an income from child labor. Both countries are characterized by high inequality, and both have made successful transitions from authoritarianism. In both, social protection is a means to reduce the path dependence of inequality and to offset the tendency of economic liberalization to raise inequality further by favoring capital over labor (certainly the case in Mexico).

Social protection also offers a means forward after war. Guatemala and El Salvador are contrasting examples. In Guatemala, poverty is very much a problem of the country's indigenous majority. Income and human development indicators are significantly lower in indigenous households than in white households.[87] These grievances fed the civil war, and little progress has been made in distributive justice. In El Salvador, which also went through a brutal civil war, the percentage of people living in poverty fell from 65 percent in the early 1990s to 41 percent by 2004.[88] Although El Salvador's tax-to-GDP ratio is Central America's lowest (12 percent, after Guatemala), tax reforms are in place to raise it.[89] A conditional cash transfer program, *Red Solidaria*, is contributing to this success.[90]

Argentina illustrates the consequences of not taking action and the need for generous international support to post-authoritarian regimes. Shortly after the end of military rule, Argentina launched a national food program (in 1984) designed to provide 30 percent of a poor family's nutritional needs.[91] This was a clear signal that the new civilian government was more concerned to protect social spending than the military. It also helped to gather support for democratic transition in what was an exceptionally difficult time for the economy, as the macroeconomic imbalances created by the military regime unwound themselves through the 1980s. In the end, the program limited, but did not prevent, the rise in Argentinean poverty (see earlier discussion). The international community could have assisted by ensuring that the debt workout was faster and more generous once the civilian government was in power, giving the latter more budgetary room for maneuver to consolidate the democratization. In the event, Argentina, like all of the 1980s debtors, faced exceptionally tough external conditions as the international community took an overly narrow view that emphasized debt repayment to the neglect of the imperative to consolidate democracy.

INTEGRATING INTO THE GLOBAL ECONOMY

A successful social compact is built on rising economic prosperity. Employment generation is a key dimension of this. Studies finding that a rise in per capita income reduces the probability of conflict are partly capturing the rise in employment that goes with increasing income.[92] This tends to reduce inequality (provided the employment is remunerative) and reduces the need to resort to crime (including warlordism). Successful integration into the global economy is central to rising prosperity, especially for small low-income economies that do not possess the import-substitution possibilities of countries with large populations. For small economies, some variant of an export-led strategy is critical, but it must spread prosperity broadly rather than reinforce the wealth of an established elite. If this outward orientation is successful, then per capita income rises and with it the tax base; if effective tax institutions are created, then this increased revenue can be collected and spent to raise state effectiveness and resolve injustice.

Entry into regional trade agreements is a key way in which economics can strengthen politics. Thus, admittance to the European Union (EU) was central to the economic success of post-Franco Spain and the rapid delivery of tangible gains to underpin a new democracy. Generous aid from the EU also reduced the political tensions in budgetary policy, and permitted a faster rise in public spending on basic services and infrastructure than domestic resources alone would have allowed. EU membership has been similarly important to consolidating the transition from communism in Eastern Europe, the benefits including not only trade and inward investment but also the migration of labor, which has set in motion a process by which wage rates will eventually converge with those in older EU member states.

The rapid rise in global commodity prices over the last five years (before the present global economic crisis) has been a mixed blessing. On the one hand, it reduced some of the budgetary pressures that transitional regimes face, and offered them the prospect of increasing public spending to create "win-win" outcomes for former belligerents. On the other hand, this fiscal largesse can be used to delay much-needed economic reform, thereby maintaining vulnerability to any subsequent fall in commodity prices (as is now occurring). Several dictatorships have consolidated themselves on the basis of oil revenues, notably in Equatorial Guinea.[93] In Angola, the elite is using oil revenues to further secure its political (and commercial) base as the country moves to democracy. Such measures as the Extractive Industries Transparency Initiative (EITI) are vital to ensuring that resource wealth is used for the benefit of the wider population, and not just for the elite. As Nigeria shows, the transition from military to civilian rule does not remove powerful mechanisms of corruption that can remain resilient and take new forms (especially as former military figures take positions in the civilian administration). Greater international action on bribery is needed, but the OECD countries have been tardy in prosecuting their nationals engaged in bribery overseas; the UK has yet to bring a single prosecution, for example.[94]

CONCLUSIONS

Authoritarian regimes leave behind an economic structure, a distribution of wealth, a style of economic policy-making, and a set of institutions. Underlying these are behaviors entailing various degrees of cooperation between individuals, groups, and the state (including respect for the law). With a few exceptions, most authoritarian states end their days with a very limited level of trust between individuals, hatred across ethnic and religious groups, and a limited belief in the capacity and honesty of the state. With the protection of property dependent upon having the right connections to the ruling authoritarian elite, and with the legal system unlikely to protect property (or life), most people look for immediate gain. The long-term outlook that underpins successful and growing economies, and which comes with political stability and freedom, is generally absent, and therefore investment and economic activity is low. This breeds a self-reinforcing cycle of underinvestment, low growth, and poverty.

Post-authoritarian governments must therefore deal with a legacy of behaviors that are destructive of prosperity and distributive justice. These behaviors are often deeply embedded in state institutions. Moreover, powerful actors with interests that they wish to preserve may remain on the stage after democratic transition. They may demand a disproportionate share of the state's finances, and they seek to preserve their economic interests, sometimes by forging new alliances within the private sector. Their economic power gives them a disproportionate influence in new democracies through media control and party influence. This can threaten democratic consolidation, as they challenge any action by legislatures and civil societies to limit their power. A country's government may therefore change with democratization, while the fundamentals of its underlying political economy do not.

These economic issues have important implications for, and must be given greater prominence in, strategies and actions to deliver transitional justice. People in authoritarian societies suffer not just from state violence but also from the poverty and hunger that economic mismanagement brings. They need social protection to ease the economic pain that the transition from authoritarianism often entails, help from the international community to prosecute the guilty who profited from running the economy into the ground, and assurance that post-authoritarian governments will deliver rising prosperity and distributive justice. Quick wins are then especially important to maintain credibility. The worst situation is when the legacy of authoritarianism is both an ineffectual state and high inequality. The country will then struggle to deliver progress, the credibility of democratic politicians will be damaged, and the country could retreat back into authoritarianism and/or descend into large-scale violent conflict. Good intentions are therefore not enough; implementation is paramount.

NOTES

1   I thank Pablo de Greiff for helpful comments. Errors remain my own.

2   Pablo de Greiff, "Theorizing Transitional Justice," in *Transitional Justice,* ed. Melissa Williams and Rosemary Nagy, Nomos XLX (forthcoming).

3   "Transitional" and "distributive" justice are distinguished—and linked—by Pablo de Greiff, "Articulating the Links Between Transitional Justice and Development," in this volume. The goals of peace, participation, and prosperity in the context of postconflict reconstruction are set out in Tony Addison and Tilman Brück, eds., *Making Peace Work: The Challenges of Social and Economic Reconstruction* (Basingstoke: Palgrave Macmillan for UNU-WIDER, 2008).

4   Chronic Poverty Research Centre (CPRC), *Chronic Poverty Report: 2008–2009* (London: CPRC, 2008).

5   On indigenous communities in Argentina that reject the "poverty label," see, e.g., Matthias vom Hau and Guillermo Wilde, "The Unintended Consequence of the 'New Politics of Recognition': Citizenship, Indigenous Mobilization, and Chronic Poverty in Argentina" (paper presented at the CPRC workshop "The Government of Chronic Poverty: From the Politics of Exclusion to Citizenship?" University of Manchester, November 26, 2008).

6   See de Greiff, "Articulating the Links Between Transitional Justice and Development," in this volume.

7   Caroline Sage, Daniel Adler, and Michael Woolcock, "Interim Institutions and the Development Process: Law and the Creation of Spaces for Reform in Cambodia and Indonesia" (paper presented at the annual meeting of the Law and Society Association, Berlin, Germany, July 25, 2007).

8   Andrew Kuper, *Democracy Beyond Borders: Justice and Representation in Global Institutions* (Oxford: Oxford University Press, 2006), 156.

9   De Greiff, "Articulating the Links," in this volume.

10 Global Witness, *An Architecture of Instability: How the Critical Link Between Natural Resources and Conflict Remains Unbroken* (London: Global Witness, 2005), 23.

11 Estimate by Paul Collier and Anke Hoeffler, "Conflicts," in *Global Crises, Global Solutions,* ed. Bjorn Lomborg (Cambridge: Cambridge University Press, 2004). This is almost certainly an underestimate; see Tony Addison, "Conflicts," in *Global Crises, Global Solutions.*

12 Alex Segovia, "Financing Reparations Programs: Reflections from International Experience," in *The Handbook of Reparations,* ed. Pablo de Greiff (Oxford: Oxford University Press, 2006).

13 Stephen L. Parente and Edward C. Prescott, *Barriers to Riches* (Cambridge, MA: MIT Press, 2000).

14 Robert Wade, *Governing the Market: Economic Theory and the Role of Government in East Asian Industrialization* (Princeton: Princeton University Press, 2003).

15 Gail E. Makinen and Thomas Woodward, "The Taiwanese Hyperinflation and Stabilization of 1945–1952," *Journal of Money, Credit & Banking* 21, no. 1 (1989): 90–105; and Herbert Werlin, "Ghana and South Korea: Lessons from World Bank Case Studies," *Public Administration and Development* 11, no. 3 (2006): 245–55.

16 Stephan Haggard and Robert Kaufman, *Political Economy of Democratic Transition* (Princeton: Princeton University Press, 1995), 95.

17 Samuel Kim, ed., *Korea's Democratization* (Cambridge: Cambridge University Press, 2003).

18 Shelley Rigger, *Politics in Taiwan: Voting for Reform* (London: Routledge, 1999).

19 Wade, *Governing the Market*, 7.

20 Gustav Ranis, "Taiwan's Success and Vulnerability: Lessons for the 21st Century," in *Taiwan in the 21st Century: Aspects and Limitations of a Development Mode*, ed. Robert Ash and J. Megan Green (New York: Routledge, 2007). Taiwan's Gini coefficient declined from 0.56 to 0.29 between 1950 and 1970 (Ranis, 44). This was a significant achievement given that inequality tends to rise during the move from low- to middle-income status (the "Kuznets" hypothesis).

21 Rudiger Dornbusch and Juan Carlos de Pablo, "Debt and Macroeconomic Instability in Argentina," in *Developing Country Debt and Economic Performance: Vol. 2 — Country Studies: Argentina, Bolivia, Brazil, Mexico*, ed. Jeffrey D. Sachs and Susan M. Collins (Chicago: University of Chicago Press for the National Bureau of Economic Research, 1990).

22 Judith A. Teichman, *The Politics of Freeing Markets in Latin America: Chile, Argentina and Mexico* (Chapel Hill: University of North Carolina Press, 2001), 198.

23 Alison Brysk, *The Politics of Human Rights in Argentina: Protest, Change, and Democratization* (Stanford: Stanford University Press, 1994), 39.

24 George Psacharopoulos, Samuel Morley, Ariel Fiszbein, Haeduck Lee, and Bill Wood, "Poverty and Income Distribution in Latin America: The Story of the 1980s," Technical Paper 351, World Bank, Washington, DC, 1997.

25 Sam Morley, "The Impact of Reforms on Equity in Latin America," Washington, DC, World Bank, 1999, 6.

26 All data from Luis Beccaria and Ricardo Carciofi, "Argentina: Social Policy and Adjustment During the 1980s," in *Coping with Austerity: Poverty and Inequality in Latin America*, ed. Nora Lustig (Washington, DC: Brookings Institution Press, 1995), 195–96.

27 Eliana Cardoso and Rudiger Dornbusch, "Brazil's Tropical Plan," NBER Working Paper W2142, Cambridge, MA, 1987.

28 Frances Hagopian, "Traditional Politics Against State Transformation in Brazil," in *State Power and Social Forces: Domination and Transformation in the Third World*, ed. Joel S. Migdal, Atul Kohli, and Vivienne Shue (New York: Cambridge University Press, 1994), 50.

29 Eliana Cardoso and Albert Fishlow, "The Macroeconomics of Brazilian External Debt," in *Developing Country Debt and Economic Performance.*

30 Luciano Martins, "The 'Liberalization' of Authoritarian Rule in Brazil," in *Transitions from Authoritarian Rule, Part 2: Latin America,* ed. Guillermo O'Donnell, Philippe C. Schmitter, and Laurence Whitehead (Baltimore: Johns Hopkins University Press, 1986).

31 Thomas E. Skidmore, *The Politics of Military Rule in Brazil,* 1964–1985 (New York: Oxford University Press, 1990), 24.

32 Walter de Oliveira, *Working with Children on the Streets of Brazil: Politics and Practice* (New York: Haworth, 2000), 49.

33 Riordan Roett, *Brazil: Politics in a Patrimonial Society* (New York: Greenwood Publishing, 1999), 226–27.

34 Eliana R. Cardoso, Paes de Barros, and Andre Urani, "Inflation and Unemployment as Determinants of Inequality in Brazil: The 1980s," in *Reform, Recovery and Growth: Latin America and the Middle East,* ed. Rudiger Dornbusch and Sebastian Edwards (Chicago: University of Chicago Press for the National Bureau of Economic Research, 1994), 151. As measured by the Gini coefficient, Brazil's income inequality increased from 0.57 in 1981 to 0.63 in 1989 (Francisco H. G. Ferreira, Phillippe G. Leite, and Julie A Litchfield, "The Rise and Fall of Brazilian Inequality, 1981–2004," Policy Research Working Paper 3867, World Bank, Washington, DC, 2006).

35 Joao R. Filho-Martins and Daniel Zirker, "The Brazilian Military under Cardoso: Overcoming the Identity Crisis," *Journal of Interamerican Studies and World Affairs* 42, no. 3 (2000): 155–70.

36 Peter H. Smith, *Democracy in Latin America* (New York: Oxford University Press, 2005), 65.

37 Rut Diamint, "The Military," in *Constructing Democratic Governance in Latin America,* 2nd ed., ed. Jorge I. Domínguez and Michael Shifter (Baltimore: Johns Hopkins University Press, 2003).

38 Smith, *Democracy in Latin America,* 69. As a consequence, Argentina's defense spending (US$1.7 billion, or 1.3 percent of GDP) is less than half that of Chile (US$3.8 billion, or 2.7 percent of GDP) (International Institute for Strategic Studies [IISS], *The Military Balance: 2006* [London: IISS, 2006]).

39 William Ascher, *Why Governments Waste Natural Resources: Policy Failures in Developing Countries* (Baltimore and London: Johns Hopkins University Press, 1999), 157.

40 Salvador Valdés-Prieto, "The Latin American Experience with Pension Reform," *Annals of Public and Cooperative Economics* 69, no. 4 (1998): 483–516.

41 Adam Przeworski, *Democracy and the Market: Political and Economic Reforms in Eastern Europe and Latin America* (Cambridge: Cambridge University Press, 1991), 78.

42 Ibid.

43 Nibaldo H. Galleguillos, "Studying Civil-Military Relations in the Post-Dictatorship Era:

An Analysis of the Chilean Experience," *Journal of Third World Studies* 17, no. 2 (2000): 93–112.

44 Lisa Baldez and John Carey, "Presidential Agenda Control and Spending Policy: Lessons from General Pinochet's Constitution," *American Journal of Political Science* 42, no. 1 (1999): 29–55.

45 Information from the Stockholm International Peace Research Institute (SIPRI) Military Expenditure Database (www.sipri.org/contents/milap/milex/mex_database1.html).

46 SIPRI, *SIPRI Yearbook 2005: Armaments, Disarmament, and International Security* (Stockholm: SIPRI, 2005), 312.

47 IISS, *The Military Balance*.

48 Richard Auty, ed., *Resource Abundance and Economic Development* (Oxford: Oxford University Press for UNU-WIDER, 2001).

49 Ascher, *Why Governments Waste Natural Resources*, 157.

50 "Chile Copper Windfall Forces Hard Choices on Spending," *New York Times*, January 7, 2007.

51 Brian Pinto, "Nigeria During and After the Oil Boom: A Policy Comparison with Indonesia," *World Bank Economic Review* 1 (1987): 419–45.

52 Transparency International, *Global Corruption Report 2004* (London: Pluto Press, 2004), 13.

53 William Case, *Politics in Southeast Asia: Democracy or Less* (London: Routledge, 2002), 38.

54 Ascher, *Why Governments Waste Natural Resources*, 61.

55 Frank Ellis, "The Rice Market and Its Management in Indonesia," *IDS Bulletin* 21, no. 3 (1990): 44–51; and Peter Timmer, "Indonesia: Transition from Food Importer to Food Exporter," in *Food Price Policy in Asia: A Comparative Study*, ed. Terry Sicular (Ithaca: Cornell University Press, 1989).

56 Peter Timmer, "Food Security in Indonesia: Current Challenges and the Long-Run Outlook," Working Paper 48, Center for Global Development, Washington, DC, 2004, 6.

57 Angus McIntyre, *The Indonesian Presidency: The Shift from Personal Toward Constitutional Rule* (New York: Rowman and Littlefield, 2005).

58 Steven R. Tabor, "General Food Price Subsidies in Indonesia: The 1997/98 Crisis Episode" (presentation at the World Bank Institute meeting "Protecting the Vulnerable: The Design and Implementation of Effective Safety Nets," Washington, DC, December 4–15, 2000).

59 Hitoshi Yonekura, "Institutional Reform in Indonesia's Food Security Sector: The Transformation of Bulog into a Public Corporation," *Developing Economies* 43, no. 1 (2007): 121–48.

60 McIntyre, *The Indonesian Presidency*, 227.

61 Timmer, "Food Security in Indonesia," 22.

62 Elizabeth Drexler, *Aceh, Indonesia: Securing the Insecure State* (Philadelphia: University of Pennsylvania Press, 2008).

63 Information from the SIPRI Military Expenditure Database.

64 Harold Crouch, *The Army and Politics in Indonesia* (Ithaca and London: Cornell University Press, 1978).

65 Human Rights Watch, *Too High a Price: The Human Rights Cost of the Indonesian Military's Economic Activities* (New York: Human Rights Watch, 2008). In addition to Indonesia, Cambodia is another transitional country in which the military is extensively engaged in private business, especially in timber and minerals. The business dealings of the People's Liberation Army, while smaller than a decade ago, may also affect any eventual democratic transition in China; see James Mulvenon, *Soldiers of Fortune: The Rise and Fall of the Chinese Military-Business Complex, 1978–1998* (New York: M. E. Sharpe, 2001).

66 See the chapter by Alexander Mayer-Rieckh and Roger Duthie, "Enhancing Justice and Development Through Justice-Sensitive Security Sector Reform," in this volume.

67 Sebastian Edwards, "The Argentine Debt Crisis of 2001–2002: A Chronology and Some Key Policy Issues" (paper presented at the National Bureau of Economic Research [NBER] Conference on Argentina, Cambridge, MA, July 2002).

68 World Bank, "Roundtable on Conceptual and Operational Issues of Lender Responsibility for Sovereign Debt," World Bank, Washington, DC, 2008, 7.

69 The Ajaokuta steel plant was begun in the 1980s with the intention of making Nigeria self-sufficient in steel. It never opened.

70 Sirkku Hellsten, "Failing States and Ailing Leadership in African Politics in the Era of Globalization: Libertarian Communitarianism and the Kenyan Experience," *Journal of Global Ethics* 4, no. 2 (2008): 155–69.

71 Michael Bratton and Nicholas van de Walle, *Democratic Experiments in Africa: Regime Transitions in Comparative Perspective* (New York: Cambridge University Press, 1997).

72 Hellsten, "Failing States and Ailing Leadership," 160.

73 Michela Wrong, *It's Our Turn to Eat: The Story of a Kenyan Whistle Blower* (New York: HarperCollins, 2009).

74 Tony Addison and Liisa Laakso, "The Political Economy of Zimbabwe's Descent into Conflict," *Journal of International Development* 15 (2003): 457–70.

75 Tony Addison, Abdur Chowdhury, and S. Mansoob Murshed, "The Fiscal Dimensions of Conflict and Reconstruction," in *Fiscal Policy for Development: Poverty, Reconstruction, and Growth*, ed. Tony Addison and Alan Roe (Basingstoke: Palgrave Macmillan for UNU-WIDER, 2004).

76 Michael Reid, *Forgotten Continent: The Battle for Latin America's Soul* (New Haven: Yale University Press, 2007), 273.

77 See Emily E. Harwell and Philippe Le Billon, "Natural Connections: Linking Transitional Justice and Development Through a Focus on Natural Resources," in this volume.

78 James K. Boyce and Madelene O'Donnell, eds., *Peace and the Public Purse: Economic Policies for Postwar Statebuilding* (Boulder: Lynne Rienner, 2007).

79   Ashraf Ghani and Clare Lockhart, *Fixing Failed States: A Framework for Rebuilding a Fractured World* (New York: Oxford University Press, 2008).

80   World Bank and Government of Nigeria, "Utilization of Repatriated Abacha Loot: Results of the Field Monitoring Exercise," World Bank and Nigerian Federal Ministry of Finance, Washington, DC, and Abuja, 2006.

81   De Greiff, "Articulating the Links," in this volume.

82   Frances Stewart, "Policies Towards Horizontal Inequalities in Post-Conflict Reconstruction," in *Making Peace Work*.

83   Saman Kelegama, "Transforming Conflict with an Economic Dividend: The Sri Lankan Experience," *Round Table: The Commonwealth Journal of International Affairs* 94 (2005): 429–42.

84   CPRC, *Chronic Poverty Report: 2008–2009*.

85   For a discussion of this strategy in the context of Guinea-Bissau, a failing state, see Jens Kovsted and Finn Tarp, "Reconstruction, Reform and State Capacity in Guinea-Bissau," in *From Conflict to Recovery in Africa*, ed. Tony Addison (Oxford: Oxford University Press for UNU-WIDER, 2003).

86   Armando Barrientos and David Hulme, eds., *Social Protection for the Poor and Poorest: Concepts, Policies and Politics* (London: Palgrave Macmillan, 2008).

87   David de Ferranti, Guillermo E. Perry, Francisco H. G. Ferreira, and Michael Walton, *Inequality in Latin America and the Caribbean: Breaking with History?* (Washington, DC: World Bank, 2004).

88   Inter-American Development Bank (IDB), *IDB Country Strategy with El Salvador* (Washington, DC: IDB, 2005), 2.

89   Ibid.

90   Fabio V. Soares and Tatiana Britto, "Confronting Capacity Constraints on Conditional Cash Transfers in Latin America: The Cases of El Salvador and Paraguay," Working Paper 38, International Poverty Centre, Brasilia, 2007.

91   Nora Lustig, "Introduction," in *Coping with Austerity*, 20.

92   Paul Collier and Anke Hoeffler, "On the Economic Consequences of Civil War," *Oxford Economic Papers* 50, no. 4 (1998): 563–73.

93   Robert Rotberg, ed., *Worst of the Worst: Dealing with Repressive and Rogue Nations* (Cambridge, MA: Brookings Institution Press/World Peace Foundation, 2007).

94   Richard Murphy and Nicholas Shaxson, "African Graft Is a Global Responsibility," *Financial Times*, June 1, 2007.

CHAPTER 4

Toward Systemic Social Transformation: Truth Commissions and Development

Rolando Ames Cobián and Félix Reátegui

Since the 1950s, the notion and practice of development has existed as an institutionally recognized path—that is, proclaimed as an official goal of states and governments, and cultivated in the centers of intellectual production—for inducing social transformation. The meaning of development can be summarized in the idea of bringing about sustained increments in the well-being of the inhabitants of a society. At the same time, in the last three decades a set of practices associated in the immediate term with problems other than development, but converging with it in the common aim of provoking ethically oriented social transformation, has been carving out an institutional existence of its own: the concepts, norms, institutions, and measures that constitute the field of transitional justice. Understood as part of "the effort to build a sustainable peace after a period of conflict, massive violence, or systematic violation of human rights,"[1] transitional justice focuses on addressing past violence by means of public truth-telling, setting in motion the machinery of criminal justice, making reparations to the victims, and introducing various institutional reforms.[2]

Though development and transitional justice have emerged and unfolded in very different conceptual and political realms, of late there is a pressing need for a dialogue between the promoters of each, and for clarification of the conceptual and practical relationship between the two fields. There are several reasons for this. From a holistic conception of human well-being, having one's needs met and the experience of being a subject with rights and a full member of the political community are equally essential. In addition, from the standpoint of public policies, it is evident that development gains require the restoration of the rule of law, which has often collapsed during periods of violence or authoritarian rule. Finally, the existence of a regime of rights is unviable if the holders of those rights are not really empowered to claim them, exercise them, and, ultimately, defend them.

Nonetheless, it is apparent that contemporary society—what has been called the "globalized" world—finds it very difficult to bring about qualitative and systemic changes. This situation affects development and transitional justice processes in similar ways, for both practices seek to bring about precisely such changes; the shared challenge is a link between the two fields that has yet to be considered. This chapter explores the relationship between transitional justice and development from the perspective of truth commissions, considering both their experience and reflections on their role.[3]

TRANSITIONAL JUSTICE AND DEVELOPMENT:
A CONCEPTUAL CHALLENGE AND QUESTION OF COLLECTIVE ACTION

The concept of *development* came into general use in the mid-twentieth century to refer, initially, to the process of economic growth, especially of the countries then gaining their independence after colonial rule. Use of the concept spread widely and rapidly, and its contents expanded to include its social implications as well as ethical-normative standards and, finally, the general debate on the relationship among modernity, economy, liberty, and social justice. The notion of development thus refers to structural changes and to the general orientation of state policies that lead to such changes, but it often continues to refer in public discourse first and foremost to economic growth ("development" is used at the same time as an analytical concept and as a journalistic term).

The opposite applies, in large measure, to *transitional justice*, a notion less well known to the public at large and whose conceptual elaboration is much more intense than its dissemination, and, above all, which does not take as its starting point a reference to macro-social processes. Rather, transitional justice has emerged as an urgent response to specific, albeit numerous, cases of massive human rights violations. Its origins lie in the need to ensure justice after situations of violence or authoritarianism, and it refers to persons affected and to other persons directly or indirectly responsible who are sought to be identified so that justice can be done.

These are clearly two fields of intervention very different in their origins, their specific subject matter, and the extent to which the public is familiar with them. Nonetheless, there is a link between them, one that becomes more visible through the concept of "human development."[4] First, the focus of human development is more on the personal experience of well-being than on national economic growth. Second, that well-being is not conceived of as access to certain goods or basic resources, but to the realization of capabilities and potentials inherent in every human being; this realization depends on the material environment, but also—and preeminently—on the institutional and cultural environment.[5] Thus, the development process is redefined as fostering societies with values that include—beyond growth—social justice and democracy, not only as a political regime but also as a way of life. Defined in these terms, one can better glean a meaningful connection between development and the broadest or most ambitious objectives of transitional justice.

An additional point of convergence is the context in which work on human development is carried out and in which transitional justice is practiced: typically societies where groups in power or privileged groups oppose the democratization of access to certain basic goods, be these economic resources, public services, or the legal protection of fundamental rights. At the same time, these are societies in which the poor account for a large share of the population, stuck with a minimal quality of life, and/or stripped of any guarantee or effective protection of their rights to life and physical integrity. These, then, are societies marked by inequalities rooted in their institutional structures or orders: culture and collective representations; social stratification and the system of opportunities; the political institutional framework; the organization of the national market and its relations with the world economy; the formation of the state and the habits and norms that govern the public administration; the instituted processes of decision-making and implementation of decisions; and other components generally found in the social structure.

In the face of these realities, transitional justice and development attempt to foster systemic changes, or at least to create the possibilities for those changes to take place. When speaking of *systemic changes* we refer to profound transformations of social organization and, ultimately, of the mechanisms and basic social arrangements by which society reproduces. The change that leads, for example, from a society that operates on the basis of hierarchical presuppositions to one that reproduces on the basis of egalitarian premises is a type of systemic transformation that involves not just the economic but also the legal, cultural, and political dimensions of collective existence. Thus, transitional justice and development are normative proposals geared to action that allude to processes already under way and which have an effective social and political impact.

Even if this transformative ambition is widely defended by scholars in normative terms, however, in a more concrete sense it runs against the currently prevailing tendencies of politics and governance. To gauge the scope of this obstacle, one would be well advised to consider the current context of *globalization*. With the increased density and power of global networks, the debate has finally emerged today as to the kind of global order that is conditioning the life of the planet. It is clear that the strength of the systems that organize the economy, information, education, and consumption patterns is such that the capacity for *agency* to reform the economy and organize power is weak. The loss of support for and legitimacy of political institutions that are fundamental for democracy, such as political parties and legislatures, is associated, for example, with the way in which power has been redistributed among economic and political actors in this form of globalization.

Indeed, the current trend to present the basic global dilemma as a tension between democracy and terrorism is dangerously mistaken for both human development and transitional justice.[6] In the plainly political realm, it is equally worrisome that the alternative positions for attaining economic equity once again consider it legitimate to sacrifice democratic pluralism and to have recourse to the imposition of force against those sectors opposed to the exclusive and official truth of the reformist governments.

For the reasons outlined here, discussions of the relationship between transitional justice and development should take stock of the weakness of agency, actors, and organizational forms that could bring about profound changes. From this perspective, one can address matters that go to the ultimate meaning of both processes as well as practical issues regarding the link between the two fields and the differentiation of their tasks and responsibilities.

The issue can be addressed from the experience of truth commissions. These commissions are highly visible public and political actors during transitions; they constitute a corps of temporary public servants with the legal and/ or moral authority to question powerful actors, and, given their nature, to appeal to public opinion from a unique position. In short, they set in motion processes of public deliberation and make their weight felt in a manner antagonistic to the established order.[7] Accordingly, a truth commission constitutes, from the standpoint of the political tensions inherent to a transition, an ad hoc actor that in its brief period of existence focuses a high degree of democratic energies. Such energies have great potential for calling attention to the systemic obstacles to justice and, ultimately, to show the need for systemic transformations.

We argue that transitional justice unfolds, ultimately, in the field of profound social transformations, and that a central aspect of those transformations is the change in collective beliefs regarding, precisely, the feasibility of achieving justice in practice. By promoting justice in those extreme cases in which it has been most clearly denied, the measures of transitional justice can alter collective skepticism or cynicism regarding the possibilities of government under the rule of law. Yet we also argue that, for this very reason, it is important that truth commissions be capable of conveying the need to launch sustainable reform processes leading to the emergence of a dominant consensus as to the feasibility and advisability of government under the rule of law— a consensus about democracy (understood in a robust sense) as the only possible option for settling disagreements and conflicts in a society and for inducing changes in it.[8]

The convergence of transitional justice and development in an analogous ultimate objective—to bring about systemic transformations—does not dissolve the specific differences between the two fields. At this point, one important difference should be noted. While much of the practice of development operates in the arena of massive and anonymous policies directed to whole categories of the population and is aimed at designing a general institutional framework, transitional justice usually takes as its starting point the domain of the particular and the concrete: bringing justice to bear in relation to serious human rights violations suffered by specific individuals.[9] In defending the life of each person, and implementing a justice measure to that end, transitional justice emphasizes the necessity and the possibility of institutional transformation as a whole. A case-by-case approach demonstrates, in the first place, the importance of personal experiences of justice for the healing of the collective body; in the second place, it reveals the shortcomings of the institutional order for providing that particular experience of justice. It is working from the particularities of suffering, redress, and healing that transitional justice brings attention to the structural inadequacies of society and to the need to change them radically. In the end, this pressing recognition of the need for institutional change encompasses not only the administration of justice but also the other institutional (structural) spheres, such as the overall economic organization, that provide the context for deprivation, exclusion, vulnerability, and abuse.

A cardinal idea of this chapter is that development agencies and truth commissions should have a clearer understanding of their shared interest in promoting not only incremental change but societal transformation, which would allow for mutual reinforcement from within their respective spaces. This reinforcement would give sustainability to the impact of each actor, which is a conceptual and practical requirement of long-term efforts geared to combating the conditions that make violence possible and not only the consequences of the violence already experienced.

Accordingly, we highlight the broader scope of the pursuit of justice during transitions, and do so from the viewpoint of truth commissions. Our focus on truth commissions reflects the fact that such initiatives—though initially defined as official bodies charged with the restoration of truth and the promotion of memory—have evolved into all-encompassing institutions that now deal with many different aspects of confronting the legacies of armed violence and authoritarian abuses.

TRUTH COMMISSIONS AS MECHANISMS OF ETHICAL AND INSTITUTIONAL CHANGE

Consistent with what has been noted about the context in which truth commissions operate—that is, a context of societies that from the standpoint of justice can be called "ill constituted"[10]—we discuss the aims of such measures by reference to three notions: the integral nature of transitional justice, without prejudice to the specificity of its components; the reality of "very imperfect" societies, in which the mere task of doing justice appears to be an immense challenge, but one with major transformative potential; and the ethnical-normative horizon underlying any justice project in the context of transitions.

Truth commissions are, in the first place, a measure of transitional justice that deals with the reestablishment or the recovery of truth about past human rights violations. They fulfill the mission of "setting the record straight" and thus of promoting the acknowledgment of abuses and the social recognition of the abused. The public exposure of truth, however, is rarely practiced for its own sake alone. In a holistic approach to transitional justice, the recovery of truth serves as both a cornerstone of justice and a triggering device for legal justice, reparations, and institutional reforms aimed at preventing massive abuses from happening again.[11] All these components should remain interrelated, given the magnitude of what transitional justice sets out to accomplish. For example, the various objectives captured in the widely disseminated notion of "Never Again" ("*Nunca Más*") include not only the need for justice with respect to past crimes, but also the need to deactivate the political, institutional, social, and cultural mechanisms that made atrocious violence possible.

The necessary interaction of these measures is better grounded by adding a second element, which we take from Pablo de Greiff.[12] Characterizing the type of society in which truth commissions tend to work helps us to understand the actual magnitude of changes that are called for. Speaking of those societies, de Greiff proposes the notion of a "very imperfect world." These are not societies in which the modern notion of government under the rule of law does not exist at all or is in a total state of collapse; such an institutional framework exists, but it has been rolled back, or its efficacy has been suspended, under the impact of authoritarianism or violence. This is important. In the societies of which we speak, the population may live outside of such normative and institutional frameworks, but that does not mean that they live in an isolated cultural world radically distinct from modern government under the rule of law. The limited relevance of institutions may reflect pragmatic reasons or reasons associated with social experience. In some societies, despite an institution's declared adherence to certain norms, collective experience teaches that the rules do not work in a timely or equitable fashion. We are talking here about a phenomenon of *learned disloyalty* to the institutional framework, rather than its nonexistence or cultural irrelevance. In de Greiff's argument, transitional justice, to have opportunities, needs in effect institutions that can survive the risks generated by the very effort to affirm certain norms. "Very imperfect worlds" are precisely those in which this is an issue.

The precarious conditions of such social worlds mean that institutions may have a nominal existence and be a reference for the population's expectations, yet lack the means to impose themselves by coercion—by the force of a consensus that takes the form of a social obligation—or by enforcement and coercive surveillance of legality. This creates a limbo that may lurk behind the acceptance of violence and the imposition and permanence of social inequalities. After all, violence and exclusion are social relationships that, if they are to prosper, need a certain institutional framework. This is what the Peruvian Truth and Reconciliation Commission (CVR) means when it situates the problem of violence and extreme vulnerability of rights not in the absence of the state but in the peculiar—and in a certain way perverse—presence of the state in certain territories.[13]

In this context of institutional ineffectiveness (or peculiar institutional presence), certain boundaries of peaceful and democratic coexistence become very fragile. The social conviction that transgressions bring sanctions is weakened until it becomes entirely insufficient to guarantee the life and physical integrity of the most vulnerable members of the population. Human rights violations become one more resource in the strategy pursued by the state and private groups for achieving their objectives. This is even more likely where human rights violations are intertwined with practices of oppression that have never come under the complete control of the law.

The notion of "very imperfect worlds" makes restoring effective law enforcement the center of the dynamics of social change. In de Greiff's terms, breaking with the habitual situation of the imposition of force—or, correlatively, breaking the chain of impunity—would imply that the social majority believes that might does *not* make right—that is, that there are legal authorities capable of bringing the de facto powers under control. Society's belief that the de facto powers can be subjected to the law makes it possible for that to happen. The social illusion of impunity as a certainty is broken down.[14] Trying to impact on collective beliefs involves vindicating the relevance of the subjective and ideological dimension of politics as a builder of new shared references, and, therefore, as a sphere of reproduction or axis of social coordination.

Highlighting the potentially profound effects of the exercise of justice, we find the possibly differential role of truth commissions. Truth commissions, by raising *unprecedented* claims to justice, make the most of that moment of rupture that is implicit in an institutional search for the truth. Accordingly, truth commissions and transitional justice would imply and demand, with their forms of discourse and their practices, a politics very different from the current one, a politics seriously embraced as the sphere in which citizens construct, all together, what their future will have in common. That politics is much more absent in ill-constituted societies than in more egalitarian and liberal societies.

Let us now consider a third notion to continue to get an overall understanding of the most general rationale of truth commissions' work: the strong *ethical-normative* nature inherent to the process. Transitional justice, following de Greiff, has as its mediate objectives recognition based on the relationship with victims and civic trust in the law and among citizens. De Greiff also identifies two final objectives that give meaning to the transitional justice project: reconciliation of society with itself and democracy. In citing objectives of this scope, de Greiff confirms that the normative character of transitional justice is not limited to an ethical-legal enunciation that merely contrasts and judges the prevailing reality. This normative framework must foster a set of sustained actions that go beyond the specific results of each transitional justice measure. This would be better understood, then, as a substantive social change project for a society whose systemic problems have been previously recognized. The search for the truth leads to visualizing a new historical form of existence for those countries.

TRUTH COMMISSIONS AND THE POSSIBILITIES OF MAKING SYSTEMIC CHANGES

Among the various measures of transitional justice, truth commissions are entrusted with casting light on past human rights violations committed in the context of armed violence or an authoritarian regime. Two fundamental characteristics of truth commissions are that they are vested with an official status that emanates from the corresponding state, or from its assent to the directives of the international community, and that they operate within a limited time frame and subject to a mandate that delimits their tasks and powers.[15]

Beyond the question of the precise definition of truth commissions, here we are interested in proposing an analysis in keeping with the broader horizon of transitional justice. Consistent with what has already been said, we underscore here that truth commissions, given their visibility and the urgency of their work, are the measure best placed to take on the role of "spokesperson" for the changes sought by transitional justice. Seen in this light, commissions would have to be geared in a more sustained fashion to the whole of public opinion in their respective societies, and not just to the actors directly involved in the conflict, who necessarily make up the public to which commissions' work refers most directly. In this role, truth commissions are a preeminent actor involved in what David Crocker has called "adversarial public action."[16] In this respect, we emphasize a point mentioned above: assuming and performing the role of strong public actor should be understood by truth commissions not only as a useful defense against possible attacks but as a requirement that goes hand in hand with the project of transitional justice on the longer horizon of social change.

A truth commission, given its specific subject matter—that is, the memory of the past and the voices of the victims who bear that memory—is the most apt transitional justice measure to impact on the symbolic design of a society, and, therefore, on its sphere of political reproduction.[17] The nexus of truth commissions, criticism of the symbolic order, and restoration of politics as a space for deliberation and decision-making can be found in the notion of "historicity" and, more generically, in a historical-social understanding of social movements and collective action. As noted by Sidney Tarrow, cultural changes are crucial for profound social transformation, but they often need a political agent to give them concrete expression and activate their transformative potential.[18]

On this point, the study and practice of truth commissions offer promising windows on the broader phenomenon of social groups and movements, so long as they both preserve their specific focus on rights and victims and assume the complexity and breadth of their political role. Inserting an exercise entailing restitution of the truth in this macro-social process requires that commissions work more on the historical-political dimension inherent in their creation. Truth commissions direct a powerful message of criticism at barbarity and make an ethical proposal of institutional and personal change. In practice, they have seen themselves as the first step in a larger process. Nonetheless, as the analysis of the processes in which they are always immersed has remained incipient, they have yet to gain clarity on all the practical consequences of being part of a project of substantive and lasting change.

Until recently, the idea predominated that the contribution of truth commissions to future change depended strictly on the successful fulfillment of their literal mandates. The enormous task of clarifying thousands of cases, establishing the foundation of complaints, designing reparations, and proposing institutional reforms, while fending off multiple attacks, tends to focus the activity of commissions; moreover, they have a very short period of time in which to do their work. Yet when truth commissions are seen as part of a process that transcends them, it is essential to take stock of the long-term project that is being initiated. This function of truth commissions, which is *charged with substantive political meaning*, would not require huge sums of resources *nor would it demand changes in the rights-based logic* with which commissions' mandates are formulated. It is a matter of attending more to public opinion: explaining and defending what a commission does, calling different actors to participate in a new experience of justice, renewing memory, and winning commitments for the conscious transformation of society. In summary, if transitional justice is understood as a project of profound social change, a critical dialogue with prevailing common sense and consideration of the macro-social context become decisive.[19] This should reinforce the work of truth commissions, rather than distract from it.

This assertion is premised on the contentious context in which truth commissions operate. After violence or authoritarianism, the collective experience of crime and impunity underscores the impression in public opinion that the use of force and relationships based on force are more effective than appealing to institutions and the law. Truth commissions have not always evaluated this belief or social intuition correctly so as to figure out how to take it as a point of departure and succeed in changing it. Since their origins and direct public audience are generally closely tied to the pro-democracy sectors of society, truth commissions run the risk of taking democratic convictions as a uniform consensus, seeing at the other extreme only the elite defenders of the old status quo, those who must be fought. This prevents them from making efforts to win over followers in the general public. Opening up to the broad public and making inroads into its common sense in order to modify indifference toward democracy and the rule of law, however, would improve the chances of successfully confronting the enemies of truth commissions, who in general are actively working on the prejudices particular to a society accustomed to mistreatment. This kind of effort implies giving more importance to the cultural aspects of social change that are needed to overcome violence. The real application of the law that truth commissions look for requires taking into account and dealing with the cultural distortions that are expressed in large sectors of the public in these societies. Once again, memory becomes relevant. In a society beset by massive violence, the model of the "memories of salvation"—focused on highlighting the merit of state security forces and, as a corollary, the inappropriateness of bringing them to trial for human rights violations—usually finds fertile ground.

The paradigmatic task of truth commissions is to set the historical record straight and to undertake a critical scrutiny of past violence and consequent human rights violations. As Daniel Pécaut has argued in relation to the need for memory of the violence in Colombia, a critical review of the past serves the purpose of impeding the "normalization" or "naturalization" of violence in the collective common sense.[20] Memory, in its role of redefining the boundaries of the social imagination regarding what is legitimate or normal for attaining one's purposes in society, has a latent and fundamentally important relationship to the need to unleash the systemic changes that we have described as a task of transitional justice.

One lesson we learned from our experience in Peru's CRV (2001–2003) relates to the fact that truth commissions often exist in a sort of tension between, on the one hand, their objectives and results and, on the other, a reality external to them over which they exercise no direct control. This gives rise to situations in which the commission affirms the urgency of justice and reparation in the face of crimes committed with impunity, but, once its work is concluded, its recommendations are implemented only partially or not at all. In the end, a declared urgency left unaddressed tends to confirm the skepticism to which those societies have a propensity.

In this regard, the mission of truth commissions should not be reduced to compliance with its legal mandate understood as a list of tasks. Instead, addressing its own extraordinary meaning in the society in which such a commission occurs will help the agents of transitional justice to explain why they, while intransigent in their struggle to apply justice, at the same time have the patience to withstand the lengthy periods of time that achievement of their mission requires. This mind-set might make it easier to understand the call for citizens to be actors in a more far-reaching process that only they can bring to completion.

As political actors, truth commissions are short-lived phenomena that give rise to an intense mobilization of wills of those committed to the fate suffered by victims, who often belong to the most underprivileged sectors. They have the potential to bring together a plurality of actors and foster intense social integration. Part of this potential is contextual in nature: truth commissions are instituted in situations in which it is more likely that public decisions will be adopted than it is in normal times. Max Weber's classic notion of *charisma* helps to explain this fact. Transitional periods are, on the one hand, instances of strategic action and negotiation; on the other hand, acute awareness of the crisis to be overcome and the enthusiasm of the democratic restoration generate a climate in which certain executive or legislative decisions become possible, along with certain agreements among various sectors of society that would not be possible in routine situations.

If making decisions for change always involves spending a certain amount of political capital, transitions and peace processes, as charismatic moments, are objective moments in which there is a high concentration of political will. At the same time, if truth commissions owe their origins to those charismatic moments, they are in a position to prolong the moment, feeding it with renewed symbolic ingredients from the past that is under review—such as memory, feelings of public shame, full exposure of discrimination as the cause of death and destruction, open discrediting of public figures, institutions, and customs—and fostering new groupings, such as victims' organizations, which in the best of cases come into the public arena with their own voices, often with the backing of international or multilateral actors, thus making possible other weighty political decisions.

In summary, a truth commission's short duration can be made most of when there is a clear understanding of transitional justice as ultimately an element of a slow and necessarily *protracted*—yet feasible—process of historical change. Without the proposal for a long-term project that can continue its work, the mission of a commission may be seen as temporary and therefore weaker. In short time frames, it is not possible to consolidate citizen recognition of those who most suffered the violence and denial of their rights.

THE NOTION OF TRANSITION AND HOW IT TIES IN WITH DEVELOPMENT

To conclude this section, we need to specify the meaning of the notion of transition as part of the very concept of transitional justice. In order for a transition to be seen as a project undertaken by broad social sectors, it is necessary to articulate the ends of the process, and distinctions should be drawn to avoid possible misunderstandings.

First, we must take a certain distance from the notion of "transition to democracy" with which transitional justice was associated from the start, particularly in Latin America. This can be relevant in the strictly institutional dimension of transitional justice—that is, insofar as we speak of "emerging from a dictatorship." But the notion of transition to democracy is insufficient. A dominant idea in the 1990s, according to which the world was beginning an almost irreversible march to democracy, it was found in the studies of post-dictatorship political processes in political science, and, what is most important, left its mark in a certain majoritarian common sense. Working from this interpretive framework, a set of factors and powerful interests combined to depoliticize social debate, considering its fundamental dilemmas resolved. There was a consensus that, since democracy was already an ongoing process and since its worldwide adoption was inevitable, no issues of systemic change were left to be faced. Seeking deeper social changes would only be necessary in countries considered extremely backward or so deeply underdeveloped as to need an outright process of state building. This kind of political assumption, which on the one hand suffers from being mechanistic and on the other hand blocks debate of still very pressing social justice problems, will not change anytime soon. It is, therefore, important to clarify that transitional justice points to issues deeper than those found in the "democratizing" paradigm that remains at the surface of political processes.

The trusted paradigm of democratization is even facing problems stemming from developments intrinsic to contemporary democracies. The difficulties of consolidating democracy in the world are, in effect, great, and not only in those countries considered "backward." One crucial difficulty lies in the field of political representation. We are witnessing a profound change in the emptying of the experience of being represented politically. Fundamental institutions, such as political parties and legislatures, have become greatly weakened, as has the commitment to public interests, accompanied by a lack of oversight of the de facto powers.

The crisis of representation can be explained, to a great extent, by the increase in social complexity. The leading role taken on at present by mixed or parastatal forms of discussion and public decision-making, such as "round-tables for dialogue," "coalitions," and, in particular, "commissions," attests to the complexity of the public scene nowadays. In other words, the reality of contemporary politics suggests that the crisis of public institutions and democracies is not restricted to the field of specifically political institutions. What is needed, then, is an approach aimed at inducing changes in the social basis of political institutions. This need is reflected in the current proliferation of new mechanisms of governance in which a diversity of actors—powerful economic actors alongside grassroots associations—are brought together in an institutional setting in order to make public choices. This new political reality poses a challenge to such fields as transitional justice and development to articulate their contribution to processes of systemic change and to the new cultural and institutional construction.

In this context, in which renewed forms are needed to reconstitute the subjects, rules, and mechanisms of political "agency," transitional justice offers a field of valuable experiences in which concrete acts of justice—in relation to persons who have been very mistreated—come together with new institutions international in scope for the defense of human rights. The feasibility of this hypothetical and desirable role for truth commissions has objective bases in the accomplishments of transitional justice internationally, nationally, and subnationally. Mobilizing populations with major unmet needs and applying to them legal criteria that go to the compensation and effective reparation of victims are extremely important. But it needs to be shown that this is the beginning of a sustained process so that barbaric acts do not recur and so as to affirm a new social treatment based on mutual respect.

Among the many measures called for by truth commissions, arguably the judicial prosecution of crimes and violations of human rights provides the symbolic, normative, institutional, and political clout needed to induce profound or systemic transformations. This is because breaking the cycle of impunity and the social illusion that no justice is available for the destitute can have a paradigm-shift quality to it: if justice can be done and if the powerful can be called to task (even if not properly punished) for their past wrongdoings, then the notion of politics as a realm where "things do happen" can prevail. As already noted, the broader aim of transitional justice is to foster and uphold the credibility of the legal institutions of the state such that they are seen to impart justice effectively and without distinctions. In the societies in question, this would be a very far-reaching positive change. One can find in transitional justice, then, the bases for restoring political processes that today seem frozen or stuck in their usual ruts.

This orientation of transitional justice must be explained with its consequences in terms of duties and rights. It involves the move from a systemic situation of imperfection and skepticism regarding the possibility of justice, to bringing about a broad and plural social commitment to establish the institutional framework for the norms and practices characteristic of the rule of law. Transitional justice thus brings together state action and culture as experienced day to day. The decision to believe that it is possible to observe human rights is based on the very practice of justice. The challenge is for that practice to encourage the majority to continue down the new road.

TRUTH, JUSTICE, AND DEVELOPMENT

We have noted the possible links between truth and justice, as promoted by truth commissions, and the institutional framing and consolidation of democracy. Operating on a case-based approach, truth commissions and transitional justice make evident the need for wide reform of the justice system and, in the end, for the transformation of other institutions. These necessary changes, if properly accomplished, have the potential to modify the way in which interpersonal relations are thought of and, ultimately, to enhance the experience of citizenship, equality, and institutional fair play among the inhabitants of the postconflict or the post-authoritarian society. It is from this societal projection of truth commission aims that arise the links with the field of development. To this end, in this third section we more forcefully underscore convergences and complementarities and better delimit the boundaries that distinguish, without totally differentiating, the specific objectives and mechanisms of action particular to each of these two major fields.

THE QUALITATIVE POINTS OF CONVERGENCE

The concept and practice of development involve, more clearly than does transitional justice, an analysis of ill-constituted societies and a proposal for intervention to change the logic of the systemic processes at work in those societies. This reality provides the historical basis for the interconnectedness of the two concepts. Poverty, inequality, and, often, ethnic-cultural discrimination offer the conditions for the outbreak of conflict and violence.[21] While it is true that internal wars cause economic and social damage of their own, one should not lose sight of what we call "the structural dimension of great imperfection"—that is, the lack of development.

This general characteristic of certain contexts explains the confluence of ultimate objectives sought by specialists in transitional justice and human development. Both find that it is not possible to sustainably overcome the problems they try to redress without correcting systemic features of the ill-constituted societies in which they work. The same is true for experts on democracy. Such notions as "transformation," "in-depth change," and "new society" are, therefore, recurrent in the recommendations of documents produced by activists and experts in these fields. Nonetheless, in general these are statements of intent, for they do not have institutions or mechanisms within reach for achieving their desired objectives.[22]

How is it possible to accomplish systemic changes when the sectors that should theoretically be most interested in them do not necessarily have the conviction or strength to propose them? This classic question in the debate on overall social change is currently its key focus, because the massive discontents that generate social instability no longer lie only within a few countries; they now occur in many countries, in an ever more interdependent global order.[23]

Having focused to this point on the relationship between transitional justice and the processes of consolidating the rule of law and democratic institutions, then, it is crucial to now engage in further study of how transitional justice relates to socioeconomic factors. The lack of development or the trend to "misdevelop" while undergoing economic growth is the great common systemic issue that affects other processes of improving the quality of life in countries with low productivity, lack of capital, poverty, and unmet basic needs in large sectors of the population.[24]

How can impartial institutions and egalitarian citizenship be achieved? The building of democracy upon everyday social practices, even against a backdrop of precariousness left by mass violence, requires that at least one of the sides involved in those practices be committed to granting fair and egalitarian treatment to the other ones. The practice of truth commissions, then, should strongly advocate this kind of treatment, which lies at the core of citizenship experience. We return to this issue below.

Before continuing, an important methodological issue needs to be addressed. Recall that the concept of development encompasses economic growth but is not reduced to it. While economic growth is a condition of development, it has been clear for decades that expanded production of goods or wealth in a society does not necessarily translate into overcoming poverty and inequality. If the growth attained by a society reproduces social relations of inequality or spoliation, the logic of growth must be reformed and reoriented, distinguishing between its favorable and unfavorable elements, however delicate and polemical this task may be. We understand economic growth as a factor of development, but one that needs to be geared to the objectives of development if it is to be considered a real public good.

Development, therefore, should be understood as a process that allows for the expansion of human capabilities for freedom and personal fulfillment, as argued by Amartya Sen, to draw on the most widely recognized proponent of the idea. What Sen calls "human development" requires effective systems of market regulation so that economic dynamics are functional to meeting the needs of people according to their cultures and the exercise of their freedom. The current economic crisis is bearing out the rejection of the notion that markets should be absolutely autonomous. If transitional justice is defined as a normative proposal, we understand that its relationship with development may be better construed by building bridges with another explicitly normative approach, that of human development.

One final point is in order on the normative affinity of the two processes. The normative framework of development should be strong enough to redirect the action of the groups in power that benefit from forms of growth that do not bring social equity. In this way, development requires a normative framework that is collectively grounded in practice. It is also a project of historical change that requires sustainability, institutional bases of support, and political will to ensure its prolonged duration. And, therefore, like transitional justice, it implies facing resistance from the groups in power that benefit from the status quo, from the institutional arrangement and from the habits and common sense of the population.

THE DIFFERENT NATURE OF THE MATTERS ADDRESSED BY TRANSITIONAL JUSTICE AND DEVELOPMENT

Having reiterated that the two projects of systemic change in question are similar in nature, we now take special note of a very big difference between them: the matters addressed by development are in one way or another broader and more numerous than those addressed by transitional justice.

The current notion of development was strengthened in a polemic with the theory of modernization, which presumed that the growth of poor countries should follow the Western path, based on the transfer of capital, technology, human resources, and know-how to produce some form of economic "take-off" that could become self-sustaining. This approach is still around, but, as we noted, there have been ever-stronger demands to understand development as improving the quality of life of the population as a whole. This does not mean that human development can disengage itself from economic problems, such as the movement of capital and goods in networks of markets that are globalized and segmented at the same time, or the regulation of a financial market that today is out of control, or the challenge of trying to reconcile conflicting demands on production. The function of human development is to guide these economic dynamics through the whole set of public policies that can make possible redistribution, equity, and an improvement in quality-of-life indicators for the entire population. Social policies are decisive to this end, yet it is mistaken to identify them with development. Development, then, occupies a field much larger than transitional justice, and in particular it has to focus first on collective processes rather than individual conduct.

Transitional justice, by way of contrast, is aimed at investigating specific human rights violations, determining responsibility and individual victims. As already noted, its first area of action is justice. Truth commission recommendations may include wide-ranging institutional reforms, for example, but they should not get into technical specifications for which they have neither the expertise nor the authority. What truth commissions need to do is explain why a given public policy or economic target should be accorded priority for making reparation for the harm caused by prolonged violence, placing special emphasis on reparations, for example, in the hardest-hit regions.

An analysis of the relationship between transitional justice and development should cast light on the specific possibilities for collaboration between those engaged in each. Accordingly, we offer some brief thoughts on the topic. The professional and volunteer personnel who work in these two types of processes may at times find themselves working side by side, in the same regions devastated by misery and violent conflict. Yet it is quite common for the practitioners of development and transitional justice, focused on the specificity of their own tasks, to be uninformed of what the nearby promoter of the other process is doing. As a result, both the material resources and the synergies that could improve the quality of the work and the public impact of what both do may be squandered. In addition, physical proximity does not always mean working with the same persons or in the same way. The victims of violence from a given locality are not necessarily the social leaders with whom the promoters of development work in that same locality. Moreover, the particular demands and needs of reparation may be invisible — or very costly to secure through a judicial process — to public policies designed for large contingents of the population. As we have said, development works more with categories of persons, while transitional justice — at least in the dimension of justice meted out by courts — is associated more with particular persons.

If one wishes to establish a framework relevant for accomplishing synergies between transitional justice and development, and to find the types of matters in which cooperation can be most important, then it seems better to go back to the qualitative aspects particular to each process. That is where we find opportunities for complementarity that involve not only direct cooperation but also, and more important, mutual reinforcement of the ultimate meaning of objectives—that is, the ambition to bring about systemic change.

THE CONTRIBUTION THAT TRANSITIONAL JUSTICE CAN MAKE TO THE MEANING OF DEVELOPMENT

The understanding of development as a process of qualitative and multidimensional change has not won a practical consensus, nor has it been the subject of specific operational definitions. A disaggregated perception of development persists—economic progress and social justice—which has ended up taking the form of a dilemma. In that dilemma, there is a tendency to decide that improving quality of life depends (exclusively) on providing the institutional framework for efficient individual effort and not (also) on the functions of government (public policies and the actions of representative parties) aimed at fostering redistribution, correcting inevitable market failures, and leveling persistent inequalities. In the face of a common sense that accepts the logic of the marketplace as the unique matrix of rational social action, the demand of social justice is tolerated as an ethical recommendation that may be respectable but remains imprecise and nonbinding.

The difficulty of situating the development agenda at the center of government processes reflects, once again, the weakening of politics indicated above. The typical locus of government decision-making during the modern period has been an intersection between competition in the political party system and adjudication in the realm of state and government. The weakening of both political spheres—those of electoral politics and, ultimately, of governance—has meant that only certain types of decisions have an opportunity to prevail, while those that require greater and more solid political will are overshadowed.[25] The decisions that development demands—like those that justice cries out for—are of this latter variety. The weakness of the party system does not allow for development to arise from an agreement among parties, as happened in Europe during the decades of the welfare state. This weakness and the discrediting of governments are part of a more complex process that includes the erosion of civic values and of the ultimate meanings of citizenship and pluralist democracy. Moreover, radical change alternatives, in their discourse, uphold values of human development, but they have yet to give rise to more holistic proposals on the scale of the complexity of the development process. A political dynamic focused on confrontation may be understandable, yet at the same time may be insufficient, ineffective, and even counterproductive in the long run for shoring up the same sectors that support these alternatives.

It is because of the existence of a political and public context of this sort that we propose that transitional justice (particularly truth-telling) and development be thought of as catalysts of far-reaching, innovative, and democratic decision-making dynamics. Trusting that sociopolitical articulations will come exclusively from the party system or civil society movements (as happened up until the early 1990s) may be a serious mistake.

In any event, both transitional justice and development are processes that convoke experts and representatives of important international and national state institutions. Both draw support from any number of interventions under way, and even though they do not necessarily articulate a novel economic project as would be desirable, mainly in the case of development, their contribution to the change in society's systemic orientation could be significant. Justice and development could be two essential main lines of political and social agreement if the urgency of moving to and consolidating systemic changes is perceived.

Nowadays, development, perhaps because it is a macro process that requires a high level of consensus, appears to be bogged down or, for some, only accessible by means of violent confrontation or authoritarianism. Transitional justice is more delimited, yet at the same time it is a point of intersection of the agendas of various state and social actors. For that reason, special note should be taken of aspects of transitional justice that could have a positive impact on the direction of societal change that all countries with ill-constituted societies require. The best support that transitional justice can give to help ensure a more consistent meaning for human development follows this logic.

Special mention should be made of acknowledging "the other," that which is different: this is a core theme in the practice of truth commissions that should receive more attention. We speak from our own personal experience with the Peruvian Truth and Reconciliation Commission, which afforded an opportunity to deal directly with fellow Peruvians who are *campesino* farmers, who have another language, ethnicity, and culture, a very uncommon occurrence even in massive political movements. To take a close look at the innocent who suffered personal harm with impunity is a painful human experience, but it is extremely valuable for better understanding the societies in which we live. It is in the nature of truth commissions and other transitional justice measures to bring about this kind of relationship between teams of experts and the victims, their family members, and the places where they live. That relationship is inherent to the professional work required to carry out this type of justice.

Furthermore, this kind of relation is precisely at the core of the ties among citizens. Their importance, therefore, is not limited to the interpersonal realm; they are necessary for democratic institutions. In Western countries, the sense of being a member of a polity occurred after people found themselves freed from ancient ties of bondage and became autonomous individuals entitled to fundamental rights. This has not been the case in postcolonial countries. It could be argued that the difficulty of building democratic institutions in these countries is closely related to the impossibility of individuals meaningfully asserting their individuality, their entitlement to private property, and, therefore, their citizen status. In such circumstances, trials and other measures called for by truth commissions are aimed at "enacting citizenship." They do so not only as a discourse but also in a performative way.

Truth commissions seek to promote the functioning of law as a form of protection for people who ordinarily have not experienced it as an effective guarantee of their rights, not even when their lives and physical integrity were at stake. A truth commission demands that the most progressive gains of contemporary law—such as, for instance, the provisions of the Rome Statute of the International Criminal Court—be applied on behalf of previously marginalized persons. For them, truth commissions call for comprehensive reparations and broad institutional reforms that ultimately deal with the basic definitions of social policy. They thus foster a positive integration among persons, cultures, and technical-professional systems that tend to ignore one another in this kind of society. Building upon the findings and recommendations made by truth commissions, transitional justice unifies the practice of the law in these countries in its best formulations, and does so working with actual individuals, with faces and names, who have been subjected to abuse. This is a core issue. Experiences of this sort open the door to new ways of understanding what the systemic changes may be, making it possible to visualize new aspects of a society's agenda and new ways of intervening. The issue is connected to the problem of how reparations and other types of services provided to the victims are delivered, a question that brings up the problems of recognition and participation. In a participatory process of redressing past wrongdoings, local micro-networks—that otherwise might go unnoticed—are empowered and allowed to gain internal consistency and to attain a broader audience. If the promoters of transitional justice find that the delivery of reparations was not experienced as an act involving the genuine recognition of dignity, they should know that something important went wrong or remained incomplete. It is not a matter pertaining exclusively to subjective sentiment, but of refined objective benchmarks and the observance of legal norms adopted to ensure justice in these types of situations.

In this way, transitional justice makes a unique contribution to the process of change, one that it should maintain at all costs: it tends to construct concretely, with each action, a new bridge over the divides that exist between the state and society. In many cases, it gives the state a presence in places where it had none and, therefore, generates universalist citizen relationships where before there were only arbitrary particular relationships marked by habits of domination and forms of subjugation accepted as *natural*. The product of transitional justice results from material and cultural factors.

It would appear clear, then, that transitional justice can contribute to a sense of association and horizontal interaction with the population being more present in the work of promoting development; in other words, the promoters of development can value the effectiveness of fostering democratic subjective and cultural changes. Transitional justice, on doing a better job of reparation and of justice, where these did not exist before, is contributing to a systemic cultural change consistent with the ultimate objective of human development.

We have found this kind of systemic change, for transitional justice, primarily in the type of social relationship or in the quality of interpersonal interactions being constructed here and now. No change in the volume of production or productivity is being sought; rather, change is being sought in another sphere, but one that is at least as important. We are referring to another way of living in society. From this point of view, transitional justice builds better-quality human relationships that can be distinguished from the logic of a society marked by the traditional domination of the strongest. It can even be said that these relationships are of better quality than the more instrumental ones of society shaped by trade in merchandise, as happens in too many realms of contemporary global society.

If the agencies that promote human development programs were to insist on making their ultimate objectives explicit, we believe it would lead to a general understanding of the importance of the recognition of the other by which citizen relations are constructed. A strong reference to this qualitative message would, finally, help bring about better coordination and mutual support between the practitioners of both processes. There is, indeed, a risk of excess isolation or "overspecialization" limiting the outlook of each. If both communities are more conscious of their shared aims, and of a confrontation, which they also share, with abiding customs that reproduce authoritarianism, forms of cooperation can be agreed upon, flexibly, in each case. This is advisable, for there is also the opposite risk: thinking that some people can do the work of all others, moving from activity to activity as if development and transitional justice were identical pursuits.

From the standpoint of those of us who have worked in truth commissions, it seems unlikely that investigations into human rights violations will expand to include an assessment of unmet needs or the framing of specific public policy proposals. The intensity of the phenomena to be addressed and the constant pressures for a timely response could not be greater. Most important, there are other projects and other professionals working in other areas. The same holds, no doubt, if one looks at things from the standpoint of promoting development.

It seems to us that being clear about the aims of each field—transitional justice and development—and about their ultimate convergence is the best way to prevent the two extreme risks: overspecialization, on the one hand, and efforts to merge the two, on the other. Excessive isolation may lead those working on justice issues, for example, to fail to perceive the need to situate the response to the problems of collective barbarity in the context of the human development of the whole country. For the victims and their next of kin, the violence they experience is generally understood as part of a situation of poverty that allows their abuse, or at least the threat of it, to stalk them all the time.

CONCLUSION

Throughout this chapter, our argument has relied on two key ideas. The first is that transitional justice and human development have their own respective spheres of action that—though they may overlap—are fundamentally different. The most significant convergence between them does not emerge from the similarity of their specific tasks, but from what each is ultimately about. Both are ethical proposals that invoke systemic processes to make necessary changes in societies described as very imperfect, where it is very difficult for changes of that sort to come about incrementally. For that reason, it is important for the promoters of both forms of justice to lay down roots as much as they can in those places where the excesses of violence and extreme poverty too often coexist.

Our second key idea has been that truth commissions are—and can be to an even greater extent—sui generis actors that, as they arise at intense, perhaps even charismatic moments, can make explicit in their discourse and practice that they seek to begin a process to make justice credible and to end impunity for the powerful, which implies making substantive changes in social relations and in the state. We have argued that the key is to affirm, through the discourse and the new capacities for agency acquired by certain groups, that each element of transitional justice is just a link in a process that must be long-lasting (even trans-generational) and coherent, lest it fizzle out.

We reiterate that the reflections herein drew on our direct experience working on a truth commission. To reflect on that commission's accomplishments and verifying its importance and the limits of its influence, more than five years after the final report was issued, has been one motivation for writing this chapter. Given the limited space, we have not set forth any specific analysis on how proposals for institutional reforms provide a space in which it is possible to link the specific charge of truth commissions with that far broader message of renewal of justice and of public life, of politics itself, in those societies. That remains a pending task for our field of endeavor.

Translated by Charles H. Roberts

NOTES

1   Paul van Zyl, "Promoviendo la justicia transicional en sociedades post-conflicto," in *Verdad, memoria y reconstrucción: estudios de caso y análisis comparado*, ed. Mauricio Romero (Bogotá: International Center for Transitional Justice, 2008).

2   The definition of transitional justice is a contested matter to this day, beginning with the very name of the field. Modifying justice by the adjective "transitional" already opens up the debate as to whether we are talking about a specific conception of justice or about forms justice takes on in certain particular circumstances. See Ruti Teitel, *Transitional Justice* (Oxford: Oxford University Press, 2000), 7; and the discussion in this regard in Pablo de Greiff, "Theorizing Transitional Justice," in *Transitional Justice*, ed. Melissa Williams and Rosemary Nagy, Nomos XLX (forthcoming).

3   The authors participated directly as commissioner and member of the technical team of the Truth and Reconciliation Commission [*Comisión de la Verdad y Reconciliación*] (CVR) of Peru (2001–2003).

4   The concept of human development has evolved intensely in a short period of time from its theoretical formulation in the work of Amartya Sen to its transformation into

an international standard for measuring development gains. See Amartya Sen, *Development as Freedom* (New York: Knopf, 1999); and United Nations Development Programme, *Human Development Report 1990* (New York: Oxford University Press, 1990).

5   Sen, *Development as Freedom*, 2 and 6; and Martha Nussbaum, *Women and Human Development: The Capabilities Approach* (Cambridge: Cambridge University Press, 2000), 1.

6   This dilemma was posed in stark terms by the internal security policy of the United States during the two presidential terms of George W. Bush. The change in administration may bring positive change with it, in view of President Barack Obama's remarks rejecting the false dilemma between security and principles (related to fully upholding the rule of law).

7   The deliberative element of truth commissions is highlighted by David Crocker in several texts. See David Crocker, "Truth Commissions, Transitional Justice, and Civil Society," in *Truth v. Justice: The Morality of Truth Commissions*, ed. Robert I. Rotberg and Dennis Thompson (New Jersey: Princeton University Press, 2000).

8   See Juan J. Linz and Alfred Stepan, "Toward Consolidated Democracy," in *Consolidating Third Wave Democracies: Themes and Perspectives*, ed. Larry Diamond, Marc F. Plattner, Yun-han Chu, and Hung-mao Tien (Baltimore: Johns Hopkins University Press, 1997).

9   Of course, we do not mean to suggest that the practice of development is uninterested in the concrete and particular or that it leaves them unchanged, or to question the significance of the multiple development actors working at the micro and meso levels, with both individuals and communities. But to see the difference (in starting points only) that we are trying to capture here, we do well to keep in mind two facts, one relating to development and one to transitional justice interventions: the majority of development interventions of bilateral donors and multilateral agencies do take place in the domain of impersonal policy-making; transitional justice interventions, by contrast, can be said to target individuals, both positively and negatively—i.e., in terms of the attribution of blame and responsibility and in terms of their expected effects on victims, starting with the anticipated results of learning the truth about individual victims to the more ambitious aim of "reconciliation," which inevitably has an individual dimension to it.

10   Historical sociology has long analyzed, mainly in poor countries with prolonged colonial pasts, the multiple causes that contribute to a society being "ill constituted." Nonetheless, the use of this concept in this chapter is related mainly to a normative horizon associated with reasonable standards of respect for and observance of human rights in general. An "ill-constituted" society would be one whose institutional organizational structure makes it very difficult to equitably enforce those rights and the function of the state and social powers in general to protect them. Hence, de Greiff's concept of "very imperfect societies" is introduced further on, referring directly to this ethical-social horizon. Both "ill-constituted societies" and "very imperfect worlds" are technical (and normative) terms meant to focus on the relationship between institutions and the

contexts in which they operate. Therefore, they are not meant to provide a *full* description of any setting, to deny that in every setting there is immense human potential and resourcefulness, or to suggest that there is such a thing as a "perfect world."

11   This is highlighted in, among others, Robert I. Rotberg, "Truth Commissions and the Provision of Truth, Justice, and Reconciliation," in *Truth v. Justice*.

12   De Greiff, "Theorizing Transitional Justice."

13   See CVR, *Informe Final, Tomo IX: Recomendaciones y Anexos* (Lima: CVR, 2004).

14   This line of argument is based on the idea that democratization is a matter not just of institutional design but also of cultural transformations, including of beliefs and of social interactions—i.e., in what Luckham, Goetz, and Kaldor call "the deep politics of society." This idea, however, does not mean attenuating the importance of institutional changes, such as those proposed by transitional justice. The authors note correctly that "where democratic institutions do stabilize themselves, in however nascent a way, they often create incentives to shape the behaviour of the political elites to be inclusive in their politics and to challenge excessive concentration of power." See Robin Luckham, Anne Marie Goetz, and Mary Kaldor, "Democratic Institutions and Democratic Politics," in *Can Democracy Be Designed? The Politics of Institutional Choice in Conflict-Torn Societies*, ed. Sunil Bastian and Robin Luckham (London: Zed Books, 2003).

15   Among the various texts that seek to define the concept of "truth commission," see, in particular, Priscilla B. Hayner, *Unspeakable Truths: Confronting State Terror and Atrocity* (New York: Routledge, 2001), 14.

16   Crocker emphasizes in an interesting way the need for an intense interrelationship between truth commissions and nongovernmental organizations as part of the effort to redefine the public space. See Crocker, "Truth Commissions, Transitional Justice, and Civil Society."

17   Félix Reátegui Carrillo, "Memoria histórica, política de la cultura y democracia en el Perú," in *Políticas culturales: ensayos críticos*, ed. Guillermo Cortés and Víctor Vich (Lima: Instituto de Estudios Peruanos, 2007).

18   Sidney Tarrow, *Power in Movement: Social Movements and Contentious Politics* (New York: Cambridge University Press, 1998), 118–22.

19   This point brings out the practical political importance of the so-called battles for memory, which are not just between victims and perpetrators but also between agents of memory, such as a commission, and a public opinion that is conformist or that actively adheres to an authoritarian memory of the conflict and its resolution. On battles for memory, see, among many others, Elizabeth Jelin, *Los trabajos de la memoria* (Madrid: Siglo Veintiuno, 2002), chap. 3; and Martha Minow, *Between Vengeance and Forgiveness: Facing History after Genocide and Mass Violence* (Boston: Beacon, 1998).

20   Daniel Pécaut, *Violencia y política en Colombia: elementos de reflexión* (Medellín: Hombre Nuevo editores, 2003).

21 On the feedback between poverty and violence, see World Bank, *Breaking the Conflict Trap: Civil War and Development Policy* (Washington, DC: World Bank, 2003). It should not be assumed, however, that development necessarily leads to peace or vice versa. See, for instance, Patricia Justino, "On the Links between Violent Conflict and Chronic Poverty: How Much Do We Really Know?" Households in Conflict Network Working Paper 18, July 2006.

22 The difficulty for contemporary society when it comes to making transformative public decisions is a major issue in sociological analysis today. See, e.g., the discussion by Alain Touraine using the notions of "rupture of societies" and "separation between actor and system" in the global world and in the socioeconomic order. Alain Touraine, *Un nouveau paradigme pour comprendre le monde aujourd'hui* (Paris: Fayard, 2005), chaps. 1 and 4. Interestingly, Anthony Giddens represents the global order as "a runaway world," emphasizing the speed and omnipresence of social changes, but it takes him to the same point as Touraine: the possibility of change that is institutionally controlled or induced in keeping with a political project—which in other theoretical traditions would be called "governability"—is very debilitated. See Anthony Giddens, *Un mundo desbocado: los efectos de la globalización en nuestras vidas* (Madrid: Taurus, 2000), chap. 5. A look at the same problem from the practice of development in the area of the right to food may be found in Jean Ziegler, *Les nouveaux maîtres du monde, et ceux qui leur résistent* (Paris: Fayard, 2002), 117–18.

23 World Bank, *Breaking the Conflict Trap*; and Francis Fukuyama, *State-Building: Governance and World Order in the 21st Century* (Ithaca, NY: Cornell University Press, 2004), chap. 3.

24 The Peruvian truth commission speaks of "unfinished modernization" or "truncated modernization" to explain the context in which it was possible for violence to be unleashed and for human rights to be highly vulnerable. See CVR, *Informe Final, Tomo I: Introducción y Exposición general del proceso* (Lima: CVR, 2004).

25 On the evolution of these two fields in the functions of governability understood as institutional control of social change, see Alan Wolfe, *Los límites de la legitimidad: contradicciones políticas en el capitalismo contemporáneo* (1977) (Mexico City: Siglo Veintiuno, 1997). Wolfe's argument, as the date of publication of his work suggests, does not take as its starting point the transformation of governability in the global and neoliberal order, but the systemic changes particular to postindustrial society.

CHAPTER 5

A Complementary Relationship: Reparations and Development

Naomi Roht-Arriaza and Katharine Orlovsky

I was detained for four months and two weeks in Puerto Barrios, all my crops, my corn, my rice disappeared, they even ate my cow, I was suffering and my children were suffering, we ended up in absolute poverty, it was all very painful and all because of the conflict we went through, we had to escape and start all over again, except this time we were always afraid.[1]

The voices of victims remind us of what is lost during periods of massive human rights violations. When such violations are committed, international law recognizes a right to reparation that, in its material components, may provide tangible goods or services to victims and survivors. As such, reparations may overlap with plans and programs to improve the material conditions of life for the population more generally. That overall process, often encapsulated under the term "development," finds concrete expression in funding, planning, and implementing programs for development cooperation. Yet reparations and development are generally conceptualized and approached independently. Reparations to individuals have for the most part been the province of human rights courts, claims commissions, and administrative programs, and advocacy on the issue has been concentrated among human rights and transitional justice organizations. Development cooperation, a much larger field, encompasses the work of international development institutions, aid agencies, financial institutions, and a constellation of development-oriented nongovernmental organizations (NGOs) and practitioners.

This chapter addresses the specific linkages between reparations and development that may exist in a post–armed conflict context or following a political transition.[2] Demands for reparations—as defined below—are becoming increasingly prevalent in postconflict negotiations, and governments, truth commissions, or other entities have responded by proposing administrative reparations programs. We concentrate on these programs rather than court-ordered or claims-commission-ordered reparations.

The victim's legal right to reparation for serious harms suffered is articulated in the UN's 2005 *Basic Principles on the Right to a Remedy and Reparation for Victims of Gross Violations of International Human Rights Law and Serious Violations of International Humanitarian Law.*[3] According to the *Basic Principles*, a victim of said violations has the right under international law to: (1) equal and effective access to justice; (2) adequate, effective, and prompt reparation for harm suffered; and (3) access to relevant information concerning violations and reparation mechanisms. Such reparation "should be proportional to the gravity of the violations and the harm suffered,"[4] and may take the form of restitution, compensation, rehabilitation, satisfaction, and guarantees of nonrepetition.[5] The right to a remedy or to reparations is also articulated in the basic human rights instruments, specialized conventions, nonbinding instruments, and the Rome Statute of the International Criminal Court (ICC).[6]

Reparations are distinct from reconstruction and from victim assistance, both of which are closely related. Reconstruction generally refers to physical and economic rebuilding after an armed conflict or other disaster. Victim assistance focuses on meeting the immediate needs (medical, psychological, economic, legal) of victims. Reparations are distinguished from both, first by their roots as a legal entitlement based on an obligation to repair harm, and second by an element of recognition of wrongdoing as well as harm, atonement, or making good. Reparations are therefore a limited category of response to harm, and generally address violations of basic civil and political rights, such as massacres or disappearances, rather than broader issues of social exclusion or denial of economic, social, or cultural rights.[7] Reparations, by their nature as a response to specific harms, also have a large symbolic component, in which the way they are carried out is as important as or more important than the material result.

Reparations may also be granted according to different methodologies. Court-ordered reparations generally entail individualized considerations of damages to each claimant based on the idea of *restitutio in integrum*—that is, putting the individual back in the position he/she would have been in absent the violation. Administrative schemes tend to operate either by providing a uniform sum to all victims or through a schedule of amounts for different violations, and do not attempt to define or repair the full amount of the losses.

Development also has multiple definitions and constituent elements. As discussed further below, we adopt the broad view of development espoused by Amartya Sen and other theorists: rather than a narrowly defined process of economic growth (whether measured by gross domestic product [GDP], foreign direct investment [FDI], or other indicators), development instead entails creating the conditions for all people to develop their fullest possible range of capabilities.[8] It is under a capabilities-centered, bottom-up approach to development that the strongest links to transitional justice generally, and reparations programs in particular, can be made.

There are obviously tensions between reparations programs and the larger development agenda. If nothing else, budgets are finite, and competition for resources is particularly fierce in a post–armed conflict or post-dictatorship context where the economy and infrastructure may be damaged or destroyed and common crime is likely to surge. Fiscal stability and a need to create a favorable investment climate may conflict with the additional social spending and need for additional government revenues that a reparations program will demand. In a number of recent examples, domestic governments, international organizations, courts, and even victims groups have moved for reparations to take the form of specific development projects, such as (re)building community structures or providing schools or health clinics. These "reparations as development" projects raise serious questions about whether such initiatives may violate the essential "character" of reparations—that is, an act done as, and that individuals in the community recognize as, atonement for past harms. The 2007 Nairobi Declaration on Women's and Girls' Right to a Remedy and Reparation has gone as far as to state that "Governments should not undertake development instead of reparation."[9]

At the same time, there are potential synergies between reparations and development. Reparations, from an individual victim's perspective, may be a necessary step toward creating a sense of recognition as a citizen with equal rights and fostering a certain level of civic trust in the government. These, in turn, are preconditions for the (re)emergence of victims and survivors as actors with the initiative, motivation, and belief in the future that drive sustainable economic activity. While all transitional justice measures share this aim, reparations constitute its most concrete, tangible, and to some degree personalized expression. Reparations payments, at least if past and current administrative programs are a guide, will never be large enough to make a difference on a macroeconomic scale. Nonetheless, reparations payments may have positive effects on rebalancing power relations within families and in local communities (though they may also, it should be noted, pose dangers of conflict and fragmentation in these contexts). Even small amounts, under certain conditions, may unleash the energy and creativity of previously marginalized sectors (especially women and indigenous peoples). Reparations in the form of services can improve health, education, and other measures of well-being that are essential to development in ways that "normal" programs for the provision of these services will miss because they are not attuned to the specific potential and needs of survivors, including the need to have their individual harms acknowledged.

Moreover, individual and collective reparations may have important spill-over effects on other aspects of development. These include linkages to other issues, such as civil registry and titling, potential strengthening of the state's ability to be an effective service provider, and the ability of civil society and business groups to interface with the state (through procurement and otherwise) in a "normal" fashion. Interactions with the state around reparations, if positive, can increase awareness of the population as rights-bearing citizens, which can spill over into a demand for access to justice and for effective (and transparent) government.

Just as reparations may affect development, however, development can also contribute to an improved ability to provide effective reparations. At the simplest level, a desperately poor country with little in the way of government infrastructure will face greater difficulties in financing and distributing reparations than a richer, more organized one. The lack of a government presence in the interior of a country emerging from conflict will make it difficult to organize the provision of reparations, or even to know what potential beneficiaries of a reparations program need or want. In particular, many reparations, especially in-kind services, require a delivery system. To the extent that these services can be channeled through already functioning pension, education, or health systems, they are more likely to be competently provided. Moreover, development efforts focused on anticorruption efforts, public administrative reform, and even security sector reform might make the state more effective in delivering reparations. This has implications for the timing of reparations: it may take some time to build up the required physical, financial, and human infrastructure to ensure an adequate reparations program. While not by any means an argument for delaying the provision of reparations, this may lead to the recognition that the benefits of reparations may accrue in part to the initial victims and survivors of the violations, and in part may be intergenerational.

The second section of this chapter examines the broader definition of development as well as the interface among certain approaches to development, social exclusion, and reparations. The third section focuses on the impact of reparations programs on the state, and on the limitations of the state that impact the delivery of reparations. The fourth section turns to some of

the particular issues raised, respectively, by collective reparations and individual reparations. We then turn, in the fifth section, to the delivery systems for
and destinations of reparations. The sixth section looks at reparations and the
international development cooperation community. Finally, in the last section,
we draw conclusions.

CONCEPTIONS OF DEVELOPMENT AND THEIR CONVERGENCE
WITH REPARATIONS

We use a broad conception of development, defining it as a process that
increases a society's prosperity, augments the welfare of its citizens, and builds
the infrastructure and the productive, civil, and political institutions necessary
to ensure its members the most fulfilling life possible, or at least a minimum
level of income or livelihood for a life with dignity. The classical view of economic development is much narrower, focusing on measures of economic
growth, such as GDP per capita or amount of investment. At the outset, we
acknowledge that even the most ambitious reparations projects will have
uncertain, and probably minimal, effects as a contributor to GDP growth—the
amount of money involved is simply too small. It may not be possible, then, to
trace the macroeconomic impact of such programs.

   Theories of development have gone through a number of evolutions, from
the presumption in the 1950s that all economies went through "stages," to the
focus on basic needs in the 1970s, to a turn in the 1980s to a stronger macroeconomic focus. During the 1980s and early 1990s, the "Washington consensus" held that growth, and thus development, were a function of opening up
economies, selling state assets, and shrinking the public sector. The result in
many countries was a contraction of economic activity and cutbacks in the services, such as public health and education, that might overlap with the efforts
of many reparations programs. In the current post-"consensus" era, even the
international financial institutions (IFIs) and donor agencies now pay lip service
to the need for increased government services in these areas and for a direct
focus on poverty alleviation (rather than regarding it as a trickle-down consequence of growth). The Millennium Development Goals (MDGs), approved by
governments in 2000, are the most well-known expression of the mainstream
policy objectives for reducing poverty and improving well-being.[10]

   In contrast to the export-led theories of past years, a new line of thinking about economic development stresses the importance of endogenous or
locally driven development. Locally driven development does not exclude

foreign investment or trade, but it focuses on creating sustained economic growth through strengthening local and regional markets. It emphasizes education (human capital development), on-the-job training, and innovation to create new niche markets that allow even small, capital-poor, and resource-poor countries to prosper. This approach leads to a stress on indigenous solutions and on education and health, and it is not hostile to using regulation to encourage innovation and linkages of domestic to global markets.[11] It coincides with theories of local control and bottom-up economic development that are gaining greater currency, especially in light of the perceived failure of the neoliberal approaches of the 1980s and early 1990s. In almost every developing/poor/global-south country, thousands of grassroots development projects, funded from local resources or NGO networks, now exist alongside, and sometimes in lieu of, centralized government efforts. One expression of this bottom-up approach, but by no means the only one, is the burgeoning microfinance and microcredit movement.[12]

In the 1990s, alongside the concern with opening up economies, came a new focus on "governance," which over time has brought the concerns and techniques of transitional justice and development experts closer together. After years of focus on markets as the sole drivers of growth, IFIs and donor governments realized that markets could not operate properly without an overarching set of rules provided by the state. They turned their attention to strengthening certain aspects of state performance, including judicial and legal system reform, anticorruption efforts, and tying external support to "good governance."[13] In particular, lending and aid agencies have focused a large amount of resources on "rule of law" programming aimed at the modernization of codes and courts to facilitate economic activity. Alongside these efforts, which have had decidedly mixed results, other programming has aimed at improving access to justice for the population, especially those who have never seen courts as a useful defender of their rights. This focus on the justice sector has also led to greater sensitivity among some development specialists to the particular needs and characteristics of postconflict societies, and to a renewed focus on the state's capacity to carry out any of the goals assigned to it, whether these involve development or justice. At the same time, those who have critiqued the emphasis on the rule of law have pointed out that improving state institutions, by itself, cannot ensure that poor people actually make use of such institutions or see them as relevant or fair.

The convergence of recent thinking on development with related paradigms of conflict transformation, human security, and rights-based approaches to development means that the concerns and ways of thinking of those involved in development work and those focusing on reparations are in many ways parallel. Practitioners of conflict transformation begin

> with a central goal: to build constructive change out of the energy created by conflict. By focusing this energy on the underlying relationships and social structures, constructive changes can be brought about.... How do we address conflict in ways that reduce violence and increase justice in human relationships? *To reduce violence* we must address both the obvious issues and content of any given dispute and also their underlying patterns and causes. *To increase justice* we must ensure that people have access to political procedures and voice in the decisions that affect their lives.[14]

Thus, for conflict transformation practitioners, dealing with the aftermath of conflict in a way that increases justice and gives affected peoples a voice in decision-making converges with the concerns of those involved in reparations programs.

Another convergent set of concerns involves the move among those involved in the security area from military security to a broader view of human security. As part of a move from a state-centered view of security to a "human-centered" one, human security "deals with the capacity to identify threats, to avoid them when possible, and to mitigate their effects when they do occur. It means helping victims cope with the consequences of the widespread insecurity resulting from armed conflict, human rights violations and massive underdevelopment."[15] Here, too, a focus on human security will dovetail with efforts to repair those consequences.

Last but not least, the approaches of development practitioners and those concerned with reparations have converged around rights-based approaches to development. As a United Nations Development Programme (UNDP) publication puts it:

> Human rights add value to the agenda for development by drawing attention to the accountability to respect, protect, promote and fulfill all human rights of all people. Increased focus on accountability holds the key to improved effectiveness and transparency of action.... Another important value provided by the application of a human rights-based approach is the focus on the most marginalised and excluded in society as their human rights are most widely denied or left unfulfilled (whether in the social, economic, political, civil or cultural spheres, and often, a combination of these). A human rights-based approach will further generally lead to better analysed and more focused strategic interventions

by providing the normative foundation for tackling fundamental development issues.[16]

All these approaches have brought the concerns, goals, and methodologies of those working in the development field closer to those of human rights or transitional justice practitioners focusing on reparations programs. A principal point of convergence is the concern with process: how programs and projects are carried out is as important as what is done. For both development and reparations programming, the issue of social exclusion, and the potential of reparations programs to combat it, is central.

DEVELOPMENT, REPARATIONS, AND SOCIAL INTEGRATION

Starting in the 1980s and increasingly today, development economists, academic experts, IFIs,[17] national and international aid agencies, and governments now recognize that growth and other macro indicators alone do not capture many of the essential aspects of a development process. The UNDP's Human Development Index has, since the 1990s, ranked countries in terms of such measures as infant morbidity and mortality, educational level, and women's rights, as well as by GDP growth. Along the same lines, development practitioners now focus on the micro as well as the macro level, looking to village-level interventions and community-driven processes as an important component of development success. Development is increasingly conceptualized not as a goal or end point but as an ongoing process, in which the agency, self-organization, and empowerment of those at the bottom of the economic pyramid are at the same time the means of reaching success and the goal itself.

There is broad agreement that the social exclusion of large sectors of a population, combined with other factors, including geography, conflict, and "governance," is a crucial variable in determining development levels.[18] Indeed, recent research explores the link between social integration and economic development. Kaushik Basu, for example, finds that "once a group of people is left outside the system or treated as marginal over a period of time, forces develop that reinforce its marginalization. The group learns not to participate in society and others learn to exclude members of this group, and participator inequity becomes a part of the economic and societal 'equilibrium.'" Therefore, because people evaluate how trustworthy or likely to succeed others may be in an economic endeavor based in part on the identity characteristics of the individual, marginalized groups (whether by race, class, or victim status) tend to stay marginalized and unable to break out of poverty. The solution, according to Basu, lies in fostering a sense of "participatory equity," such that the marginalized belong to their society and also have rights like others.[19]

Along similar lines, the UNDP recognizes the importance of social integration, participation, and accountability for the overall development process:

> [P]articipation is not simply something desirable from the point of view of ownership and sustainability, but rather a right with profound consequences for the design and implementation of development activities. It is concerned also with access to decision-making, and the exercise of power in general.... The principles of participation and inclusion means that all people are entitled to participate in society to the maximum of their potential. This in turn necessitates provision of a supportive environment to enable people to develop and express their full potential and creativity.[20]

It is this vision of development, especially as it concerns the life conditions and chances of excluded or marginalized sectors, where the clearest overlap with reparations occurs.

Reparations programs present an opportunity to establish trust, specifically by creating a consciousness of survivors as rights holders. The goals of reparations programs, especially of administrative programs, generally do not include returning beneficiaries to where they had been prior to the violation—even if such a thing were possible. Rather, the goals include recognition that a harm needs to be remedied, expressing social solidarity, and (re)creating civic trust.[21] What distinguishes reparations from assistance is the moral and political content of the former, positing that victims are entitled to reparations *because* their rights have been violated by the state (through acts or omissions). Thus, those receiving reparations are by definition rights holders, with a claim against the state. Once sectors of the population start thinking of themselves as rights holders, rather than as passive recipients of whatever benefits the government chooses to provide, the demonstration effect may be significant. Rights holders can demand their rights, and they are more likely to seek ways of doing so in non-reparations-related contexts as well. Thus, reparations can serve as a jumping-off point for efforts at social inclusion that are key to development.

REPARATIONS AND THE STATE

Reparations are unique among transitional justice measures in requiring adequate performance from a wide range of government entities. Unlike truth commissions, which are set up on an ad hoc basis, or even trials, which involve either special chambers or at most police and justice ministries, a complex reparations program requires input and participation from numerous government ministries, including health, education, land, housing, planning, and finance. It may also involve bodies at the national, regional/provincial, and local levels. The more a reparations program is "integrated"—that is, complex or combining different types of benefits—the greater role there is for multiple existing state organs. At a minimum, because funds must be not only collected but also disbursed, financial ministries and an administrative structure must be involved. This broad government involvement required to implement a reparations program is a source of both tensions and, potentially, synergies with longer-term development.

Post–armed conflict states are generally weak, and in many cases the weakness of the state, particularly the central state, was a contributing factor to the conflict. Administrative systems—outside the internal security sector—are generally inefficient, cumbersome, corrupt, and concentrated in the capital. In countries emerging from dictatorship, the state may not be weak per se, but its institutions and functions have been skewed toward internal security and the benefit of those in power, to the exclusion of the majority. In both cases, state services rarely reach large sectors of the population, and those that do are low-quality and enmeshed in corruption and patronage systems. Doctors and teachers have often abandoned rural posts, medicine has been diverted from local clinics, and the poor, especially indigenous people, ethnic minorities, and women, are treated with disdain and condescension. Access to any kind of government benefit usually requires several trips to the capital, any number of signatures, stamps, side payments, and extensive delays.

This is the system and the warped development patterns facing the governments that design and implement reparations programs, and they are slow to change. One of the biggest hurdles to the programs in both Peru and Guatemala, for example, has been the need to channel a transitional justice strategy through existing state structures that are ill suited for the purpose, to the extent they exist at all. In addition to a lack of resources and, often, preparation, government ministries tend to operate in separate "silos" without much communication with other ministries (and often in mistrustful, competitive relations with them), making it even more difficult to create integrated programs. This has led to long delays, to frustrations for victims in dealing with a slow and often unfeeling bureaucracy, and to problems operationalizing the delivery of money and services. The "normal" problems of a weak state unable to deliver benefits or services effectively are exacerbated when infrastructure has been neglected or destroyed during armed conflict or military buildup, and needed professionals have been killed or exiled or have emigrated. They are further exacerbated when the message is supposed to be one of valuing the recipients as equal citizens and creating a new dispensation in which they are fully integrated. Indeed, the wrong message may be sent, angering and retraumatizing the ostensible beneficiaries of a reparations program.

Thus, the more development focuses on strengthening the services that will most likely be used by reparations beneficiaries, the more effective the reparations program or project is likely to be. More generally, a focus on service delivery to the poor, or on the anticorruption and administrative reform efforts needed to make sure those services actually arrive, will have important positive repercussions on the eventual delivery of reparations, and will expand the range of benefits that reparations programs could provide. The limitations of the state become obvious when, for example, it has committed to provide medical and psychosocial services where existing networks for service provision are patently inadequate. How exactly will it do that—using existing delivery systems or setting up a new, parallel system dedicated to victims? Either approach has drawbacks. In Peru, for example, the incipient reparations program— the Comprehensive Reparations Plan [*Plan Integral de Reparaciones*] (PIR)— provides medical services through the existing social health insurance network. But that network only has facilities in major cities, is already overburdened, and did not initially cover many of the chronic diseases common among victims and survivors.[22] In Guatemala, where Inter-American Court–ordered collective reparations—for example, in the *Plan de Sánchez* case—have included mental health services, the state responded by sending therapists with no experience dealing with victims of massive crimes into rural areas, where they were completely ineffectual. Moreover, local people complained that the doctors who were sent to staff the local health clinic as part of reparations to the affected community were just as racist and dismissive of their complaints as the doctors they had previously encountered, so much so that many victims no longer visited the clinic.[23]

One solution might be to avoid dysfunctional ministries altogether by setting up new service delivery providers, in a parallel to the establishment of special chambers or special courts for war crimes and crimes against humanity to bypass a dysfunctional judicial system. This was indeed the response in Guatemala, where NGOs supported by the UNDP and other agencies initiated the Psycho-social Assistance to War Victims [*Programa de Dignificación y Asistencia Psicosocial a las Víctimas del Enfrentamiento Armado*] (DIGAP) project, which provided psychosocial counseling and support services around exhumations of mass graves years before the National Reparations Program [*Programa Nacional de Resarcimiento*] (PNR) got under way. Development efforts as well have turned to this solution: the Venezuelan *Misiones*—health and welfare services provided outside the normal government bureaucracy—may be the best-known example. However, setting up dedicated services for victims is more feasible where victim populations are concentrated rather than dispersed, and it raises concerns about creating new stigmatization of, or new resentments against, those able to use the system if it is exclusively for designated victims. Creating new, temporary parallel structures may also simply reproduce old patterns of dependence and elite capture. Although general predictions are difficult, it may make more sense to create new structures where the old ones are hopelessly compromised, and to try to integrate reparations into existing administrative structures where the "transition" is more pronounced or where such structures need to be (re)built almost from the ground up. A related concern involves the stability and permanence of a reparations program itself, especially in politically volatile situations. Where possible, such programs will be more stable if they are backed by legislation and multiyear budgets rather than simply by executive orders.

DYNAMICS BETWEEN THE STATE AND REPARATIONS PROGRAMS

COMPLEMENTING EXISTING STATE FUNCTIONS

Just as development might support a reparations program by focusing on strengthening the government structures that will deliver reparations, reparations programs may in turn play a small role in strengthening certain state functions. An example comes from the plans of the Guatemalan PNR. Sensitive to the criticism that providing services as reparations is not really a reparations program at all, the PNR decided to shy away in its planning from duplicating or funneling its resources into existing health, education, or infrastructure programs. Rather, it aims to complement those programs by focusing on training and support for traditional (Mayan) medicine, preventative health education, teen health education, preschool education, domestic violence prevention, and the like—programs not currently carried out by the relevant ministries. This initiative has been framed as a way of creating sustainable, culturally relevant change while addressing both root causes and survivors' immediate needs.[24] Unfortunately, these plans are, as of December 2008, just plans: actual outlays have focused on individual cash payments (although 2009 programming moves away from this approach to focus on community-led nonmonetary actions). But the idea of complementing, not duplicating, existing state functions is a useful one.

CREATING MODELS OF CIVIC INTERACTIONS WITH THE STATE

Another potentially beneficial dynamic involves the programs and projects started under the auspices of reparations serving as demonstrations of civic interactions with the state. Ideally, these projects can serve as models of a new way of relating to beneficiary populations, and of a new set of priorities that can be folded into existing government programs and ministries. For this to happen, planning and training must start years earlier, so that the ethos and accountability of a highly public and closely watched reparations program is diffused throughout the state. Of course, the danger is that the converse will happen, that the existing state's "business-as-usual" approach will overwhelm efforts at reparations. But, if done consciously and carefully, reparations programs can spearhead change throughout a larger part of the state apparatus. Reparations may constitute the first time affected populations have interacted positively with the state, which is an important step toward (re)building social integration.

There are both promise and pitfalls in embedding reparations programs within much larger existing ministries, however, as exemplified by the Chilean Program of Reparations and Comprehensive Health Care for Victims of Human Rights Violations (PRAIS). This program, which emerged from the recommendations of Chile's Truth and Reconciliation Commission, and with an initial grant from the United States Agency for International Development (USAID), was designed to provide comprehensive physical and psychological health care to those who had suffered human rights violations during the military dictatorship and their family members. PRAIS granted free access to the existing public health service and priority access where there were delays in service provision, using specially trained personnel who were absorbed into the existing service. This allowed for a stable source of funding and a high level of service, but over time the dedicated teams stopped providing exclusive care to victims and began incorporating domestic violence victims into the service, thus diluting the reparatory effect. It took active mobilization and lobbying by the program's beneficiaries to reestablish the emphasis on reparations. As Elizabeth Lira puts it, "the program depended greatly on the individual motivation of the professionals who formed its teams, rather than on institutional compliance with its objectives."[25]

One way to potentially resolve the conundrum of strengthening existing state institutions versus creating new specialized ones is to place within existing agencies at all levels personnel whose job it is to serve as go-betweens, facilitators, and advocates for the beneficiaries of reparations. Such people could serve as a focal point for the specific needs of survivors, help them access the necessary services and navigate confusing or indifferent bureaucracies, and generally be the "friendly face" of the state with respect to victims and survivors.[26]

STRENGTHENING LOCAL AND REGIONAL GOVERNMENTS

Another possible positive spillover effect of reparations programs may be in the potential to strengthen local and regional governments in the context of greater democratization. Much of the literature on decentralization stresses the greater ease with which local governments can connect to constituents, tailor priorities to local needs, experiment, and be responsive to citizen participation. This is not necessarily true, of course: local government can also more easily be captured by elite interests and exclude women, youth, and/or minority or indigenous populations. However, at least potentially, a participatory and accountable local government may do better in creating bottom-up development.

In Peru, implementation of the reparations program has been spearheaded by provincial and municipal administrations, which are setting their own priorities and budgets, with national and local government funding. While some provinces have done little, a few have extensive and ambitious plans and have engaged in substantial consultation with local communities on priorities. For example, the regional government of Huancavelica in 2006 programmed more than 2.5 million new soles (US$837,500) to create its Victims Registry, strengthen local victims' associations, train educators and health personnel, and the like.[27] This effort served as an example and a catalyst for other regional initiatives as well as for the central government. The infusion of resources and attention that the Peruvian PIR has brought to municipal and provincial governments may allow those governments to become more effective service providers across the board, strengthening and deepening decentralization.

In Morocco, reparations are specifically intended to address communities in regions that were marginalized or ostracized. After holding a national forum on reparations, planned state-supported initiatives at a local level are intended to repair communities previously punished for standing up to the repressive regime or for being home to a secret detention center. The uses of reparations funds are thus to be decided by local councils, based on local priorities. In Guatemala, after several years of experience with a centralized program run from regional offices and the capital, the revamped program is now focusing on pilot projects proposed by local villages. In South Africa, the Khulumani survivors' organization proposed a partnership between organized victims' groups and local government to "build citizen and community competence" through local development efforts focused on the communities most heavily affected by the wrongs of apartheid. This effort would build on constitutional and legal provisions regarding public participation in municipal planning and budgeting. Local development would move beyond

> investment in productive assets and infrastructure to re-thinking Child, Health and Education Rights so that public funding becomes pro-gramme rights and associated budgets within registered communities. These are either first spent to create local demand, rewarding local pro-duction, to bind all adults together to protect and to secure the develop-ment of all children (and thus parents and pre-schools), to use School Feeding monies to fuel a local agricultural revolution by buying locally, or to remove the false dichotomy between public and private health and education that ruins both systems and denies community members and parents (now financially secured by Investment rights) from playing key roles as policy requires.[28]

STRENGTHENING CIVIL SOCIETY

Reparations discussions may also stimulate the creation and growth of civil society organizations. The time frame for reparations programs tends to be up to a dozen years, which is enough time for various constellations of local organizations, victims' groups, advocacy organizations, and professionals to coalesce around lobbying and implementation activities centered on the pro-grams. The prospect of resources and concerns about their fair distribution provide an incentive for many people to initially organize and learn how to engage with the state. Those concerns over time spread to work around jus-tice, development, or other related issues. Above all, to the extent that repara-tions programs emphasize the goals of social solidarity, recognition, and equal citizenship, they can provide conduits for people to begin to exercise that citi-zenship in myriad ways. Thus, it is crucial that reparations programs allow for participation by victims' groups and other civil society organizations in formu-lating policies and monitoring progress; such participation can create habits of interaction with the state that will carry over. The phenomenon of civil society organizations flourishing as interlocutors of reparations programs exemplifies the ability of such programs to reconceptualize victims as citizens—that is, as persons with rights who are able to make demands on the state.

Examples include the key role of the Human Rights Advisory Council (CCDH) in formulating and delivering the reparations ordered by the Moroccan truth commission, and the reliance on civil society intermediaries for carrying out the projects of the Victims' Trust Fund (VTF) of the International Criminal Court. In Peru, civil society organizations, such as the *Asociación Pro Derechos Humanos* (APRODEH), have played a key role in ongoing monitoring of the implementation of community-level reparations. These organizations have worked with both government and local survivors' groups in order to address the shortcomings of existing reparations and to advocate for greater involvement of marginalized sectors, especially women.

BRINGING FOCUS TO BUDGETING, OVERSIGHT, AND PROCUREMENT

A related potential effect of reparations programs comes from the budgeting, oversight, and procurement areas. State reparations programs mobilize and energize a relatively large and involved constituency to focus on government funding and budgeting practices. In the process, they can prepare people to deal with government as an institution, not just an adversary. Participatory budgeting is a promising development tool, allowing service recipients to oversee and influence how government monies are allocated. Reparations programs can serve as a training ground for methodologies of participatory budgeting, which can then be transferred to other areas. This is beginning to happen with the PIR in Peru, where NGOs have been particularly concerned with the ability to distinguish exactly which funds in ministry budgets are dedicated to reparations as a separate line, in order to avoid having reparations funds simply folded into existing ministry affairs. This provides training to NGOs and other civil society actors in understanding budgets and budgeting, and to the government in having civil society oversight of what has generally been a rather opaque process.[29] Similarly, committees set up to contribute to or oversee reparations programs might extend their lifespan as local development committees, and vice versa. For example, the World Bank increasingly requires such community councils as part of the implementation of a country development plan; in at least one case, a preexisting community council in Aceh, trusted by both sides in the armed conflict there, served as a mechanism to verify eligibility of widows for special assistance.[30]

Procurement practices initiated as part of reparations programs may also have longer-term effects. In Guatemala, the PNR has turned to NGOs as providers for specialized services, such as exhumations, psychosocial counseling, and legal services for victims. NGOs, long accustomed to an outsider, reactive role vis-à-vis the state, have had to deal with government bureaucracies in procurement as well as planning. While NGO representatives complain about bureaucratic requirements and the slow pace of government actions, they are learning how to assume a proactive stance and, at least potentially, infusing the agencies with which they collaborate with a new spirit and a new set of priorities. On the other hand, outsourcing service functions to NGOs may result in continuing weakness in the state, or may divert NGO resources and attention from watchdog or activist roles to a competition for service provision contracts. Nor will nonstate actors necessarily be able to manage programs of this magnitude.

STIMULATING THE CREATION OF REGISTRIES

While the above effects largely concern the service provision aspects of reparations schemes, other types of spillover effects could arise from individual compensation and restitution programs. For example, one of the most difficult issues faced by the Peruvian and Guatemalan programs is the inability to easily prove the existence and family connections of those who were killed. In both armed conflicts, the warring parties destroyed city halls, churches, and other places where birth, baptismal, and marriage certificates were kept; few death certificates for those killed were ever issued. Truth commissions could not, within the time and resources allotted, register many victims by name.[31] How, then, to prove that one's father or child was killed as a result of the armed conflict? Even if the existence of the victim can be proven (through testimony accepted by a truth commission or a court, for example), the names and relationships of the next of kin may be impossible to document.

This creates a terrible dilemma. If the programs demand too much documentation, they will exclude large numbers of eligible victims and survivors, especially those from rural areas who were hardest hit; they will retraumatize victims and undermine any reparatory effect of the compensation. On the other hand, in countries with few jobs and extensive poverty, it would be surprising if the promise of money did not elicit all kinds of fraudulent behavior, including false claims of victimhood. To benefit the true beneficiaries, reparations programs that include individual payments must establish ways to weed out false claims. This is especially true when the resources are coming from the state. States not only have to meet their own budgeting and administrative rules, but also have to show other states, IFIs, debtors, and investors that they have adequate controls on state funds and are actively combating corruption. This has become a more salient concern as the fight against government corruption and for financial transparency has become a centerpiece of the programmatic work of the World Bank, among others. Establishing adequate mechanisms to register victims has thus caused enormous delays in the distribution of compensation in both Peru and Guatemala.

In these countries, the state has responded to this dilemma by trying to create registries for victims and their next of kin. Eventually, programs will have to find innovative ways—including the use of witnesses, elders, or in some cases simply circumstantial evidence of time and place—to establish eligibility for reparations payments through a register of victims. From a development standpoint, these efforts may pay off in the long term, yielding the core of a larger civil registry and staff trained in its operation. In turn, this could facilitate broader efforts at a census, as well as documentation and formalization of generally document-poor populations. This should make it easier for the poor to engage in the formal economy, obtain loans, and the like.[32]

STIMULATING LAND TITLING AND RESTITUTION

Similar frustrations, and similar potential, attend the issue of land restitution. Thousands are forcibly displaced during armed conflicts, and sometimes their land is resettled by others. The process of land restitution is often complicated because those displaced had no title, deficient title, or based ownership on indigenous community landholding norms not recognized by the state. Where the land has been resettled, equivalent lands must be found and adequately titled, and the formal title then must be respected in practice. The frustration comes from the fact that land distribution and titling agencies are extremely underfunded, slow, disrespectful of customary or collective landholding practices, and unable to access much viable land in the absence of broad agrarian reform, thus leaving land restitution programs largely in limbo. The potential arises from the possibility of a new way of working or from putting additional political heat on these agencies to speed up the pace and improve the quality of titling and distribution activities.[33] The South African Land Claims courts, among others, have pioneered an approach to establishing facts of ownership and identity through the use of oral traditions, evidence of witnesses, and other nonwritten sources; a similar approach might be acceptable in other similar circumstances.[34] By putting increased resources into restitution accompanied by titling, reparations programs can indirectly unleash access to credit for the new owners.[35] They can also serve as the catalyst for reforms to ensure women's access to land and title or to recognize the land rights of indigenous or traditional communities as such, which may have important symbolic as well as practical implications.

COLLECTIVE AND INDIVIDUAL REPARATIONS

Practitioners and scholars have often distinguished between individual and collective reparations as preferable approaches. We start from the premise that both individual and collective reparations are important components of a sufficiently complex and integrated reparations effort. Individual reparations serve as recognition of specific harm to an individual, and of an individual's worth as a rights-bearing citizen. Such recognition, which is integral to (re)gaining civic trust, may not be otherwise satisfied. Individual recognition becomes especially important where the government has previously treated the affected population as an undifferentiated mass or as second-class citizens. Collective reparations may serve other, albeit overlapping, functions: to respond to collective harms and harms to social cohesion (especially in places with a strong sense of collective identity), to reestablish social solidarity, and to maximize the effectiveness of existing resources. The objective is not to choose one form of reparation over another, but to understand the strengths and limitations of each and to combine them in a culturally appropriate and creative manner.

Individual reparations need not be limited to monetary compensation; they can also take the form of restitution—of land, other property, jobs, pensions, civil rights, or good name—and of physical, mental, and legal rehabilitation. Individual reparations may be symbolic as well as material; for example, the Chilean government's delivery of a personalized copy of the Truth and Reconciliation Commission's report with a letter indicating where the name of each individual victim could be found had a profound reparative value for the individuals involved.[36] Other individual reparations may include the exhumation and reburial of those killed, apologies to individual survivors or next of kin, or the publication of the facts of an individual case. Individual reparations can also take the form of government service packages, such as enrollment in government health plans, preferential access to medical services, or scholarships.

The concept of collective reparations is more complicated, in part because it is used to mean different things in different contexts. In practice, collective reparations have most often been conceptualized as either nonindividualized modalities of distribution or public goods tied to specific communities—either basic goods, such as schools, health clinics, roads, and the like, or extra funds targeted at specific regions deemed to have suffered most during the period of conflict, as in Peru or Morocco. Thus, while access to scholarships or hospital privileges would constitute an individual reparation, the building of schools or health clinics in affected communities, open to all residents, would be a collective reparation. Some modalities of reparations are collective in form but are still largely limited to victims, and may be targeted at group-based harm.[37] Examples include psychosocial accompaniment for groups of victims, exhumations of mass grave sites in specific communities, titling of collective lands, restitution of sites of communal worship, and microcredit or other producer-targeted projects for groups of widows and the like.

As with individual reparations, these forms of collective reparations may include material as well as symbolic measures, and restitution, satisfaction, and compensation. Fundamentally, collective reparations consider the individual in the context of societal ties. Use of the term "collective reparations" may refer to reparations to a particular social, ethnic, or geographical group, or simply to a community that suffered harm to its cohesion and social fabric as such and thus is being repaired qua community. This approach, of course, raises the difficulty of assigning victims to groups or communities for reparations purposes, a problem magnified by demographic and social shifts during the course of an armed conflict, especially those caused by widespread displacement and migration.

Most existing proposals and programs, at least in theory, combine both individual and collective components. The South African Truth and Reconciliation Commission (TRC), for example, called for a reparation and rehabilitation policy that was "development-centred," to actively empower individuals and communities to take control of their own lives.[38] In particular, the community rehabilitation measures included health and social services, mental health services, education, housing, and institutional reform.[39] But the TRC also called for individual awards, which were eventually distributed, although the amounts involved were far smaller than those the TRC recommended.

The law creating the Peruvian PIR specifies multiple modalities, including restitution of civil rights; reparations in health, education, and housing; symbolic and collective reparations; and others.[40] Reparations may be paid to individual victims or their next of kin, or to collectivities, defined as:

The peasant and native communities and other population centers affected by the violence, that present certain characteristics such as: a concentration of individual violations, destruction, forced displacement, breaks or cracks in local authority structures, loss of family or communal infrastructure; and organized groups of non-returning displaced, who come from the affected communities but have resettled elsewhere.[41]

A pilot process in Peru grants hard-hit communities around 100,000 soles (US$33,500) each for development projects of their choosing. The first 440 of these ranged from projects for irrigation, electrification, water, and school and road improvements to projects to raise small livestock (*cuyes*, or guinea pigs), improve tourist infrastructure, and create a computer center for a small town. It is too early to evaluate the long-term effectiveness of these projects or the process by which they were allocated support, although an initial monitoring project found a number of shortcomings in the way in which the projects were chosen.[42] On a conceptual level, the projects had no tie to the nature or type of harms they were supposed to be redressing, which led to a lack of understanding of their purported purpose among beneficiaries. In practical terms, although the PIR design called for community participation in choosing the projects, in practice those with connections to local government or existing leaders tended to be most active in the discussions about potential projects, with little participation of women. Of course, these local-level power dynamics can exist more broadly in setting local development priorities. Reparations programs can take advantage of the lessons learned in this area by development practitioners in crafting ways of ensuring more widespread participation.

The Guatemalan truth commission recommended either individual or collective reparations, depending on the violation. To facilitate reconciliation without stigmatizing victims or perpetrators, it mandated that collective measures "should be carried out within a framework of territorially based projects to promote reconciliation, so that in addition to addressing reparation, their other actions and benefits also favor the entire population, without distinction between victims and perpetrators."[43] The Guatemalan PNR in theory includes both an individual compensation component and a large collective reparations component, including psychosocial and cultural reparations, productive projects for women, and education, health, and housing benefits for affected communities. In practice, to this point the major component of actual disbursements has been in individual reparations and in support for exhumations of mass graves, although in 2008 the program was being revamped.

In Morocco, the reparations paid by the Equity and Reconciliation Commission will include collective reparations focused on building infrastructure, including schools, clinics, and women's centers in the hardest-hit areas of the country. Individual reparations in Morocco took the form of compensation granted to individuals and were distributed through their local post office, along with a personalized letter of apology and acknowledgment, an explanation of the ruling in their individual case, and an application form for health coverage.[44] In Ghana, while most of the recommendations of the truth commission focused on individual payments, collective reparations, in the form of reconstruction of a destroyed market, were also part of the proposal.[45]

RELATIVE ADVANTAGES AND LIMITATIONS

The most effective and legitimate reparations program will be, generally speaking, one that combines individual and collective reparations of some kind (not necessarily monetary) and in which the reparative value of both types is paramount. For the most part, human rights practitioners and theorists writing about reparations have discouraged the use of nonexclusive goods and services as the principal, or even *a* principal, form of reparations. Such an approach may appeal as a practical and fail-safe approach to addressing mass violations, but there are a number of related problems. Among them is the concern that, at an individual level, social reconstruction as reparations will have a limited psychological impact, especially for those seeking individual reparations. In addition, survivors (and community members generally) may consider the upgrading of their communities to be a right provided by citizenship. Brandon Hamber notes that genuine reparation and healing do not occur only or primarily through the delivery of an object or acts of reparations, but also through the process that takes place around the object or act.[46] Advocates have pointed out that using reparations funds to provide nonexclusive goods or services to underserved populations (including but not limited to victims) allows the government to get off too easy: it need only do what it should be doing anyway and slap a reparations label on it.[47] Moreover, the beneficiaries are likely to consider the results as a product of official largesse rather than a legally defined obligation.

Nonetheless, governments tend to prefer the use of collective reparations, often for pragmatic reasons. Collective reparations may allow them to funnel programs into existing ministries, seem more efficient and less likely to be politically sensitive, require less new bureaucracy, and seem more acceptable to budget-conscious managers and creditors. Nonexclusive reparations also avoid problems associated with singling out victims or creating new resentments. Aid agencies also prefer to speak of "victim assistance" but not of reparations.

Indeed, despite the limitations of nonexclusivity and the danger of confusion outlined above, there may be some substantial advantages to collective reparations in the context of longer-term development, especially if used to complement some kind of individual reparations. First, in conditions where there is resource scarcity and a large number of victims, the choice may be between, on the one hand, collective reparations and, on the other hand, no material reparations at all, or individual compensation so meager as to be insulting. The provision of services, such as health and education, is at least of some concrete benefit to beneficiary populations. Moreover, by avoiding the creation of new resentments or the singling out of victims, nonexclusive access for larger segments of an affected population, including victims and perpetrators, can avoid the stigmatization and continuing marginalization that victim-only programs may engender.

Collective reparations can be designed to maximize their symbolic impact (although they often are not), through naming ceremonies, in combination with symbolic reparations of different kinds, or the like. It is important, in that sense, that collective reparations be explicitly tied to the nature of the harms, something that has been largely absent, for instance, in the Peruvian program. Moreover, the dangers of governments downplaying the rights-based, obligatory nature of reparations, allowing them to be perceived as merely largesse, are not limited to collective reparations, nor to reparations in the form of infrastructure improvements and service delivery. This risk may be just as applicable to individual compensation payments. In Guatemala, for example, victims' groups have complained that checks to victims of human rights violations are perceived as equivalent to checks issued at the same time to civil patrollers (who were often human rights violators) for forced labor. In that situation, there are also (with rare exceptions) no symbolic or apologetic aspects to the handover of funds, and groups report that people are confused and upset by different amounts being handed out to different families, notwithstanding the fact that the differing amounts had a clear logic behind them.[48]

Individual reparations in the form of lump-sum cash payments can create other types of difficulties. Anecdotal evidence about reparations negotiated in or ordered by the Inter-American System suggests that large payments (admittedly, an order of magnitude larger than those offered by most administrative reparations programs) have provoked community dislocations: historic leaders were abandoned in favor of a host of newcomers promising that they could obtain more and better reparations; towns were flooded with hucksters promising fast checks; long-lost and unknown family members suddenly appeared; and some recipients were assaulted or threatened into turning over the proceeds of their check.[49] Intra-family dynamics were also impacted: while in some cases women were empowered by receiving disposable cash in their names, in other cases male family members quickly laid claim to the compensation paid to their wives and mothers.[50]

A judicious combination of individual and collective reparations, however, may have potential positive impacts from a development standpoint beyond any impact on the state. It may, for example, help rebalance power at the local level by altering the dynamic between victims and the local power structure. After many armed conflicts, the victors constitute the local (official or de facto) leadership: they have the most resources (often as a result of appropriating the resources of victims), they are protected by rampant impunity from any kind of accountability, and they have sometimes morphed into local mafia or crime bosses. Victims, on the other hand, tend to be among the worst-off members of the community, because of a lack of one or more breadwinners, a lack of land, and/or health problems. Despite the return of peace, they tend to continue to be largely powerless and marginalized. As described earlier, this creates difficulties in fully engaging a substantial sector of the population in development efforts.

Under these circumstances, a well-designed reparations program can help rebalance local power. Most obviously, it can put much-needed resources into the hands of the worst off, which in turn may underscore and make public the state's recognition that those people have suffered disproportionately. But even such services as schools, roads, or health centers, which will benefit everyone living in the area, including perpetrators, bystanders, and rescuers as well as victims,[51] may help rebalance power in favor of victims. If needed services for all come to the community because of the needs—and, even better, the efforts—of victims and survivors, it provides them with a source of status and pride in the eyes of their neighbors. One source of status in many cultures and communities is the ability to bring resources to bear for the common good, to be a benefactor.[52] By making clear that victims are the reason that services arrive, even if those services benefit everyone, collective reparations can begin to address an existing power imbalance. This may, in turn, allow for broader participation by the victims in local governance.

Ideally, reparations programs should maximize the relative advantages of both the individual and collective approaches in combining them. Experiences dealing with the reintegration of ex-combatants may be helpful here. According to the World Bank's Sarah Cliffe, one planned modality of reintegration payments to demobilized combatants in Aceh involved a small individual cash payment, a somewhat larger voucher for individual services, such as school fees or vocational training, and a third component of community development vouchers. These vouchers, given to each ex-combatant, entitled him (and rarely her) to pool the resources represented by the voucher with others to fund community programs. The vouchers had no redeemable cash value except when combined with others, and could only be used for collective purposes.

This sort of scheme has a number of potential advantages when applied to reparations for victims. It allows for small individualized payments to be made, while at the same time focusing the bulk of resources elsewhere. It makes victims the agents of positive change in their communities, with positive impacts on local power dynamics. In this instance, that effect is strengthened because it is victims, collectively, who decide which projects are a priority, and these projects are clearly differentiated from regular government spending. It also creates a mechanism for collective decision-making that may outlive a reparations program, especially in communities with large numbers of victims. It maximizes the potential of collective reparations, while minimizing the drawbacks.

DELIVERY SYSTEMS AND DESTINATIONS OF REPARATIONS

As mentioned earlier, on a macro scale it is probably impossible to detect the economic contribution of reparations programs, if any, to development. However, on the community, family, and individual levels, the type of reparations, how monetary compensation or service packages are provided, and the possibility of using even modest amounts of money to jump-start local demand or local productive capacity may be significant. This is especially true given the baseline level of poverty of most beneficiaries. In this section, we examine some of the implications for using different modalities and delivery systems of reparations.

IN-KIND AND MONETARY REPARATIONS

The development impact of reparations may in some cultural contexts be different depending on whether reparations are made as in-kind restitution for losses or through cash payments as compensation. Restitution in kind includes housing materials, farm or grazing animals, seeds, and work and domestic implements, such as hoes and pots. While economists will argue that providing goods rather than cash is inefficient,[53] there are a few reasons why augmenting restitution in kind might have a differing impact on both the reparatory effect and on long-term development.

First, the symbolic values are different: replacement goods are a tangible connection to what was lost, whereas money is generic. This is why international law traditionally favors restitution if at all possible, and considers monetary compensation only for goods (and people) that cannot be replaced. Second, the relative values of money and goods in certain societies are different. Of all the potential types of reparations, money is the most controversial: in some places, monetary reparations for the death of a loved one is considered "blood money"; in others, cash is associated with colonial impositions and the necessity of wage labor; and in some places, wealth and worth are measured by money, while in others wealth is measured in cattle, pigs, or other goods, and personal worth is a function of giving away assets to the community rather than saving them. In many traditional non-Western cultures, different kinds of money have different uses, with cash often associated with more crass, commercial dealings, and other products (*pom*, shells, cattle, and offerings, among others) seen as valuable in solemn contractual or important interpersonal dealings.[54] While, in many cases, these differences may be nothing more than residual at this point, when highly symbolic, emotion-fraught goods are at stake they may resonate. Thus, in Rwanda, reparations paid from one community to another shortly after the genocide under traditional notions of gacaca[55] took the form of cattle—the traditional marker of wealth in east Africa—not cash. In East Timor, reparations for property and personal damage under the community reparations procedures included young pigs or chickens and ceremonial beads.[56]

At the same time, the line between personal and property losses may not be the same in all societies. In some places, domestic animals may be seen as sentient beings more akin to extended family, while in others even crops and domestic goods may have spirits. This is especially true in the cosmovision of indigenous cultures. Thus, the loss of these things may be felt as more than the loss of "mere" property. It is quite striking in the testimonies of victims the number of times people enumerate losses of crops, domestic animals, and tools with great specificity, even decades after the losses took place, as the testimony of the K'ekchi survivor in the opening quote of this chapter suggests.

Third, restitution in goods rather than compensation may change the intra-family and gender-based effects of the payment. The domestic economy tends to be the sphere of women, while the cash economy is that of men. Control over resources will then tend to depend on whose sphere they belong to, so that the provision of goods will more likely retain them in the hands of women. Domestic animals in particular are more likely than cash to be used for improving the family's nutrition or to augment an income stream under the control of women. In turn, studies show that income controlled by women is more likely to be spent on nutrition and the education of children.[57]

Admittedly, restitution in kind may not be practicable in urban areas, nor may it have the same resonance in all cultures, even rural ones. But even there, care should be taken to think about culturally appropriate and economically beneficial forms of noncash individual payments, whether these be housing materials or tools that would give victims the means to live with dignity. Thought should also be given to the nature and size of available markets: if the things people most need cannot be bought locally, cash payments may end up benefiting urban or foreign elites and not creating any kind of multiplier effect at the local level. They may even serve to drain the local economy of human resources, as when people use their reparations payments to send their young abroad to work as migrant labor.

CASH PAYMENT DELIVERY SYSTEMS

Most individual compensation programs have issued checks for the full value of the promised compensation. Two alternatives to lump-sum payments are bond issuance and periodic pensions. As a compensation distribution strategy, bonds allow the government to make an early statement that a wrong was done, and that reparation will be paid, while allowing the payment to be amortized over a number of years, thus lessening the fiscal impact. This allows a cash-strapped government to make larger payments to victims, at least in principle. For example, Argentina financed relatively large payments (on average close to $224,000) to the families of the disappeared by issuing bonds to them, payable in full over a sixteen-year period in 120 monthly payments, including interest and principal, after a 72-month grace period.[58]

While allowing for larger payments and an important early commitment to repair, however, issuing bonds creates two major problems: it forces the victims to bet on the government's future financial probity, and it forces them to wait a long time to be paid in full. Both problems surfaced in Argentina, when the 2001 financial crisis temporarily led to the suspension of the payment of bond proceeds, and forced many victims to sell their bonds on secondary markets for less than face value in order to obtain needed cash.[59] Thus, richer and younger recipients were able, in practice, to receive more than those who were poorer, older, or with fewer alternative sources of funds.

The Chilean reparations program provided for a periodic pension rather than a single lump-sum payment for the families of those killed or disappeared.[60] The payment, calculated according to average civil servant wages, is divided in fixed percentages among the spouse, parents, and children of the deceased or disappeared, with each child receiving the stipulated percentage until age twenty-five, even if the total exceeds 100 percent. Where adequate infrastructure for distribution of a pension exists, it may be preferable because some income will accrue to each family member, rather than running the risk of a lump sum being appropriated by the strongest. A pension is also a continuing reminder of the state's commitment to make good on the harm, even if the actual sums involved are far from adequate for support (as is the case in Chile). However, it also puts on the victims the risk that the state will decline to continue paying, leaving them with a smaller overall recovery. Periodic payments also require an ongoing administrative structure; in countries with other pension systems, pensions to victims may simply be folded into an existing administration, but where such programs are incipient or badly managed, victims may suffer.

On a national scale, the amounts involved in reparations payments are relatively small, but if those payments are relatively regionally concentrated and injected into otherwise cash-poor areas, they could make a significant difference at the local and regional level. They could result in a short-lived burst of spending that flames out in a year or two, leaving its recipients no better off; they could stimulate increased crime against recipients; or they could simply provide the means for larger numbers to flee the area and resettle in the United States, Europe, or large cities. In either case, the development impact at the local level will be minimal (except perhaps for eventually stimulating remittances from successful migrants).[61] On the other hand, reparations in the form of a small, regionally focused infusion of cash could serve as the catalyst for locally generated productive investment, local demand, and sustainable livelihoods, maximizing the impact of small amounts of money and tapping into local capabilities in ways that can be similar to the injection of micro-lending.

To encourage a link between such a reparations program and sustainable development would involve a process of education, training, and planning around finances and small investment opportunities, encouraging recipients to use local vendors when possible. It may also involve stimulating the creation of mini–credit unions or other local (formal or informal) banking systems with initial capital formed from reparations payments, which could give beneficiaries both access to credit and shares in a potentially profitable enterprise.[62]

Cash payments disbursed as part of disarmament, demobilization, and reintegration (DDR) programs regularly include training in both concrete skills and financial management, but with reparations programs little seems to be done beyond, at most, opening a bank account for recipients. Governments may object that it is paternalistic to tell people how to spend their money, but surely laying out options and possibilities is not the same as coercive limits to spending.[63] Indeed, when given the option early enough in a reparations process, beneficiaries may well see advantages to a community-development-centered approach that entails aspects of financial management.

To date, productive activities make up only a small part of the plans of reparations programs. In Guatemala, the PNR has set aside a small fund for productive activities and is beginning to explore how the program could support investments in, for example, solar energy. It also has a proposed fund for women structured along the model of a communal bank. Women would receive small amounts ($300 to $350) for productive activities, along with literacy classes. The program is still not under way, although several other (private) microcredit schemes are operating within the most hard-hit areas. Several of the Peruvian community projects referenced earlier involve productive activities, from planting pasture and buying grazing animals to a handicrafts center, although most focus on the basic infrastructure necessary for agriculture and rural life. In South Africa, the private sector Business Trust, in collaboration with local governments, is providing skills training and cofinancing for tourism and other productive projects in communities heavily affected by apartheid, including several that have recently recovered land. However, although the goals include reconciliation and reconstruction, the program is billed as an antipoverty rather than a reparations initiative.[64]

TRUST FUNDS

Reparations may also come from a trust fund created for the purpose of funding reparations to individuals, through service providers, or in the form of projects that benefit a community. Given that any reparations program requires time to lay its groundwork (at a minimum, the time needed to identify victims and projects and to acquire and distribute funds), the establishment of a trust fund at the beginning of a reparations process furthers at least four objectives. These objectives should be of interest both to development professionals and transitional justice professionals.

First, establishing a trust fund gives victims a concrete institution to focus on, both for advocacy and accountability, and lets them know that a definite pool of money exists for reparations. This should strengthen the demand for transparency and accountability with respect to that specific institution, which should assist the community to define the process of reparations and any resulting development impacts. This is very much in keeping with Sen's emphasis on development as freedom, which advocates for the right of a community to define its own development goals.

Second, establishing a trust fund allows the funding of discrete projects by application, potentially involving civil society and victims in a dialogue about how reparations could be best used in their particular situation. The involvement of civil society actors as intermediaries with a trust fund may also strengthen and promote civil society (although it may also create competition for funds and put less vocal communities at a disadvantage). Representatives of survivor communities can be included on the governing body of a trust fund to serve as links to those communities.

Third, a trust fund can maintain the flexibility to fund both collective and individual reparations as needed. As discussed above, a combined approach may maximize the impact of such programs, both in terms of dignification and in terms of development objectives. Without a trust fund, the flexibility to adjust to the local situation may be lost; for example, the reparations program may be defined at the outset as purely collective or purely individual in nature.

Fourth, a trust fund could be funded and managed by both domestic and international sources and actors, creating the possibility that the international community, especially those countries that may have had some connection to the conflict, could make a contribution to reparations for victims. A measure of international oversight may also be especially useful when domestic governance structures are weak. A major challenge for any trust fund, as with any reparations program, will be in securing adequate funding to fulfill its mandate. A number of government-created trust funds have had little success to date in attracting sufficient sources of capital.[65] At times, however, the trust fund form may prove useful in channeling resources from a wide variety of sources.

One prominent example of a trust fund is the Victims' Trust Fund (VTF) of the International Criminal Court, which, although connected to a court, may provide a useful model for trust funds in other situations.[66] The VTF was established by the Assembly of States Parties of the ICC in September 2002,[67] as provided for in Article 79 of the Rome Statute, which mandates that a trust fund be established for the benefit of victims of crimes within the jurisdiction of the court, and of their families. The VTF is therefore limited to serving victims of genocide, war crimes, and crimes against humanity. Victims, in this case, may include organizations and institutions as well as individuals.[68] The VTF has two mandates, the first to provide reparations to victims participating in cases before the court, upon a conviction, and the second to use "other resources" to provide interim assistance to affected communities, again for crimes within the jurisdiction of the court. The VTF may receive fines and forfeitures from convicted persons, but it may also receive funds from, among other sources, voluntary contributions from governments, international organizations, individuals, corporations, and other entities.[69]

The VTF may not undertake projects that would predetermine any issue before the court, cause prejudice to the rights of the accused, or compromise any of the issues related to the participation of victims in the situation, and it must receive the approval of the relevant chamber for its activities.[70] However, the fund otherwise retains discretion with respect to the form that this second mandate should take, and has decided to focus on projects of physical rehabilitation, psychological rehabilitation, and material support. Projects are selected from proposals solicited by the VTF Secretariat, in an increasingly formalized process, and are carried out by local partners, usually civil society groups. Although the VTF's work is in its early stages, its projects in the Democratic Republic of Congo and Uganda are expected to include microcredit programs targeted at reintegrating and supporting victims of rape and sexual violence and physical mutilation, as well as vocational training and counseling.[71]

As noted above, with a trust fund private actors could be involved in the funding of reparations, which may be especially appropriate where a link can be drawn between high profit margins and the origins or continuation of conflict. There are some precedents for private funding for reparations, although most of the examples are underscored by the reluctance of private actors to take any actions that could be construed as admitting culpability for the victims' harms. The South African TRC recommended that the private sector pay a one-time levy on corporate income and a donation of 1 percent of market capitalization of public companies, a retrospective surcharge on corporate profits, and a "wealth tax" to make repairs for the excess profits generated by apartheid-era wages and restrictions on labor, but the private sector refused; although, as noted above, the Business Trust has provided funds to hard-hit communities without naming them as reparations.[72] The Peruvian PIR is financed in part by the "óbolo minero," a voluntary contribution of 3 percent of net profits to the government by mining companies, but it is not specifically tied to reparations and has many claimants; a windfall profits tax on mining in

Peru was rejected. Private funds could also come from the tracing and confiscation of the assets of perpetrators and the ill-gotten gains of former leaders. The Peruvian PIR is also partially financed (15 million new soles for 2007, or approximately US$4,745,334) from a special fund set up to hold monies recovered from former government officials accused of embezzlement from the state.[73] However, there are multiple demands on the fund's assets, and once the current assets are depleted it is unclear where more will come from.

REPARATIONS AND THE INTERNATIONAL DEVELOPMENT COMMUNITY

To serve their expressive and symbolic function, reparations should come primarily from the parties responsible for the violations. Thus, in cases of state-sponsored human rights violations, it is important that reparations come from the state, rather than from outside agencies. However, this does not mean that IFIs, aid agencies, and private actors have no role to play. As donors, they provide funding and technical assistance that may determine which postconflict initiatives are implemented, either through the international community directly or by internationally assisted local partners. Transitional justice initiatives, in the form of prosecutions, truth-telling, and especially security sector reform and DDR, have been heavily dependent on external support and funds from multilateral and bilateral donors.

Reparations programs have also benefited from external support, but to a much lesser extent. This may in part be because it is difficult to show the necessary favorable payback periods and rates of return on investment in a reparations program, given its focus on intangibles, such as dignification and inclusion. At the same time, however, there may be risks, especially with large, multilateral donors, in allowing the conceptual basis or practical implementation of reparations projects to be too closely linked to or dependent on the other agendas of a donor. A bias in the culture, expertise, and mission of these institutions may lead to excessive focus on the monetizable aspects of programs, or to the imposition of unrealistic cost-benefit evaluation rubrics. Furthermore, in implementing their other agendas, donors may also make reparations programs more difficult: too strong a focus on cutting budget deficits and state payrolls to meet externally imposed structural adjustment, for example, will undermine a government's ability to fund any kind of reparation scheme.

On the other hand, an understanding among donors of the potential and purposes of reparations programs may overcome opposition and free up resources for such programs. For IFIs—and the World Bank in particular—the trend appears to be an increase in their postconflict work, and support for reparations programs could in theory become part of this growing postconflict agenda.[74] However, several of those involved in World Bank activities agreed that until now, at least, reparations projects have been mostly off the Bank's radar. In part, little is known about how reparations programs have worked and might work outside the context of post–World War II Germany, and there is therefore a sense that such programs are a luxury that poor countries cannot afford. In addition, reparations programs seem unnecessarily political: Why take the chance of exacerbating tensions between beneficiaries and those left out, or seeming to take sides in the past conflict, when the problem can be avoided by terming the provision of resources to those injured by the conflict "victim assistance" rather than "reparations"? A clear explanation of the rationale behind reparations programs and the difference between court-ordered tortlike remedies and the kinds of reparations possible after massive conflict would help bridge the gap between transitional justice practitioners and World Bank personnel, with the hope that in time economic actors would make room for and support reparations efforts alongside victim assistance.

At the same time, while most donors have been slow to provide significant material or technical support to reparations programs in a postconflict setting, they do provide significant support for DDR and for the reform of the security sector. Donors justify this focus by framing the reintegration of former combatants and the removal of arms from circulation as a security issue, which has been shown to have major implications for the stability of society and the economy. One recent study of aid patterns after conflict in Rwanda and Guatemala showed that, over the eleven-year period in question, security sector reform, including DDR, received the bulk of aid that went to transitional justice measures — more aid than went to criminal prosecutions, truth commissions, traditional justice mechanisms, or reparations.[75] However, it is not clear that this very strong emphasis on DDR, possibly to the detriment of other approaches, is the best means to stabilize the society and the economy.

While there are benefits to donors taking on DDR, there are also tensions if the demand for reparations is not taken up simultaneously. DDR often works by creating incentives for former combatants to turn in their weapons and reintegrate into society in a nonmilitaristic role. However, reparations, because it is not framed in terms of security, may be pushed off for months, if not years, after a conflict. This can create the perception that combatants or perpetrators will be compensated and given social benefits, whereas the victims may receive nothing. It is hard to advance goals of either reconciliation or social (re) integration or an end to the exclusion of marginalized groups without better attention to this imbalance. Indeed, as de Greiff has noted, at a rhetorical level some DDR efforts have begun to reflect this criticism, noting the broader context in which they operate while maintaining the primary aim of promoting security.[76] But, while working with different populations—combatants and victims—DDR and reparations programs share certain similar challenges. Both types of programs must, for example, define beneficiaries, benefits, and the goals of the program.

Reparations and development agency agendas overlap during the period of planning and programming after a conflict has ended, when there is an opportunity for donors to understand the extent to which national funds will need to be committed to reparations programs, and to hold governments accountable for promises to institute reparations initiatives. Bilateral agencies and the UNDP have provided significant support for reparations initiatives within the context of support for transitional justice generally. As a percentage of overall development aid, though, support for transitional justice has been minor—in the study referred to above covering Guatemala and Rwanda, aid for all transitional justice came to about 5 percent of all development aid.[77] About 20 percent of all aid to transitional justice in Guatemala went to reparations—for mental health, exhumations, and assistance in setting up the PNR—while in Rwanda the figure was 5 percent—and was used for mental health program support and commemorative museums and sites.

In addition, the UNDP in some situations has served as the administrative vehicle for national and international funds related to reparations.[78] Together with the German cooperation agency GTZ, the UNDP has been involved in the conceptualization of the reparations program in Guatemala and especially with the psychosocial aspects of working with hard-hit communities.[79] The UNDP identifies reparations programs as one of the "four pillars" of transitional justice and recognizes both financial and nonfinancial measures as reparations. In practice, however, the UNDP does not initiate programs but responds to government requests. If a reparations program has, for instance, been included in a peace agreement or the recommendations of an official truth commission, the UNDP can follow up, but otherwise it is limited to serving as an "honest broker" with strong government connections in a dialogue between government and civil society.

The most important contribution that international development actors could make to creating viable reparations programs would be to build consideration of reparations into the initial discussions of government budgets for the immediate post–armed conflict years. Setting up reparations discussions at the point of negotiation of peace accords or initial government plans would, for example, allow them to become part of a UNDP assistance framework, which would then permit follow-up and would make it more difficult for governments to cite budgetary impossibility as a reason not to implement reparations. To the degree that development actors play a role in the peace accords and initial government plans, they should ensure that reparations are at least a viable possibility.

CONCLUSIONS AND RECOMMENDATIONS

It is under a capabilities-centered, bottom-up approach to development that the strongest links can be made to transitional justice generally, and reparations programs in particular. Like development more broadly, reparations is a process, not a deliverable. The most important determinant of success is how things are done—that is, whether the discussion and delivery of reparations are set up in a way that makes the goals of acknowledgment, respect, restoration of dignity, and civic interest in the betterment of lives a felt reality for survivors.

A well-designed and implemented reparations program can have follow-on and spillover effects that affect longer-term development. Such a program can help to create sustainable, culturally relevant change while addressing both root causes and survivors' immediate needs. Reparations can play an important role in changing citizens' relationship to the state, in strengthening civic trust, and in creating minimum conditions for victims to contribute to building a new society. At the same time, the resources—human, institutional, and financial—available for reparations will obviously vary depending on the level of development. While the two processes are different and should not be conflated or merged, there are a number of ways in which they can strengthen and complement each other. Indeed, care should be taken to ensure that reparations programs *complement* development efforts (and related state functions) rather than *duplicate* them.

For development experts, especially those in aid agencies and IFIs, the needs and contours of a reparations program need to be considered early on, in initial donor conferences or during negotiations for a post–armed conflict government. Governments need to consider both a budget and the specificity of programming as early as possible. Those funding DDR should simultaneously think about funding reparations. For both DDR and reparations programs, if individuals receive cash, they should also receive some training in budgeting and investing so as to maximize the long-term return. Transitional justice experts need to better understand the financing process and engage with banks, governments, and donors early enough to influence budget allocations for the three- to five-year planning period. Post–armed conflict reconstruction and initial economic development planning will overlap with the time frame in which reparations are being negotiated for the victims of the conflict—after initial emergency and humanitarian aid has ended but before a business-as-usual phase sets in. The lack of adequate provision and sequencing has meant that many reparations programs only come about twenty or more years after the end of the violations they are meant to redress, when both their material and symbolic effect is attenuated. It may be, however, that a time lag is inevitable, and that reparations should be conceived of as a multigenerational effort that takes into account the multigenerational effects of trauma.[80] Thus, reparations for the first generation could focus on livelihood reconstruction, psychosocial and medical assistance, and dignification, while for the second and third generations a focus on education and social empowerment would be appropriate.

Both collective and individual reparations can contribute to dignification—or not. Collective reparations should not be automatically rejected by human rights groups and NGOs. Rather, they should be designed to maximize both the perception that victims are contributing to their community and the ability of victims' and survivors' groups to establish priorities for social spending. While individual reparations are important, they need not be entirely, or even mostly, made up of a one-time cash award. In particular, in-kind restitution of domestic animals, housing materials, seed, and tools may have more positive effects in rural communities. Conversely, reparations must have at least some individualized component to fulfill its goals—the provision of basic services, no matter how needed or how well executed, will not serve the same functions.

In this context, those designing reparations programs should make conscious efforts to rebalance power after a process of victimization, making the survivors and their descendants empowered to shape and take ownership over the process of reparation. Those affected by violence should ideally see themselves as and be agents of positive change, with the capacity to organize around solving shared problems.

States planning reparations programs should think about service provision that does not duplicate existing services but rather improves these for all while providing tailored and complementary help to victims and survivors. They should also maximize the ability of such programs, where needed, to eventually merge into the regular government (and budget). They should use NGO providers, where needed, to infuse programs with new knowledge and energy, in the areas of community mental health, exhumations/forensics, or participatory budgeting, for example.

Reparations cannot, and should not, replace long-term development strategies. But they can be designed to be the initial "victim-friendly" face of the state, creating habits of trust and rights possession among their target population that will set the stage for a more positive long-term interaction between the state and a sizeable group of its citizens.

NOTES

1   Testimony of K'ekchi survivor, Guatemala, in Carlos E. Paredes, *Te Llevaste Mis Palabras: Efectos psicosociales de la violencia política en comunidades K'ekchi'es* (Guatemala: Equipo de Estudios Comunitarios y Accion Psicosical [ECAP], 2006), 195 (author's translation).

2   At the outset, we acknowledge that both reparations and development may take place in other contexts. For example, reparations have been awarded to groups in nonconflict settings in the United States and Canada. Reparations and development may intersect in such cases as well, in that such groups — for example, indigenous peoples or immigrant groups — may be relatively economically disadvantaged in the context of a more developed country. Reparations may be ordered by courts or may be part of an administrative scheme; we focus here on the latter. For the sake of simplicity, this chapter will not address those issues, but will try to more thoroughly address a smaller set of issues. Moreover, we acknowledge at the outset the shortcomings of "post–armed conflict" and "transitional" as labels. We use them as shorthand for situations where massive violations of humanitarian law or serious human rights violations have occurred in the recent past, with a particular focus on cases where there have been large numbers of victims, followed by a change in regime or a negotiated end to the fighting. We also acknowledge that there may be significant differences between "postconflict" and "postdictatorship" situations, which we take up in the third section. Finally, it is important to recognize at the outset that most large-scale reparations programs, especially after armed conflict, remain in their infancy, and so descriptions must be based largely on plans and proposals, and any evaluation of their effectiveness is premature.

3   United Nations, *UN Basic Principles and Guidelines on the Right to a Remedy and Reparation for Victims of Gross Violations of International Human Rights Law and Serious Violations of International Humanitarian Law* (hereafter *Basic Principles*), A/RES/60/147, March 21, 2006,

VII, 11. For a thorough examination of the *Basic Principles* and other sources of the right to reparation in international law, see Dinah Shelton, "The United Nations Principles and Guidelines on Reparations: Context and Contents," in *Out of the Ashes: Reparations for Victims of Gross and Systematic Human Rights Violations*, ed. K. De Feyter, S. Parmentier, M. Bossuyt, and P. Lemmens (Antwerpen-Oxford: Intersentia, 2005).

4   *Basic Principles*, IX, 15.

5   Ibid., IX, 19–23.

6   See Naomi Roht-Arriaza, "Reparations Decisions and Dilemmas," *Hastings International and Comparative Law Review* 27, no. 2 (2004): 160–65.

7   This is not to argue that reparations for violations of economic, social, and cultural rights are not possible, simply that no program to date labeled as reparations has attempted to redress such violations in the absence of concurrent violations of basic civil and political rights.

8   Amartya Sen, *Development as Freedom* (New York: Knopf, 1999).

9   The Nairobi Declaration on Women's and Girls' Right to a Remedy and Reparation, March 2007, sect. 3(B).

10 The Millennium Development Goals (MDGs) were developed out of the eight chapters of the United Nations Millennium Declaration, signed in September 2000. The eight goals are: eradicate extreme poverty and hunger; achieve universal primary education; promote gender equality and empower women; reduce child mortality; improve maternal health; combat HIV/AIDS, malaria, and other diseases; ensure environmental sustainability; and develop a global partnership for development. For the most part, the goals are to be achieved by 2015.

11 See, e.g., Paul Romer, "Endogenous Technological Change," *Journal of Political Economy* 98, no. 5 (October 1990): 71–102; and, more generally, William Easterly, *The White Man's Burden: Why the West's Efforts to Aid the Rest Have Done So Much Ill and So Little Good* (New York: Penguin Press, 2006).

12 See, e.g., International Monetary Fund, "Microfinance: A View from the Fund," January 25, 2005, 2, www.imf.org/external/np/pp/eng/2005/012505.pdf; and Thomas Dichter, "Hype and Hope: The Worrisome State of the Microcredit Movement," Microfinance Gateway, www.microfinancegateway.org/content/article/detail/31747. A number of countries in Latin America, including Brazil, Ecuador, and Bolivia, have been experimenting with economic development strategies based on the "glocal"—that is, an articulation of markets and production starting at the local level and creating linkages upward. See, e.g., Alberto Acosta, *Desarrollo Glocal* (Quito, Ecuador: Corporacion Editora Nacional, 2005).

13 See, for instance, the Millennium Challenge Account.

14 John Paul Lederach and Michelle Maiese, "Conflict Transformation," October 2003, www.beyondintractability.org/essay/transformation.

15 Shahrbanou Tadjbakhsh, "Human Security: Concepts and Implications with an Application to Post-Intervention Challenges in Afghanistan," Centre d'études et de recherches internationals, No. 117–118, September 2005, www.ceri-sciencespo.com/publica/etude/etude117_118.pdf.

16 UNDP, "A Human Rights-Based Approach to Development Programming in UNDP—Adding the Missing Link," Geneva, August 2001, www.undp.org/governance/docs/HR_Pub_Missinglink.pdf.

17 The most important IFI for purposes of this discussion is the World Bank Group, itself divided into a commercial arm, the International Finance Corporation (IFC), making market-rate loans, and the International Development Association (IDA), which loans at below-market rates to very poor countries for both projects and support of government budgets. Regional banks, such as the Inter-American Bank and the Asian Development Bank, also provide project finance. The International Monetary Fund (IMF), in contrast, does not provide project finance but serves as a lender of last resort in cases of currency or commercial imbalance. The IMF sets conditions on its loans that are often echoed by the World Bank as well as by commercial and state lenders, in effect making it very difficult for states that defy its prescriptions to borrow money. That is slowly beginning to change with the advent of such states as Venezuela and China willing to lend under different conditions, but it is still the norm. See James M. Cypher and James L. Dietz, *The Process of Economic Development*, 2nd ed. (London: Taylor and Francis, 2004), chap. 17.

18 See, e.g., Jeffrey Sachs, *The End of Poverty* (New York: Penguin Press, 2005); for the World Bank's account of the causes and measurements of poverty, see web.worldbank.org/WBSITE/EXTERNAL/TOPICS/EXTPOVERTY/0,,contentMDK:20153855~menuPK:373757~pagePK:148956~piPK:216618~theSitePK:336992,00.html.

19 Kaushik Basu, "Participatory Equity, Identity, and Productivity: Policy Implications for Promoting Development," Center for Analytic Economics (CAE) Working Paper No. 06-06, Cornell University, May 2006.

20 UNDP, "A Human Rights-Based Approach to Development Programming," 7.

21 Pablo de Greiff, "Justice and Reparations," in *The Handbook of Reparations* (hereafter *The Handbook*), ed. Pablo de Greiff (Oxford: Oxford University Press, 2006).

22 In subsequent regulations implementing the program, specific medicines likely to be needed by victims/survivors were listed and covered.

23 See Marcie Mersky and Naomi Roht-Arriaza, "Guatemala," in *Victims Unsilenced: The Inter-American Human Rights System and Transitional Justice in Latin America*, ed. Due Process of Law Foundation (Washington: Due Process of Law Foundation, 2007).

24 Interview with Leticia Velásquez, Technical Assistant Director, PNR, Guatemala City, July 10, 2007.

25 Elizabeth Lira, "The Reparations Policy for Human Rights Violations in Chile," in *The Handbook*, 71.

26 This idea emerged from a discussion of one of the authors with Christian Correa of ICTJ, for which we are grateful.

27 José López Ricci, "Vigilancia de Proyectos y Actividades Relacionados con el Plan Integral de Reparaciones en Huancavelica," Instituto de Defensa Legal, June 2006.

28 Tlhoki Mofokeng and Marjorie Jobson, "Repairing the Past: Reparations and Transitions to Democracy: Debates on Transitional Justice: Where Are We in South Africa?" Khulumani Support Group, Cape Town (March 2004): 9.

29 Mofokeng and Jobson, "Repairing the Past."

30 Interview with Sarah Cliffe, World Bank, Washington, DC, June 8, 2007.

31 In earlier efforts in the Southern Cone and in South Africa, the commissions did create at least an initial roster of victims.

32 See Hernando de Soto, *The Mystery of Capital* (New York: Basic Books, 2000), on the advantages of formalization. Of course, de Soto's theory that formalization of title will result in unleashing capital for productive use has been subject to critiques. Formalization may be more easily taken advantage of by elites better able to "work the system," and the poor may end up worse off if formalization results in easy credit that leads to increased indebtedness and eventual asset loss.

33 See also the chapter by Chris Huggins, "Linking Broad Constellations of Ideas: Transitional Justice, Land Tenure Reform, and Development," in this volume.

34 On the Land Claim courts process, see, e.g., Joan G. Fairweather, *A Common Hunger: Land Rights in Canada and South Africa* (Calgary: University of Calgary Press, 2006), 109–11.

35 De Soto, *The Mystery of Capital*.

36 Lira, "The Reparations Policy for Human Rights Violations in Chile."

37 Ruth Rubio-Marín, "Gender and Collective Reparations in the Aftermath of Conflict and Political Repression," in *The Politics of Reconciliation in Multicultural Societies*, ed. Will Kymlicka and Bashir Bashir (Oxford: Oxford University Press, 2008).

38 Truth and Reconciliation Commission of South Africa Report, vol. 5, para. 46, reproduced in *The Handbook*, 800.

39 Ibid., paras. 94–155, in *The Handbook*, 810–13.

40 Ley No. 28592, Ley que crea el Plan Integral de Reparaciones (PIR), in Lisa Magarrell and Julie Guillerot, *Reparaciones en la Transición Peruana-Memorias de un Proceso Inacabado* (Lima: Asociación Pro Derechos Humanos [APRODEH] / ICTJ / OXFAM-GB, 2006), 259.

41 Ibid.

42 APRODEH-ICTJ, "Sistema de Vigilancia a Reparaciones," Reporte Nacional de Vigilancia del Programa de Reparaciones Colectivas, 2008, www.aprodeh.org.pe/reparaciones/sistema/reparaciones/reportenacional.pdf.

43 Report of the Commission for Historical Clarification, Conclusions and Recommendations, pt. III, Reparatory Measures, para. 10, shr.aaas.org/guatemala/ceh/report/english/recs3.html.

44   International Center for Transitional Justice, "Truth-Seeking and Reparations in Morocco," ICTJ Reparations Unit Country Summary, April 2008.

45   National Reconciliation Commission Report (Accra, Ghana, April 2005).

46   Brandon Hamber, "Narrowing the Micro and Macro: A Psychological Perspective on Reparations in Societies in Transition," in *The Handbook*, 580.

47   See Roht-Arriaza, "Reparations Decisions and Dilemmas"; de Greiff, "Justice and Reparations"; and Rubio-Marín, "Gender and Collective Reparations."

48   Amounts depended on the nature of the violation (i.e., whether the victim was killed) and also on how many family members suffered the violation, in order to deal with situations where entire extended families were nearly wiped out. Amounts ranged from Q20,000 to Q44,000 (US$2,608 to $5,737).

49   Mersky and Roht-Arriaza, "Guatemala." Elizabeth Lira notes a similar result in the Mapuche areas of Chile, where "in very poor communities the economic reparations distorted family relations of solidarity and negatively affected family and community networks." Lira, "The Reparations Policy for Human Rights Violations in Chile," 63.

50   This information is based on discussions in Guatemala regarding reparations paid as a result of Inter-American cases, especially interviews with Olga Alicia Paz of ECAP and with massacre survivors in Plan de Sanchez. See also Mersky and Roht-Arriaza, "Guatemala."

51   These categories are obviously fluid: the same individual may fall into more than one category by, e.g., rescuing some people while attacking others; within families there are often representatives of all of them. It may be impossible to benefit only the "right" victims; Peru's PIR, e.g., excludes members of subversive groups, but this provision has raised a host of criticisms that the exclusion is discriminatory and sweeps much too broadly.

52   This phenomenon takes different forms in different cultures. It is (derogatorily) talked about as the ability to act as a godfather, big man, or mover and shaker, but the same impulse motivates, at least in part, large wedding feasts and hefty donations to the ballet or new hospital wing.

53   Welfare economists stress the ability of cash recipients to satisfy a wider range of preferences and the smaller administrative costs of cash disbursements. Daniel M. Hausman and Michael S. McPherson, "Beware of Economists Bearing Advice," *Policy Options* 18, no. 7 (September 1997): 16–19.

54   There is a vast literature on commodities, gifts, and currencies and their meaning. See, e.g., Andrew Strathern and Pamela J. Stewart, "Objects, Relationships and Meanings," in *Money and Modernity: State and Local Currencies in Melanesia*, ed. David Akin and Joel Robbins (Pittsburgh: University of Pittsburgh Press, 1999), speaking of the Nuer of East Africa: "Limits on the interconvertibility of money and cattle are based on the idea that money 'has no blood' and does not carry the procreative power that cattle do. The fact

that humans and cattle do have blood is given by Nuer as the reason why cattle can stand for people in reproductive exchanges (bridewealth, blood payments) as pigs do in New Guinea." See also C. A. Gregory, *Gifts and Commodities* (London: Academic Press, 1982).

55 We do not refer here to the "legal gacaca" created to hold low-level perpetrators accountable, but to the spontaneous version that sprung up in the years immediately following 1994.

56 See Patrick Burgess, "A New Approach to Restorative Justice: East Timor's Community Reconciliation Processes," in *Transitional Justice in the Twenty-First Century*, ed. Naomi Roht-Arriaza and Javier Mariezcurrena (New York: Cambridge University Press, 2006).

57 Sen, *Development as Freedom*, 195–98.

58 María José Guembe, "Economic Reparations for Grave Human Rights Violations: The Argentinean Experience," in *The Handbook*, 40–41.

59 Ibid.; see also Marcelo A. Sancinetti and Marcelo Ferrante, *El Derecho Penal en la Protección de los Derechos Humanos* (Buenos Aires: Hammurabi, 1999).

60 Law 19.123 of February 8, 1992, cited in Lira, "The Reparations Policy for Human Rights Violations in Chile," 59.

61 Pablo Fajnzylber and J. Humberto López, eds., *Remittances and Development: Lessons from Latin America* (Washington, DC: World Bank, 2008).

62 See Hans Dieter Seibel with Andrea Armstrong, "Reparations and Microfinance Schemes," in *The Handbook*, 676.

63 The debate over whether training in financial planning and legal protection should accompany individual reparations or whether this would imply that recipients cannot be trusted with the money was also present in South Africa. See Christopher J. Colvin, "Overview of the Reparations Program in South Africa," in *The Handbook*, 192.

64 See discussion of the Trust's Community Investment Program at www.btrust.org.za/index.aspx?_=127&id=9&sid=4.

65 Alexander Segovia, "Financing Reparations Programs: Reflections from International Experience," in *The Handbook*.

66 See also the example of Sierra Leone's Special Fund for War Victims.

67 Information on the VTF is at www.iccnow.org/?mod=vtfbackground.

68 Rome Statute, Rules of Procedure and Evidence, Rule 85.

69 Resolution ICC-ASP/1/Res.6.

70 Regulation 50 requires the board to notify the court, and to wait for a response from the relevant chamber, or the expiration of the requisite time period, before undertaking a project. See, e.g., the filings made in the situations of the Democratic Republic of Congo and Uganda: www.redress.org/reports/2008%20March%20April%20Legal%20Update.pdf; www.icc-cpi.int/iccdocs/doc/doc470235.PDF; www.icc-cpi.int/iccdocs/doc/doc459788.PDF.

71 "Trust Fund for Victims Program Overview," 2008, on file with the authors.

72 Colvin, "Overview of the Reparations Program in South Africa," 209.

73 The Fondo Especial de Administración de Dinero Obtenido Ilícitamente a Perjuicio del Estado (FEDEDOI) holds funds recovered from ex-president Alberto Fujimori and his officials. According to the National Human Rights Commission, it has been used for the PIR. Informe CCDDHH 2006, citing Proyecto de Ley 110-2006-PE.

74 World Bank, "The Role of the World Bank in Conflict and Development: An Evolving Agenda," no date, 9, web.worldbank.org/servlets/ECR?contentMDK=20482342&sitePK=4 07546.

75 Ingrid Samset, Stina Petersen, and Vibeke Wang, "Foreign Aid to Transitional Justice: The Cases of Rwanda and Guatemala, 1995–2005," in Kai Ambos, Judith Large, and Marieke Wierda, eds., *Building a Future on Peace and Justice: Studies on Transitional Justice, Peace and Development* (Heidelberg: Springer, 2009).

76 Pablo de Greiff, "DDR and Reparations: Establishing Links Between Peace and Justice Instruments," in *Building a Future on Peace and Justice: Studies on Transitional Justice, Peace and Development: The Nuremberg Declaration on Peace and Justice*, ed. Kai Ambos, Judith Large, and Marieke Wierda (Heidelberg: Springer, 2009).

77 Samset, Petersen, and Wang, "Maintaining the Process?" 13.

78 The UNDP undertakes a wider range of support activities in the field of transitional justice—coordination, program management and implementation, situation analysis and needs assessments, facilitation of national dialogue processes, technical assistance and fund management, capacity development, and information management. Examples of UNDP transitional justice support include support for the Timor-Leste Commission for Reception, Truth and Reconciliation; a role in the creation of the Sierra Leone Truth and Reconciliation Commission; and support for the Truth and Reconciliation Commission in Peru, where the UNDP acted as a channel for donor funding. The UNDP was also involved in Guatemala's Historical Clarification Commission and was key in funding psychosocial support in the context of exhumations and in keeping Guatemala's PNR alive when the bank holding the program's funding collapsed in 2006. UNDP Bureau for Crisis Prevention and Recovery, "UNDP and Transitional Justice: An Overview," January 2006, 5–8.

79 Informe de la Evaluación Conjunta del Programa Nacional de Resarcimiento y de los Programas de Apoyo al PNR de GTZ y PNUD, Guatemala, December 14, 2007, www.berghof-peacesupport.org/publications/Informe%20final%20EC%20PNR.pdf.

80 For a discussion of the multigenerational effects of genocide, repression, and other trauma, see generally Yael Danieli, ed., *International Handbook of Multigenerational Legacies of Trauma* (New York: Springer, 1998).

CHAPTER 6

Enhancing Justice and Development Through Justice-Sensitive Security Sector Reform

Alexander Mayer-Rieckh and Roger Duthie[1]

Security and development are increasingly understood as being linked, particularly in countries emerging from armed conflict. This can be seen in the emergence in the late 1990s and the growing use and acceptance since then of the concept of security sector reform (SSR). While it does not necessarily refer to new practices or ideas employed or thought up only among donors, SSR as a concept linking security and development did originate in the donor community. From its inception, SSR has been articulated explicitly in terms of its connection to development. It is, most would agree, a development concept. SSR is also a notion from which a number of links can be drawn to transitional justice. The clearest example of this might be vetting measures aimed at excluding human rights abusers from security sector institutions, but others are explored below. While this is acknowledged in the field of SSR, however, the links between SSR and transitional justice have received much less attention than those between SSR and development. There is much less consensus that SSR also is a transitional justice concept.

In this chapter, we seek to map out some of the links between transitional justice, SSR, and development. We first review the concept of SSR from a development perspective, and then examine it from a transitional justice perspective. Our main argument is that while in practice transitional justice and SSR have often seemed to be in tension, there is potential for them to complement each other as well, and to a certain extent to converge in the notion of a justice-sensitive approach to SSR. On the one hand, development-focused SSR is a critical tool in the prevention of the recurrence of widespread and serious abuses, which is an important long-term objective of transitional justice, and it is a directly enabling factor for certain transitional justice measures, such as prosecutions and truth-telling. On the other hand, we suggest that a justice-sensitive SSR—one that takes seriously the concerns of transitional justice and directly deals with past serious human rights abuses—conceptually fits within the broad framework of SSR as a development tool.

In addition, we propose that a justice-sensitive approach may have the potential to enhance the developmental impact of SSR by improving the legitimacy of security institutions and promoting the inclusion of citizens. Justice-sensitive SSR may serve to improve legitimacy in the long term by endorsing a more holistic concept of accountability, encouraging not only structural but also symbolic reforms, and making a case for coherence of SSR with other transitional justice measures. A justice-sensitive approach also seeks to reinforce the inclusion of all citizens, but in particular of victims and other marginalized groups, by advancing their representation among the security sector's personnel, encouraging the establishment of structures that meet their specific security needs, and having a keen interest to directly empower them as citizens. At the same time, though, a justice-sensitive approach to SSR in transitional and developing contexts will be subject to the same constraints and challenges as all SSR work, including those related to coherence, capacity, and local ownership and politics. In this sense, transitional justice practitioners engaged in SSR should learn from the experiences of SSR and development actors. Dialogue and coordination are called for in order to promote mutual reinforcement of transitional justice and SSR.

SECURITY SECTOR REFORM

There is no commonly agreed upon definition of the concept of security sector reform. Two of the most accepted but somewhat different definitions are those articulated by the United Nations (UN) and by the Organisation for Economic Co-operation and Development's Development Assistance Committee (OECD DAC). The UN's definition of security sector, as contained in a 2008 report of the UN secretary-general, refers to the range of "structures, institutions and personnel responsible for the management, provision and oversight of security in a country." Security sector reform, according to the report, "describes a process of assessment, review and implementation as well as monitoring and evaluation led by national authorities that has as its goal the enhancement of effective and accountable security for the State and its peoples without discrimination and with full respect for human rights and the rule of law."[2] The OECD DAC uses the term "security system," which is broader than the UN's concept of security sector and includes core security actors, management and oversight bodies, justice and the rule of law institutions, and nonstatutory security forces.[3] The OECD includes both the judicial sector and nonstate actors in the security system; the UN, on the other hand, states that elements of the judicial sector "in many instances" are included, and that nonstate actors "could be considered part of the security sector." In both definitions, the idea of providing security both effectively and accountably is key. The two major categories of SSR activities are "measures aimed at restructuring and improving the capacity of the security forces and justice institutions" and "measures aimed at strengthening civilian management and democratic oversight of the security forces and justice institutions."[4] Both the UN and the OECD stress the importance of national or local ownership of the process, and the OECD also emphasizes sustainability as a key principle.[5]

In this chapter, we use the term "security *sector* reform" because we wish to focus our analysis primarily on security institutions, but we do not disagree with the OECD DAC definition and the idea of a holistic and coherent approach to addressing security and justice issues.[6] We also focus on SSR in particular contexts—postconflict and post-authoritarian situations—which allows us to link it to transitional justice. "What makes post-conflict SSR different" from SSR in other contexts, explains the SSR expert Heiner Hänggi, "is the fact that [in addition to aiming at effective and accountable security] it has to tackle a third objective, namely, to address the specific legacies of violent conflict and to focus on issues that are rarely pursued in SSR programmes." These include the need "to redress past crimes and atrocities and to promote reconciliation."[7] As will be discussed below, little attention has been paid to this third objective of SSR, and how it relates to transitional justice, beyond the acknowledgment that dealing with the legacies of the violent past is important to the contribution that SSR can make to governance.[8]

THE DEVELOPMENT APPROACH TO SSR

The reform of security institutions has been practiced at many times, in developed and developing countries, and before, during, and after armed conflicts and periods of authoritarian rule. The specific notion of "security sector reform"—reforming the security sector so that it provides effective security for citizens through a democratically accountable process with the long-term goal of contributing to sustainable development—originated in the 1990s as an explicit development concept. SSR "provided an overarching concept that intellectually justified the development community's venture into security-related activities."[9]

When Clare Short, the then UK secretary of state for International Development, used the term in 1999, she spoke of poverty reduction as the main development priority, and of "bloated, secretive, repressive, undemocratic and poorly structured security sectors" as a principle obstacle to poverty reduction. They were seen as an obstacle because they divert resources from development purposes; because their involvement in the economy leads to gross inefficiency, corruption, and lower levels of investment; and because they are a source of insecurity, armed conflict, and human rights abuses—which have enormous development costs—rather than security, which she described as an "essential prerequisite for sustainable development" and a priority of the poor, who need it for purposes of work, education, and health. "We are therefore entering this new area of security sector reform in order to strengthen our contribution to development."[10] The UK Department for International Development's (DFID) use of SSR as a development concept[11] subsequently spread throughout the donor and international community.

Currently, the UN and the OECD DAC both understand SSR similarly to DFID in terms of its developmental objectives. The secretary-general's report on SSR speaks fairly broadly about security as a prerequisite for development, security sectors as an obstacle to development, and reform of these sectors being aimed at contributing to development. "The most fundamental lesson for the United Nations"—regarding SSR—"is that security is a precondition for sustainable peace, development and human rights," argues the report. "In development contexts," however, "an inefficient and unaccountable security sector can be a major obstacle to democratic governance and can undermine the implementation of poverty reduction strategies." Therefore, the "goal of the United Nations in security sector reform is to support States and societies in developing effective, inclusive and accountable security institutions so as to contribute to international peace and security, sustainable development and the enjoyment of human rights for all."[12] The OECD DAC refers to security system reform as a "development approach," similarly centered on the idea of security (and the provision of security) being a precondition of development: "A democratically run, accountable and efficient security system helps reduce the risk of conflict, thus creating an enabling environment for development." Just as with health and education, security is a question of service delivery that is "of critical importance for supporting sustainable development."[13] SSR appears in certain developing countries' Poverty Reduction Strategy Papers (PRSPs) as well. Liberia's PRSP, for example, states that the "central goal for the security sector is to create a secure and peaceful environment, both domestically and in the sub-region, that is conducive to sustainable, inclusive, and equitable growth and development."[14]

Analysts outside the UN and donor community also refer to SSR as fundamentally linked to development. Hänggi, for example, describes it as being "driven by the understanding that an ineffective, inefficient and poorly governed security sector represents a decisive obstacle to sustainable development, democratisation, conflict prevention and postconflict peacebuilding."[15] According to Michael Brzoska, the SSR agenda has a "clear normative and practical commitment to development. Reform is thus ideally planned and implemented in a way that maximizes its contribution to development."[16] Brzoska is more specific, though, about the specific links between SSR and development—that is, about how SSR may contribute to development. He cites four main intermediate goals of SSR that may lead to poverty reduction, which we paraphrase here:

- reduction of spending on security forces, which makes resources available for poverty-reduction activities;
- improved security/protection for individuals and their property; crime and violence can lower growth rates, destroy livelihoods, and reduce confidence in savings and investment, and, importantly, they affect poor people more than others;
- improved contribution of the security sector to conflict prevention and management, as armed conflict is seen as a major cause of poverty; unreformed security forces can be a source of conflict; and
- greater participation of poor people in decision-making and oversight related to the security sector and greater access to security and justice.

According to Brzoska, these links are well established, but there are acknowledged gaps and the various objectives are not without internal tensions.[17]

In terms of the first point, a World Bank and International Monetary Fund (IMF) study has shown that higher levels of military expenditure do on average lead to lower growth rates and income levels, especially in developing countries. The economist Paul Collier argues that this expenditure can be reduced in ways that do not increase the risk of conflict.[18]

The second two points are based on the connections between security and development, and the idea that more effective and accountable security institutions will increase security. At the individual and community level, Frances Stewart contends that, in addition to security leading to development, security is itself an "intrinsic aspect of development." If the objective of development is "the enlargement of human choices" (human development), then security, even defined narrowly as relating to interpersonal violence or the risk of it, is part of development because insecurity "cuts life short and thwarts the use of human potential."[19] That lack of physical security is a major concern of the poor, and that such institutions as the police are often seen by the poor as sources of that insecurity, has been an extremely important finding of World Bank poverty assessments.[20] The broader notion of "human security" has also influenced SSR as a concept and provides a conceptual link to development: human security posits the protection of the individual as its primary goal and recognizes either that violent threats to individuals are "strongly associated with poverty, lack of state capacity and various forms of socio-economic and political inequity" (conceived narrowly), or that threats to individuals "include hunger, disease and natural disasters" (conceived more broadly).[21] Some, indeed, are critical of the concept of human security precisely because it is so broad as to overlap with or even be indistinguishable from human development.[22] There is a growing literature on the relationships between security and development (the "security-development nexus") and, more narrowly, conflict and economics, which suggest that the relationship works in both directions—that is, security can facilitate development, and development can facilitate security. The theoretical mechanisms underlying this relationship are contested and knowledge gaps are acknowledged, and it is beyond the scope of this chapter to enter that discussion, except to say that progress in interpreting the relationship is important for determining policies that are able to set priorities effectively in given contexts.[23]

Finally, and as is discussed in a number of other chapters in this volume, the fourth link Brzoska identifies between SSR and development is about participation, a critical element of the "rights-based approach" to development, and is based on the claim that the processes supported by development assistance are as important, if not more so, for development as their immediate outcomes. These processes should be "participatory, accountable, and transparent with equity in decision-making and sharing of the fruits or outcome of the process."[24]

The development approach to SSR faces certain challenges and constraints. According to the *OECD DAC Handbook on Security System Reform*, the main (and interrelated) challenges to donors include a lack of coherent strategy, a lack of capacity, and ensuring local ownership.[25] This is worth emphasizing, because justice-sensitive SSR has to face the same challenges and may in fact have implications for how such challenges are addressed overall, as is discussed more below. There would appear, then, to be opportunities for lessons learned from and coordination with the experiences of SSR and development actors in dealing with such issues.

A coherent strategy is difficult, because in any given context there may be multiple donor countries involved, with representatives from multiple agencies within each donor government, attempting to engage with multiple actors from different domestic institutions and sectors in a wide range of activities, while balancing multiple and sometimes competing or contradictory objectives and priorities. Increasing operational capacity, for example, may sometimes be in tension with improving overall accountability and transparency. The development approach does not always provide the guidance necessary to resolve these tensions. "Although poverty reduction provides a solid, but very broad, framework within which a great number of security-related activities can be usefully placed," argues Brzoska, "such activities cannot be easily prioritised or sequenced."[26]

Lack of capacity affects both donors and the societies whose security sectors are being reformed, particularly in contexts of poverty and postconflict transition where institutions are weak and resources scarce. As Hänggi points out:

> The socio-economic context will have a direct bearing on openings for SSR. States with higher standards of living are more likely to establish sustainable security. However, states that are the subject of statebuilding and reconstruction efforts tend to be characterized by limited social and economic capital, including reliance on humanitarian and development assistance, coupled with an absence of infrastructure and skills. These factors, exacerbated by long-standing governance deficits, represent significant barriers to security sector reconstruction.[27]

Based on an OECD DAC survey of security reform in African countries, Eboe Hutchful and J. Kayode Fayemi conclude that capacity constraints should suggest a lowering of expectations:

> Indeed, given the institutional and resource constraints that characterise African countries, there is a real possibility that the elevated benchmarks often associated with SSR will represent overkill. A set of more modest core goals, such as gradual and monitorable improvements in transparency, in sensitivity to human rights issues, and in the quality of defence and security management, would be more realistic.[28]

Lack of capacity has implications for coherence, because it may affect the ways in which the different priorities of SSR will be set, and it has implications for the degree of local ownership that is possible as well, because local actors may not be able to implement reform without capacity.[29]

But local ownership will be affected by political constraints as well. "Like any other policy," observes Brzoska, "security sector reform has winners and losers, and, more often than not, powerful actors stand to lose from security sector reform programmes. Under such circumstances it is difficult to find local actors who are both willing to support reform and are in a position to actually implement it."[30] Coherence, capacity, and local ownership, then, are some of the challenges facing donors in SSR work, especially in developing and postconflict contexts.[31] These are challenges that must be kept in mind when thinking about a justice-sensitive approach to SSR, which we turn to in the next section.

JUSTICE AS SECURITY: SSR AND TRANSITIONAL JUSTICE

"Transitional justice is a response to systematic or widespread violations of human rights."[32] SSR, on the other hand, is not limited to circumstances in which systematic or widespread human rights violations occurred. As noted in the previous section, SSR is also applied in development contexts and even in developed societies that are not confronted with a legacy of serious human rights abuse but face a need to improve the effectiveness or accountability of their security sectors.[33] However, in societies emerging from conflict or authoritarian rule in which serious abuses took place, practices of SSR and transitional justice regularly occur alongside each other and are often supported by some of the same domestic and international actors. Nevertheless, the fields rarely interact, either in practice[34] or in theory. In relevant writings, the other field is often not referred to, discussed at a level of generality that is almost void of meaning, or even misunderstood. Conversations between the two fields are commonly deadlocked around the tedious and often ill-framed peace versus justice debate.[35] In the SSR literature, transitional justice is regularly meshed together or even equated with judicial reform.[36] The report of the UN secretary-general on SSR does not discuss or reference transitional justice.[37] The secretary-general's report on the rule of law and transitional justice, on the other hand, provides only a fleeting reference to security sector reform and does not explain it or link it to or distinguish it in any detail from the core concepts of the rule of law, justice, and transitional justice that are defined and discussed in the report.[38] The report devotes an entire section to vetting the public sector to screen out abusive officials but fails to situate vetting in its broader context of public sector or security sector reform.[39] In another example, the UK Department for International Development (DFID), in a recently published briefing note on justice and accountability, provides an overview of how justice systems contribute to accountability. The note makes brief reference to transitional justice, which is defined as a means to pursue accountability for the worst abuses in periods of transition. The note limits transitional justice to criminal prosecutions, truth and reconciliation processes, and reparations and restitution, but does not include or refer to SSR (or institutional reform more broadly).[40]

SSR and transitional justice experts and practitioners not only fail to understand each other, but significant cultural and institutional barriers also persist between the two communities. Transitional justice actors generally come from and see their origins in the human rights community, which is often perceived as soft, lofty, and unreasonably idealist by security actors. The SSR community, on the other hand, continues to be dominated by former uniformed personnel and political strategists, who are often perceived as too narrowly focused on operational concerns and overly realist by transitional justice and human rights actors. Few are those who attempt to cross the line and engage in constructive conversations with the other community, and they are often viewed with suspicion in their own community.[41]

In actual transitional settings, transitional justice and SSR frequently share some of the same historical catalysts (such as poverty, access to resources, and identity conflicts), face some of the same social and political barriers to reform, and target some of the same institutions and individuals in their programs. At the same time, the immediate aims of SSR and transitional justice may diverge, and transitional justice and SSR programs can get in each other's way during implementation. SSR and transitional justice practices frequently also compete for the same resources. For instance, a threat to criminally prosecute senior security officials may mobilize the security establishment against the reform process; the disarmament, demobilization, and reintegration (DDR) of former combatants may draw away resources from a reparations program for victims; a memorial commemorating victims may provoke intransigent reactions among security officials; or resources dedicated to a transitional justice measure may delay or undermine the development of effective permanent state institutions. Both transitional justice and SSR will, then, be genuinely interested to preempt negative repercussions of the other's practices on their own programs. However, these unavoidable actual interactions establish a relationship that remains at the level of *competition* and is determined by defensive postures on both sides.

But from a transitional justice perspective, this cannot be the last word. SSR is not just another field with which transitional justice de facto interacts and competes in transitional settings; it is a field in which transitional justice has an intrinsic interest. In the SSR community, transitional justice is frequently mis-understood to be based on no more than a narrow, backward-looking, mor-alist notion of accountability.[42] But such an understanding misses out on an important dimension of justice in transitional societies. Not only does account-ability on its own provide for forward-looking, political justifications, but the concept of accountability by itself cannot fully capture the various aims that transitional justice pursues.[43] For instance, if we were to live through a perfect transition[44] in which we criminally prosecuted all abusers, documented and fully acknowledged the truth about all past abuses, and repaired all victims, but did not at the same time stop the continuation of the same abuses and did not build the rule of law, we would not provide justice. Preventing the recur-rence of systematic or widespread human rights abuses is a significant aspect of effectively addressing their legacy and, therefore, of transitional justice.

In transitional societies, efforts to prevent the recurrence of massive and serious human rights abuses and build the rule of law will include a range of measures, which will vary significantly according to the context and will have to be coordinated in order to complement rather than to obstruct each other. They will include peacekeeping and peacebuilding efforts; DDR programs; poverty reduction; constitutional, legislative, and administrative reforms; pub-lic sector reforms and development efforts; economic development programs; curriculum and other educational reforms, and others.[45]

Obviously, SSR will generally be central among the measures designed to effectively prevent the recurrence of systematic or widespread abuses and build the rule of law. More often than not, it is security agencies (including armed forces, law enforcement agencies, special forces, and intelligence ser-vices), unofficial armed groups (such as insurgents, rebel groups, and freedom fighters), mercenaries and private military companies (contracted by security agencies or unofficial armed groups), and other security actors that have com-mitted the most serious abuses during the conflict or period of authoritarian rule. At the same time, the security sector, with its management and oversight structures, has primary responsibility to protect and respect some of the most basic human rights, including the rights to life, security, liberty, and personal integrity. Reforming abusive security structures and building a security sec-tor that effectively provides security without violating fundamental human rights, and that builds a society's "capacity to manage conflict without vio-lence," then, is a central concern of transitional justice.[46] Without SSR, it will be far more difficult for transitional justice to achieve some of its key mediate aims, in particular providing recognition to victims and building civic trust. As a result, transitional justice without SSR is considerably less likely to help attain reconciliation and democratization, which represent core final ends of transitional justice.[47] Transitional justice without SSR to prevent recurrence can only be incomplete justice.[48]

Rather than understanding SSR as a competitor, it should be understood that SSR fundamentally matters to transitional justice. Transitional justice, therefore, should be interested in integrating SSR into a comprehensive and coherent strategy and ensuring that its various measures—particularly criminal prosecutions, truth-seeking, reparations, memorialization, and the range of guarantees of nonrecurrence including SSR—do not obstruct each other, but instead *complement* and mutually reinforce each other.[49] If the outcome of an SSR process is an effective and accountable security sector that provides security, respects human rights, and sanctions instances of abuse, then the credibility of other transitional justice measures, as well as of a transitional justice project as a whole, will be enhanced. For instance, a truth-seeking effort is less likely to be perceived as "cheap talk" and reparation payments are less likely to be understood as an unacceptable effort to buy off victims of abuse when these transitional justice measures are accompanied by an SSR process that contributes to preventing the recurrence of the same abuses and to providing effective security to all population groups, including those who were previously victimized, marginalized, or excluded.

Other transitional justice measures can also benefit from SSR in that it fulfills an enabling function for these measures. For instance, vetting of security institutions could remove spoilers from positions of power that were used to obstruct other transitional justice measures, such as prosecutorial efforts, reparations, and truth-telling.[50] Or, more generally, the building of an effective and accountable security sector, including police forces and prison systems—which is what SSR at its best promises—could enable and accelerate the prosecution of those who committed the worst human rights abuses in the past. In this sense, then, development support to SSR in transitional contexts can contribute to a more comprehensive and coherent transitional justice program. And the more comprehensive and coherent the transitional justice effort is, the more it can redress the legacy of serious human rights abuse and, therefore, help to give "currency to [the] human rights norms that were systematically violated."[51]

TOWARD A JUSTICE-SENSITIVE SSR

So far, our aim has been to argue that the relationship between SSR and transitional justice is better understood in terms of potential complementarity rather than competition. But stating that transitional justice needs SSR is far from claiming that transitional justice could make a contribution to SSR. Indeed, except for promoting a coherent approach that recognizes the potentially mutually reinforcing character of SSR and transitional justice, it may appear advisable to keep the two fields apart because the institutional cultures, operational challenges, and reform methodologies and techniques applied have little in common and require widely different expertise and skill sets.[52] Any interaction across the two fields can easily be perceived as unprofessional and even arrogant interference by incompetent outsiders.

Nevertheless, in addition to the potential correlations between SSR and transitional justice, we propose that SSR itself can actually benefit from a closer examination of both the normative framework of and the practices applied in transitional justice. This is not to say that such an examination would lead to a new or entirely different concept of SSR that would oppose or replace existing concepts and approaches. We suggest, rather, that an examination of transitional justice can enrich common understandings of SSR, strengthen their normative foundations, and provide supplementary tools to more effectively conduct SSR in transitional societies in which security actors were involved in serious human rights abuses.[53] We start this examination with a cursory exploration of three key terms that are used in both the SSR and the transitional justice literatures: accountability, prevention, and the rule of law. On this basis, we consider more closely how SSR and transitional justice take different approaches to dealing with the past. Finally, we begin to explore a justice-sensitive approach to SSR that understands that the past—as a concrete and specific past—matters in SSR.[54]

DIFFERENT APPROACHES TO DEALING WITH THE PAST

The terms "accountability," "prevention," and "the rule of law" appear and play relatively important roles in key documents of both the SSR and the transitional justice literatures. An exploration of the understanding and use of these terms in both fields, however, reveals differences that can help to elaborate the potential contribution transitional justice can make to SSR. The exploration is limited to a review of the UN secretary-general's reports on SSR and on the rule of law and transitional justice. While a more in-depth analysis of relevant literature would be necessary to draw definitive conclusions, this fairly superficial review already provides certain interesting findings.

The term "accountability" is central in the secretary-general's 2008 report on SSR.[55] The term or a variation of it appears eighteen times throughout the report. In most instances, it appears within such phrases as "effective and accountable security institutions" or "effective and accountable security sector" and describes one of the two central qualities successful SSR aims to achieve. Accountability in the report refers basically to the existence of a legal framework and of functioning discipline, oversight, management, and governance mechanisms that ensure the legitimate use of force and financial propriety.[56] It is accountability *to laws and structures* to ensure good governance and full respect for human rights in the future. "Accountability" is also a key concept in the secretary-general's 2004 report on the rule of law and transitional justice,[57] where the term and variations thereof also appear eighteen times. In the sections that discuss the rule of law, the meaning of accountability is along the lines of its meaning in the report on SSR.[58] But the term takes on a somewhat different meaning when it is used in the context of transitional justice. There, it does not refer generally to the establishment of structures that ensure accountability in the present and future but specifically to accountability for serious or widespread abuses that occurred in the past.[59] It is accountability *for specific acts* and expresses a way to obtain justice in redressing past abuses and to confront a culture of impunity.

The term "prevention" or a variation of it appears seven times in each report. In the secretary-general's report on SSR, the term refers to preventing specific categories of future abuses[60] or to preventing countries from relapsing—in general, unspecific terms—into conflict.[61] The secretary-general's report on the rule of law and transitional justice uses the term "prevention" along similar lines.[62] However, where it is used in the specific context of transitional justice, the term takes on a more precise meaning and refers to preventing the recurrence of certain serious violations of human rights and humanitarian law that occurred in the past.[63] Through the term "prevention," both SSR and transitional justice share a common concern for a peaceful, secure, and just future. But whereas SSR as introduced by the secretary-general has little interest in the past, transitional justice draws links to the concrete, unjust past and holds that it is better to deal with this past for building a just future.

The concept of "the rule of law" is also central in both reports and appears many times. The secretary-general's report on SSR sets out to develop a "vision of security based on the rule of law" and emphasizes that "security, human rights and development . . . can only be achieved within a broad framework of the rule of law."[64] The SSR report also cites a part of the definition of the rule of law given in the secretary-general's report on the rule of law and transitional justice referring to a "principle of governance in which all persons, institutions and entities, including the State, are accountable to laws that are publicly promulgated, equally enforced and independently adjudicated and that are consistent with international human rights norms and standards."[65] Nevertheless, the definition of the rule of law provided in the latter report is richer, including specific references to, among other things, the principles of equality before the law, accountability to the law, separation of powers, and participation in decision-making.[66] The concept as it is used in the rule of law report is more substantive than the rather formalist notion in the SSR report.[67] Also, the rule of law report generally refers to the rule of law and justice in the same breath,[68] emphasizes that both the rule of law and transitional justice are mandated by international law,[69] and argues that "[j]ustice and peace are not contradictory forces … [but] promote and sustain each other."[70] Unlike the SSR report, the rule of law report links the rule of law with transitional justice and articulates a strong relation between the two concepts.

This cursory review of the use of the terms "accountability," "prevention," and "the rule of law" in the report of the secretary-general on SSR, on the one hand, and the report of the secretary-general on rule of law and transitional justice, on the other, reveals, among others, differences in dealing with an abusive past in the two fields. In SSR, the past matters differently than in transitional justice. By and large, SSR is interested in the past only insofar as it manifests itself as a performance or structural deficit in the present. Beyond the identification of existing deficits that are the consequences of past shortcomings, SSR is largely willing to draw a "thick line" between the past and the present,[71] and to start—or pretend to start—anew from a clean slate. The aim is to build an effective and accountable security sector for the present and future; the past matters only insofar as it led to a deficient present state of the security sector that SSR aims to overcome. But comprehensively confronting an abusive past is generally perceived as a distraction to this endeavor, a waste of resources, or, even worse, an impediment to reform. Transitional justice, on the other hand, argues that preventing recurrence is important but not enough to overcome the scale of harm inflicted by systematic or widespread human rights violations. Transitional justice offers a range of approaches to confront comprehensively such a legacy, thereby contributing to reconciliation and democratization.[72] If addressing an abusive past can actually contribute to achieving these ends, and if transitional justice can help SSR overcome some of the direct effects of an abusive past, particularly the delegitimization of the security sector and the exclusion of victims and other marginalized groups, would it then not be in the interests of SSR to learn from transitional justice for its own sake? In what follows, we offer a few concrete suggestions on how SSR could benefit from transitional justice and begin to develop what we call a "justice-sensitive SSR."

JUSTICE-SENSITIVE SSR

SSR can learn from transitional justice that the past as a concrete, abusive past actually matters in the present and that comprehensively addressing rather than ignoring the abusive past makes for better SSR. For instance, a well-managed and well-governed police department with highly skilled and properly equipped personnel cannot function effectively if it is not trusted because abusive police officers remain employed. As a result, citizens might not rely on the police but resort to other means to resolve their conflicts and perhaps even return to violence. For SSR, the slate cannot be clean: the abusive history of a security sector represents a burden that can significantly impact on the sector's present performance. The burden of an abusive past consists, among other things, in the continued presence of abusive security agents and nonstate security actors who undermine the legitimacy of the security sector and may block reform efforts; the persistence of structures within which individual security agents carried out and continue to carry out abuses; the ongoing victimization of specific population groups and segments, and their exclusion from the security sector; and, as a result of these different factors, deep distrust in a security sector that was involved in serious abuses but fails to address them.[73]

Concretely, transitional justice can help SSR in its efforts to address the systemic and political *causes* of an abusive past that contributed to the need for SSR in the beginning.[74] This help may include providing a better understanding of such causes, drawing attention to them, and mobilizing support for appropriate reform. An important concern of transitional justice is revealing and acknowledging the abuses that took place and explaining their causes, which include institutional weaknesses and structures. As Rolando Ames Cobián and Félix Reátegui explain in their chapter in this volume, truth commissions in particular, as highly public and political actors, can call attention to the need for systemic transformation in a society.[75] Prosecutions as well, to the extent that they demonstrate the systemic nature of past abuses, can serve the same purpose. As explained by the UN Office of the High Commissioner for Human Rights' rule-of-law tool for prosecutions, the investigation of "system crime"—genocide, crimes against humanity, and large-scale war crimes, all of which require a certain degree of organization—"requires a detailed exploration of the system itself, and not merely of the results." System crime is most often committed by state and nonstate security forces, and so its investigation requires "appropriate analysis of the ways in which such organizations are legally required to work, as well as how they actually operated during the time in question." Unfortunately, few investigative bodies have had the necessary techniques and resources to investigate such crime effectively.[76] Nevertheless, both truth commissions and prosecutions may be able to highlight the need for SSR to address the systemic causes of abuses, and may also mobilize broad institutional and public support behind such reform efforts.

In addition, transitional justice can direct the attention of SSR efforts toward those who know best what abuses occurred and are in greatest need of a reform of the security sector: the direct victims of the systematic or widespread abuses and other groups that were marginalized during the abusive past.[77] Transitional justice may also provide tools for SSR to better understand some of the systemic causes of conflict and abuse. Official truth-seeking processes or broad-based public consultations that are regularly applied in transitional justice programs can inform an SSR review or assessment about some of these systemic causes. Truth-seeking experts could be integrated into SSR processes in contexts where no truth-seeking efforts take place or where the timing does not allow an SSR review or assessment to benefit from such efforts.

Transitional justice may help SSR not only in its efforts to address some of the systemic causes of an abusive past but also to begin to effectively address a *legacy* of abuse in SSR. Addressing an abusive legacy calls for a particular focus on the following four areas of reform: the establishment of effective accountability structures that draw no artificial lines between past and present abuses; the inclusion of victims and other marginalized groups, in particular by ensuring their participation in the design and implementation of SSR processes, by building their representation in the security sector, and by empowering them to know, make known, and enforce their rights and needs toward the security sector; the promotion of the security sector's legitimacy through both structural and symbolic reforms; and coherence between all aspects of SSR, as well as with other transitional justice measures.

The creation of effective accountability mechanisms represents a central feature of established SSR doctrine and encompasses setting up legal and constitutional frameworks, as well as putting in place institutionalized systems of governance and management.[78] Nevertheless, SSR practice often remains too heavily focused on providing skills training, supplying resources, and increasing organizational efficiency to overcome capacity deficits of the security sector. However, building the organizational and operational capacities of an abusive security sector is not only insufficient but can even represent a risk of making it more effective in carrying out abuses. In fact, abusive security agencies are often remarkably "efficient" in using their skills and resources for abusive purposes. The Yugoslav police, for instance, was a founding member of Interpol; nevertheless, these police forces were arguably efficient not only in imposing "ethnic cleansing" during the internal Yugoslav conflicts but also in undermining the return of refugees and displaced persons after the conflicts had ended.[79] Justice-sensitive SSR reinforces the need to carefully coordinate capacity development with building effective accountability structures to discourage, prevent, and sanction abuses, and emphasizes that one cannot come at the expense of the other.[80] In addition, a justice-sensitive SSR proposes a *more holistic conception of accountability* than common SSR approaches, which focus largely on establishing effective accountability mechanisms for future abuses.[81] A legacy of systematic or widespread abuse commonly results in a pervasive culture of impunity. In order to overcome impunity and to make a security sector trustworthy in the wake of such abuses, SSR has to establish accountability not only for present and future abuses but also for the most serious past abuses. For instance, vetting to exclude from public service the biggest criminals helps not only dismantle abusive structures that were established during the period of conflict or authoritarian rule but helps also to build trust in the security sector by reaffirming that its members are not above the law.[82] Establishing accountability not only in the present and future but also for the past gives stronger "currency" to basic norms and values.[83]

Common approaches to SSR generally emphasize that it should be shaped and driven by local actors,[84] based on an assessment of the security needs of the people, and focused on improving delivery of security services.[85] SSR should be "people-centered" and "locally owned."[86] The practice of SSR remains, however, frequently marked by an absence of public *participation* in SSR processes.[87] Justice-sensitive SSR stresses the need to include in the design and implementation of SSR processes the local population generally, and victims of systematic or widespread abuses and other marginalized groups in particular. This can be done, for instance, in broad-based population surveys, by linking SSR processes with truth-seeking efforts, or by designing SSR assessments in a way that ensures consultation with victims and other marginalized groups.[88] Subjects of oppression, violence, and abuse have a clear understanding of what needs to be reformed, and their involvement in SSR will also be critical to build trust in the security sector.

Justice-sensitive SSR not only promotes the participation of victims and other marginalized groups in SSR processes but also highlights the need to involve them in the provision of security itself. Systematic or widespread human rights abuses aim at and have the effect, among others, of excluding individuals and groups from a political community and its resources.[89] One aspect of this process is the exclusion from service in the security sector, which in turn facilitates the commission of abuses. Justice-sensitive SSR is, therefore, particularly concerned to advance the *representation* of marginalized groups among the staff members across all ranks of security institutions.[90] Adequate representation provides for internal checks and balances within security institutions, helps to overcome the pursuit of single group interests, and improves the overall distribution of power and resources. A more representative security institution will also better understand the concerns of all population groups because its representatives will speak their languages, comprehend their cultures, and appreciate their traditions. As a result, a more representative institution will better serve and respond to the needs of all population groups, including those who were previously victimized, marginalized, or excluded, and respect them as rights-bearing citizens.[91] Justice-sensitive SSR also has a keen interest in the establishment of structures that meet the *specific security needs* of victims and other marginalized groups (such as dedicated mechanisms to respond to gender-based violence).[92] In the Democratic Republic of Congo (DRC), for example, where sexual crimes are so prevalent that impunity for them "raises the question as to the extent to which women can participate in a democracy as fully rights-bearing citizens," justice-sensitive SSR could make an important contribution to addressing both the necessity to reform security institutions to protect and serve the population and the related question of sexual and gender-based violence in the country, "including and beyond the security system."[93]

In addition to promoting the participation of victims and other marginalized groups in both SSR processes and in the provision of security itself, justice-sensitive SSR also promotes their *empowerment* as citizens.[94] While common SSR approaches focus on and use as entry points the reform of the providers of security—that is, the security sector and its actors (including related non-state actors)—justice-sensitive SSR also targets the local population directly, particularly victims and other marginalized groups, who are the recipients of security—or of insecurity, for that matter. The marginalization and exclusion of victims that accompany systematic or widespread human rights abuses disenfranchise victims of their rights and infringe on their status as citizens.[95] A justice-sensitive approach to SSR acknowledges the relational nature of security delivery—it is provided by someone for someone—and aims not only to reform the security providers but also to directly *empower* victims and other marginalized groups to know, make known, and enforce their rights and needs toward the security sector.[96]

In the absence of totalitarian oppression and surveillance, a security sector depends in many ways for its effective functioning on the trust of citizens.
People cooperate with security agencies because "they view them as legitimate legal authorities, entitled to be obeyed."[97] Trust in a security institution
"amounts to knowing that its constitutive rules, values, and norms are shared
by its members or participants and that they regard them as binding."[98] Without such trust, citizens are unlikely to report crimes, are not likely to turn to
the police and the courts to resolve their conflicts, and will hardly seek police
assistance for their security. Trust is earned when a security sector effectively
and fairly provides security. Involvement in systematic or widespread abuses,
on the other hand, undermines the legitimacy of a security sector, resulting
in a fundamental crisis of trust.[99] Particularly those who suffered violence and
oppression will find it difficult to gain or regain trust in such a security sector.
Establishing or reestablishing its *legitimacy* is, therefore, a complex undertaking
to convince the citizens that the security sector is again, or for the first time, *at
their service* and hence worthy of their trust.[100] Public consultations about security and reform needs, public participation in the design and implementation
of SSR processes, human rights training, and structural reform activities that
promote accountability and adequate representation help to build the legitimacy of the security sector (see above). Efforts to increase the sector's capacity and effectiveness through skills training, better equipment, and improved
management will also contribute to strengthening the legitimacy of the security sector. But such measures may not be sufficient to restore civic trust, particularly among victims, in a security sector that was involved in systematic or
widespread abuses. Specific and targeted legitimacy-building measures might
be necessary—in addition to inclusion in SSR processes, training, and structural reforms—to overcome this profound trust deficit and help to transform
a trustworthy security sector into a trusted one. Such measures can include,
for instance, apologies by representatives of security institutions that were
involved in serious abuses;[101] memorials, commemorative days, and museums
that remember victims and acknowledge the involvement of specific security
institutions in abuses; the renaming of streets and public places that bear the
names of security officials or institutions with histories of abuse; the changing
of coats of arms, insignia, and uniforms that are associated with an abusive
past; and institution-based truth-seeking efforts. These targeted legitimacy-
building measures *verbally or symbolically reaffirm* a commitment to overcome
the legacy of abuse and an endorsement of democratic norms and values.
Unlike inclusion in SSR processes, training, and structural reforms, these measures do not "promote trust through action," but they do so by acknowledging

past abuses, by expressing a turning away from an abusive past, and by reaffirming a commitment to fundamental norms and values.[102]

These specific legitimacy-building measures cannot, of course, replace reforms that require actual individual or structural changes. Stand-alone verbal or symbolic reaffirmations of norms that are not accompanied by actions to give effect to these norms lack credibility. Such "empty promises" are unlikely to convince citizens to trust a security sector. Nonetheless, reaffirmations may usefully complement other reforms that by themselves may be insufficient to build trust in a security sector that was involved in systematic or widespread abuses. Such acknowledgments of past abuses and expressions of commitment to norms may help to convince citizens, particularly victims and other marginalized groups, of the sincerity of other reform efforts, and to move them from distrusting to trusting a trustworthy security sector.[103]

Finally, justice-sensitive SSR is premised on the assumption that *coherence* contributes to its effectiveness. SSR can be more effective if it is *internally coherent* and responds holistically to the reform needs of a specific transitional context, including structural and symbolic reform measures and civic empowerment. Common approaches to SSR emphasize the need to be coherent and comprehensive. As indicated, the basic SSR principles articulated by the OECD and the UN highlight the need for SSR to ensure both the accountability and effectiveness of security. But justice-sensitive SSR reaches beyond the confines of SSR per se. At the beginning of our exploration, we found that transitional justice is fundamentally interested in SSR to reinforce its other measures. We now see that the reverse also holds: SSR will be more effective if it is *externally coherent* and forms part of a comprehensive transitional justice policy that also includes other measures, such as criminal prosecutions, truth-seeking, and reparations to victims.[104] For instance, it will be easier to build trust in security institutions if an SSR process is accompanied by programs that provide direct support to victims, such as a reparation program. Without such support, the SSR process is likely to be perceived as yet another instance to provide preferential treatment to security actors and to further disserve those who have already been victimized and marginalized.[105]

Transitional justice can make a limited but important contribution to SSR. Transitional justice does not replace but enhances existing SSR approaches and helps SSR to understand better how an abusive past matters. In doing so, it draws the attention of SSR to certain important areas of reform that are less considered in common SSR approaches. These include, in particular, accountability for past and present abuses; participation, representation, and empowerment of victims; promotion of legitimacy; and coherence of SSR with other transitional justice measures.

CONCLUSION: JUSTICE-SENSITIVE SSR AND DEVELOPMENT

Having both reviewed the broad development approach to SSR and articulated a justice-sensitive approach as well, we conclude by discussing some of the specific ways in which the two approaches might relate to each other. It is argued here that SSR and transitional justice can be understood to complement each other in ways that have received little attention so far, and that bringing in a substantive and direct focus on past abuses can make a useful contribution both at the conceptual and at the practical level to the development approach to SSR.

As explained above, SSR was from its beginning a development concept. At the broadest level, the term "SSR" describes measures aimed at creating an effective and accountable security sector that contributes positively to sustainable peace and development. An effective security sector requires the operational capacity to provide security to both citizens and the state, and an accountable security sector requires it to be governed democratically, such that it provides this security while respecting the human rights of its citizens. An effective and accountable security sector, then, requires both capacity and governance. More specifically, SSR has been argued to contribute to poverty reduction and therefore development through its reallocation of resources from military spending to poverty-reduction activities, through its increased provision of security for individuals and property, through its contribution to conflict prevention and management, and through the greater participation of poor people in the security sector. Among the challenges faced by SSR practitioners are those related to capacity, local ownership, and coherence, which we return to below.

While SSR and transitional justice are often understood to be in tension with one another, we have suggested that there is much potential for them to be complementary as well. For one thing, even with a purely development-oriented approach, SSR can serve to reinforce one of the primary long-term objectives of all transitional justice efforts: the prevention of the recurrence of widespread and serious human rights abuses. SSR is a critical tool in such prevention, which means that, in the absence of SSR, transitional justice is less likely to achieve its final goals of democratization and reconciliation. Furthermore, SSR at its best provides for effective and accountable security institutions, which are often required for the successful implementation of transitional justice measures, such as criminal prosecutions and truth-telling. In both of these ways, then, development support to SSR can facilitate and reinforce transitional justice.

We have also argued that a justice-sensitive approach to SSR differs from standard SSR work in its direct concern with the past, and specifically past human rights abuses. This is evident in the different understandings of such concepts as "accountability," "prevention," and "the rule of law" in key SSR and transitional justice documents. Justice-sensitive SSR, then, may make a contribution to SSR—that is, help SSR to achieve its own goals, which at a broad level include development—by calling attention to the systemic causes of abuses and mobilizing support behind systemic reform efforts that address such causes, and by helping SSR programs to effectively address the legacies of such abuses. Addressing these legacies through SSR involves measures aimed at accountability for past abuses; participation, representation, and empowerment of victims and other marginalized groups; the legitimacy of institutions; and coherence of SSR efforts with transitional justice measures.

What, then, are the implications of a justice-sensitive approach to SSR from a development perspective? We suggest the following. First, broadly speaking, justice-sensitive SSR can affect the security sector in terms of both effectiveness and accountability, possibly altering the balance of priorities between the two elements. As explained above, SSR that takes seriously the concerns of transitional justice will use the notion of "accountability" differently than most SSR work—that is, to include past abuses rather than just current and future ones. Furthermore, in practice, justice-sensitive SSR may involve some degree of a shift of focus away from increasing operational capacity and more toward improving the accountability or governance side of things. At the same time, however, it would be incorrect to assume that a justice-sensitive approach cannot also improve the effectiveness of security actors: as explained above, one of the key potential contributions that justice sensitivity brings to public institutions is greater legitimacy—that is, increased levels of trust among citizens, which is critical for the effective functioning of security institutions. Thus, if effective and accountable security institutions can contribute to sustainable development, there is reason to think that justice-sensitive SSR has a role to play.

Second, justice-sensitive SSR concerns may also have implications for the specific links to development aims, such as poverty reduction. In terms of resources being freed up to spend directly on development activities, vetting processes involve the removal of personnel from institutions, and can be coordinated as part of larger downsizing efforts and a reduction in security spending. Security, as we have seen, is the main link identified by SSR documents and experts between SSR and development. Security at the individual and communal level has been argued to be both an element of development in itself and a precondition for development needs, such as income, education, and health. Security has also been linked to development through the immense developmental costs of armed conflict—lack of security being a cause of poverty—which means that conflict prevention can play an important role in poverty reduction. As we have seen, both standard SSR and transitional justice are concerned with prevention, although with somewhat different meanings. SSR is generally concerned with the prevention of conflict, while transitional justice is concerned with the prevention of the recurrence of systematic or widespread human rights violations. The increased security that SSR can provide can both reinforce transitional justice and contribute to development. At the same time, because the type of prevention that transitional justice is most concerned with is different than general conflict prevention, justice-sensitive SSR may contribute to a deeper kind of security, and therefore a more sustainable development, in the long run; although, in the short run, there may be tension between these two types of prevention. Again, we do not know enough about the theoretical links between security and development to fully resolve the issue; nevertheless, there are reasons to think that justice-sensitive SSR can contribute positively in this regard. We have also made it clear that participation is a key objective of both standard SSR and justice-sensitive SSR, although again with slightly different but potentially overlapping meanings. Participation, as it is used in poverty-reduction terms, refers to poor people in general, while in justice-sensitive terms it refers to the victims of human rights violations and other marginalized groups. It is therefore possible that efforts to increase the participation of victims in SSR and the provision of security, as proposed here, will be mutually reinforcing with efforts to increase the participation of the poor. Not only will victim groups and the poor overlap, but the reaffirmation of human rights norms achieved by justice efforts may have inclusionary effects beyond immediate victims.[106]

Third, however, it is important to remember that justice-sensitive SSR is subject to the same constraints and has to face the same challenges as any SSR work, including those related to coherence, capacity, and local ownership. As pointed out, justice-sensitive SSR requires coherence not just within SSR efforts, which is difficult enough, but also with transitional justice measures as well. As argued in this chapter, there are important reasons to think that this type of coherence is possible and desirable. At the same time, however, there are cultural and institutional barriers between transitional justice and SSR practitioners that may be difficult to break down, and there will be situations in which the various objectives of SSR being done from both a development and justice perspective do not in fact reinforce each other and may be in tension. As with SSR in general, this will be affected by the second challenge, a lack of capacity both among donors and within security institutions.

Justice-sensitive SSR is constrained by resources and capacity limitations, and competition with other SSR activities is not always avoidable. Vetting of any public institution, for example, may, in certain cases, lead to the dismissal of "unacceptably large number of employees,"[107] or "governance vacuums,"[108] doing harm to the capacity of institutions — capacity that less-developed countries may not be able to do without.[109] Furthermore, such justice-sensitive reform measures as vetting can be "complex, time-consuming, and resource-intensive exercises requiring multidisciplinary skills, in particular when they concern institutions with large numbers of employees."[110] This can lead to competition for resources. In Sierra Leone, SSR activities were ranked on a numerical scale in terms of their ability to deliver the objectives of the PRSP framework, the primary one of which being the provision of an "enabling environment for poverty reduction." Only those activities scoring very high on this scale had a chance to receive funding.[111] Even if a case can be made that justice-sensitive activities can contribute to development goals, it is unlikely that such activities would score among the highest on such a scale, which is not a positive outcome from a justice perspective.

Finally, although participation, representation, and empowerment have been argued to be key objectives of justice-sensitive SSR, local ownership of the process is likely to remain a difficult challenge. Local ownership can be constrained by local capacity, which is often lacking in transitional and developing country contexts. Furthermore, SSR is a political process, not a technical one, and as such faces resistance or lack of will. Justice and development initiatives, as repeatedly emphasized throughout this book, are both inherently political projects. They affect power dynamics within countries and communities and can be sensitive issues. Justice-sensitive SSR is no different, and it should not be expected that it will go without resistance, manipulation, and competition.[112]

In the end, our argument is as follows. In making the attempt to deal with an abusive past more central to the notion of SSR, a justice-sensitive approach remains within the broader understanding of SSR as a development concept, in that it can be conducive to broader development goals. But, importantly, a justice-sensitive SSR may even enhance the long-term development impact of SSR through its effect on the main SSR principles of accountability and effectiveness. Potentially, dealing with the past can improve the legitimacy of security institutions and promote the inclusion of all citizens, in particular of victims and other marginalized groups. At the same time, though, it is important to remember that justice-sensitive SSR faces the constraints and challenges of all SSR work, and, since justice and development objectives will not always align in the short run, tensions may exist in terms of resources, methods, and priorities. Thus, what is called for is more dialogue and coordination, to ensure that SSR and transitional justice are mutually reinforcing in the way we believe they can be, instead of only being in tension, as they are often currently seen to be.

NOTES

1   The authors would like to thank Pablo de Greiff and Undine Kayser-Whande for comments on earlier versions of the chapter, Tracy Vienings for discussions on the topic at the conceptual stage, and the participants at the project meeting in Bonn for their feedback on a draft of the chapter. The views expressed here do not necessarily represent those of the ICTJ.

2   United Nations, *Securing Peace and Development: The Role of the United Nations in Supporting Security Sector Reform, Report of the Secretary-General*, A/62/659-S/2008/39, January 23, 2008, paras. 14, 17.

3   OECD DAC, *OECD DAC Handbook on Security System Reform (SSR): Supporting Security and Justice* (Paris: OECD, 2007), 5.

4   Heiner Hänggi, "Security Sector Reform," in *Post-Conflict Peacebuilding: A Lexicon*, ed. Vincent Chetail (Oxford: Oxford University Press, forthcoming 2009). A full description of the wide range of activities involved in SSR is beyond the scope of this chapter, but according to the OECD, the categories of SSR-related activities include: activities aimed at improving civilian security force relations, increasing civilian input into security policy-making, and preparing the terrain for reform; activities aimed at improving governance of the armed forces and intelligence services; activities involving the justice and internal security apparatus (including police, courts, prisons, etc.); activities involving nonstate security forces, such as private security companies; activities involving civil oversight mechanisms; activities aimed at strengthening the functioning of civil management bodies; activities aimed at civilian capacity building; activities involving regional initiatives; and activities in the area of disarmament, demobilization, and

reintegration (DDR). OECD DAC, *Security System Reform and Governance*, DAC Guidelines and Reference Series (Paris: OECD, 2005), 35.

5 United Nations, *Securing Peace and Development*, para. 17; and OECD DAC, *OECD DAC Handbook*, 21.

6 Both terms are frequently used interchangeably in the literature, and the use of the terms in this chapter often depends on the source that it refers to. A separate chapter in this volume by Muna Ndulo and Roger Duthie, "The Role of Judicial Reform in Development and Transitional Justice," looks specifically at links between judicial reform and transitional justice.

7 Hänggi, "Security Sector Reform."

8 Heiner Hänggi, "Establishing Security in Conflict-Ridden Societies: How to Reform the Security Sector" (paper presented to the Aspen European Strategy Forum "International state-building and reconstruction efforts—experience gained and lessons learned," September 18–21, 2008, Bonn, 23); and Michael Brzoska, "Development Donors and the Concept of Security Sector Reform," Geneva Centre for the Democratic Control of Armed Forces (DCAF), Occasional Paper No. 4, Geneva, November 2003, 32.

9 Hänggi, "Security Sector Reform."

10 Clare Short, "Security Sector Reform and the Elimination of Poverty," Centre for Defence Studies, King's College, London, March 9, 1999.

11 For DFID's guidelines on SSR, see DFID, "Understanding and Supporting Security Sector Reform," DFID, 2002, www.dfid.gov.uk/Pubs/files/supportingsecurity.pdf.

12 At the broadest level, security, human rights, and development are seen as "interdependent and mutually reinforcing conditions for sustainable peace." United Nations, *Securing Peace and Development*, paras. 1, 35, 28, 45(a).

13 OECD DAC, *OECD DAC Handbook*, 13, 15.

14 "Liberia: Poverty Reduction Strategy Paper," International Monetary Fund (IMF) Country Report No. 08/219, July 2008, 50, www.imf.org/external/pubs/ft/scr/2008/cr08219.pdf. See also "Sierra Leone: Poverty Reduction Strategy Paper," International Monetary Fund (IMF) Country Report No. 05/191, June 2005, 80, www.imf.org/external/pubs/ft/scr/2005/cr05191.pdf.

15 Hänggi, "Security Sector Reform."

16 Brzoska, "Development Donors and the Concept of Security Sector Reform," 16.

17 Ibid., 25–28.

18 Paul Collier, "War and Military Expenditure in Developing Countries and Their Consequences for Development," *Economics of Peace and Security Journal* 1, no. 1 (2006): 9–13; the study cited is in M. Knight, N. Loayza, and D. Villanueva, "Military Spending Cuts and Economic Growth," World Bank Policy Research Working Paper 1577, 1996.

19 Frances Stewart, "Development and Security," Centre for Research on Inequality, Human Security and Ethnicity (CRISE) Working Paper 3, Oxford University, 2004, 2–4,

www.crise.ox.ac.uk/pubs/workingpaper3.pdf.

20 Deepa Narayan et al., *Voice of the Poor: Crying Out for Change* (Oxford: Oxford University Press / World Bank, 2000). This research is cited by many of the documents and much of the literature on SSR in linking the security sector and poverty.

21 The definition provided here comes from *Human Security Centre, Human Security Report 2005: War and Peace in the 21st Century* (Oxford: Oxford University Press, 2005), viii. The importance to SSR is pointed out in Nicole Ball and Dylan Hendrickson, "Trends in Security Sector Reform (SSR): Policy, Practice and Research" (paper prepared for the workshop "New Directions in Security Sector Reform," International Development Research Centre [IDRC], Ottawa, Canada, November 3–4, 2005, 7).

22 Maria Derks, "Security Sector Reform as Development: A Closer Look at the Link Between Security and Development" (paper prepared for the International Studies Association Annual Conference, March 28, 2008, 9–11).

23 See, e.g., Stewart, "Development and Security"; Derks, "Security Sector Reform as Development"; Christopher Blattman and Edward Miguel, "Civil War," *Journal of Economic Literature* (forthcoming); Patricia Justino, "On the Links Between Violent Conflict and Chronic Poverty: How Much Do We Really Know?" Households in Conflict Network Working Paper 18, July 2006; and Paul Collier et al., *Breaking the Conflict Trap: Civil War and Development Policy* (Washington, DC: World Bank and Oxford University Press, 2003).

24 Arjun Sengupta, *Right to Development*, Note by the Secretary-General, 55th Session of the General Assembly, A/55/306, August 17, 2000, quoted in Peter Uvin, *Human Rights and Development* (Bloomfield, CT: Kumarian Press, 2004), 138.

25 OECD DAC, *OECD DAC Handbook*, 13–14.

26 Brzoska, "Development Donors and the Concept of Security Sector Reform," 33–34.

27 Hänggi, "Establishing Security in Conflict-Ridden Societies," 16.

28 Eboe Hutchful and J. Kayode Fayemi, "Security System Reform in Africa," in OECD DAC, *Security System Reform and Governance*, 87.

29 Hänggi, "Security Sector Reform."

30 Brzoska, "Development Donors and the Concept of Security Sector Reform," 45.

31 For discussions of SSR challenges and constraints, see also Herbert Wulf, "Security Sector Reform in Developing and Transitional Countries," in *Security Sector Reform: Potentials and Challenges for Conflict Transformation*, ed. Clem McCartney, Martina Fischer, and Oliver Wills, Berghof Handbook Dialogue Series No. 2 (Berlin: Berghof Research Center for Constructive Conflict Management, 2004); and Ball and Hendrickson, "Trends in Security Sector Reform."

32 International Center for Transitional Justice, "What is Transitional Justice?" December 2008, www.ictj.org/en/tj/.

33 We have seen above that SSR is actually a development concept. The *OECD DAC*

Handbook on SSR, for instance, situates SSR in the broader context of development and includes a separate chapter on SSR in postconflict situations. See OECD DAC, *OECD DAC Handbook*, 100–111.

34   The Center for the Study of Violence and Reconciliation (CSVR) in South Africa and ICTJ are examples of organizations engaging directly with both fields.

35   A recent overview of the peace versus justice debate is provided in Kai Ambos, Judith Large, and Marieke Wierda, eds., *Building a Future on Peace and Justice: Studies on Transitional Justice, Peace and Development: The Nuremberg Declaration on Peace and Justice* (Heidelberg: Springer, 2009).

36   For instance, in an important article on the concept of security sector reform, Brzoska states that "there is a danger that traditional security sector reform activities might be crowded out by judicial sector reform activities such as transitional justice and access to justice which are highly worthy in themselves but have little to do with the provision of physical security in a narrow sense" (Brzoska, "Development Donors and the Concept of Security Sector Reform," n. 7). Along similar lines, the *OECD DAC Handbook* on SSR discusses transitional justice in its section on justice reform, and puts it among justice reform's "particular features of post-conflict settings" (OECD DAC, *OECD DAC Handbook*, 194). Transitional justice is, however, also described—albeit differently and not cross-referenced—as a separate postconflict activity with which SSR is linked (ibid., 107).

37   United Nations, *Securing Peace and Development*, except for a passing reference to the secretary-general's report on the rule of law and transitional justice in para. 12. In another example, DFID, which has been and continues to be at the forefront of developing and promoting the concept of SSR, makes no reference to transitional justice in its most recent and comprehensive publication on SSR (DFID, "Understanding and Supporting Security Sector Reform").

38   United Nations, *The Rule of Law and Transitional Justice in Conflict and Post-Conflict Societies, Report of the Secretary-General*, s/2004/616, August 3, 2004, para. 5.

39   Ibid., paras. 52–53. Both for practical and normative reasons, vetting should be understood as a measure of institutional reform (generally security system or justice sector reform). As a stand-alone program, it is generally not executable and can generally not achieve the aims for which it is established. See Alexander Mayer-Rieckh, "On Preventing Abuse: Vetting and Transitional Reforms," in *Justice as Prevention: Vetting Public Employees in Transitional Societies*, ed. Alexander Mayer-Rieckh and Pablo de Greiff (New York: Social Science Research Council, 2007).

40   See DFID, "Justice and Accountability: A DFID Practice Paper" (May 2008), www.dfid.gov.uk/pubs/files/justice-accountability-briefing.pdf.

41   A few academics have begun to make efforts to relate the two fields to each other. This conversation remains, however, at a fairly high level of abstraction, with little impact

on programming. The SSR Program of the International Center for Transitional Justice aims to make both conceptual and practical contributions to the conversation between SSR and transitional justice.

42   See R. A. Duff, *Answering for Crime* (Oxford: Hart Publishing, 2007).

43   See Pablo de Greiff, "Deliberative Democracy and Punishment," *Buffalo Criminal Law Review* 5, no. 2 (2002): 373–403.

44   Needless to say, this is a thought experiment only with no relevance in the real world. Transitional justice finds its natural place in "a very imperfect world"—i.e., one in which it is not just that there is no generalized compliance with norms, but also in which the very effort to enforce norms generates risks to the existence of enforcing institutions. See Pablo de Greiff, "Theorizing Transitional Justice," in *Transitional Justice*, ed. Melissa Williams and Rosemary Nagy, Nomos XLX (forthcoming).

45   See, e.g., the list of guarantees of nonrecurrence of violations in the *Updated Set of Principles for the Protection and Promotion of Human Rights through Action to Combat Impunity*, E/CN.4/2005/102/Add. 1, February 8, 2005, 17–19.

46   See Elizabeth M. Cousens, "Introduction," in *Peacebuilding as Politics: Cultivating Peace in Fragile Societies*, ed. Elizabeth M. Cousens and Chetan Kumar (Boulder: Lynne Rienner Publishers, 2001), 12. Cousens argues convincingly that "the most effective means to self-enforcing peace is to cultivate political processes and institutions that can manage group conflict without violence but with authority and, eventually, legitimacy."

47   Pablo de Greiff distinguishes between the immediate, mediate, and final aims of transitional justice. These terms do not relate to proximity or distance in time but in causal chains; mediate aims cannot be brought about by one transitional justice measure alone—the intervention of a number of different measures will be required to achieve them. Final ends are causally even further removed from the transitional justice measure in question. The realization of final ends, then, depends on a range of other measures and factors, and the transitional justice measure can make only a relatively small contribution to their attainment. See de Greiff, "Theorizing Transitional Justice."

48   SSR in its broadest sense, as a process to establish an effective and accountable security sector, can be understood to prevent the recurrence of massive and serious abuses. For instance, enhancing a security sector's capacity to deliver security is likely to increase the public's trust in and the public's reliance on the security sector in resolving its conflicts and is, therefore, likely to decrease the probability of a relapse into violence. But transitional justice will be most interested in those measures of SSR that directly redress a legacy of massive human rights abuse and are necessary to reform an abusive security system. In this sense, transitional justice is particularly interested in and will prioritize those SSR practices that represent measures of *corrective* justice. See de Greiff, "Theorizing Transitional Justice."

49   A caveat about the potential complementarity of SSR and other transitional justice

measures is in order here. While the various measures have the potential to reinforce each other, there are also many ways in which they can get in each other's way and make the implementation of other measures even more difficult. The complementarity of these various measures is only potential and certainly not a given in the "very imperfect" contexts of transitional justice. On the potentially mutually reinforcing correlations between various transitional justice measures but also on potential negative repercussions, see, e.g., Pablo de Greiff, "Vetting and Transitional Justice," in *Justice as Prevention*, 527–30.

50   De Greiff, "Vetting and Transitional Justice," 528–29.

51   De Greiff, "Theorizing Transitional Justice."

52   But in varying degrees, this is true for all transitional justice practices: they share goals but not approaches, means, and techniques!

53   SSR is of course not limited to such contexts. As noted earlier, SSR can also be relevant in development and developed contexts, in which transitional justice does not play a role.

54   It is hoped that these reflections can help to make the link between transitional justice and SSR less elusive. See also Charles T. Call, "Conclusion," in *Constructing Justice and Security after War*, ed. Charles T. Call (Washington, DC: US Institute for Peace, 2008), 398.

55   United Nations, *Securing Peace and Development*.

56   Ibid., para. 15.

57   United Nations, *The Rule of Law and Transitional Justice*.

58   See, e.g., ibid., paras. 5, 6, 36.

59   This is expressed in United Nations, *The Rule of Law and Transitional Justice*, in particular, in such phrases as "accounting for the past" (para. 21), "accountability for perpetrators" (para. 39), "accountability for serious violations of international human rights and humanitarian law by civilian and military leaders" (para. 40), and "hold violators to account" (paras. 41, 48). See, e.g., paras. 7, 21, 25, 39, 40, 41, 48, 50.

60   For instance, United Nations, *Securing Peace and Development*, refers to "preventing conflict" (para. 6), "crime prevention" (paras. 20, 50), "violence-prevention initiatives" (para. 31), or "prevention of sexual and other forms of gender-based violence and organised crime" (paras. 45, 50).

61   In United Nations, *Securing Peace and Development*, para. 3, the report refers to "the importance of a professional, effective and accountable security sector for the consolidation of peace and security, in preventing countries from relapsing into conflict and in laying the foundations for a sustainable peace." While this is a reference to the past, it remains unspecific and noncontextual.

62   For instance, United Nations, *The Rule of Law and Transitional Justice*, states that "prevention is the first imperative of justice" (para. 4), or refers to the "prevention of wrongs"

(para. 7) and "crime prevention" (para. 24).

63   In United Nations, *The Rule of Law and Transitional Justice*, para. 38, the report states that one of the main objectives of establishing special criminal tribunals is "bringing to justice those responsible for serious violations of human rights and humanitarian law, putting an end to such violations and preventing their recurrence.... "

64   United Nations, *Securing Peace and Development*, paras. 1, 4.

65   Ibid., para. 12.

66   United Nations, *The Rule of Law and Transitional Justice*, para. 6.

67   Following Jürgen Habermas, de Greiff distinguishes between a purely formalist conception of the rule of law and a richer conception of the rule of law that articulates the internal links between constitutional democracy and the rule of law, and that is one of transitional justice's final ends. See de Greiff, "Theorizing Transitional Justice."

68   See, e.g., United Nations, *The Rule of Law and Transitional Justice*, paras. 3, 4.

69   Ibid., paras. 9, 10.

70   Ibid., para. 21.

71   The term "thick line" was used in this way by Tadeusz Mazowiecki, the first post-communist prime minister of Poland, in his opening speech to parliament in 1989.

72   See de Greiff, "Theorizing Transitional Justice."

73   Indeed, why would one trust a political project that lightly accepts impunity for atrocities and is built on the assumption that as long as you are powerful and accommodating you can get away with the worst crimes while their victims are ignored? Such a lack of commitment to basic norms fundamentally impacts on the trustworthiness of the security sector. See de Greiff, "Vetting and Transitional Justice," 535–36.

74   The UN secretary-general acknowledges the need to attend to root causes but says little on how to identify or address them. See United Nations, *Securing Peace and Development*, para. 6.

75   Rolando Ames Cobián and Félix Reátegui, "Toward Systemic Social Transformation: Truth Commissions and Development," in this volume.

76   Office of the UN High Commissioner for Human Rights, *Rule-of-Law Tools for Post-Conflict States: Prosecution Initiatives* (New York and Geneva: United Nations, 2006), 11–13.

77   Eric Scheye and Gordon Peake diagnose that SSR practice frequently does not take seriously "the needs or wishes of the recipients of reform" and propose that SSR needs to refocus on the "concrete demand by the national recipients of SSR for a tangible outcome: to arrest insecurity.... By focusing on insecurity, attention is focused on those who suffer from it and seek its alleviation." See Eric Scheye and Gordon Peake, "To Arrest Insecurity: Time for a Revised Security Sector Reform Agenda," *Conflict, Security & Development* 5, no. 3 (December 2005): 300–301. Transitional justice can help SSR to do so.

78   The *OECD DAC Handbook* on SSR defines "effective governance, oversight and

accountability" as one of four principles of SSR. See OECD DAC, *OECD DAC Handbook*, 21. See also United Nations, *Securing Peace and Development*, paras. 15, 17; and Nicole Ball, Michael Brzoska, Kees Kingma, and Herbert Wulf, "Voice and Accountability in the Security Sector," Bonn International Center for Conversation, Paper 21 (Bonn, 2002). Some SSR experts even prefer the term "security sector governance" over the term "security sector reform." See Heiner Hänggi and Fred Tanner, "Promoting Security Sector Governance in the EU's Neighbourhood," Chaillot Paper 80 (July 2005), 11–16.

79   For an account of the practices of the police in Bosnia and Herzegovina, see Alexander Mayer-Rieckh, "Vetting to Prevent Future Abuses: Reforming the Police, Courts, and Prosecutor's Offices in Bosnia and Herzegovina," in *Justice as Prevention*.

80   Effective accountability structures include both internal mechanisms (disciplinary procedures, management and budget processes) and external governance mechanisms (parliament and other formalized oversight, judicial oversight, and informal oversight by the media and civil society). One approach to keep the two dimensions together is the capacity and integrity framework to assess institutional reform needs and develop realistic programs. See OECD DAC, *OECD DAC Handbook*, 60–61. The capacity and integrity framework was developed by Alexander Mayer-Rieckh and Serge Rumin.

81   Also the United Nations Principles to Combat Impunity, which embrace a comprehensive approach to addressing a legacy of systematic or widespread human rights violations. See United Nations, *Updated Set of Principles*, principles 1 and 35 ff.

82   De Greiff, "Vetting and Transitional Justice," 536; and Mayer-Rieckh, "On Preventing Abuse," 484–85.

83   See de Greiff, "Theorizing Transitional Justice."

84   See, e.g., Laurie Nathan, *No Ownership, No Commitment: A Guide to Local Ownership of Security Sector Reform* (Birmingham: University of Birmingham, 2007).

85   See OECD DAC, *OECD DAC Handbook*, 21, 41 ff.

86   OECD, *Security System Reform and Governance*, 22.

87   The exclusion of civil society from SSR efforts in Liberia following the 2003 peace agreement is a case in point. See Adedeji Ebo, "The Challenges and Opportunities of Security Sector Reform in Post-Conflict Liberia," Geneva Centre for the Democratic Control of the Armed Forces, Occasional Paper No. 9, Geneva, 2005. In general, see Call, *Constructing Justice and Security*, 401–04 and n. 77.

88   For a recent example of a justice survey, see Patrick Vinck, Phuong Pham, Suliman Baldo, and Rachel Shigekane, *Living with Fear: A Population-Based Survey on Attitudes about Peace, Justice, and Social Reconstruction in Eastern Democratic Republic of Congo* (New York: International Center for Transitional Justice, 2008).

89   See de Greiff, "Theorizing Transitional Justice," on inclusion and recognition.

90   Art. 25(c) of the International Covenant on Civil and Political Rights provides that every citizen shall have the right to "have access, on general terms of equality, to public service

in his country."

91 United Nations, *Code of Conduct for Law Enforcement Officials*, preambular para. a (noting that "every law enforcement agency should be representative of and responsive and accountable to the community as a whole"). For an overview of arguments for broad representation, see Mary O'Rawe and Linda Moore, *Human Rights on Duty: Principles for Better Policing — International Lessons for Northern Ireland* (Belfast, Northern Ireland: Committee for the Administration of Justice, 1998), 20–61.

92 For a comprehensive discussion of gender and SSR, see Megan Bastik and Kristin Valasek, eds., *Gender and Security Sector Reform Toolkit* (Geneva: DCAF, 2008).

93 Laura Davis, "Justice-Sensitive Security System Reform in the Democratic Republic of Congo," Initiative for Peacebuilding, International Alert, International Center for Transitional Justice, February 2009, 14, 30.

94 "[Democratic self-determination] is inclusive in that such a political order keeps itself open to the equal protection of those who suffer discrimination and to the *integration* of the marginalized, but without *imprisoning* them in the uniformity of a homogenized ethnic community." Jürgen Habermas, "On the Relation Between the Nation, the Rule of Law, and Democracy," in *The Inclusion of the Other*, ed. Ciaran Cronin and Pablo de Greiff (Boston: MIT Press, 1998), 139.

95 De Greiff, "Theorizing Transitional Justice."

96 On transforming a relation, see Call, *Constructing Justice and Security*, 387, 393. For efforts to strengthen civil society, see Call, *Constructing Justice and Security*, 403.

97 Tom Tyler, *Why People Obey the Law* (Princeton: Princeton University Press, 2006), 84.

98 Here we follow Pablo de Greiff's conception of "vertical trust" between citizens and the institutions that regulate their common lives. See de Greiff, "Vetting and Transitional Justice," 533–37.

99 Hannah Arendt's distinction between violence, on the one hand, that is instrumental in character and uses tools to multiply natural strength, and institutionalized power, on the other, that enables a group to think and act and that draws its legitimacy from the group, is helpful here. "[V]iolence itself results in impotence. Where violence is no longer backed and restrained by power, the well-known reversal in reckoning with means and ends has taken place. The means, the means of destruction, now determine the end — with the consequence that the end will be the destruction of all power." Hannah Arendt, *On Violence* (Orlando: Harcourt Brace and Company, 1970), 54.

100 For a discussion of civic trust as a mediate end of transitional justice, see de Greiff, "Theorizing Transitional Justice."

101 For a comprehensive analysis of the function of apologies in transition, in particular their norm-affirming function, and how apologies can complement other transitional justice mechanisms, see Pablo de Greiff, "The Role of Apologies in National Reconciliation Processes: On Making Trustworthy Institutions Trusted," in *The Age of Apology:*

Facing Up to the Past, ed. Mark Gibney et al. (Philadelphia: University of Pennsylvania Press, 2008). See also Ruti G. Teitel, "The Transitional Apology," in *Taking Wrongs Seriously: Apologies and Reconciliation*, ed. Elazar Barkan and Alexander Karn (Stanford: Stanford University Press, 2006).

102 de Greiff, "The Role of Apologies."

103 See ibid.; de Greiff, "Theorizing Transitional Justice"; and Arendt, *On Violence*.

104 Additionally, SSR and transitional justice work can be mutually reinforcing with other tools, such as those included under the term "conflict transformation," which aims to transform the structural causes of conflict, and which has "a deeply social side of transforming century old organizational cultures in a world where military thinking (and in that sense forceful/violent) and means are still the dominant paradigm" (Communication with Undine Kayser-Whande, February 17, 2009). "Working with institutional reform reveals how much the old and the new are entangled. It shows how much transformation is also a new 'battlefield' over images and perceptions, and how hard it is to build legitimacy and maintain integrity while the people working inside the institutions often remain a blend of old and new 'guard' dealing with their own pain, loss, insecurities and ambitions." Undine Kayser-Whande and Stephanie Schell-Faucon, "Transitional Justice and Civilian Conflict Transformation: Current Research, Future Questions," Study for the Centre for Conflict Studies (CCS), University of Marburg, Germany, and the Ministry for Economic Cooperation and Development (BMZ), Bonn, Germany, 2008, 22.

105 See Pablo de Greiff, "DDR and Reparations," in *Building a Future on Peace and Justice*.

106 See Pablo de Greiff, "Articulating the Links Between Transitional Justice and Development," in this volume.

107 "Vetting Public Employees in Post-Conflict Settings: Operational Guidelines," in *Justice as Prevention*, 558.

108 De Greiff, "Vetting and Transitional Justice," 528.

109 South Africa, e.g., according to Maryam Kamali, chose not to implement a formal vetting process in part for such practical reasons: it "could not afford to dismiss large numbers of its professionals until a new generation of qualified professionals became available." Germany, on the other hand, could afford vetting because it "had cadres of willing and qualified unemployed professionals in the western part of the country ready to take over." Maryam Kamali, "Accountability for Human Rights Violations: A Comparison of Transitional Justice in East Germany and South Africa," *Columbia Journal of Transnational Law* 40 (2001): 136.

110 "Vetting Public Employees," 552.

111 Mark White, "The Security and Development Nexus: A Case Study of Sierra Leone 2004–2006," Security System Transformation in Sierra Leone, 1997–2007, Working Paper Series, Paper No. 4, October 2008, 9.

112 See "Vetting Public Employees," 549, 553.

CHAPTER 7

The Role of Judicial Reform
in Development and Transitional Justice

Muna B. Ndulo and Roger Duthie[1]

Armed conflicts weaken the authority of the state, breed insecurity, and erode institutions of governance and civil society. Postconflict societies are characterized by a lack of the rule of law, past and present gross human rights violations, impunity, and economic devastation and decay. The official end of conflict does not automatically bring peace, security, or an end to violence and human rights violations. There is always a continuing risk that conflict might resume, alongside the need to rebuild society. One legacy of conflict shared by many postconflict societies is a lack of national institutions to deal with past and present human rights violations, to advance good governance, to deal with massive poverty, violence, and displaced populations, and to support socioeconomic development. The lack of legal infrastructure is often at a very basic level, with damage sustained in conflict and key personnel having fled, been killed, or been compromised by association with the previous regime. It is widely acknowledged that the performance of courts is hampered by the shortage of both human and operational resources,[2] which tends to undermine the public's confidence in the courts' ability and suitability as forums for the protection of human rights and the advancement of the rule of law.[3]

In response to past human rights violations, a variety of measures have been developed, including prosecutions at both international and domestic levels, truth commissions, and reparations for victims. All these options need strong institutions. The most common criticism of prosecutions, for example, is that they are driven by vengeance[4]—a criticism that can be deflected by having judicial institutions that are independent and fair and that respect and guarantee due process of law and the presumption of innocence. In the context of postconflict societies, this requires reforming or rebuilding the judicial system and its supporting services. At the same time, prosecutions in domestic or hybrid tribunals can have an enduring effect on the local justice systems and in norm articulation. Long-term improvement of the justice system helps the development of a culture of justice and accountability and ensures that norms established during the prosecution of past human rights violations will not vanish when the tribunal or specific trial is over. The judicial system can be strengthened and legitimized for its long-term role of protecting the constitution, ensuring the rule of law, and facilitating development. Reforming judicial institutions is a core task in postconflict societies.[5]

This chapter seeks to draw connections between judicial reform, transitional justice, and development in transitional contexts. Specifically, it uses the relatively narrow notion of judicial reform to link the broader notions of transitional justice and development. The first section briefly looks at some of the key elements of an effective and legitimate judicial system that judicial reform should work toward in postconflict contexts. The second section then reviews two ways in which judicial reform conceptually relates to development—namely, both as an integral part of a broad notion of development and as something that relates in complex ways to other elements of development through such concepts as the rule of law, governance, and social capital. This section also introduces some of the challenges faced by development practitioners working with judicial reform and rule of law programs—challenges that are also relevant to transitional justice, particularly with regard to the legitimacy of judicial institutions. The third section similarly outlines two ways in which judicial reform conceptually relates to transitional justice—namely, again, both as a part of transitional justice and as something that relates in complicated ways to specific elements (or measures) of transitional justice, such as criminal prosecutions for human rights violations. The point of the chapter is not to establish causal connections but to show how the various notions of judicial reform, development, and transitional justice can be thought to fit together as part of a broad and coherent response to justice and development concerns in transitional contexts. Drawing on some of the main issues that arise in the previous sections, the final section makes some broad recommendations for both development and transitional justice actors.

As with some other subjects discussed in this volume, it is important to acknowledge that the notion of "judicial reform" is not unproblematic. Some note that it is sometimes used interchangeably with the broader notion of the rule of law, leading to practice that neglects other important ways in which the rule of law in a society can be strengthened or undermined. Others point out that judicial reform can lead to too much emphasis being placed on top-down approaches to reforming formal institutions of the state, while ignoring the ways in which civil society actors interact with judicial institutions or the access that marginalized communities actually have to justice.[6] Others claim that it makes the most sense to consider the reform of judicial institutions together with the reform of security institutions and all oversight institutions, either as part of the concept of security sector (or system) reform (SSR) or as part of the concept of justice and security sector reform (JSSR). These are all valid criticisms and arguments, and they are taken into account here as much as possible. Nevertheless, since judicial institutions narrowly considered can be important for transitional justice efforts and for development, we believe it is useful to think about these relationships.[7]

ELEMENTS OF AN EFFECTIVE AND LEGITIMATE JUDICIAL SYSTEM IN A POSTCONFLICT CONTEXT

Judicial systems and their reform are related in important ways to both development and transitional justice. Before examining those connections, however, we begin by reviewing some of the key elements of an effective and legitimate judiciary that reform efforts should seek in postconflict contexts. These are independence, accountability, representativeness, oversight, gender sensitivity, and access to justice.

JUDICIAL INDEPENDENCE

Judicial independence is recognized in many international and regional human rights instruments[8] as constituting one of the cornerstones of the rule of law and good governance.[9] It involves two principles: (1) judicial power must exist as a power separate from and independent of executive and legislative power; and (2) judicial power must repose in the judiciary as a separate organ of government, composed of persons different from and independent of those who compose the executive and legislature. While discussion of the independence of the judiciary in rule of law discourse often centers on the higher courts, we must also recognize that magistrates require comparable protection, not least because it is they who deal with the vast majority of cases, both criminal and civil, and it is in them that much of the public confidence in the legal system resides. The main pillars of judicial independence are institutional and financial autonomy. These encompass the need for an appropriate appointment procedure, security of tenure, satisfactory conditions of service that the executive cannot adversely affect, the provision of adequate financial resources, and appropriate terms and conditions for all those involved in the administration of justice.

JUDICIAL ACCOUNTABILITY

Judicial independence and accountability are closely related. A society must support and protect the judiciary because judges remain an easy target for those wishing to generate partisan political capital. In return, society can expect judges to accept fair and temperate criticism of judgments and to maintain appropriate standards of ethical behavior. To help maintain the sensitive balance between independence and accountability, several states have developed codes of judicial ethics, an extremely desirable means of establishing the parameters for public expectations and criticism of judicial conduct. Given its potential relevance to so many, the development of a code is best undertaken as a result of a cooperative effort on the part of judges, the legal profession, legal academics, and civil society,[10] preferably based on internationally agreed standards.[11] Such a code should deal with the exercise of both judicial duties and extrajudicial activities, and, in particular, should require judges to disclose their assets, which is essential to guard against potential corruption. While many codes lay down rules that are seemingly straightforward and obvious to lawyers, they provide the public with a clear statement as to what they can expect from their judges. The effectiveness of such codes largely depends on their wide public dissemination.[12] To maintain public confidence, it is necessary also to offer appropriate protection for judges against unfounded criticism. One suitable approach is the establishment of an independent judicial ombudsman. A transparent and independent removal procedure is also essential. While any person or body is entitled to call for removal, arguably the initiation is best left to an independent judicial service commission (or judicial ombudsman) or the chief justice.

A FULLY REPRESENTATIVE JUDICIARY

Upholding the judicial oath of office to administer justice *to all persons* represents a considerable challenge for judges, who are inevitably the product of their social conditioning, education, gender, and ethnicity. If they are to discharge fully their judicial oaths and to enjoy the confidence of the people, they must be drawn from a wide array of backgrounds to ensure a better understanding of the experiences of those with whom they will be dealing.[13] The need to maintain a gender balance within the judiciary is now widely recognized.[14] Encouraging equality requires states to identify and tackle the factors that inhibit the entry of women onto the bench; for example, not imposing the duty upon women to go on circuit or be posted away from their home areas.

The "fast-tracking" of appropriate candidates is also necessary, although this should not be at the expense of applying less rigorous qualification requirements, for the principle that judicial appointments are made on merit is inviolable. Arguably, the appropriate approach to redressing imbalances is for all levels of the judiciary to have as an objective a selection system based on "merit with bias"—that is, where two candidates are of equal merit the bias should be to appoint a woman or member of an underrepresented minority.

OVERSIGHT BODIES

A key project in postconflict countries is the development of oversight institutions and mechanisms over and above the courts designed to promote and protect human rights and the concepts of good governance, accountability, and the rule of law.[15] These institutions include human rights commissions, anticorruption commissions, and ombudsman.[16] The international community has increasingly recognized the importance of national human rights institutions to promote transparency and the rule of law. In postconflict and conflict-affected countries, where the judicial system is weak, slow, or otherwise incapacitated, national human rights institutions provide a viable forum for the investigation and resolution of human rights complaints.[17] Another important oversight institution that can be useful in a postconflict situation is the office of ombudsman, particularly in strengthening the civil service. The prime role of the office of the ombudsman is to investigate complaints from members of the public about "maladministration" on the part of the public officials.[18] Several factors may affect the effectiveness of oversight bodies: independence; defined jurisdiction and adequate powers; accessibility; cooperation; operational efficiency and accountability; the behavior of government in not politicizing the institution, and in having a receptive attitude toward its activities; and the credibility of the office in the eyes of the populace.[19]

GENDER SENSITIVITY

It is important to ensure that national legal systems provide accessible and gender-sensitive redress for women who are victims of human rights violations. National institutions must respond to women's needs, concerns, and experiences, and must include special measures for victim and witness protection—especially of crimes of a sexual and violent nature—as well as specially trained staff (including prosecutors and investigators). There is also a need to deal with the aspects of custom and customary law that undermine women's rights.

This is particularly important in postconflict states in Africa, as the majority of the people in these countries regulate their lives in accordance with customary law whose procedures sometimes fail to accord with human rights norms. The majority of the people in some countries use customary law and its institutions instead of the modern statutory law and its courts because customary law and its institutions are cheap, familiar, and accessible. But the customary system is open to abuse and pervasive gender discrimination. People complain of corruption, highhandedness, and manipulation of the system by traditional leaders. A major challenge, therefore, which is often ignored in judicial reform, is the reform, regulation, and integration of the customary law and its procedures.

ACCESS TO JUSTICE

Access to the judiciary and other watchdog and oversight institutions remains a key element for the functional rule of law, albeit one that is often elusive in postconflict states, where the majority of people can neither assert nor defend their legal rights in criminal or civil matters.[20] Access to justice in postconflict societies is notoriously hampered by delays in all stages of proceedings in the law courts. The legal system is not perceived by many as protecting the rights of all citizens equally and effectively. The poor and marginalized groups in society have generally received poor protection from the law; the general perception is that corruption and economic status play a major role in one's ability to access justice. This should be a major concern in postconflict countries where the majority of people live below the poverty line. Such difficulties tend to undermine the public's confidence in the ability and suitability of the courts to act as a check on the executive, and as forums for the protection of human rights, the resolution of disputes, and the advancement of the rule of law. Accessibility requires that courts and other agencies charged with the promotion and protection of human rights be accessible to the population that the institutions are designed to protect. It is determined in part by such factors as public knowledge of the institution, physical location, and diversity of composition,[21] as well as awareness of the possible remedies that exist under the law—that is, levels of legal literacy. Access to justice means that justice should be affordable to all, and those who cannot afford it should be provided the means through legal aid assistance. The challenge for national institutions is to develop mechanisms to facilitate accessibility using such strategies as circuit courts and the establishment or strengthening of legal aid schemes.

JUDICIAL REFORM AND DEVELOPMENT

Judicial reform refers to measures intended to reform courts, prosecutors' offices, and other institutions that make up the judicial system.[22] Many developing countries throughout the world receive development assistance to engage in such reform, at least in part because it is widely understood by donors to be good for development purposes. Indeed, official development assistance to judicial and legal development increased from approximately US$142 million in 2002 to US$895 million in 2007.[23] Judicial reform can be thought to relate to development in two main ways—constitutively and instrumentally[24]—and through a number of broader concepts—legal reform/development, the rule of law, governance, and social capital.

First, as Amartya Sen articulates it, judicial reform as an element of a broader program of legal reform or legal development can be considered a constitutive part of development. "The claim here is not so much that, say, legal development causally influences development tout court," explains Sen, but that

> development as a whole cannot be considered separately from legal development. Indeed, in this view, the overarching idea of development is a functional relation that amalgamates distinct developmental concerns respectively in economic, political, social, legal and other spheres. This is more than causal interdependence: It involves a constitutive connection in the concept of development as a whole.[25]

Development, understood broadly, has "a strong association of meanings that makes a basic level of legality and judicial attainment a constitutive part of it."[26]

Second, again according to Sen, judicial reform is related to other specific elements of development. "Legal and judicial reform," he argues, "is important not only for legal development, but also for development in other spheres, such as economic development, political development, and so on, and these in turn are also constitutive parts of development as a whole."[27] Conversely, judicial reform can be facilitated by developmental progress in these others spheres.[28] The UK Department for International Development (DFID) (at the time the ODA) echoes Sen on this broad point. "Law is a crucial element of both good government and the wider development agenda," it states. "A sound and well-enforced legal framework provides benefits which are often desirable ends in themselves but also help provide a framework within which economic and social development may be achieved."[29]

In what ways is judicial reform important to other elements of development? According to Stephen J. Toope, at a general level, "stable and just legal systems support the promotion of security, equity, and prosperity," while more specifically, "reform of legal institutions and processes is integral to the promotion of human rights, democratic development, and good governance," facilitates private economic activity, assists in promoting the participation of women, and is necessary for the establishment of a framework for environmental protection.[30] One particularly common development-related justification for judicial reform is that it will positively affect economic growth/development. "Whatever the rationale for judicial reform," explains Richard Messick, "it is widely believed that reform will significantly improve economic performance." There are two ways in which this can happen: one is through "the importance of the judicial system in enforcing property rights, checking abuses of government power, and otherwise upholding the rule of law"; and the second, narrower one is through "the judiciary's effect in enabling exchanges between private parties."[31] Others emphasize that a limited degree of certain kinds of legal reform may have more positive effects on economic development than extensive but untargeted reform.[32]

There is little concrete evidence, however, of how legal and judicial reform contribute to the broader development agenda.[33] "Although few now question the importance of judicial reform for development," observes Messick, "little is known about the impact of the judicial system on economic performance. Nor is there any agreement on what makes for a successful judicial reform project."[34] Messick contends that the relationship between judicial reform and economic performance is best modeled as "a series of on-and-off connections, or of couplings and decouplings. At some stages in the development process, the two may be interdependent, while at other stages they may be autonomous."[35] Empirical evidence does not settle the question of the direction of causality (whether reform leads to development or the other way around) or whether both are caused by something else.[36] Again, however, while the precise nature of the relationship is unclear, it seems that there is indeed some form of relationship. "Can sustainable social and economic development take place at the macro level in the absence of functioning legal systems?" asks Toope. "Increasingly, the answer, backed up with some tentative empirical work, is 'no.'"[37]

At a broader conceptual level, judicial reform can be thought to relate to other elements of development through notions such as the rule of law, governance, and social capital. First, as indicated above, one way in which judicial institutions are thought to relate to development is in their role in upholding the rule of law. There is debate, however, as to what is meant by the rule of law and in what specific way it can relate to development. To some, the rule of law and judicial reform call for the elimination of wide discretionary authority from government processes,[38] because greater discretion tends to encourage less predictable and less principled decision-making. To others, the rule of law means acknowledging formal rules that do not involve a choice between particular ends or particular people, but which are there for the use of everyone;[39] this conception assumes that individuals have inalienable rights and liberties that governments should not violate, and that when these are violated courts should provide remedies.[40] To some extent, "the essence of the rule of law lies in its juxtaposition to 'the rule of men.' "[41]

The rule of law connotes the use of state power through legislation to establish the economic and social system agreed upon by the people through constitutionally sanctioned representative institutions or other acceptable surrogates. The rule of law implies the assurance of some sort of predictability in the conduct of state officials by the prior existence of a basic law covering the subject matter that falls within their fields of operation.[42] It demands precise definition of the roles and status of such public officials by law.[43] It commends the creation of control devices to ensure that public officials abide by these norms, and that, if they do not, their actions will be invalidated by courts of law.[44] The rule of law refers to a regulation of both state and private power, and, crucially, it guarantees recourse for those whose rights have been violated.

In postconflict countries, the establishment of the rule of law has generally been accepted as essential for reconstruction and long-term stability. Development and peacebuilding actors now engage in extensive rule of law projects, based on the belief that promoting the rule of law will contribute to good governance, conflict resolution, protection of human rights, and economic development.[45] The law can further contribute to development and reform by conferring impersonality, legitimacy, and to some extent stability on the political structure of the nation-state. The strengthening of the state is an important indirect contribution of the legal order to the development process because the state provides at once: (1) a national market; (2) a centralized source of general decision-making and long-range planning; and (3) a more impersonal and less restrictive center of social gravity than the primary group, which might in fact exacerbate conflict.

Judicial institutions are important to the rule of law; as B. O. Nwabueze has observed, "the one institution above all others essential to the preservation of the rule of law has always been and still is an honest, able, learned, and independent judiciary."[46] But the rule of law should not be equated only with judicial systems or their reform. The rule of law is not just made up of courts and other institutions, points out Thomas Carothers; it also includes norms: "Law is also a normative system that resides in the minds of the citizens of a society. As rule-of-law providers seek to affect the rule of law in a country, it is not clear if they should focus on institution-building or instead try to intervene in ways that would affect how citizens understand, use, and value law."[47] Similarly, Peter Uvin contends that there are three main mechanisms for promoting improvements in the rule of law: legal and judicial changes at the state level, the presence and resources of the aid machinery, and "any and all mechanisms that increase the capacity to and willingness of citizens to know the laws, to be aware of when their rights are being violated or circumvented, and to seek redress." The rule of law is important to a rights-based approach to development because "it empowers ordinary people."[48] Michael J. Trebilcock and Ronald J. Daniels, in examining how the rule of law relates to development, use a procedural conception of the rule of law, focusing on process values (transparency, predictability, stability, and enforceability), institutional values (independence and accountability), and legitimacy values.[49] In his conceptual chapter in this volume, Pablo de Greiff emphasizes the legitimacy of the rule of law: "the authority of law depends, ultimately, upon its legitimacy, something that a law gains precisely in virtue of the fact that we can consider it to be *our* rule (ownership), one that we give to ourselves—via recognized procedures—where the 'ourselves' keeps growing (inclusion)."[50] While we focus on judicial institutions in this chapter, we do so recognizing the importance of their place within the larger concept of the rule of law. Effectiveness, independence, accountability, and legitimacy are discussed throughout, but legitimacy is seen as especially crucial from a transitional justice perspective.

Empirically, however, the rule of law should not be reduced to a precondition for development. "Simplistic assertions such as have become common among aid agencies to the effect that 'the rule of law' *grosso modo* is necessary for development," Carothers warns, "are at best badly oversimplified and probably misleading in many ways."[51] It appears, others have generalized, that while the rule of law can be improved, it is weakly linked to economic growth in the short term.[52]

Judicial reform and the rule of law can also be linked to development through the still broader concept of governance, which became the focus of development strategies in the early 1990s. According to this notion, "the state is indispensable in formulating and implementing a wide range of economic and social policies that bear on human well-being," and "failures of governance in many developing countries are an important explanation for many of the characteristics of low levels of development."[53] Empirical work by Daniel Kaufmann and others at the World Bank—work that includes the rule of law ("measuring perceptions of the extent to which agents have confidence in and abide by the rules of society, and in particular the quality of contract enforcement, property rights, the police, and the courts, as well as the likelihood of crime and violence") as one of six elements of governance, the others being voice and accountability, political stability and the absence of violence, government effectiveness, regulatory quality, and control of corruption—demonstrates a strong positive and causal effect of governance on economic development.[54]

The concept of social capital[55] is another way to link judicial systems and their reform to development. According to Christiaan Grootaert and Thierry van Bastelaer, social capital can be characterized by its scope, its forms, and its channels. In terms of scope, social capital can exist at the micro level, the meso level, and the macro level, the last of which expands the concept to cover "the social and political environment that shapes social structures and enables norms to develop," including "the most formalized institutional relationships and structures, such as the political regime, the rule of law, the court system, and civil and political liberties," also referred to as "government social capital," as opposed to "civil social capital." In terms of form, social capital exists as a structural type—that is, "established roles and social networks supplemented by rules, procedures, and precedents"—and as a cognitive type—that is, "shared norms, values, trust, attitudes, and beliefs." Social capital's channels refer to the ways in which it affects development, which depend on the interaction between its different levels and forms.[56] The idea that social capital leads to economic progress and development is contested. According to the World Bank economist Stephen Knack, however, "a consensus has developed on the importance of government social capital for economic performance; a similar consensus is rapidly developing on civil social capital."[57] As a contributing factor to social capital, then, judicial institutions may affect development.

Writing broadly about rule of law reform and its relationship to development, Trebilcock and Daniels propose three broad categories of major potential impediments. The first two of these are technological or resource-related impediments and political-economy-based impediments, which, as will be seen, are important challenges from a transitional justice perspective as well.[58] The third category of impediments faced by developing countries, however, "relates to a variety of factors that might loosely be placed under the rubric of social-cultural-historical factors that have yielded a set of social values, norms, attitudes, or practices that are inhospitable" to rule of law reform.[59] In discussing the judiciary, they write about the importance of independence, accountability (which are both discussed in more detail below), and, crucially, legitimacy. "Successful judicial reform also requires public acceptance of the judicial institution. Courts must be perceived as legitimate because they occupy a powerful position vis-à-vis the public." Without legitimacy, citizens may opt not to use the system, reducing compliance and making enforcement more difficult.[60] One way in which the legitimacy of judicial institutions can be impeded, then, is through social-cultural-historical factors, which, we emphasize, can include the role of those judicial institutions in past abuses. This, we argue, is where an important role can be played by transitional justice measures, as they may shape judicial reform in a way that helps it overcome historically related obstacles. We note here that in addressing such social-cultural-historical factors in judicial reform, transitional justice can be seen to be part of the broader notion of conflict transformation, an important part of the development discourse, which addresses both "direct and attitudinal manifestations of conflict, but also their deeper structural sources."[61]

JUDICIAL REFORM AND TRANSITIONAL JUSTICE

Having briefly reviewed the relationship between judicial reform and development, in this section we outline the relationship between transitional justice and judicial reform, which we argue exists at three levels. First, judicial reform can constitute an element of transitional justice. Second, judicial reform may facilitate transitional justice, and in some instances may be a precondition of certain justice measures, particularly criminal prosecution for human rights violations. Third, transitional justice may contribute to judicial reform efforts. It is argued here that this relationship can be one of mutual reinforcement, and that there are numerous lessons that can be learned from the field of development that are of relevance to transitional justice in its engagement with judicial reform.

TRANSITIONAL JUSTICE AS JUDICIAL REFORM

Under some conceptions of security sector (or system) reform (SSR), as noted above, such as that used by the Organisation for Economic Co-operation and Development's Development Assistance Committee (OECD DAC), judicial reform is part of SSR. Since a justice-sensitive approach, as articulated elsewhere in this volume,[62] can be considered to be part of transitional justice as well, at a broad level one can argue that, conceptually, transitional justice includes certain elements of judicial reform under the notion of justice-sensitive SSR. Even if one does not take judicial reform to be part of SSR, however, there is still one type of institutional reform that can be considered a direct form of transitional justice, and which can be applied directly to the judicial system: vetting, the process of screening for and dismissing human rights abusers from public institutions. Thus, vetting can conceptually be considered to be both a transitional justice measure and a development measure.

Vetting in the judicial sector has generally not been undertaken in developing countries emerging from conflict or authoritarianism, at least in part because of the frequent incapacitation or virtual nonexistence of judicial institutions in those contexts. Most instances of vetting in the judiciary have occurred in such places as Bosnia and Herzegovina, Greece, and the formerly communist countries of Eastern and Central Europe.[63] Nevertheless, the lessons to be learned from such experiences correspond to some of the main issues that have emerged from the study of judicial reform from the perspectives of development and transitional justice, and are discussed more below.

JUDICIAL REFORM AS AN ENABLING CONDITION OR PRECONDITION OF TRANSITIONAL JUSTICE

Some judicial reform may facilitate transitional justice or may be necessary before it can be pursued. This is most likely to be the case with domestic criminal prosecutions and other forms of legal accountability for perpetrators of massive human rights abuses, which require the institutions and infrastructure of the judicial system more so than other transitional justice measures. Judicial systems in developing countries emerging from conflict and/or authoritarian rule, however, are often virtually nonexistent, weak, corrupt, and without the trust of citizens, damaged by years of physical destruction and the fleeing or murder or complicity of judges, lawyers, and other personnel. Rwanda, East Timor, Sierra Leone, and Cambodia would be examples of such countries. As Etelle R. Higonnet puts it:

> It is undeniable that local courts and governance structures in most postconflict contexts are too flawed and face too many financial and logistical limitations to cope effectively with massive war crimes trials. In the immediate aftermath of conflict, the inability of many post-atrocity local courts to cope with war crimes trials is often due, at the most

basic level, to crippling damage sustained by physical infrastructure by bombing, shelling, arson, looting, or neglect. In addition, key personnel may have fled abroad, been killed, or been compromised by association with a prior regime which failed to prosecute or convict murderers, torturers, or ethnic cleansers. In some other cases, a new regime may have replaced the old personnel almost completely, resulting in an enormous skill and experience deficit, as well as the danger of show trials and overly zealous prosecution for past crimes.[64]

Such judicial systems, which require "an entire set of functioning institutions to investigate, prosecute, and punish individuals who commit human rights violations" with some degree of due process, may need to be built or reformed before they can deal with cases of massive abuses. This process can take months, years, or decades.[65] "Emphasis on the prosecution of past violations is justifiable, therefore," argues Tonya Putnam, "only if accompanied by parallel efforts at building institutions capable of punishing human rights abuses perpetrated in the postconflict environment and of helping to prevent future abuses." While choices about trade-offs and timing may in fact be best left to particular societies themselves, as Putnam contends,[66] a key point here is that it may not be appropriate to pursue criminal accountability for massive human rights violations through domestic judicial systems in developing countries with fragile states emerging from armed conflict or authoritarian rule.[67] For the purposes of the discussion to follow, it is also important to distinguish those institutions that lack capacity because their personnel were tainted by association with the prior regime from those that lack capacity for other reasons, such as lack of trained personnel and/or physical infrastructure; each circumstance involves different levels of mistrust to overcome.

From a transitional justice perspective, this general lack of capacity in judicial institutions presents the possibility of impunity at the domestic level, at least in the short term, for those who committed serious crimes. From an international justice perspective, it presents the possibility that developing countries are more likely to become the subject of proceedings before the International Criminal Court (ICC). If a case or a situation in a country falls within the ICC's jurisdiction, whether through referral by a state, being investigated by the ICC of its own action, or even being referred by the UN Security Council, the ICC is more likely to admit (or accept) a case arising from those countries on the grounds that they are unwilling or unable genuinely to carry out the prosecution. While the ICC's response predominantly depends on its focus on only the most serious cases and on those most responsible, William Schabas has noted the danger of the ICC being perceived as a "mechanism directed essentially at poor or under-developed countries," thus potentially reducing its legitimacy in those countries.[68]

From a development perspective, donors can respond to a lack of domestic capacity by providing development support directly to transitional justice measures, such as vetting or prosecutions. According to one recent study, for example, from 1995 to 2005 Rwanda received US$111 million in aid to transitional justice measures, roughly 20 percent of which went to criminal courts, and Guatemala received US$140 million, roughly 3 percent of which went to criminal courts.[69] The United Nations Development Programme (UNDP) has provided capacity development to the gacaca process in Rwanda and the War Crimes Chamber in Bosnia and Herzegovina.[70] Importantly, however, development assistance for judicial reform can play an important role in strengthening domestic judicial systems such that, at some point, they will have the capacity to engage in transitional justice efforts. Support to vetting, even if conceived only as a measure of judicial reform, can still serve to facilitate other types of transitional justice efforts. As de Greiff articulates it, "vetting may be thought of as an 'enabling condition' of other transitional justice measures." Although he makes the point with regard to security institutions, it is not unreasonable to think that judicial institutions vetted of complicit judges and prosecutors would be more likely to prosecute perpetrators of massive abuses.[71]

TRANSITIONAL JUSTICE CONTRIBUTIONS TO JUDICIAL REFORM

Transitional justice efforts can be dependent on judicial systems, but they may also contribute to the reform of those systems as well. A mutually reinforcing relationship, then, is possible. "Domestic prosecution for past crimes and judicial reform are in many ways interdependent," writes Eirin Mobekk.

> There needs to be a level of judicial reform for domestic trials to be held, yet these can also affect long-term judicial reform. Judicial reform is a long-term process—how long-term is dependent upon the state of the judicial system—which can be contrary to the immediate demands for justice arising within a post-conflict setting. However, it is not necessary to fully reform or restore a judicial system prior to conducting domestic prosecution for past abuses, on the contrary domestic trials can also contribute to the development of rule of law, as long as the minimum requirements of a fair trial are guaranteed.[72]

How might this contribution to judicial reform be made, specifically? First, transitional justice efforts may reinforce judicial reform (and thereby development) by contributing to the rule of law and social capital. Jane Strom-seth, David Wippman, and Rose Brooks, for example, argue that "account-ability proceedings" for atrocities can have a long-term impact on the rule of law—which, again, includes judicial institutions but is not limited to them—in three ways:

> first, the effective disempowerment of key perpetrators who threaten stability and undermine public confidence in the rule of law; second, the character of the accountability proceedings pursued, particularly whether they demonstrate credibly that previous patterns of abuse and impunity are rejected and that justice can be fair; and third, the extent to which systematic and meaningful efforts at domestic capacity-building are included as part of the accountability process.[73]

In terms of specific transitional justice measures, de Greiff, in his chapter in this volume, summarizes the various contributions to strengthening the rule of law roughly as follows: criminal trials demonstrate the generality of law through procedural guarantees and the application of justice to those in power; truth-telling provides the basis on which legal systems can behave in the future by contributing to an understanding of how legal systems failed to protect the rights of citizens in the past; reparations signify a commitment to the notion that legal norms matter; and institutional reform measures help to make rule of law systems operative.[74]

Remaining at a broad level, transitional justice can be thought to reinforce judicial reform efforts by promoting civic trust as well. Again, as de Greiff articulates it: prosecutions can promote civic trust by reaffirming the relevance of the norms that perpetrators violated, norms that turn natural persons into rights bearers; truth-telling may be seen by victims as an effort to initiate a new political project around shared norms and values; reparations can foster civic trust by demonstrating the seriousness with which institutions now take the violation of their rights; and vetting can induce trust by "re-peopling" institu-tions and demonstrating a commitment to systemic norms.[75] Thus, transitional justice measures may reinforce judicial reform programs—and their contribu-tion to development—by strengthening the rule of law and improving gover-nance, and by increasing levels of trust between citizens and the state, thereby raising levels of macro or government social capital. In both ways, transitional justice efforts may reinforce judicial reform primarily by improving the legiti-macy of those institutions.

At a more direct level, prosecutions and truth-telling in particular can make contributions to judicial reform. Hybrid tribunals or courts (combined domestic and international efforts)—the main justifications for which, in addition to those cited for general prosecutions, are lack of capacity and fears of bias or lack of independence[76]—for example, are one avenue through which transitional justice efforts can potentially affect domestic judicial systems. Indeed, the term that has been coined for this potential impact is "legacy," which is defined by the Office of the UN High Commissioner for Human Rights (OHCHR) in *Rule-of-Law Tools for Post-Conflict States* as a "court's lasting impact on bolstering the rule of law in a particular society, by conducting effective trials to contribute to ending impunity, while also strengthening domestic judicial capacity."[77] According to the *Rule-of-Law Tools*—and echoing Stromseth and others above—legacy includes: a court's "demonstration effect"—that is, its promotion of a culture of rule of law and human rights through adhering to a set of standards, including fair trial standards, prosecutorial standards, detention and imprisonment standards, transparency, and gender issues; a court's contribution to human-resource and professional development within the domestic judicial system, through recruitment, training, and skills transfer; a court's physical infrastructure, including facilities, evidence, and court records; and a court's contribution to law reform.[78] At the international level, prosecution efforts, such as the International Criminal Tribunal for the former Yugoslavia (ICTY), the International Criminal Tribunal for Rwanda (ICTR), and the ICC, can potentially assist, encourage, and/or leverage domestic prosecutions and capacity building (although this potential is inherently limited).[79]

Truth commissions may also contribute to the development of a country's legal system and the establishment of the rule of law in a number of ways. These include appraising the role of the judicial system in past abuses and exposing compromised personnel, making specific recommendations to improve the efficiency and independence of the judiciary, promoting the rule of law by helping to fulfill international legal obligations, promoting a richer understanding of the rule of law, stimulating debates about what constitutes a "good society," and promoting trust in the institutions of the judicial system.[80] In El Salvador, for example, a number of postconflict reforms to the judicial system—related to the appointment, oversight, and removal of judges, and including a new Criminal Procedures Code—were, according to Priscilla Hayner, "a direct outcome of recommendations made by the El Salvador truth commission." Reforms had been pushed there by nongovernmental organizations (NGOs) and other governments before, "but the truth commission report focused attention and pressure on them."[81] Rubén Zamora agrees that the truth commission in El Salvador "created a greater public sense of the need for reform."[82] More broadly speaking, but still including judicial institutions,

Eric Brahm observes that "in a number of instances truth commission reports appear to have provided reform blueprints that have had varying degrees of success."[83] And as with other potential benefits of transitional justice measures, combined or holistic approaches tend to have more impact. "Combined approaches that also include truth and reconciliation mechanisms," it is argued, "are more likely to produce more effective and far-reaching demonstration effects and capacity-building than trials alone."[84]

A positive impact on domestic judicial systems cannot, of course, be assumed.[85] Transitional justice efforts could have negative, negligible, or non-existent effects on judicial reform. Trying to uphold international standards of justice without institutional preconditions could undermine legal norms by demonstrating their ineffectiveness.[86] As the OHCHR *Rule-of-Law Tools* acknowledges, there is a potential "negative legacy" of a hybrid tribunal: for example, "if it drains domestic capacity as local professionals try to move to the hybrid court, diverts the focus away from investment in the necessary domestic legal reforms or contributes to negative perceptions of the local legal system" (although these effects have not necessarily happened and can be short term).[87] Truth commissions may also undermine judicial reform. For example, while it is contested whether or not truth commissions should name the names of perpetrators, doing so without giving the accused the opportunity to defend him/herself could be viewed as "contravening the principle of due process," thus setting "a negative example for a judicial reform process aimed at ensuring a fair system."[88]

Whether transitional justice measures actually have positive, negative, or no impact on judicial reform will depend, of course, on a number of contextual factors, both internal and external to the justice measure itself. Internally, those designing and implementing a trial or truth commission can take steps to maximize the positive and minimize the negative effects. With hybrid courts, for example, legacy will depend on the extent to which and the way in which the court's core mandate is achieved, but it will also depend on whether a specific legacy strategy is adopted—whether legacy is incorporated into the mandate, whether it is planned for, whether it receives support from the core budget, whether outreach is effective and comprehensive—and whether that strategy is realistic.[89] The ICTY and the ICTR both "could have done much more to assist domestic capacity-building" with "more effective outreach to domestic audiences, and by more systematic efforts to design focused, well-conceived domestic capacity-building programs."[90] For truth commissions, the naming of names is a complicated question that cannot be addressed here, but commissions can take steps to improve procedural fairness through, for example, guaranteeing judicial review of findings against named individuals.[91]

In seeking to strengthen domestic judicial systems, there are lessons that can be learned from development practitioners' experiences with judicial reform and rule of law programs. As the *Rule of Law Tools* stresses, and as is often stressed in the development literature, especially on the rights-based approach to development, "*how* it is done is as important as *what* is done."[92] As Uvin contends, "the process is as important if not more important than the product in most development work." At the heart of this is the idea of a participatory approach, one that

> ought to respect the dignity and individual autonomy of all those it claims to help, including the poorest and the most excluded, including minorities and other vulnerable, often-discriminated against groups; it ought to create opportunities for their participation—opportunities that are not dependent on the whim of a benevolent outsider but rooted in institutions and procedures. This means we are talking about a particularly strong and deep form of participation here....[93]

From a transitional justice perspective, this can mean two things. First, it means ensuring local participation in the design and implementation of transitional justice measures themselves. The OHCHR *Rule-of-Law Tools* on the various transitional justice measures all call for broad consultations with civil society and victims groups. "Because of their proximity to victims," states the prosecutions tool, "NGOs can and should develop programmes that allow victims to participate meaningfully in the prosecution process."[94] "Broad consultations with civil society and an opinion survey," states the OHCHR tool on vetting, "will ensure a comprehensive identification of the public needs. Particular attention should be paid to the needs of victims, women, minorities and vulnerable groups."[95] Second, it means encouraging the reform of judicial institutions such that long-term access to justice for the poor and marginalized is increased and improved, as previously noted. There are, then, steps that transitional justice practitioners can take to improve the judicial systems in the countries in which they work, and in doing so they can draw on the approaches and experiences of, and coordinate with, development practitioners working toward similar goals.

Externally, however, the impact on judicial reform will depend on such factors as the political context in which justice measures are designed and implemented, and whether international donors' support is substantial, extended, coordinated, and strategic enough to implement such things as outreach campaigns to accompany locally driven processes.[96] Just as with all judicial reform and rule of law work, transitional justice efforts are inherently political projects that may be resisted by certain groups within society that stand to be sanctioned or lose power as a result of such projects. Vetting is a good example, again because it is in itself a type of institutional reform: it is often subject to both political resistance and political manipulation.[97] Other transitional justice measures, which in themselves might not constitute institutional reform, can also be subject to political resistance and misuse, particularly if they may lead to institutional reform. In El Salvador, the implementation of some judicial reforms recommended by the truth commission did happen, but not easily, and only after several years of the legislature's "internal debate, deadlock, international pressure, and finally mediation by a senior UN representative."[98] The truth commission there had recommended the resignation of the entire Supreme Court, to which the president of the court responded (incorrectly) that "only God" could remove him.[99] As Hayner notes, in addition to the push from civil society and the leverage of external actors, "in the end, the implementation of reforms recommended by a truth commission depends on the interest and political will of those in power."[100]

Perhaps most important for the argument made by this chapter, the impact of transitional justice measures will depend on *other reforms* to the judicial system and *other efforts* related to the rule of law and conflict transformation.[101] The *Rule-of-Law Tools* explicitly state that while legacy is defined as a contribution to the rule of law, it should be "differentiated from the broader effort to rebuild the rule of law in a particular context, which may take many years"; hybrid courts should be part of a "multifaceted intervention." "There is obviously," it declares, "a need for simultaneous investment in hybrid courts and domestic judicial systems.[102] Even vetting, which is itself an institutional reform measure, will be more effective in achieving one of its own goals—that is, preventing the recurrence of abuses—if it is "integrated into a coherent institutional reform strategy." Other reform measures aimed at promoting institutional integrity and legitimacy, which should accompany vetting, according to Alexander Mayer-Rieckh, include "structural reforms to provide accountability, build independence, ensure representation, and increase responsiveness, as well as verbal and symbolic measures that reaffirm a commitment to overcome the legacy of abuse and an endorsement of democratic norms and values."[103] As mentioned above, conflict transformation processes seek these types of structural reforms, but they also aim to change relationships, interests, and discourses among the people within institutions as well. Transitional justice efforts that seek to change institutions then by dealing with the past can be reinforced by other types of conflict transformation work.[104] Institutional reform in the judicial sector in the aftermath of conflict and human rights abuses, then, is a complex process in which interventions in the fields of transitional justice, development, the rule of law, or conflict transformation will to a certain degree depend on each other.

Empirically, however, there is not a strong case that transitional justice measures other than vetting actually do make a substantial contribution to judicial reform. The experiences of Timor-Leste, Kosovo, Sierra Leone, and Bosnia and Herzegovina, for example, have shown that the "demonstration effects and capacity-building impact of these diverse hybrids, in fact, have varied widely." The effects on the rule of law have been "mixed, complex, and often unclear, and more research is needed to fully understand their long-term impact." The subject is "surprisingly underanalyzed."[105] According to Charles T. Call, there has recently been "some recognition of the need to integrate these two perspectives — past accountability and present judicial development — but written analysis has lagged." A series of case studies edited by Call on justice and security in postconflict contexts did determine that in countries where violence was particularly widespread, such as Rwanda, Timor-Leste, and parts of Bosnia, "perceptions of justice for past abuses affected popular acceptance of present-day justice in some countries." The studies did not, however, establish a "robust, empirical connection between justice for past abuses and the quality and accessibility of justice in the future." Instead, they found that "deficiencies of justice under new postconflict regimes varied greatly across the cases...but they seemed rooted in institutional choices, political decisions, and the context of war termination more than in the decision about how to deal with perpetrators of past atrocities."[106]

Despite the lack of empirical evidence, there appear to be legitimate reasons to think that transitional justice may make a modest contribution to the judicial reform process. Furthermore, in engaging with judicial reform directly or indirectly, justice practitioners must contend with some of the same challenges as development actors, such as those related to resources and capacity, political context, process (and participation), and coherence with broader reforms. Again, much of the discussion here depends on the existence of a judicial reform program itself.

CONCLUSIONS AND RECOMMENDATIONS

In this chapter, we have attempted to draw some connections between judicial reform, development, and transitional justice. To summarize, we have argued the following: judicial reform is a part of one element of development (legal development), and it is related to other elements of development; judicial reform itself can be a measure of transitional justice (vetting or justice-sensitive SSR), and it can be a precondition or enabling condition for transitional justice elements, especially criminal prosecutions; transitional justice may contribute to judicial reform (mainly by improving the legitimacy of the legal order and promoting the rule of law, and depending on a number of internal and external factors), and, taking this into account, transitional justice practitioners must face—and may learn from—many of the same challenges and issues as development actors in their engagement with judicial reform. We conclude by making several broad recommendations based on these connections.

- Given the state of the empirical evidence and the myriad other factors involved, the links between judicial reform, development, and transitional justice discussed here should be viewed in terms of modest expectations for outcomes.
- Transitional justice and development practitioners should consider how their contribution to judicial reform may impact each other's work. In particular:
  - Transitional justice measures, such as prosecutions, should be designed and implemented giving consideration to the issues of feasibility and timing that may depend on judicial reform and on development support to judicial reform; transitional justice actors should also develop specific strategies, when appropriate, for contributing positively to judicial reform;
  - Development actors should consider directly supporting transitional justice efforts, such as prosecutions, that may have an impact on judicial reform; they should also consider the potential value from a justice perspective in providing support for judicial reform.
- Ideally, transitional justice and development actors whose work may impact judicial reform should acknowledge the strong need for dialogue, coordination, and joint planning of activities with an eye to maximizing mutual reinforcement and minimizing tensions between each other's work.
- Transitional justice and development actors should learn from each other as they face similar challenges:
  - *Resources/Capacity:* Resources and capacity are central concerns of both transitional justice and development engagement with judicial reform, in terms of the constraints that they create, the shared aim of building capacity, and the competition for resources that may have a negative impact on capacity.

- *Political Context:* Both transitional justice and development actors must remember that judicial reform is a political project, not a technical one. Local political dynamics, including resistance and manipulation, must be taken into account.
- *Process:* For both transitional justice and development efforts, process can be as important as outcomes. It is important, for example, to undertake both types of efforts in ways that prioritize broad and deep participation, including that of victims, the poor, and the marginalized.
- *Legitimacy:* As has been pointed out by many others, institutional reform affects and is affected by less tangible things, such as relationships, norms, values, and trust. One of the main obstacles faced by judicial reform and rule of law programs is overcoming a lack of legitimacy; by bringing a consideration of past abuses into the process of judicial reform, transitional justice can help to overcome this obstacle.
- *Coherence with Broader Reform:* Reform of judicial institutions in the aftermath of massive abuses is a complex, interdependent process. Transitional justice and development engagement with judicial reform should be approached as part of a broader and coherent program of institutional reform, the rule of law, governance, and conflict transformation.

NOTES

1 The authors would like to thank Pablo de Greiff, Undine Kayser-Whande, and Caitlin Reiger for comments on earlier versions of the chapter. The views expressed here do not necessarily represent those of the ICTJ.

2 UN Centre for Human Rights, *National Human Rights Institutions: A Handbook for the Establishment and Strengthening of National Institutions for the Promotion and Protection of Human Rights*, Professional Training Series No. 4 (New York and Geneva: United Nations, 1995), 18.

3 Linda C. Reif, "Building Democratic Institutions: The Role of National Human Rights Institutions in Good Governance and Human Rights Protection," *Harvard Human Rights Journal* 13 (2000): 1–70.

4 Office of the UN High Commissioner for Human Rights (OHCHR), *Rule-of-Law Tools for Post-Conflict States: Prosecution Initiatives* (New York and Geneva: United Nations, 2006).

5 See generally UN Security Council, *The Rule of Law and Transitional Justice in Conflict and Post-conflict Societies, Report of the Secretary-General*, S/2004/616, August 23, 2004.

6   See, e.g., Thomas Carothers, "Promoting the Rule of Law Abroad: The Problem of Knowledge," Working Paper No. 34, Rule of Law Series, Carnegie Endowment for International Peace, January 2003; and Stephen Golub, "The Rule of Law and the UN Peacebuilding Commission: A Social Development Approach," *Cambridge Review of International Affairs* 20, no. 1 (2007): 47–67.

7   The chapter in this volume by Alexander Mayer-Rieckh and Roger Duthie, "Enhancing Justice and Development Through Justice-Sensitive Security Sector Reform," is intended to complement this one.

8   "Everyone is entitled to a fair and public hearing by an independent tribunal...." Universal Declaration of Human Rights, art. 10; "...everyone shall be entitled to a fair and public hearing by a competent, independent and impartial tribunal established by law." International Covenant on Civil and Political Rights, art. 14.1. See also African Charter on Human and Peoples' Rights, art. 7(1).

9   Its significance has also led to the development of the *United Nations Basic Principles on the Independence of the Judiciary*, which are designed to "secure and promote" judicial independence (para. 1). *Basic Principles on the Independence of the Judiciary*, adopted by the Seventh United Nations Congress on the Prevention of Crime and the Treatment of Offenders held at Milan from August 26 to September 6, 1985, and endorsed by General Assembly resolutions 40/32 of November 29, 1985, and 40/146 of December 13, 1985. See also the similar views of the International Commission of Jurists, *States of Emergency: Their Impact on Human Rights* (Geneva: International Commission of Jurists, 1983), 434–37; and Julius Nyerere, *Freedom and Socialism* (Dar es Salaam: Oxford University Press, 1968), 109–14.

10 A suitable body for drafting, revising, and overseeing the working of the code is therefore a fully representative Judicial Service Commission.

11 *Bangalore Principles of Judicial Conduct*, drawn up by the Judicial Group on Strengthening Judicial Integrity in February 2001, whose drafting committee included senior judges from Uganda, Tanzania, and South Africa, and as revised at the Round Table Meeting of Chief Justices held at the Peace Palace, The Hague, November 25–26, 2002. The code highlights six values: propriety (propriety and the appearance of propriety are essential to the performance of all the activities of a judge); independence; integrity; impartiality; equality (ensuring equality of treatment to all before the courts); and competence and diligence.

12 For example, ensuring a copy of the code in all the major languages is readily available to all litigants.

13 See, e.g., para. 7 of the Bloemfontein Statement of 1993: "...it is fundamental to a country's judiciary to enjoy the broad confidence of the people it serves: to the extent possible, a judiciary should be broad-based and therefore not appear (rightly or wrongly) beholden to the interest of any particular section of society."

14 One of the principles enshrined in the *Latimer House Guidelines* states: "It is recognized that redress of gender imbalance is essential to accomplish full and equal rights in society and to achieve true human rights. Merit and the capacity to perform public office regardless of disability should be the criteria of eligibility for appointment." The *Basic Principles on the Independence of the Judiciary* state that in the selection of judges there shall be no discrimination against a person on grounds of sex (para. 10).

15 UN Centre for Human Rights, *National Human Rights Institutions*, 5.

16 Reif, "Building Democratic Institutions," 67.

17 Human Rights Watch, *Protectors or Pretenders? Government Human Rights Commissions in Africa* (New York: Human Rights Watch, 2001), 11.

18 Reif, "Building Democratic Institutions," 67.

19 Ibid., 23.

20 Muna Ndulo, "The Democratization Process and Structural Adjustment in Africa," *Indiana Journal of Global Legal Studies* (Winter 2003): 315–67.

21 Human Rights Watch, *Protectors or Pretenders?*, 20.

22 Richard E. Messick, "Judicial Reform and Economic Development: A Survey of the Issues," *World Bank Research Observer* 14, no. 1 (February 1999): 117–36.

23 Organisation for Economic Co-operation and Development (OECD), International Development Statistics Online, www.oecd.org/dac/stats/idsonline (accessed February 12, 2009).

24 The point is made about the rule of law more generally by Michael J. Trebilcock and Ronald J. Daniels, *Rule of Law Reform and Development: Charting the Fragile Path of Progress* (Cheltenham, UK: Edward Elgar, 2008), 4.

25 Amartya Sen, "What Is the Role of Legal and Judicial Reform in the Development Process?" (paper presented at the World Bank Legal Conference on the Role of Legal and Judicial Reform in Development, Washington, DC, June 5, 2000), 8.

26 Ibid., 9.

27 Ibid., 13.

28 Ibid., 15.

29 UK, ODA, Government and Institutions Department, *Law, Good Government and Development* (Guidance Paper) (January 1996), 1, 12, cited in Stephen J. Toope, "Legal and Judicial Reform through Development Assistance: Some Lessons," *McGill Law Journal* 48 (2003): 360.

30 Toope, "Legal and Judicial Reform through Development Assistance," 360–61.

31 Messick, "Judicial Reform and Economic Development," 120.

32 "[E]conomic progress is possible with little—perhaps no—law," Richard Posner argues, "and can be stifled by excessive investment in public-sector projects, including legal reform. A small expenditure on law reform can increase the rate of economic growth, which will in turn generate additional resources for more ambitious legal reforms later."

It is more important, he contends, to focus on "creating substantive and procedurally efficient rules of contract and property rather than on creating a first-class judiciary or an extensive system of civil liberties." Richard A. Posner, "Creating a Legal Framework for Economic Development," *World Bank Research Observer* 13, no. 1 (February 1998), 8–9.

33   Toope, "Legal and Judicial Reform through Development Assistance," 360.

34   Messick, "Judicial Reform and Economic Development," 117.

35   Ibid., 123.

36   Ibid., 122.

37   Toope, "Legal and Judicial Reform through Development Assistance," 363; and Posner, "Creating a Legal Framework for Economic Development," 3: "If it is not possible to demonstrate as a matter of theory that a reasonably well-functioning legal system is a necessary condition of a nation's prosperity, there is empirical evidence showing that the rule of law does contribute to a nation's wealth and its rate of economic growth."

38   See Richard H. Fallon, Jr., "The Rule of Law as a Concept in Constitutional Discourse," *Columbia Law Review* 97 (1997): 1–56.

39   Tawia Ocran, "The Rule of Law as the Quest for Legitimacy," in *Law in Zambia*, ed. Muna Ndulo (Nairobi: East African Publishing House, 1984), 297.

40   Ibid., 297.

41   Ibid., 299.

42   Ndulo, "The Democratization Process," 339.

43   Ocran, "The Rule of Law as the Quest for Legitimacy," 303.

44   Ibid., 305.

45   International Monetary Fund (IMF), *Good Governance, The IMF's Role* (Washington, DC: IMF, 1997); Economic Commission for Africa, *Good Governance in Africa 2005* (Addis Ababa: Economic Commission for Africa, 2005), 2; and World Bank, *Good Governance: The World Bank's Experience* (Washington, DC: World Bank, 1994). Messick, "Judicial Reform and Economic Development," 117, observes that the recognition that good governance is essential for economic growth has sparked renewed interest. Since 1994, the World Bank, the Inter-American Development Bank (IDB), and the Asian Development Bank have either approved or initiated more than $500 million in loans for judicial reform projects in twenty-six countries.

46   B. O. Nwabueze, *Ideas and Fact in Constitution Making: The Morohundiya Lectures* (Ibadan: Spectrum Books, 1993), 189.

47   Carothers, "Promoting the Rule of Law Abroad," 8.

48   Peter Uvin, *Human Rights and Development* (Bloomfield, CT: Kumarian Press, 2004), 155–56.

49   Trebilcock and Daniels, *Rule of Law Reform and Development*, 29–37.

50   Pablo de Greiff, "Articulating the Links Between Transitional Justice and Development," in this volume.

51   Carothers, "Promoting the Rule of Law Abroad," 7.

52   "Order in the Jungle," *Economist*, May 13, 2008.

53   Trebilcock and Daniels, *Rule of Law Reform and Development*, 4.

54   See Daniel Kaufmann and Aart Kraay, "Growth Without Governance," World Bank Policy Research Working Paper No. 2928, November 2002; and Daniel Kaufmann, Aart Kraay, and Massimo Mastruzzi, "Governance Matters VII: Aggregate and Individual Governance Indicators 1996–2007," World Bank Policy Research Paper No. 4654, June 2008, 7. There are, according to Trebilcock and Daniels, reasons to be cautious about these empirical measures. Trebilcock and Daniels, *Rule of Law Reform and Development*, 9.

55   See de Greiff, "Articulating the Links," in this volume.

56   Christiaan Grootaert and Thierry van Bastelaer, "Introduction and Overview," in *The Role of Social Capital in Development: An Empirical Assessment*, ed. Christiaan Grootaert and Thierry van Bastelaer (Cambridge: Cambridge University Press, 2002), 2–4.

57   Stephen Knack, "Social Capital, Growth, and Poverty," in *The Role of Social Capital in Development*, 73.

58   Trebilcock and Daniels, *Rule of Law Reform and Development*, 39. See also Laure-Hélène Piron, "Time to Learn, Time to Act in Africa," in *Promoting the Rule of Law Abroad: In Search of Knowledge*, ed. Thomas Carothers (Washington, DC: Carnegie Endowment for International Peace, 2006). Piron presents five main challenges to "justice sector reform" work: enhancing resources in ways that promote ownership and sustainability; adopting a coherent sectoral approach; understanding the political context; involving non-state actors; and improving donor habits and incentives. On the political challenge, see also Barbara Oomen, "Donor-Driven Justice and Its Discontents: The Case of Rwanda," *Development and Change* 36, no. 5 (2005): 887–910.

59   Trebilcock and Daniels, *Rule of Law Reform and Development*, 39.

60   Ibid., 65–66.

61   Veronique Dudouet, "Transitions from Violence to Peace: Revisiting Analysis and Intervention in Conflict Transformation," Berghof Report No. 15, Berghof Research Center for Constructive Conflict Management, November 2006, 4.

62   See Mayer-Rieckh and Duthie, "Enhancing Justice and Development," in this volume.

63   For case studies on these and other countries, as well as thematic studies, see Alexander Mayer-Rieckh and Pablo de Greiff, eds., *Justice as Prevention: Vetting Public Employees in Transitional Societies* (New York: Social Science Research Council, 2007).

64   Etelle R. Higonnet, "Restructuring Hybrid Courts: Local Empowerment and National Criminal Justice Reform," *Arizona Journal of International and Comparative Law* 23, no. 2 (2006): 357. See also Tonya Putnam, "Human Rights and Sustainable Peace," in *Ending Civil Wars: The Implementation of Peace Agreements*, ed. Stephen John Stedman, Donald Rothchild, and Elizabeth Cousens (Boulder: Lynne Rienner Publishers, 2002); and Eirin

Mobekk, "Transitional Justice and Security Sector Reform: Enabling Sustainable Peace," Geneva Centre for the Democratic Control of Armed Forces (DCAF), Occasional Paper No. 13, Geneva, November 2006.

65 Putnam, "Human Rights and Sustainable Peace," 238, 248.

66 Ibid., 251.

67 See also Jack Snyder and Leslie Vinjamuri, "Trials and Errors: Principle and Pragmatism in Strategies of International Justice," *International Security* 28, no. 3 (Winter 2003/2004): 5–44.

68 William A. Schabas, "Addressing Impunity in Developing Countries: Lessons from Rwanda and Sierra Leone," in *La voie vers la Cour pénale internationale: tous les chemins mènent à Rome*, ed. Hélène Dumont and Anne-Marie Boisvert (Montréal: Les Éditions Thémis, 2004), 162.

69 Ingrid Samset, Stina Petersen, and Vibeke Wang, "Maintaining the Process? Aid to Transitional Justice in Rwanda and Guatemala, 1995–2005" (paper prepared for the conference "Building a Future on Peace and Justice," Nuremberg, Germany, June 25–27, 2007, 10, 15). The percentages of the total amounts might be misleading, since aid to "transitional justice" in the study includes aid to security sector reform, a very broad category of activities, only some of which are usually considered to qualify as transitional justice.

70 UNDP Bureau for Crisis Prevention and Recovery, *UNDP and Transitional Justice: An Overview* (January 2006), 5.

71 Pablo de Greiff, "Vetting and Transitional Justice," in *Justice as Prevention*, 528–29.

72 Mobekk, "Transitional Justice and Security Sector Reform," 15.

73 Jane Stromseth, David Wippman, and Rose Brooks, *Can Might Make Rights? Building the Rule of Law after Military Interventions* (New York: Cambridge University Press, 2006), 254.

74 De Greiff, "Articulating the Links," in this volume.

75 Ibid.

76 Office of the United Nations High Commissioner for Human Rights (OHCHR), *Rule-of-Law Tools for Post-Conflict States: Maximizing the Legacy of Hybrid Courts* (New York and Geneva: United Nations, 2008), 4–5.

77 Ibid. See also UN Security Council, *The Rule of Law and Transitional Justice in Conflict and Post-conflict Societies*, para. 46. When establishing the Special Court for Sierra Leone (SCSL), the United Nations Security Council recognized the need to adopt a model that could leave a strong "legacy" in Sierra Leone, including improved professional standards. Indeed, the Security Council referred specifically to the "pressing need for international cooperation to assist in strengthening the judicial system of Sierra Leone," UN Doc. S/RES/1315 (August 14, 2000).

78 OHCHR, *Rule-of-Law Tools: Maximizing the Legacy*. See also Higonnet, "Restructuring Hybrid Courts," 347–435, esp. 350, 354, and 361–71; and Dustin N. Sharp, "Prosecutions,

Development, and Justice: The Trial of Hissein Habré," *Harvard Human Rights Journal* 16 (2003): 147–78.

79   Stromseth et al., *Can Might Make Rights?*, 274, 305; and OHCHR, *Rule-of-Law Tools: Maximizing the Legacy*, 2.

80   Priscilla B. Hayner, *Unspeakable Truths: Facing the Challenge of Truth Commissions* (New York and London: Routledge, 2002), 102–06. Pablo de Greiff, "Truth Telling and the Rule of Law," in *Telling the Truths: Truth Telling and Peace Building in Post-Conflict Societies*, ed. Tristan Anne Borer (Notre Dame, IN: University of Notre Dame Press, 2006).

81   Hayner, *Unspeakable Truths*, 166–67.

82   Rubén Zamora with David Holiday, "The Struggle for Lasting Reform: Vetting Processes in El Salvador," in *Justice as Prevention*, 101.

83   Eric Brahm, "Uncovering the Truth: Examining Truth Commission Success and Impact," *International Studies Perspectives* 8 (2007): 28.

84   Stromseth et al., *Can Might Make Rights?*, 308.

85   Ibid., 253.

86   Snyder and Vinjamuri, "Trials and Errors."

87   OHCHR, *Rule-of-Law Tools: Maximizing the Legacy*, 15.

88   Mobekk, "Transitional Justice and Security Sector Reform," 46.

89   OHCHR, *Rule-of-Law Tools: Maximizing the Legacy*, 5–9, 18–21.

90   Stromseth et al., *Can Might Make Rights?*, 265, 274. See also Higonnet, "Restructuring Hybrid Courts," 347–435, esp. 427.

91   See Mark Freeman, *Truth Commissions and Procedural Fairness* (New York: Cambridge University Press, 2006), 291–300.

92   OHCHR, *Rule-of-Law Tools: Maximizing the Legacy*, 6.

93   Uvin, *Human Rights and Development*, 137–39. For a much more detailed discussion on links between the rights-based approach to development and transitional justice generally, see Marcus Lenzen, "Roads Less Traveled? Conceptual Pathways (and Stumbling Blocks) for Development and Transitional Justice," in this volume. See also Higonnet, "Restructuring Hybrid Courts," 347–435, esp. 360.

94   OHCHR, *Rule-of-Law Tools: Prosecution Initiatives*, 6, 11, 17, 27.

95   Office of the United Nations High Commissioner for Human Rights (OHCHR), *Rule-of-Law Tools for Post-Conflict States: Vetting: An Operational Framework* (New York and Geneva: United Nations, 2006), 14.

96   OHCHR, *Rule-of-Law Tools: Maximizing the Legacy*; and Higonnet, "Restructuring Hybrid Courts," 410.

97   As ICTJ's "Vetting Guidelines" explain: "Vetting processes regulate access to positions of power and are highly political undertakings, in particular in post-conflict situations. Resistance to reform is a regular feature in countries emerging from conflict and the position of post-conflict governments is often tenuous. Individuals who risk losing

power through a vetting process will resist its implementation." At the same time, vetting can be politically manipulated: "A vetting process can be misused for partisan political purposes. For example, vetting of judges could be used to undermine the independence of the judiciary. Removals can be based on group or party affiliation, rather than
on individual conduct, target political opponents, and degenerate into political purges.
Such processes undermine, rather than reinforce, human rights and the rule of law, create resentment among those affected by the process, and are unlikely to achieve the necessary reform goals. International human rights standards have to be respected in the
implementation of a vetting process itself in order to avoid its political misuse." "Vetting
Public Employees in Post-Conflict Settings: Operational Guidelines," 549, 553.

98   Hayner, *Unspeakable Truths*, 166.

99   Zamora with Holiday, "The Struggle for Lasting Reform," 101.

100 Hayner, *Unspeakable Truths*, 30.

101 As Stromseth et al. put it with regard to Sierra Leone's Special Court: "Ultimately, however, whether the Special Court's capacity-building efforts—the professional skills
development of its own staff, the ripple effects of working with local NGOs, and the
training and sharing of expertise with local jurists and legal personnel—will make a
lasting and sustainable impact on Sierra Leone's domestic justice system and political
culture will depend on longer-term reforms within Sierra Leone." Stromseth et al., *Can
Might Make Rights?*, 298.

102 OHCHR, *Rule-of-Law Tools: Maximizing the Legacy*, 1–2, 15–16.

103 Alexander Mayer-Rieckh, "On Preventing Abuse: Vetting and Other Transitional
Reforms," in *Justice as Prevention*, 483.

104 As Undine Kayser-Whande and Stephanie Schell-Faucon argue: "work with people in
institutions shows (at the micro-level) just how difficult it is to make a clean cut with
the past, or even to speak about the 'pre'- and 'post'-conflict eras. Working with institutional reform reveals how much the old and the new are entangled. It shows how
much transformation is also a new 'battlefield' over images and perceptions, and how
hard it is to build legitimacy and maintain integrity while the people working inside the
institutions often remain a blend of old and new 'guard' dealing with their own pain,
loss, insecurities and ambitions." Undine Kayser-Whande and Stephanie Schell-Faucon,
"Transitional Justice and Civilian Conflict Transformation: Current Research, Future
Questions," Study for the Centre for Conflict Studies (CCS), University of Marburg, Germany, and the Ministry for Economic Cooperation and Development (BMZ), Bonn, Germany, 2008, 22.

105 Stromseth et al., *Can Might Make Rights?*, 275, 307. For more detail on these case stud-
ies, including discussions on legacy, see ICTJ's Prosecutions Case Studies Series: Bogdan
Ivanišević, *The War Crimes Chamber in Bosnia and Herzegovina: From Hybrid to Domestic
Court* (ICTJ, October 2008); Tom Perriello and Marieke Wierda, *The Special Court for Sierra*

Leone Under Scrutiny (ICTJ, March 2006); Tom Perriello and Marieke Wierda, *Lessons from the Deployment of International Judges and Prosecutors in Kosovo* (ICTJ, March 2006); and Caitlin Reiger and Marieke Wierda, *The Serious Crimes Process in Timor-Leste: In Retrospect* (ICTJ, March 2006).

106 Charles T. Call, "Introduction" and "Conclusion," in *Constructing Justice and Security after War*, ed. Charles T. Call (Washington, DC: United States Institute of Peace Press, 2007), 14, 398–99.

CHAPTER 8

Natural Connections:
Linking Transitional Justice and Development
Through a Focus on Natural Resources

Emily E. Harwell and Philippe Le Billon

Natural resources are a natural "connecting point" for postconflict development and transitional justice. Resources play a major role in the economies of many postconflict countries[1] and contribute to the well-being and livelihoods of local populations—both directly as means of subsistence or providing labor opportunities and indirectly by funding state capacity to deliver services. Well-managed resources can make significant contributions to postconflict development and help build and protect human security in all its forms, including human dignity and citizenship in its fullest meaning.

However, when mismanaged, valuable natural resources are not simply a lost opportunity but in fact endanger both long-term economic development and human security, as well as justice and basic freedoms. Misappropriated revenues from natural resources can undermine economic performance and the quality of governance, thereby increasing the risk of armed violence and human rights abuse.[2] For example, failure to control extraction of lucrative resources results in competition that can itself become an armed struggle. Likewise, inequity in access to subsistence resources often is an organizing point for grievances that lead to armed conflict, or it functions as the punishment waged against victims of aggression. An abundance of natural resources is not a predictor of positive performance.[3] Understanding the specific role of natural resources in the maintenance of authoritarian regimes and the facilitation of armed conflicts is therefore central to transitional justice's aim of understanding and repairing the context of victimization and repression of past regimes, as well as to development workers' goals of addressing impoverishment and poor governance.

The first section of this chapter introduces the concept of vulnerability as a multidimensional condition and argues that addressing these various forms of vulnerability is a common aim of both transitional justice and development. The subsequent section builds on this commonality by discussing in deeper detail the role that natural resources play in authoritarian regimes and armed conflicts. The chapter then moves to an empirical examination of how transitional justice's traditional areas of intervention—legal accountability, truth commissions, reparations, and security sector reform—have engaged with natural resource issues. We examine normative arguments for why an expansion of the transitional justice mandate in key areas to more directly engage resource issues would be fruitful and how this might work operationally, as well as the challenges posed by such an expansion and how these challenges might be met.

However, even at its most successful, the expansion of transitional justice measures to include natural resources would only make a modest contribution to the prevention of future abuses due to the differing scope and capacities of transitional justice and development programs. In comparison, both the programmatic scope and resources available for postconflict development are much broader and therefore more likely to make a lasting impact, particularly in the area of institutional reform, not only of the security and judicial sectors, which are the current focus of transitional justice, but also of resource extraction and financial sectors.

Consequently, we suggest some forms of achieving "external coherence" between the two arenas[4]—that is, how development and transitional justice might collaborate by using natural resources as one key focal point. Additionally, we offer some concrete suggestions for how postconflict development programming can also address "internal coherence"—that is, ways that workers from different development programs might productively coordinate *among themselves* to pursue both development's and transitional justice's common goals of addressing vulnerabilities. We close with some recommendations on strategic ways to make both development and transitional justice interventions most effective, given the large scale of problems needing attention in transitional contexts.

DEVELOPMENT AND JUSTICE TOOLS FOR ADDRESSING VULNERABILITY

In this chapter we define *development* as encompassing both macroeconomic reforms and capacity building undertaken with the goal of increasing economic growth (we refer to this aspect as "economic development"), as well as efforts to address conditions of impoverishment and to improve human physical and intellectual well-being (we call this aspect "human security"). We use the concept of *vulnerability* to articulate the relationship between material deprivation (the traditional focus for development) and the effects and modalities of armed violence and oppression (the focus of transitional justice). Our major point here is fourfold: (1) vulnerability has several planes—economic, social, political, and physical; (2) these planes reinforce one another to produce both poverty and violence; (3) both programmatic arenas of transitional justice and development have often failed to adequately grasp the complexity and interaction of vulnerability in their respective interventions; and (4) this misapprehension has often compromised the effectiveness of the interventions.

Drawing on extensive literature on vulnerability to "natural hazards" (that is, famines and natural disasters), we conceptualize vulnerability as a composite of exposure (to risks), capacities (to cope), and potentiality (for recovery).[5] The concept of vulnerability has been deployed widely since the 1980s in relation to economic and physical deprivations that lead to poverty and famine. We follow later thinkers in the political ecology field in considering the multifaceted nature of vulnerability, in particular its intimate relationships not only with economic and material deprivation but also with armed violence and oppression.[6] People who are socially vulnerable—excluded from society and from access to adequate resources for subsistence—are therefore economically vulnerable—trapped in cycles of hunger and disease—and are also politically vulnerable—with little opportunity to participate meaningfully in their government. The cycle is perpetuated because the politically voiceless are unable to affect the economic and social conditions that hold them in poverty. In turn, society's outcasts are either deserted by the institutions of the state, or, more menacingly, they are the target of state attention not as constituents or citizens but as threats to public order, and are subjected to various forms of violence and oppression. People living at the margins of society are also targets of violence from nonstate actors who thrive in the vacuum, including gangs, insurgents, and unaccountable corporations.[7]

A focus on natural resources can help articulate the linkages between development and transitional justice, particularly in the areas of conflict prevention (physical vulnerability), equity (economic vulnerability), building civic trust and community reconciliation (social vulnerability), and democratization (political vulnerability). This orientation to the role of natural resources is more complex than simply asserting that one's human security is a direct function of how many resources one controls. As Amartya Sen has observed, poverty is more usefully thought of as a result of impaired capacities or freedoms rather than simply not having enough money. We likewise view the most useful analysis of the role of natural resources to be how they mediate or obstruct those "functionings."[8] Natural resources, when wisely managed, can help reduce vulnerability by strengthening the capacity to cope with stressors and the potential to recover at (1) the national level, as high-value resources supply investment and economic growth, and (2) at the local level, as farming, forest-product collection, fishing, and hunting resources provide subsistence and artisanal livelihoods. Although the proportion of the world economy made up of raw natural resources has sharply declined over the past thirty years, half of developing countries still rely on less than four commodities for half of their export earnings.[9] This economic dependence means that resource sectors play a critical role in investments, tax revenues, employment, and infrastructure creation in these countries.

However, resource-dependent countries often underperform economically, due to weak institutions for accountability and neglect of nonresource sectors.[10] Resources can also play central roles in decreasing capacities and resilience and in increasing risks, thereby increasing vulnerability to material deprivation as well as physical violence, as we explore in the following section.

In order to effectively prevent conflict and address victims' needs, traditional transitional justice measures of legal accountability, truth-seeking, reparations, and security sector reform must be contextualized within the larger reality facing most postconflict societies. In countries dependent on primary resources, contexts of vulnerability often center around the political and economic benefit derived from control of natural resources and the negative impacts of state control on civilians. In truth-seeking, an awareness of the role of natural resources might involve direct investigation of injustices that supported authoritarian regimes or contributed to the onset and fueling of armed conflict or the targeting of people for abuse. In the realm of transitional judicial accountability, a resource focus might contribute to bringing legal cases against the worst perpetrators of economic crimes in key resource sectors that are directly linked to human rights abuses. Such cases, whether criminal or civil, could yield the recovery of stolen assets that could be used for reparation for victims. In reform of the security sector, a resource focus might support the vetting of the perpetrators from future concession licenses or positions of authority in resource ministries, and the reform of structures that enabled the corrupt control of resource revenues by security personnel.

These transitional justice interventions could contribute to the prevention of conflict and remove fear (addressing physical vulnerability), create a deterrent to corruption and help to build equity (addressing economic vulnerability), and remove natural resources as a "honey pot" to reward client networks, thereby restoring accountability to governance (addressing political vulnerability). Truth-seeking and legal accountability around natural resource crimes, in particular, undercut impunity and help generate public discussion and build awareness, which all help build civic trust, facilitate democratization, and make a contribution to reconciliation (addressing social and political vulnerability). The proposed expansion of the transitional justice mandate in these respective areas will be discussed in detail later in the chapter.

While transitional justice is narrowly focused in its interventions, programs falling under the general rubric of postconflict "development" are varied indeed. Given the boom in interest in postconflict development, many of these programs in fact consider themselves to be fields of their own. They include such disparate focuses as security, internally displaced persons (IDPs) and refugee resettlement, ex-combatant disarmament and reintegration, legal reform, humanitarian aid, macroeconomic and fiscal reform, rebuilding physical infrastructure, elections and civic education, civil society building, natural resources sector reform... the list goes on. Development agencies from the UN, bilaterals, international financial institutions, and nongovernmental organizations (NGOs) descend en masse to a postconflict country, many with staff possessing only scant knowledge of the local context, each organization with its own goals, funding, contacts, and methodologies. Although organizations working in the same programmatic area aim to coordinate themselves, sometimes through formal bodies, such as the Humanitarian Information Center (HIC), given the scope of operations and staff available and the scale of problems to be dealt with, coordination is most often an intention rather than a reality; many consequently work at cross-purposes. Ex-combatants are trained for farming livelihoods when no farmland is available[11] or for urban trades for which an insufficient market exists,[12] legal reformers craft new forestry laws while indigenous land tenure remains legally insecure,[13] or new mining concessions are put up for bid to generate rapid foreign exchange before fiscal transparency regulations are in place.[14] Some suggestions to improve coordination in order to achieve "internal coherence" are made in the final section of this chapter.

However, more fundamentally than failed coordination, development often suffers from an epistemic duality that is most easily revealed in natural resource reform—that is, the duality of development as both top-down macroeconomic reform and bottom-up improvement of human welfare. This duality clashes in the operations of transitional governments, whose officials feel the pressure from local business constituents (and many international advisors) to quickly issue concessions for high-value resource extraction before subsistence resources issues, such as overlapping and legally uncertain land tenure, are adequately addressed. The window of opportunity for reforms in transitional contexts is often truncated, with half of all postconflict countries returning to war within a decade.[15] At the same time, the scale of reconstruction and repair needed in these contexts is massive. The difficulty, therefore, in reaching a balance between these two "faces" of development is challenging in the extreme.

NATURAL RESOURCES, AUTHORITARIAN REGIMES, AND ARMED CONFLICT

Weak governance institutions for natural resources relate to violence and massive human rights abuse in three major ways. First, as noted above, high-value resources can sustain repressive or neglectful political regimes by providing excess revenues that can insulate the ruling elite from the rest of the economy and accountability to its citizenry. Such regimes use resources to maintain power, and do so by routinely violating human rights, as has been the case in many so-called petro-states, such as Iraq, Saudi Arabia, Nigeria, Equatorial Guinea, and Angola.[16]

Second, resource exploitation can result in direct human rights abuses, such as targeted violence and looting by security forces against communities in extraction areas, forced labor, and the forced and brutal displacement of local residents, as was the case in Sierra Leone, the Democratic Republic of the Congo (DRC), Liberia,[17] and by pulp producers in Sumatra in order to gain access to forest resources.[18]

Finally, resources can motivate, sustain, and aggravate human rights abuses committed by armed groups, notably by financing and rewarding their activities. Gems, timber, and narcotics, but also cash crops and oil, have sustained numerous rebel movements, especially when these resources can be easily extracted, transported, and sold. Revenues have also been indirectly obtained from resource sectors through extortion and kidnappings. With the end of the Cold War and the decline in "superpower" financing of insurgencies, more belligerents have come to rely on revenues from such resources, particularly those considered to be "lootable" (easily accessible without high-technology extraction operations).[19] Between 1989 and 2006, an estimated 640,000 persons died in battles in which at least one of the belligerents was financed by resource revenues.[20] These numbers do not account for the total number of deaths related to the context of conflict, which is generally much larger. Nor do these numbers account for other types of human rights abuses, such as forced displacement, rape, torture, and arbitrary detentions, or the use of starvation as a weapon of war.

Thus, "conflict commodities" are understood as not only financing hostilities but also as motivating conflicts through "greed" or "grievance" mechanisms, weakening states, and aggravating human rights abuses.[21] This aggravation first relates to resources prolonging hostilities, especially when these resources are easily accessible to the weaker party.[22] Sometimes funds are obtained even before the resources are under the control of the belligerent party, a practice Michael Ross has called "booty futures." This practice facilitates insurgencies by funding rebels to attack governments and lengthens conflicts by providing embattled governments with funds for counterinsurgencies.[23] Consequently, the longer the war goes on, the more likely massive and indiscriminate human rights abuses will take place as a result of revenge, a growing normalization of violence, the fragmentation and individualization of motivations, and/or the undermining of discipline and the rule of law.[24]

Resource revenues can also dissociate armed groups from the necessary support of and accountability to both the civilian population and the international community. The lack of a need for civilian support for food and housing can lead to insular encampments, where combatants develop contempt for civilians and child soldiers are indoctrinated.[25] Moreover, belligerents may coerce labor or displace populations to gain control of resources. Resource revenue, particularly when belligerents have no real political manifesto other than control of these financial flows, affects the pattern of recruitment, the type of leadership, and the internal discipline of an armed group. Resources may entice the recruitment of economically rather than politically motivated members, or of leaders who pursue short-term political strategies and are thus less preoccupied with the political effects of massive human rights abuses.[26] Finally, resource revenues increase rights abuses by allowing both sitting governments and insurgents to wage wars without the diplomatic pressure to avoid human rights abuses that might come with financial support from foreign governments.

TRANSITIONAL JUSTICE'S PAST AND POTENTIAL ENGAGEMENT WITH NATURAL RESOURCES

Transitional justice measures of legal accountability, truth-seeking, reparations, and security sector reform have only rarely engaged issues relevant to natural resources, focusing instead on gross violations of civil and political rights (CPR). We believe that, in cases where resources are relevant, this has been a missed opportunity to more fully capture the nature of authoritarian belligerent power or of armed conflict, and the experience of victims under the old regime or during war. Likewise, we believe that this partial apprehension of injustices thereby contributes to only partial solutions that may in fact be counterproductive when joined with other transitional programs as a whole, as we will describe in turn in the following sections. Rectifying this shortcoming, however, is not without costs and risks (the magnitude of which varies with each context), and we examine these challenges and how they might be addressed as we look at each justice measure in turn.

LEGAL ACCOUNTABILITY

One of the traditional focuses for transitional justice advocacy has been to facilitate legal accountability for crimes committed during the conflict. However, these cases have rarely addressed crimes associated with natural resource extraction (hereafter referred to as "resource crimes"), which include:

- massive corruption in issuing extraction and export licenses;
- embezzlement of resource-derived revenues from state coffers;
- violence, looting, and forced displacement of communities in extraction areas;
- forced labor for resource extraction;
- trade of UN-sanctioned commodities;
- trade of resource commodities in exchange for arms and military materiel in violation of UN arms sanctions and/or arms conventions/ moratoria; and
- extraction in contravention of domestic laws for resource licensing, use, and payment of resource taxes/fees and extraction labor.

There are several sound arguments for broadening the traditional focus of transitional justice efforts to pursue legal accountability to include these resource-related crimes. First, as detailed in the previous section, the pattern of control and criminality in authoritarian regimes and among violent belligerents is intimately tied to the financial rewards of crimes in the resource sectors. Therefore, as both a conceptual and practical matter, efforts to pursue accountability for civil and political abuses are rendered less effective by the neglect of economic crimes that facilitate and motivate that abuse.[27] Additionally, when impunity continues for economic crimes of corruption, which are arguably more widespread and have broader societal effects, this sends the counterproductive message that there is still no rule of law in the "new" society. Finally, trial testimony, evidence, and arguments can generate needed momentum for change by raising public awareness about these issues, their connection to massive abuses and atrocities, and the need for institutional reforms. This is especially true when care is taken to make trials broadly accessible through live radio feeds.

In this section, we review some of the potential and past engagements in legal accountability for resource crimes and the challenges illustrated by some of the failed attempts to win convictions for these crimes.

INTERNATIONAL TRIBUNALS

Judicial systems in transitional governments frequently lack capacity and are too politically freighted to try cases effectively, particularly where they implicate actors still able to wield power. If domestic courts are incapable of successful prosecutions, ineffective trials can be worse than none at all because they send the message that impunity still reigns. In such scenarios, international courts are the last, best resort for legal accountability.

However, there are limited examples of trials dealing directly with resource-related crimes. For resource crimes related to corruption, some have argued that the dearth in cases is not due to preference of civil and political crimes but rather to the weakness in international law to address these crimes in comparison to relatively robust legal tools for human rights prosecutions.[28] However, some resource-related crimes are in fact human rights violations in themselves, and there are legal tools available for prosecutions of these crimes, including:

- humanitarian law prohibitions against pillage;[29]
- human rights and humanitarian law prohibitions against forced labor and attacks against civilians by security forces guarding resource extraction operations;[30]
- Rome Statute of the International Criminal Court (ICC) prohibitions against the destruction of property and pillage, forced labor, and displacement;[31] and
- UN Security Council resolutions prohibiting the trade in particular commodities.[32]

Although amnesties granted during a peace process may apply to domestic violations, such claims to amnesty have been disallowed for violations of international law (see the Sierra Leone Special Court discussion below).

At present, the most developed tools for prosecuting certain resource crimes are those prohibiting violation of UN sanctions (which can be tried domestically by some UN member states)[33] and those for prosecuting human rights crimes. The Hague Regulations, the Geneva Conventions, and the Additional Protocols regulate the conduct of hostilities in international and non-international armed conflicts. These bodies of law explicitly prohibit pillage. The Hague Regulations, for instance, stipulate that "pillage is formally forbidden,"[34] whereas the Geneva Conventions state that "pillage is prohibited."[35] In the context of military occupation during an international conflict, however, the Hague Regulations, although still prohibiting pillage, allow a series of exceptions (Articles 48–56).[36] Nevertheless, in situations other than the particular circumstances of an occupied state during an international conflict, the Geneva Convention and Additional Protocol prohibitions against pillage still apply and bear no such limitation.

The Geneva Convention's prohibition against pillage[37] requires no systematic state strategy. The International Committee of the Red Cross (ICRC) commentary notes that the prohibition applies to "the ordering as well as the authorization of pillage," and to "all types of property, whether they belong to private persons or to communities or the State."[38] Pillage is also not limited to the seizure of assets by force. The ICRC notes that courts have deemed pillage to include acquisitions through contracts based on intimidation, pressure, or a position of power derived from the surrounding armed conflict. In other cases, the ICRC observes that knowingly receiving goods obtained against the will of the true owner was also judged to constitute pillage.[39]

Further, the conventions apply the prohibitions to everyone, including nonstate actors, such as insurgents, corporations, and individual citizens. For example, the United States Military Tribunal (USMT) at Nuremberg prosecuted defendants from several major industrial conglomerates: IG Farben, the Krupp firm, and the Friedrich Flick Concern.[40]

Special Court for Sierra Leone. The mandate of the Special Court for Sierra Leone (SCSL) granted the authority to prosecute those "who bear the greatest responsibility for serious violations of international humanitarian law and Sierra Leonean law committed in the territory of Sierra Leone since 30 November 1996."[41] The language of the indictments is exemplary in that it explicitly recognizes the role of valuable resources, especially diamonds, in contributing to the conflict and makes charges for crimes in direct association with the struggle for control of the mines.[42] The Revolutionary United Front (RUF) defendants and former Liberian president Charles Taylor were charged with "joint criminal enterprise of trying to take control of Sierra Leone territory, especially diamond mining areas...and the reasonable foreseeable outcomes of that enterprise including crimes of unlawful killings, use of child soldiers, physical and sexual violence, abduction, forced labor (in mines), looting and pillage of civilian property." The court, therefore, recognized the key role of extracting diamonds for funding insurgencies and targeting victims, but chose not to charge with the actual war crime of pillage due to a lack of familiarity with the necessary elements of the charge and the desire to quickly issue the Taylor indictment during the peace negotiation in Accra.[43]

International Court of Justice. A landmark 2005 civil case in the International Court of Justice (ICJ), brought within the context of increasing attention to "conflict commodities" in policy circles and the UN Sanctions Committee in particular, has revitalized the attention to the justiciability of the pillage of natural resources as a war crime. The ICJ found in *Democratic Republic of the Congo v. Uganda, Armed Activities on the Territory of Congo (DRC v. Uganda)*[44] that although there was no evidence of a state strategy to use its military to pillage DRC's resources, the Ugandan state nevertheless failed in its obligation as an occupying power to prevent pillage of natural resources by its armed forces and through their nonstate collaborators in the occupied Congolese province of Ituri, which is rich in gold and other minerals. The court relied heavily for evidence on the findings of the Judicial Commission of Inquiry into Allegations of Illegal Exploitation of Natural Resources and Other Forms of Wealth in the Democratic Republic of the Congo, set up by the Ugandan government in May 2001 and headed by Justice David Porter (hereafter the Porter Commission; see the following section).[45]

However, the damages due DRC pursuant to this ruling are still under bilateral negotiation because the court did not award damages and analysts say it will be nearly impossible to enforce a compensation ruling. Experts warn that the negotiation could be so protracted that a settlement might take many years to conclude, but believe that the case nevertheless represents a positive step toward peace (Uganda accepted the judgment), and was therefore also a step toward legal accountability, although part of a larger process.[46] We revisit the question of the enforcement of damages later in the chapter.

Dutch Federal Court. Some domestic courts have responded to crimes committed in conflict zones by bringing cases against their own citizens for behavior while conducting business abroad. Guus Kouwenhoven, a Dutch logger who operated the Oriental Timber Corporation in Liberia during Taylor's regime, was convicted in federal court for arms trafficking in contravention of the

UN arms ban and African arms conventions.[47] He was also charged with war crimes for the massacre by his company security of the village of Youghbor, located in the logging concession area.[48] There is forensic evidence and admission by the accused that he deposited money into Taylor's personal account (for which he received a tax receipt).[49] Kouwenhoven maintained his innocence, arguing that such exchanges and engagement of armed militia were simply the way one had to do business in Liberia under Taylor.[50] This view of compliance with Taylor's demands for bribes in circumstances of armed conflict simply as a "way of doing business" underlines the importance of addressing the role of natural resource extraction and corrupt governance in human rights abuses and the relevance of focusing on resource extraction as a means of breaking impunity for human rights abuses.

Kouwenhoven's conviction was ultimately overturned on appeal due to mishandling of the prosecution and inconsistencies in the statements of witnesses, some of whom the appeals court found had questionable credibility.[51] The judge noted that the most compelling evidence was forensic evidence and the admission by the accused that he bought a helicopter for Charles Taylor from the known arms dealer Sanjivan Ruprah,[52] in apparent contravention of UN sanctions[53] and regional arms treaties[54] against the trade of military materiel. The judge further noted that this evidence was inexplicably never presented in court.[55]

These cases indicate that although there are legal tools available for prosecuting crimes associated with natural resources, there are also significant obstacles to evidence gathering, limitations of prosecutorial knowledge regarding existing statutes for bringing cases and winning convictions, and—most problematic—often a lack of political will.

OTHER LEGAL INSTRUMENTS

The above cases were brought against insurgents or neighboring or occupying states. Although a far less developed area of legal accountability, emerging legal remedies are available for the more protracted problem of predatory states that pillage their own country's natural assets (either directly or through corporate partnerships) and impoverish their own people. One mechanism for accountability that is receiving growing attention is the use of civil charges and asset recovery that could benefit victims. Although many of these cases do not directly involve natural resources, they offer a promising model for advocates seeking to hold predatory heads of state accountable for pillage of national assets.

Civil suits against corporate partners of predatory states could be brought for abuses suffered by foreign nationals. One such tool is the Alien Torts cases brought in U.S. courts that have agreed to hear such suits against corporations (including UNOCAL, Exxon-Mobil, Texaco, and Chevron) and individuals (including Ferdinand Marcos) for potential complicity or direct involvement in human rights abuses. In a domestic civil action, Indonesian courts recently sought to hold former Indonesian president Suharto accountable for massive corruption and government embezzlement of one of his family's foundations, Supersemar. Although this case was not directly related to natural resources, a similar case could be made for other types of embezzlement and corruption of numerous similar foundations that received kickbacks in exchange for lucrative extraction rights for logging, plantation agriculture, mineral resources, and oil and gas. Transparency International estimated the Suharto family foundations amassed between US$15 billion and $35 billion (more than Marcos, Mobutu Sese Seko, and Sani Abacha combined).[56] Suharto died while the Supersemar case was still under way, but Indonesians were encouraged when the court found against Supersemar. However, this optimism was tempered when the damages ordered were surprisingly low—US$105 million from a foundation that was said to have misappropriated over US$420 million.[57]

When domestic political will exists for civil suits to recover stolen assets, there are other potential tools, such as the recent increase in domestic criminal charges under money laundering and racketeering laws, and the Stolen Assets Recovery unit of the UN Convention Against Corruption (UNCAC), a new instrument that, with international assistance in forensic accounting, has already assisted in tracking and repatriating over US$2 billion of assets stolen by the now deceased Nigerian dictator Sani Abacha. Parties to the convention are enjoined to enact banking reforms and anticorruption legislation including "know your customer" rules with enhanced oversight for those in public office and their families.[58] Recent forensic evidence that the former Liberian president Charles Taylor moved some US$1 billion through a U.S. bank account over a six-year period[59]—at a time when the entire gross domestic product (GDP) of Liberia was around half that amount—suggests possible space for a money-laundering charge in U.S. courts.

Special Commissions of Inquiry: One possible means to pursue accountability is the establishment of special commissions of inquiry. These commissions might include generalized anticorruption commissions or can be specific to a particular issue or sector. While political will and prosecutorial capacity to bring such cases may be limited in a politically charged atmosphere, special commissions, which might be domestic or with international experts as advisors or members, are often able to provide an intermediate measure between truth-seeking and accountability. They most often do not have sentencing authority but can make recommendations for prosecutions and revocation of concession licenses. Often they also have powers of subpoena that some (but not all) truth commissions lack. Additionally, they provide information that can generate public awareness and evidence to facilitate prosecutions.

Two examples of such domestic inquiries in the DRC are the successive Lutundula Parliamentary Commission (2005) and the Inter-Ministerial Commission (2007), with the latter bringing sixty mining companies under review for the legality of contracts issued during the war.[60] The interministerial review is still under way, but it should examine the legal requirements that must be met when concessions are granted by a sitting administration or its officials. In a similar example of domestic review of resource extraction during wartime, the Porter Commission examined involvement by the Ugandan military in the extraction of mineral resources and attendant violence against civilians in the mining regions of DRC.[61] Its findings were relied on heavily by ICJ judges in the case brought by DRC against Uganda. These investigations help build momentum for other forms of legal accountability and reform, and might have benefited from transitional justice expertise regarding investigations and evidence gathering.

CHALLENGES

The promise of such tools aside, as many of these cases illustrate, there are numerous challenges to the notion of using legal accountability—for these types of resource crimes in particular—as a means to promote transition. One argument against pursuing legal accountability for resource-related crimes is that the legal instruments available for prosecuting such crimes are weak. As we have noted, however, while this may be true for some, there is nevertheless a sound legal basis for prosecuting those resource crimes that also constitute war crimes. Yet prosecutors have (so far) only rarely used these tools, whether due to a lack of familiarity with the necessary elements or a lack of political will. As a result, those seeking to advocate for such cases will likely face resistance from some prosecutors and judges who are less familiar with the standards. The underdeveloped arena of pillage, in particular, merits further legal analysis to determine the viability of this as a transitional justice strategy and the most strategic contexts in which to pursue this avenue of remedy.

Some have argued that the nature of evidence collection and witness cooperation for economic crimes might simply be beyond the capacity of courts and transitional justice experts.[62] Certainly these issues pose serious obstacles in postconflict environments. The SCSL and the Kouwenhoven cases demonstrate that this type of case does present significant logistical challenges to the investigators, even if they have the appropriate expertise. Obstacles to prosecuting such cases include witnesses and evidence being physically located far from the court; witnesses who are impossible to protect adequately and have good reason to fear retaliation; and circumstances of widespread criminality that make the credibility of most witnesses impeachable by the opposing counsel. However, dealing with such difficulties is beyond the capacity of these actors only if the uniqueness of the cases is not taken seriously and planned for in advance. (We return to this discussion in the following section.) Furthermore, these challenges of evidence and witness cooperation are common to most human rights cases for postconflict countries being brought in international courts. They are not exclusive to resource-related or economic crimes. For international courts, more effort and resources should be directed toward in-country investigations and evidence collection, coordination between prosecutors and investigators, and witness protection measures.

On the question of the charges being rarely used by prosecutors, some have argued that this is due to a "cultural acceptance" of economic crime. In fact, some argue that the slow development of legal tools for dealing with economic crime in general is a reflection of an attitude of leniency toward this type of criminality.[63] Certainly cynicism and inaction are common obstacles to reform in countries suffering widespread corruption and economic predation, yet these seem surprisingly defeatist and overly relativistic arguments against pursuing legal accountability. Horrifying practices are often protected under the guise of "cultural acceptance" when in fact they are "accepted" only by the status quo and forced upon the rest, who are powerless to resist.[64] In fact, no one would credibly argue that the unabashed sacking of public assets to the impoverishment of millions is "acceptable," only that "everyone is doing it," which is hardly a reason to further delay accountability.

It seems to us more likely that the dearth in prosecution for crimes of this type is due to the slipperiest of all fish: political will. Given the resources available, not all crimes for which there is a legal basis for prosecution will be brought to trial. Prosecutors make strategic choices about what cases they can win and what the overall benefit will be (and the risks of an acquittal). In cases of economic crimes that are often widespread and systematic, this selectivity will often be used (or seen to be used) as political score settling, thereby generating cynicism rather than civic trust and reconciliation. Further, there is the question of whether prosecuting economic crimes is more politically feasible for public trial than grave human rights abuses. The convictions of Augusto Pinochet and Suharto for economic crimes while they remained unaccountable for their involvement in widespread human rights violations suggest it might be more feasible, at least in those particular cases. On the other hand, some have argued that in some contexts powerful interests disenchanted with the brutality of the old regime might be allies for a transition but might block it if they feel they will be implicated in prosecutions for economic crimes.[65] Such actors, if they believe their economic interests are at stake, may undermine efforts for legal accountability or truth-seeking around resource crimes and thereby undercut these initiatives for other types of abuse. In short, political will is both highly contextual and dynamic and must be weighed empirically.

A more general challenge to legal accountability for resource crime as a means to transitional justice and development goals is that outcomes from trials are inherently uncertain, making them a risky vessel in which to house too much hope for transition. They are, as authors elsewhere have argued, at best only partial solutions that leave untouched large sectors of actors who participated in some way in the crimes, including the uncharged perpetrators, the international actors who facilitate if not directly aid and abet crimes, and the larger community of bystanders who do nothing to intervene. Trials are not intended to deal with these communities of wrongdoers and provide only partial repair to problems of violence and criminality. There are other, often more useful, tools at hand, including those discussed below, which can provide a more complete picture of criminality, harm, and the way forward to repair.[66]

Clearly the prevailing lack of judges' and prosecutors' familiarity with the applicability of international standards to resource crime presents an obstacle to bringing successful cases. However, we argue that the most serious challenges to legal accountability for natural resources crimes—the problems of political will, the difficulty of investigations, and providing only partial solutions—in fact are similar to the challenges to legal accountability for human rights violations more generally. Legal accountability is but one hammer in the tool box, yet it is nevertheless an essential tool. Victims and perpetrators themselves have commented in East Timor that truth-seeking and reconciliation measures without accountability are unsatisfying, and, in fact, the failure to bring the most responsible to trial can undermine the progress of these measures by breeding resentment among those who participate that "the big fish" still remain free.[67] While bearing in mind the need for using other measures in concert, careful selection of a few key cases can help generate needed momentum by fueling public debate and awareness of how these different arenas connect and the direction that reforms should take.

TRUTH COMMISSIONS

Truth commissions have an advantage over judicial procedures in their ability to focus both on individual responsibility as well as on broader institutional or structural injustices at the root of abuses and violence. Truth commissions can ask broader questions of how and why abuses occurred, while trials ask only if individual charges have been adequately proven. While mass atrocities may rightly be the primary focus of commissions' work, as broad arenas for "truth recovery" they provide a useful opportunity for exploring the multifaceted role of natural resources in violence. Such an ancillary focus can help address questions of why particular people were targeted and what circumstances enabled the violence to take place. It can illuminate vulnerability in all its forms. Truth commissions can be an avenue for revealing the resource/economic dimensions of the very abuses that people suffered (for example, losses of livelihood when people were displaced or resources destroyed, conscription as forced labor to extract resources, the dangerous and underpaid conditions of labor and housing, and lost education opportunities suffered when people are forced to work in resource sectors), as well as how the mismanagement and destruction of resources and the unequal distribution of benefits from their extraction has endangered livelihoods and disempowered people, who then become targets for other kinds of abuses (arrest, intimidation, and physical violence) because they resist or simply because they are voiceless.

However, this rich vein of insight into contexts of vulnerability and power has most often been underutilized by truth commissions, which have generally focused their investigations narrowly on civil and political (CPR) violations. With a few recent exceptions, most notably Sierra Leone, East Timor, and Liberia, truth commissions have not conducted primary investigations of resources' role in violence and the targeting of victims for abuse. Truth commissions also have only rarely (the exception being Sierra Leone, East Timor, South Africa, and Liberia) investigated violations of economic and social and cultural rights (ESCR) that stem from these linkages, including rights to control one's own resources, to adequate livelihood, food, housing (from displacement from extraction areas), health, and education (from coerced extractive labor, especially of school-aged children, and squalid conditions of labor camps). Nor have truth commissions (with the exception of Sierra Leone) tended to make recommendations for the reform of resource institutions in order to prevent such abuses.

There are several possible reasons for this inattention. First, the mandate of many truth commissions limits them to the investigation of gross civil and political abuses. In the recent wake of physical brutality against civilians, truth recovery regarding grave abuses (particularly the lingering uncertainty of forced disappearances) is seen as most urgent in the pursuit of reconciliation. Additionally, the narrow focus on CPR violations can be the result of a desire to limit the scope of inquiry given limitations foreseen in budget, time, and/ or staff that would preclude detailed investigation into such seemingly prosaic matters as illegal logging and diamond smuggling. However, even a mandate that limits truth commissions to CPR violations does not preclude investiga- tion of the *context* of these violations, which can include structural inequi- ties and ESCR violations. Some truth commissions have indeed explored this arena, but have left natural resources under-examined, even though in agrar- ian societies ESCR violations are tightly linked to natural resources.

Finally, no two conflicts are the same, and the role of natural resources in violent oppression is not always a prominent one. In some countries (for example, Chile, Argentina, Northern Ireland, and Bosnia), the context of vic- timization was primarily political and a substantive investigation of economic influences and natural resources would be largely missing the point. But in other contexts, such as South Africa, Peru, Guatemala, and Sudan, victimiza- tion was intimately linked to the social and economic marginalization of spe- cific segments of the population, particularly through a lack of access to natu- ral resources with which to make their livelihood. In still others, such as East Timor, DRC, Sierra Leone, and Liberia, the very conflict itself was fueled by eco- nomic inequities and political and economic competition for lucrative natural resources. In these latter countries, natural resources provide fertile ground for a truth commission investigation of marginalization and victimization.

The Sierra Leone Truth and Reconciliation Commission (TRC) was exem- plary in its incorporation of the political economy of resource extraction into its conception of the conflict—its contexts, how and why it unfolded, and who suffered most from it. The TRC was mandated to investigate economic violations, and the final report included a detailed chapter entitled "Mineral Resources, Their Use and Their Impact on the Conflict and the Country," which observed that because Sierra Leone's economy depends on revenues from its mineral resources, the management of these state resources is central to the quality of governance. The commission, therefore, deemed it important to examine how mineral resources were used by successive governments and how they may have contributed to the war. Furthermore, the commission set out to explore the extent to which the combatant groups exploited mineral resources to sustain themselves and replenish their war-making supplies.[68]

The commission argued that the misuse of diamond resources in "an essentially single-product economy like Sierra Leone's has created huge disparities in socioeconomic conditions. While the elite and their business associates in the diamond industry have lived in grandeur, the poor have invariably been left to rue the misappropriation of the collective wealth." Revenue from diamond production allowed armed belligerents to buy weapons, which in turn allowed them to capture more territory, which they could convert into diamond-mining fields. The report concludes that this use of diamonds to expand economic, military, and geographic control gradually became the main motivating factor for all the armed groups and many local commanders, thus triggering further conflict.[69] Crucially, the report found that diamonds and their particular form of extraction were important in developing profiles of victims of violence. The report concludes that communities in diamond-mining areas became targets of violence as different forces struggled to control the mines, plundered the financial resources of the diggers, forcibly recruited labor for digging, and harvested coffee and cocoa to further fund the conflict and enrich commanders.

As a result of its findings, the Sierra Leone TRC's final report recommended detailed reforms in the mining sector, including revenue transparency, anticorruption measures, a rough diamond chain-of-custody system to certify point of origin (known as the Kimberley Process),[70] and earmarking of diamond revenues for rural social spending. By the time these recommendations were made, most of them were already in place or in the making, thereby contributing to momentum on implementing these reforms. By 2001, the government of Sierra Leone had established the first diamond certification scheme in the world, and a tax-revenue distribution scheme for mining areas was set up for community-interest projects (Diamond Area Community Development Fund), although it was initially characterized by misspending and embezzlement.

In another example, the conditions of South African apartheid provide a rich context for examining the multiple meanings of vulnerability, including the economic exploitation of the black population. The mandate of the South African TRC, however, was to examine gross human rights violations, which was interpreted to preclude a direct and in-depth investigation of abuses around the extraction of gold and the exploitation in the mines of a cheap labor pool that led to the victimization and impoverishment of the black underclass of apartheid. Nevertheless, the report analyzed information the TRC collected in its various public hearings on the political, economic, and social environment that gave rise to gross human rights violations. In particular, a chapter on business and labor explores the role of white business and black labor during apartheid and examines issues of culpability, collaboration, and involvement[71] and the costs and benefits of apartheid.[72] Further, in its chapter on reparations, the report addresses these issues through an argument that business should pay communal reparations due to their responsibility for and direct benefit from abuses of land dispossession, exploitive labor practices, and impoverishment of miners.[73]

In Peru and Guatemala, as noted by Pablo de Greiff earlier in this volume, truth commissions documented how rural indigenous communities suffered the overwhelming majority of abuses from both insurgents and state security. In Guatemala, the final report of the Commission for Historical Clarification found a correlation between "social exclusion" — or lack of human development (life expectancy, child malnutrition, literacy, access to social services) — concentrations of indigenous ethnic communities, and incidences of violence committed by both rebel and state armed forces.[74] The final report of the Peruvian commission argued that the marginalization of the indigenous population was such that the majority of the Peruvian population was practically indifferent to the violence until eight journalists from Lima were massacred and a car bomb exploded in a wealthy neighborhood of the capital.[75] The Peruvian and Guatemalan commissions made significant contributions to the idea of vulnerability and how its different forms — social, political, economic, physical — reinforce each other. Their findings reveal how the prevailing indifference to physical violence against rural ethnic minorities is a reflection of social exclusion and political voicelessness, and how these inequalities mutually enable the tolerance of economic deprivation. A process of ethnic exclusion has shut out indigenous populations from "Peruvian" and "Guatemalan" societies, while at the same time there was a subsequent absence of state presence in the indigenous communities that left them exposed to violence.[76]

These findings notwithstanding, the Peruvian report views vulnerability to violence as primarily a function of political and social disempowerment. Natural resources enter into the analysis only tangentially, in an overview of agrarian political history of social and political control of the nineteenth century that was based on private control of land, indigenous labor, and local elite family patron-client relationships.[77] Overall, however, the conclusions of the report rest on social and political marginalization and do not refer to the specific modalities of economic vulnerability, which remain in the background of the commission's analysis. This gap in analysis of the specific role of natural resources is unfortunate because both the Guatemalan and Peruvian victimized minority populations are largely agrarian and, paradoxically, live in geographical proximity to high-value mineral, oil, and timber resources. As a result, the Peruvian commission recommended collective reparations for affected rural communities, to be used on development projects to address economic deprivation, but did not specifically explore how that deprivation occurred and how it contributes to social conflict and societal fractures. Recommendations for institutional reform therefore concentrated on judicial and educational institutions that would strengthen development of a diverse civil society, democratic participation, and recognition of diversity.[78] Recommendations for democratic reform did not include measures to improve economic development and equity in benefits from natural resources as a means of addressing the fractures in Peruvian society.

In contrast, East Timor provides an example in which natural resources were not part of the original mandate or research of the Commission for Reception, Truth and Reconciliation (CAVR), but the course of the work revealed them to be important factors.[79] Specifically, the commission found that trading companies with direct links to the Indonesian military and government deliberately and systematically underpaid coffee smallholders, "thereby abridging their right to an adequate livelihood."[80] One key finding was that the Indonesian-Chinese businessman Robbie Sumampow, like the Dutch citizen Guus Kouwenhoven during the Liberian war, provided transport for food and materiel for the war effort in exchange for access to resources. Sumampow, who transported military materiel because "we just want to do something for the government," was rewarded with exclusive access to the East Timor coffee supply. He later expanded this exclusive access into a monopoly on sandalwood oil and lucrative construction contracts.[81]

However, although the commission made specific findings regarding the abuses related to the occupation government's misappropriations of natural resources and the benefits from their extraction, no recommendations were made for resource-management reforms or prosecutions for crimes related to illegal resource exploitation. Indeed, recommendations for prosecutions would undoubtedly have found little traction, given the lack of political will, either domestically or internationally.[82] Additionally, the CAVR opted not to consider victims of ESCR violations as beneficiaries for reparation, for reasons of "feasibility and needs based prioritization."[83] This was a prudent decision, given that the massive numbers of people who were displaced and lost homes and property meant that virtually everyone in the country would be eligible for the few funds available.

Overall, with the exceptions of Sierra Leone, South Africa, and East Timor (and possibly Liberia, although the results remain to be seen), the role of natural resources in the character of the conflicts and profile of victims has received little attention in truth commission analyses. For the commissions that have engaged natural resources, only Sierra Leone made any significant recommendations related to resource management. Some argue that making wide-ranging recommendations for economic and natural resource reform, if a commission is not specifically mandated to do so, would be seen as overreaching its mandate, expertise, and authority.[84] This critique might be accurate when recommendations are too utopian and too broad and when the need to empanel the necessary expertise to conduct investigations is not taken seriously from the outset. However, as with all recommendations, when resource-related recommendations are kept specific and flowing directly from the analysis and findings, this difficulty can be minimized. As is true for all recommendations, the ones with the best chance for success are those that build on momentum from popular support and other efforts for reform.

Many argue that expanding the mandate of truth commissions to include an investigation of natural resource or economic issues could overstretch scarce resources and risk producing "watered down" findings due to a lack of depth.[85] In truth commission practice so far, there appear to be real reasons for concern. One such concern is the possibility that a focus on resource crime might spark resistance to the commission from those who continue to have economic interests under the transition and who are reluctant to have those interests closely scrutinized. This is a particular worry in contexts where the truth commission is mandated to make recommendations for prosecutions and where such prosecutions might actually materialize. Such actors are likely to wield considerable influence even under the new government and could take steps to undermine the commission's work. At the same time, in Liberia, for example, such contexts often also present considerable desire among the general public to see these crimes addressed, popular support that has propelled the political momentum forward. Thus, there is a delicate balance between not giving in to political bullying and cover-ups while also weighing the timing of truth commissions for maximum momentum and effectiveness. The context-specific nature of this calculus and its possible unintended consequences should be taken seriously by transitional justice advocates, for both investigations of widespread human rights crime and resource crime. Transitional justice advocates, like development workers, should seek to avoid cookie-cutter solutions.

These political obstacles notwithstanding, investigation of resource crime is not beyond the inherent capacity of truth commissions, which are by definition ephemeral bodies, formed and staffed explicitly for the purposes of carrying out their mandate. Trouble arises when natural resources are not included in the vision from the outset, and are instead squeezed onto the research agenda with existing staff and deadlines. This is a recipe for mediocrity. When relevant, truth commission mandates should specifically include the investigation of natural resources and crimes associated with their extraction that contributed to the maintenance of the old regime and the targeting of victims, so that experts can be recruited to undertake technical investigations, within appropriate time frames. When done in this proactive manner, the possibilities can be promising, as demonstrated in the Sierra Leone case. Transitional justice advisors to truth commissions should encourage commissioners and research staff to engage experts early in the process to ensure adequate coverage of these issues is not left until the last minute. Some have argued for a separate chamber within the commission or even a separate commission to deal exclusively with economic crimes, in order to avoid overtaxing the traditional human rights focus.[86] While this may seem an expedient solution, we believe such a proposal does not inherently address the alleged problem of insufficient resources and would only further solidify the artificial separation between civil and political rights violations and the patterns of resource criminality and kleptocracy that characterize the regimes under investigation.

Perhaps the most serious challenge for truth commission recommendations in this area is again the problem of political will—the lack of ability to ensure that recommendations are enacted. Although public acknowledgment of crimes committed and harms suffered are one of the goals of truth commission investigations, if recommendations are shelved, victims may feel that the commission has done little more than repeat what is already well known. Reform of the revenue streams that financed the conflict goes against the economic interests of many in the ruling elite, and such recommendations often meet with considerable political resistance. Therefore, resource reform requires considerable popular pressure, effective international expertise, and oversight. The policy leverage or momentum provided by UN commodity sanctions has proven to be an effective way of applying pressure for institutional reform, as explained in the final section of this chapter.

REPARATIONS

An in-depth discussion of whether development projects can be usefully deployed as reparations is discussed elsewhere in this volume.[87] Here we briefly note two aspects of reparations related to natural resources. First, the South African and Sierra Leonean truth commission final reports directly addressed the question of structural inequities as a direct result of crimes committed in association with natural resource extraction and how reparations might be used to address development deficits among victim communities.[88] The Sierra Leone TRC proposed that income from the mining sector and assets seized from convicted persons "who profited from the conflict" be used for reparations.[89] The South African commission proposed "contributions" (or taxes) on businesses—focused on the mining sector—that benefited from apartheid to be used for reparations.[90] This discussion of who benefited and who suffered from these inequities and criminality focused most directly on the displacement of farming communities to access a captive labor population for the mines and dangerous working conditions and union busting for mine workers. Although the proposals for corporate taxes found little traction, these analyses provided useful contributions to awareness of the issues and generated some momentum for further investigation later undertaken under the aegis of the National Anti-Corruption Forum in South Africa[91] and Sierra Leone's mining reforms and the establishment of Diamond Area Community Development Fund (discussed above), and may yet generate civil suits that could produce damages for reparations.

As we noted previously, the return of stolen assets from resource crime through trials or the UNCAC might be used to support frequently underfunded reparations programs, as was intended in key rulings on cases of returned stolen assets of Augusto Pinochet (US$9 million),[92] Alberto Fujimori (US$97.2 million),[93] and Ferdinand Marcos (US$2 billion), and through the ICC's Trust Fund for Victims. The attention to asset recovery and money laundering is growing, particularly in the United States in association with the increasing number of cases brought under the Patriot Act.

Although symbolically important, to date the actual record on the recovery of stolen assets from resource crime is poor.[94] This raises again the persistent challenge of insufficient political will to alter economic conditions favoring the political elite and the question of leniency toward these types of crimes. However, some have suggested that transitional justice could aid this recovery through an incentive-based truth commission process (similar to the Philippine Commission on Good Government), whereby perpetrators of less serious resource crimes could offer evidence leading to the recovery of stolen assets of the worst offenders in exchange for criminal amnesty for their own crimes (although not obviating the need to repay their own fiscal arrears).[95] In addition, although asset recovery has (so far) proved difficult to enforce, as noted above, legal proceedings have the added benefit of aiding truth-seeking by raising awareness and opening up evidence of abuses in the trial process as well as adding momentum behind a formal truth commission.[96]

Another reason to remain cautious about the potential of returned stolen assets from resource crime is the low likelihood that such assistance could produce significant development effects. In part, this is because returned assets are often not specifically earmarked for reparations or development spending. For example, the UNCAC mechanisms for international technical assistance in the recovery of stolen assets are conditional on the level of development of the victim country[97] but *also* on the lack of earmarking for returned funds.[98] Likewise, the SCSL statute stipulates that seized assets be returned to "rightful owners" or to the government of Sierra Leone, without specification of the final use of the funds.[99] Further, even if the designated recipients for reparations are the more limited pool of victims of gross human rights violations rather than the much larger group of people who suffered economic and social rights violations (such as rights to housing, livelihood, education, and health, which are likely to be the entire population of the transitional country), any funds available are likely to be modest. Given the breadth and depth of deprivation faced by the underclass of developing countries, recovered assets are unlikely to make a significant contribution to mitigating these conditions. However, this insufficiency for the magnitude of the task is not unlike reparation programs more generally, which are most significant in their ability to bring recognition of harm rather than material repair for wrongs committed.

SECURITY SECTOR REFORM

The engagement of transitional justice in institutional reform has traditionally been in the field of security sector reform (SSR), involving the vetting of human rights abusers and reforms to make law enforcement and armed forces more responsive and accountable to the citizenry. In the realm of natural resources, these measures can also be positive steps toward restoring the rule of law for enforcement of sound and equitable resource management and trade regulations, and legitimacy of state control of resources.

In addition to the role of old-regime armed forces as the primary beneficiaries of (often criminal) resource-extraction activities, police and military personnel are often also engaged as security for extraction operations, and often commit serious rights abuses while serving in this capacity. For example, during the Taylor regime, the Liberian timber company Maryland Wood Processing Industries (MWPI) engaged one of Taylor's former rebel commanders, General William Sumo, and his troops as company security. While in this capacity, Sumo's troops committed grave human rights abuses, including the massacre of at least 200 people in the community of Youghbor.[100] It was common practice throughout the Taylor period for extraction companies to employ government armed forces as company security, and many of these actors are accused of committing atrocities while in the companies' employ. Transitional justice measures for vetting could be extended to ensure that resource-extractive companies that win concessions do not employ those who have credible allegations of rights abuse as security or silent partners.

Some argue that vetting can actually compromise institutional capacity by removing trained and experienced officials.[101] This is undoubtedly true for indiscriminate purging of entire government institutions, such as the "De-Baathification" of the post–Sadaam Hussein Iraqi government, which as a form of collective punishment had the additional negative effect of generating more grievances. However, if vetting for the most egregious resource crimes (not widespread petty corruption) is used against those most responsible, the offenders tend to be top political appointees with little legitimate operational or technical expertise. The use of targeted vetting facilitated by transitional justice investigations, along with the implementation of oversight and accountability mechanisms crafted by development programs (see below), will help both preserve capacity and prevent criminality.

LINKING DEVELOPMENT AND TRANSITIONAL JUSTICE THROUGH A FOCUS ON RESOURCES

Development and transitional justice can productively coordinate on a few key natural resource issues to improve progress toward the common goals of preventing conflict and gross rights abuses (reducing physical vulnerability), building democratization (reducing political vulnerability), building civic trust and reconciliation (reducing social vulnerability), and improving efficiency and equity in the distribution of benefits from resource extraction (reducing economic vulnerability). In this section, we offer some broad outlines for the nature of that coordination, using the case of Liberia's forestry reform as an illustration.

First, it is helpful to understand that the forms development interventions take in transitional countries often change over time as the transition evolves through three generalizable stages:[102]

- "disaster" aid (refugee and IDP aid and return/resettlement; security/ peacekeeping; disarmament and demobilization of ex-combatants);
- reconstruction aid (macroeconomic reconstruction; election systems preparations; humanitarian aid; ex-combatant training and reintegration); and
- institutional reform (security sector reform; legal reforms, including constitutional and decentralization lawmaking; fiscal reform; natural resources management and land tenure reform; anticorruption; civil society building).

In order to better coordinate among programs *within* development programs and *between* development and transitional justice arenas, attention should be paid to the concepts of coherence and momentum. One of the lessons of the review of initiatives in this chapter has been the overarching problem of insufficient political will. There is, therefore, an urgent need to be strategic, given the breadth of problems to be addressed in brief time frames and the entrenched political and economic interests at play. Actors from both arenas should seek to build off each other's efforts in ways that raise awareness within constituencies who feel ownership over the agenda and will use their own networks and social capital to push for reform.

Build consensus, not cookie cutters. Frequent and varied public consultations can help build consensus around goals and priorities for resource management in order to avoid arbitrary decision-making that enables corruption. Resource sectors, as we have shown, often play a central role in facilitating conflicts. Therefore, reforms of resource extraction and trade are designed to affect financial flows to armed parties, which makes them inherently highly political, particularly reforms for redistribution (such as land tenure laws and reviews of extraction concessions) and accountability (such as prosecutions or vetting of war profiteers). If not undertaken in a principled way, these reforms will be seen as political punishment by the "winners" of the conflict against the "losers."

As demonstrated by the Liberian forest reforms outlined below, an assessment of management options that seeks to address the political vulnerability of the voiceless should seek broad participation in clarifying objectives and developing principled and transparent processes for resource allocation to maximize effectiveness, equity, and broad developmental benefits. Assessments and policies should focus on building structures and processes for revenue transparency and accountability.

Transitional justice measures—in particular truth-seeking and legal accountability—can provide investigations into and increase awareness around the role of natural resources in facilitating violence and targeting victims so that policy targets can be fine-tuned to those most in need, rather than used in a cookie-cutter approach. Development programs should help build locally specific knowledge, perhaps facilitated by transitional justice experts, as a required part of their programming so that actors better understand the context in which they work. However, as noted above, transitional justice advocates should also avoid the cookie-cutter approach and take seriously the importance of context and timing in considering the potential unintended consequences of truth commissions, prosecutions, and vetting.

Do no harm. Development workers often see themselves as offering solutions to problems of deprivation and underdevelopment. However, the international community has an ethical obligation to first ensure that it is not part of the problem—that is, it must minimize its own negative impacts on transitional countries.[103] Without diluting the attention to poor governance and responsibility of individuals for criminal behavior, development programs should also focus on the impact of the international community on the conflict through markets and the contribution of donor money. In particular, what was the role of international buyers of natural resources and the foreign corporations involved in extraction or its financing as drivers of demand and extraction practices? This approach has the added strategic advantage of building momentum by drawing in international interests. Development workers should seek coherence of reform by encouraging buyers and financiers to use their influence to push for reforms that promote human security and conflict prevention through sound resource management, equity, and transparency of resource flows.

The Kimberley Process for the certification of origin for diamonds is an example of an initiative that came from this international focus and the coordination of human rights and development concerns around a natural resource. Investigations and advocacy campaigns by such human rights groups as Global Witness contributed to increased global awareness of the use of luxury diamonds sold on the international market to fund the brutal civil wars in Africa (especially in Sierra Leone and Angola), which were causing widespread crimes against humanity. This awareness resulted in UN sanctions on the trade of diamonds from a number of conflict-ridden African countries. Diamond marketers, such as De Beers, panicked about the potential decline in sales, and resource-dependent countries worried that their income would dry up if consumers became reluctant to buy "blood diamonds" when their origin could not be traced. Consequently, diamond-producing countries and marketers joined forces, with participation from human rights advocates, to produce a system for the certification of origin that allows diamond-producing countries with sound institutions, such as Botswana and South Africa, to share in the economic benefits of diamond extraction, while helping[104] to protect against the human rights abuse that stems from unregulated sales.

Don't sacrifice good governance and human security for quick economic recovery. As mentioned previously, the frequent duality of development priorities means that macroeconomic priorities often trump measures to protect human security. Transitional contexts present particular challenges to mobilizing natural resources for both economic development and the improvement of social welfare.[105] But the urgency to put in place initiatives believed to speed economic recovery should not be undertaken without consideration of the unintended consequences. For example, entitlements over resources are often redefined during conflicts as people are displaced and new concessions issued, often on top of old ones. Transitions are often characterized, at times under the facilitation of development experts, by a rush on resources under the guise of "economic rehabilitation," a rush that further disadvantages the politically voiceless, whose resource rights are overlooked. Under ephemeral transitional governments, there are high incentives for corruption for those with the means to quickly secure access to land and resources.

Likewise, transitional governments often neglect accountability for crimes committed under the past regime for the sake of "political stability," again often under the advice of international experts. At times, in the interest of "stability," such controversial initiatives as concession reviews and land reforms are put on the back burner until after the most lucrative natural resource rights are issued to powerful players. As we have shown, given the proven role of resources in funding conflict, this "pragmatic" approach is actually not a conflict-prevention strategy but a conflict-creation strategy.

As with conflict zones, postconflict zones attract the most risk-tolerant companies, which are more inclined to use bribery and deploy private armed protection, thereby undermining steps toward respecting human rights and eradicating corruption. Again, as we have demonstrated, entrenched corruption that rewards bribe payers instead of those who follow sound resource management and taxation regulations in fact does not advance economic growth over the long term, but rather saps government revenues and encourages inefficient resource management. A major challenge is thus to ensure that the path of revenue allocation consolidates both economic recovery and good governance. Resource allocation and oversight mechanisms can, when equitably and effectively designed and enforced, foster a sense of entitlement over revenues among the population, building incentives and accountability mechanisms to protect revenues from misallocation by governments and extractive industries.[106]

THE LIBERIA FOREST INITIATIVE:
AN EXAMPLE OF COHERENT INSTITUTIONAL REFORM

The Liberia Forest Initiative (LFI) is one example of a creative and broadly effective initiative for assisting comprehensive institutional reform in the Forest Development Authority (FDA), following from the recognition of the role that timber played in fueling violence. The LFI is a collaborative, multi-stakeholder forum that included donors, the Liberian government, and civil society, whose aim was to implement forest sector reform in postconflict Liberia. While it is not surprising that, after decades of violence, Liberia remains challenged in its reform efforts, we underscore here the possibilities for coordination between investigations of past abuse and building strong institutions for the future, and the effective use of windows of opportunity.

We have often referred in this chapter to the importance of creating momentum for effective reform. One important form of momentum is the incentive for implementing institutional reform that comes from UN sanction conditionalities. These reforms may include improved resource management and institutional operations; increased fiscal transparency; legislative review and drafting of resource management and tenure laws and regulations; review of extraction concessions and subsequent renegotiation or cancellation of such contracts; and disbarment for bad actors.

Other sources of external momentum in the Liberia case were the strong interest of international actors—the U.S. government in particular—in pushing for change and influence in the process (the LFI was administered in-country by U.S. forest service staff, with participation from the World Bank, the UN Food and Agriculture Organization [FAO], and others). George W. Bush's Presidential Initiative on Illegal Logging, although an unfunded mandate, brought interest and funding from key U.S. State Department and U.S.

Agency for International Development (USAID) players. The U.S. ambassador to Liberia had particular interest in pushing for change in the timber sector and sought expertise from USAID on how to do so in a productive way. At the same time, there was increasing interest in "conflict commodities" following on the awareness of diamonds and the Kimberley Process in Sierra Leone and coltan[107] in DRC. These sources of external momentum were capitalized on by the active involvement of government, donors, industry, civil society organizations, and communities in the reform process. These factors combined with a general enthusiasm for and attention to the new Liberian president, Ellen Johnson-Sirleaf, the first African woman elected head of state and a Harvard-trained development economist. Further, the indictment of Charles Taylor raised awareness around the conflict, generating momentum for successful transition.

Timber played a central role in financing armed violence in Liberia. At the end of Charles Taylor's regime in 2003, forestry accounted for an estimated 22 percent of GDP and half of exports.[108] Forests are also important to ordinary Liberians, most of whom rely on charcoal for cooking and the forests for subsistence, shifting agriculture. However, forests have also been linked with instability.[109] Over the past two decades, timber funded conflict and the security forces of logging companies engaged in widespread human rights abuses, including massacres of local communities. To eliminate the role timber played in the regional conflict, in 2003 the UN Security Council sanctioned the import of forest products from Liberia. Reform of the forestry sector was relatively uncharted territory because, unlike diamonds and the Kimberley Process, there was not an existing set of criteria to judge when sanctions could be lifted safely. The UN specified that the necessary reforms for lifting sanctions must be consistent with good governance, including government control over forest resources and the use of forest revenues for legitimate development purposes.

One of the first steps taken by the LFI and the FDA was to review the existing logging claims. When all concessions were mapped, the claims were 2.5 times greater than the area of forest in the entire country. Successive governments had used forestry as a source of patronage, ignoring prior contracts, leading to overlapping concessions. The review committee received a writ of search and seizure to examine financial records of Liberia's Central Bank and other private banks. These records revealed that only 14 percent of taxes were paid, with more than $64 million in arrears. (Although due to underreporting and smuggling, arrears are likely three to four times greater.) Furthermore, of the seventy-two contracts, not one company could meet the minimum legal requirements to operate,[110] even for a single year. Consequently, the first executive order of President Johnson-Sirleaf was to declare all prior logging contracts null and void.

In addition to the concession review, the National Forestry Law was reformed in 2006 as a precondition to lifting sanctions. The reforms included competitive bidding for contract allocation, community involvement in decision-making, disclosure requirements, comprehensive public access to information, and a chain-of-custody (COC) system to track the origin of timber from stump to export in order to ensure legality and the payment of taxes (COC immediate operations have been contracted out to the European inspection company SGS Group).

The reforms culminated in 2008 with the allocation of the first new logging contracts. The challenge now is the proper implementation of the new procedures. To that end, the Liberia Extractive Industries Transparency Initiative[111] (EITI) is the first such initiative to incorporate forestry (in other countries, EITIs are normally restricted to the reporting of revenues from oil, gas, and mining companies). Likewise, the European Community has asked Liberia to join in a Voluntary Partnership Agreement (VPA) to license all shipments of Liberian forest products to Europe to assure legality; European customs agents would then bar all unlicensed imports as a way of reinforcing the above reforms.

Such reforms are invariably slow to be implemented in the wake of conflict, with government institutions challenged by a lack of capacity and traditions of crony politics and corrupt resource use. At the same time, full implementation of reform is often hampered by the urgency of demands for economic rehabilitation. Postconflict countries need capital influxes to rebuild infrastructure and public services, create employment, and build a peacetime economy in order to maintain peace. In such scenarios, foreign direct investment is seen as the fastest way to meet these needs for capital.

Underscoring the way in which transitional justice and development measures call for one another, capital influxes can arguably have negative effects if there is not vetting of bad actors, and if the process for granting contracts is arbitrary rather than following strict principles for tendering and auction. In the absence of both sets of measures, foreign investment can have negative impacts on governance and give investors the impression of "business as usual." In addition, prioritizing the extraction of resources by foreign companies over local resource use has adverse impacts on local entitlements and livelihoods of rural resource-dependent communities, which can contribute to local grievances and ultimately to renewed violence.

Transitional justice efforts and concerns overlapped in a number of ways with the Liberian Forest Initiative. It is worth noting that the chair of the Liberian TRC was also a member of the concession review board. Additionally, investigations and evidence collected by the concession review were used by the SCSL prosecution of Charles Taylor to assist in the investigations to trace his stolen assets (and his claims of indigence, which entitle him to aid for his defense). This information is also being submitted to the Liberian TRC, which can then use the information not only as part of the widely accessible public record, but also to recommend prosecutions and further institutional reforms.

Additionally, human rights advocates who sat on the concession review committee went out to communities in the logging concession areas and collected statements regarding the abuse they suffered at the hands of logging companies and their security during the war. These findings contributed to the decision to establish a vetting policy for concession bidders.[112] The TRC could keep the process going by investigating and substantiating the claims of abuse from the concession review as part of their investigations on economic crimes. These findings, in turn, could generate more momentum to implement this debarment policy, support SSR and prosecutions, and help to target reparations for victims.

Liberia's vetting policy for forest concessionaires is graduated. The first step is suspension from the bidding process of either companies or individuals that "have defaulted on their financial obligations."[113] There are two types of debarment. For individuals or companies wishing to bid on forest concessions, the regulation for qualification for concession bidding debars any persons (including legal persons) "who have aided or abetted civil disturbances involving the use of weapons."[114] The specific criteria for identifying the precise meaning of "aided and abetted" and "involving the use of weapons" have not yet been identified by the FDA due to faltering political will. For individuals providing security for forest companies, the criteria are based on those established by the UN Civilian Police's consultative process for vetting the Liberian National Police.[115] These criteria involve not being among those most responsible in the war or who have credible allegations of abuse against them, which some of the accused claim is a violation of due process. The LFI partners countered that, given the key role played by timber in the conflict, it was in the best interests of Liberia to err on the side of caution in the vetting process.

Transitional justice also played a role in the FDA's reform process, as potential concession winners were required to offer statements to the TRC about their activities during the war in order to prequalify for concession bidding. The goals of this were both to support truth-seeking about the nature of the

timber sector's role in the conflict and its impacts on victims as well as to hold
the perpetrators accountable by gathering information that could be shared
with the FDA for the debarment of those who committed rights abuses.

Although there are many challenges remaining—primarily the problem
of political will for implementation—the forest sector reform in Liberia is an
encouraging example of how transitional justice and development can productively collaborate to the benefit of each arena's core agendas.

CONCLUSION: RETHINKING NOTIONS OF VULNERABILITY, ACCOUNTABILITY, AND JUSTICE

Natural resources are central to both national economic development and to
local livelihoods in many conflict-affected countries. Further, resource mismanagement in economies dependent on primary commodities can undermine
good governance and fund armed violence as well as contribute to entrenched
poverty and deprivation. Resources can therefore be the catalyst for both positive development as well as the facilitator of rights abuses. Resources, then, in
many cases are a natural focus and a convenient leverage point for coherent
programs focused on development and justice in their fullest meanings, as well
as for prevention of conflict that further victimizes the poor.

In contexts where natural resource extraction plays a key role, legal
accountability for pillage as a war crime is an underused tool for holding war
profiteers to account. The recent ICJ conviction of Ugandan state involvement, even without a systematic state strategy of plunder, in the rapacious and
brutal exploitation of DRC's embattled Ituri region is a positive sign that the
legal charge of pillage as a war crime may be increasingly used to bring war
profiteers to account and foster a climate that respects the rule of law in which
resources are not viewed as booty for the taking. Nevertheless, whether there
will be sufficient political will to use the courts to seek relief for pillage cannot
be assumed, as the overlap between economic and political interests at stake in
crimes dealing with stolen assets may prevent successful convictions.

Because of the scope of the research and expertise that well-funded truth
commissions can marshal, truth recovery can be perhaps the most useful way
to publicly reveal the linkages between resources and abuses, as a way of generating momentum—public support for reform and even legal action. Truth
commissions with a mandate to focus beyond civil and political violations to
include natural resources allow a fuller understanding of how abuse happens
and how to avoid it in the future. A focus on the role of resources provides a

more complete picture of the extent and modalities of state rule and victimization. Through truth-seeking in particular, transitional justice can make several concrete contributions to development through investigations that help target aid toward victims, and contribute to momentum for prosecutions and institutional reforms that build accountability and the capacity of government law-enforcement institutions. In turn, development can contribute to transitional justice by undertaking reforms that capitalize on the information gathered to help prevent future abuse and violence and to promote equity and transparency in natural resource benefits. These steps build civic trust, help restore legitimacy and capacity of government, and work toward reconciliation.

Therefore, where the circumstances are relevant and the political climate permits, we advocate for a modest expansion of the transitional justice mandate to include:

- rigorous truth-seeking investigation into the role of natural resources in facilitating the conflict and targeting victims, the linkages between this form of economic criminality and human rights abuses, and specific institutional weaknesses that enabled resource crimes; and
- key prosecutions of those most responsible for certain crimes associated with natural resource extraction—those who are also closely linked to gross human rights abuses.

However, although attention to political realities is important in weighing what measures will be effective, without external pressure the power of the status quo is likely to prevent meaningful change. We emphasize that when transitional justice and development advocates pay attention to building momentum, they can help *bring about* the political climate for change rather than simply waiting for it to occur. Such momentum is aided by attending to building external and internal coherence. We urge transitional justice advocates to build external coherence by coordinating with development workers using information derived from truth-seeking and trials to:

- improve natural resource and fiscal institutional reform to prevent armed conflict and improve equity and the sustainability of resource management;
- coordinate SSR and institutional vetting to exclude both human rights abusers and the worst perpetrators of resource crime from politically exposed positions; and
- encourage the use of seized assets from resource crimes for reparations.

We encourage development workers to build internal coherence by working among themselves toward the goals they share with transitional justice to:

- respond to local context, not cookie-cutter directives;
- recognize and minimize the negative impact of the international community on transitions; and
- not sacrifice good governance for economic recovery.

A coordinated transitional justice program that takes into account institutional reform of the management of natural resources enriches its understanding of the vulnerability of victims, and it expands accountability and reconciliation beyond immediate individual perpetrators to institutions. A coordinated approach to institutional reform that promotes transparent, accountable, and equitable management of natural resources as part of postconflict programming provides a contribution to the repair and recovery of conflict-affected societies through the promotion of good governance, the rule of law, democratization, citizenship, social inclusion, social capital, the fight against impunity, and respect for human rights in all their complexity—the whole range of civil and political, as well as economic and social, rights.

NOTES

1   Since 1989, one-third of postconflict countries have had gross domestic products (GDPs) more than 30 percent dependent on extractive sectors (excluding foreign grants and loans) in the years following conflict termination (information culled from International Monetary Fund [IMF] country reports and Peace Research Institute in Oslo conflict dataset).

2   Michael Ross, "What Do We Know About Natural Resources and Civil Wars?" *Journal of Peace Research* 41, no. 3 (2004): 337–56; and Philippe Le Billon, *Fuelling War: Natural Resources and Armed Conflicts*, Adelphi Paper 373 (London: Routledge and IISS, 2005).

3   See, e.g., Nancy Peluso and Michael Watts, *Violent Environments* (Berkeley: University of California Press, 2001).

4   On the use of the notions of external and internal coherence, see, e.g., Pablo de Greiff, "Justice and Reparations," in *The Handbook of Reparations*, ed. Pablo de Greiff (New York: Oxford University Press, 2006).

5   Michael J. Watts and Hans G. Bohle, "The Space of Vulnerability: The Causal Structure of Hunger and Famine," *Progress in Human Geography* 17, no. 1 (1993): 43–67; Greg Bankoff, Georg Frerks, and Dorothea Hilhorst, *Mapping Vulnerability: Disasters, Development and People* (London: Earthscan, 2004); Andrew Kirby, ed., *Nothing to Fear: Risks and Hazards in American Society* (Tucson: University of Arizona Press, 1990); Michael Watts, *Silent*

Violence: Food, Famine and Peasantry in Northern Nigeria (Berkeley: University of California Press, 1983); and Michael Watts, "On the Poverty of Theory: Natural Hazards Research in Context," in *Interpretations of Calamity*, ed. Kenneth Hewitt (London: Allen and Unwin, 1983b).

6   Ben Wisner, Piers M. Blaikie, Terry Cannon, and Ian Davis, *At Risk: Natural Hazards, People's Vulnerability and Disasters* (London: Routledge, 2003); Ben Wisner and Maureen Fordham's Web site, Radical Interpretations of Disaster, www.radixonline.org/index. htm; Peluso and Watts, *Violent Environments*; Sue Lautze and Angela Raven-Roberts, "The Vulnerability Context: Is There Something Wrong With This Picture?" (paper presented at the Food and Agriculture Organization [FAO] International Workshop "Food Security in Complex Emergencies: Building Policy Frameworks to Address Longer-term Programming Challenges," Tivoli, September 23–25, 2003, ftp://ftp.fao.org/docrep/fao/meeting/009/ae509e.pdf).

7   Emily Harwell, *Without Remedy: Human Rights Abuse and Indonesia's Pulp Industry* (New York: Human Rights Watch, 2003).

8   Amartya Sen, *Development as Freedom* (Oxford: Oxford University Press, 2001).

9   United Nations Conference on Trade and Development (UNCTAD), *Development and Globalization: Facts and Figures* (Geneva: UNCTAD, 2008).

10   See, e.g., Michael L. Ross, "The Political Economy of the Resource Curse," *World Politics* 51, no. 2 (1999): 297–322; and Richard M. Auty, ed., *Resource Abundance and Economic Development* (New York: Oxford University Press, 2001). For a counterargument, see Christa N. Brunnschweiler, "Cursing the Blessings? Natural Resource Abundance, Institutions, and Economic Growth," *World Development* 36, no. 3 (2008): 399–419.

11   Patricia Gossman, "Disarmament and Transitional Justice in Afghanistan," Country Study (New York: ICTJ, 2009).

12   In Sierra Leone, many ex-combatants who chose skills training for urban livelihoods in trades, such as carpentry and auto mechanics, over farming found few job opportunities and wound up selling the tools they were given as part of the reintegration benefits package. See Jeremy Ginifer, "Reintegration of Ex-Combatants," in *Sierra Leone: Building the Road to Recovery*, ed. Mark Malan et al. (Pretoria: Institute for Security Studies, 2003).

13   Sustainable Development Institute, "Clarifying Forest Ownership in Liberia: The Way Forward to Integrate Economic Growth with Social Justice in the Forest Sector," Occasional Briefing #03/2007, October 2007.

14   Global Witness, "Heavy Mittal? A State within a State: Inequitable Mineral Development Agreement Between the Government of Liberia and Mittal Steel Holdings NV," Report by Global Witness, October 2006.

15   Jean-Paul Azam, Paul Collier, and Anke Hoeffler, "International Policies on Civil Conflict: An Economic Perspective" (unpublished working paper, December 2001, users.ox.ac.uk/~ballo144/azam_coll_hoe.pdf).

16   Michael L. Ross, "Does Oil Hinder Democracy?" *World Politics* 53, no. 3 (2004): 325–61. Several quantitative studies suggest a link between oil and a higher risk of conflict onset due to weakened state institutions (compared to countries with equivalent GDP per capita). See James D. Fearon, "Primary Commodity Exports and Civil War," *Journal of Conflict Resolution* 49, no. 4 (2005): 483–507; and Paul Collier and A. Hoeffler, "Greed and Grievance in Civil War," *Oxford Economic Papers* 56, no. 4 (2004): 563–95.

17   Al Gedicks, *The New Resource Wars: Native and Environmental Struggles Against Multi-national Corporations* (Cambridge, MA: South End Press, 1993); and Francis O. Adeola, "Environmental Injustice and Human Rights Abuse: The States, MNCs, and Repression of Minority Groups in the World System," *Research in Human Ecology* 8, no. 1 (2001): 39–59.

18   Harwell, *Without Remedy.*

19   Alluvial minerals and gems that can be easily exploited with low technology often escape the grasp of institutional control. Countries economically dependent on these types of easily tapped resources often have thriving informal untaxed sectors that undermine the capacity of the state to develop strong institutions. It is noteworthy that Botswana's and South Africa's diamonds are almost exclusively kimberlite, deep subterranean pipes that require expensive mining technology to access, while Sierra Leone's vast diamond resources are almost exclusively shallow alluvial deposits, which can be extracted by low-skill laborers equipped with no more than a bucket and shovel. Francois Jean and Jean-Christophe Rufin, eds., *Economies des Guerres Civiles* (Paris: Hachette, 1996); Michael L. Ross, "How Do Natural Resources Influence Civil War? Evidence from 13 Cases," *International Organization* 58, no. 1 (2004): 35–67; Ross, "What Do We Know?"; and Carolyn Nordstrom, *Shadows of War: Violence, Power, and International Profiteering in the Twenty-First Century* (Berkeley: University of California Press, 2004).

20   Based on figures from Bethany Ann Lacina and Nils Petter Gleditsch, "Monitoring Trends in Global Combat: A New Dataset of Battle Deaths," *European Journal of Population* 21, no. 2–3 (2005): 145–65.

21   Karen Ballentine and Jake Sherman, eds., *The Political Economy of Armed Conflict: Beyond Greed and Grievance* (Boulder: Lynne Rienner, 2003); David Keen, *The Economic Functions of Violence in Civil Wars* (Oxford: Oxford University Press for the International Institute of Strategic Studies, 1998); and Jeremy M. Weinstein, *Inside Rebellion: The Politics of Insurgent Violence* (New York: Cambridge University Press, 2007).

22   Ross, "What Do We Know?" For a contrary finding, see Macartan Humphreys, "Natural Resources, Conflict, and Conflict Resolution," *Journal of Conflict Resolution* 49, no. 4 (2005): 508–37.

23   Michael Ross, "Booty Futures: Africa's Civil Wars and the Futures Market for Natural Resources" (paper presented at the annual meeting of the American Political Science Association, Boston, Massachusetts, August 28, 2002).

24 See, e.g., Herfried Münkler, *The New Wars* (Cambridge: Polity, 2005).

25 Weinstein, *Inside Rebellion.*

26 Ibid.

27 Ruben Carranza, "Plunder and Pain: Should Transitional Justice Engage with Corruption and Economic Crimes?" *International Journal of Transitional Justice* 2, no. 3 (2008): 310–30; and Roger Duthie with Pablo de Greiff, "Transitional Justice and Economic Crimes," ICTJ document, November 2007, 4.

28 Duthie with de Greiff, "Transitional Justice and Economic Crimes," 6.

29 The Hague Convention IV respecting the Laws and Customs of War on Land and its annex: Regulations concerning the Laws and Customs of War on Land (hereafter referred to as H.R.), The Hague, October 18, 1907, arts. 46, 52, 53; Article 33, Convention (IV) relative to the Protection of Civilian Persons in Time of War, Geneva, 12 August 1949; and Article 4, sect. 2(c) of the Protocol Additional to the Geneva Conventions of 12 August 1949, and relating to the Protection of Victims of Non-International Armed Conflicts (Protocol II), 8 June 1977. It should also be noted that pillage is a crime in most domestic jurisdictions also (thanks to James Stewart for this point).

30 UN Covenant on Civil and Political Rights, arts. 6, 7, 9, 17; H.R., art. 25; and Geneva Convention (IV), art. 3(1)(a)(b)(c)(d).

31 Rome Statute of the ICC, arts. 7(1)(c) and (d), 8(2)(e)(v, xii), and 25(3)(d).

32 National-level legislation for the enforcement of UN Charter, Chapter VII, arts. 41, 42, 48. Not all countries have such legislation in place, which provides a loophole for sanction busters (e.g., the case of Leonid Minin, arrested in Italy but acquitted for lack of territorial jurisdiction, nevertheless had his European-based assets frozen; see Judgment of the Court of First Instance [Second Chamber] of 31 January 2007: *Leonid Minin v. Commission of the European Communities*).

33 Emily Harwell and Arthur Blundell, "Achieving Accountability in Conflict and Post-Conflict Countries: Improving Coordination between Prosecutors and other Investigators" (unpublished paper submitted to the Canadian Department for Aid and International Trade, Human Security Program, 2007).

34 H.R., art. 47.

35 Fourth Geneva Convention, art. 33.

36 Occupying states are allowed usufructuary use of natural resources in order to support the occupation and provide for the civilian population. Interpretations of the nature of the usufructuary duty of occupying powers are the subject of heated debate. Usufruct rights allow the holder to enjoy products and benefits as long as they do not diminish or damage the substance of the asset. See, e.g., R. Dobie Langenkamp, "What Happens to the Oil? International Law and the Occupation of Iraq," January 2003, www.beg.utexas.edu/energyecon/documents/behind_the_gas_pump/Langenkamp_FullPaper.pdf. The prevailing interpretation has been that "renewable" resources, such as timber, may be

extracted, and already open mines (oil, gas, minerals, gems) may be exploited but new
ones may not be opened. This latter concept is known as the U.S. "Open Mine" Doctrine and is based on Roman law. See Edward R. Cummings, "Oil Resources in Occupied
Arab Territories Under the Law of Belligerent Occupation," *Journal of International Law
and Economics* 9 (1974): 533–93; and William W. Buckland and Arnold D. McNair, *Roman
Law and Common Law*, 2nd ed., rev. F. H. Lawson (Cambridge: Cambridge University
Press, 1952), 130. More controversially, James Stewart and colleagues at the Open Society Justice Initiative Pillage Project now argue that, in fact, occupying powers have no
defensible right to extract resources because none are truly "renewable" (James Stewart,
telephone interview, April 23, 2008). A further question as to the legality of resource
extraction centers on whether the profits from the resource extraction are directed
toward the costs of administering the occupied territory and not toward the enrichment
of individuals or of the occupying state or use by the home population of the occupying
state. This point, as laid out in the Hague Regulations, was explored in some detail in the
Nuremberg trials against World War II Nazi war criminals. See *Trials of the War Criminals before the Nuremberg Military Tribunals under Control Council Law No. 10*, Nuremberg,
October 1946 – April 1949, vol. v (Washington, DC: Government Printing Office, 1950),
avalon.law.yale.edu/subject_menus/imt.asp; "USA v. Oswald Pohl et al indictment,"
Count 2 — War Crimes, point 13, Nuremberg, January 13, 1947, avalon.law.yale.edu/imt/
indict4.asp; *Nazi Conspiracy and Aggression*, Volume 1, Chapter XIII — "Economic Aspects
of the Conspiracy: Germanization and Spoliation," avalon.law.yale.edu/imt/chap_08.
asp; and *Judgment of Nuremberg International Military Tribunal against German War Criminals*, "Judgment relating to war crimes and crimes against humanity," avalon.law.yale.
edu/imt/judwarcr.asp.

37   Article 33 of the Fourth Geneva Convention, and later art. 4, sect. 2.c, of the Second
Additional Protocol on non-international conflicts.

38   Commentary on Article 33, Geneva Convention (IV) Relative to the Protection of
Civilian Persons in Time of War, August 12, 1949, www.icrc.org/ihl.nsf/COM/380-
600038?OpenDocument.

39   International Committee of the Red Cross (ICRC), *Business and International Humanitarian Law: An Introduction to the Rights and Obligations of Business Enterprises under International Humanitarian Law* (Geneva: ICRC, 2006), 22.

40   Although not specifically dealing with natural resources, the USMT cases against the
industrialists Krupp and Farben supported the prohibitions against permanent seizure
under the "illusion of legality" without fair compensation, and for the purposes of misappropriation for self-enrichment rather than administering the territory. The International Military Tribunal (IMT) also prosecuted the individual German banker and war
profiteer Karl Rasche, who was convicted of looting and spoliation.

41   Agreement Between the United Nations and the Government of Sierra Leone on the

Establishment of a Special Court for Sierra Leone, art. 1.

42 For a review of diamonds relations with armed conflicts, see Philippe Le Billon, "Diamond Wars? Conflict Diamonds and Geographies of Resource Wars," *Annals of the Association of American Geographers* 98, no. 2 (2008): 345–72.

43 In an effort to address this gap, James Stewart and colleagues at the Open Society Justice Initiative have drafted guidelines and have conducted legal training for prosecutors on the crime of pillage (James Stewart, telephone interview, April 23, 2008).

44 See *Armed Activities on the Territory of the Congo (Democratic Republic of the Congo v. Uganda)*, Judgment, International Court of Justice, December 19, 2005, www.icj-cij.org/docket/files/116/10455.pdf.

45 Ibid., para. 242. In its judgment, the court quotes liberally from the commission findings that Brig. Gen. Kazini, commander of Uganda forces (UPDF) in the DRC, was "clearly aware" of the involvement of officers under his control doing business in the DRC, including the use of military aircraft in "gold mining and trade, smuggling and looting of civilians." The court cited commission findings that "exploitation had been carried out, *inter alia*, by senior army officers working on their own and through contacts inside the DRC; by individual soldiers taking advantage of their postings; by cross-border trade and by private individuals living within Uganda." Further, Kazini was found to be "an active supporter" of Victoria, an organization engaged in smuggling diamonds from the DRC through Uganda, and "it is difficult to believe that he was not profiting for himself from the operation." The court considered the commission report to present "ample credible and persuasive evidence to conclude that officers and soldiers of the UPDF, including the most high-ranking officers, were involved in the looting, plundering and exploitation of the DRC's natural resources and that the military authorities did not take any measures to put an end to these acts."

46 Henry Wasswa, "Will Uganda Pay Up for Congo Occupation?" Institute for War and Peace Reporting, July 26, 2007, www.globalpolicy.org/intljustice/icj/2007/0726ugandapayup.htm. "Armed Activities on the Territory of the Congo: The ICJ Judgment in the Context of the Current Peace Process in the Great Lakes Region," summary of a meeting of the International Law Discussion Group at Chatham House on January 27, 2006; participants included lawyers, regional experts, academics, and representatives of NGOs and of UK government departments, www.chathamhouse.org.uk/publications/papers/download/-/id/336/file/3306_ilp270106.doc.

47 For example, the Economic Community of West African States (ECOWAS) Convention on Small Arms and Light Weapons, www.ecosap.ecowas.int/. For the text of the convention, see www.iansa.org/regions/wafrica/documents/CONVENTION-CEDEAO-ENGLISH.PDF.

48 The village was allegedly attacked for interfering with the security militia's plundering raids of another village of the same ethnic group. Kouwenhoven was acquitted on this

charge, as the judge deemed there to be insufficient evidence of his direct involvement or abetting the crime. Kouwenhoven claimed innocence to this charge, as he was out of the country at the time, admitting he was in violation of the UN travel ban against him.

49 Report of UN Panel of Expert to Liberia, s/2007/340, Annexes III–V, June 7, 2007.

50 Marian Husken and Harry Lensink, "Guus Kouwenhoven: Dit is een absolute nachtmer-rieâ," *Vrij Nederland*, March 31, 2007.

51 Official translation in English: Guus Kouwenhoven Case, Judgment Court of Appeal in The Hague, Cause-list Number: 22-004337-06, Public Prosecutor's Office Number: 09-750001-05. Date Judgment: March 10, 2008.

52 Report of UN Panel of Experts to Liberia, para. 116, Annex XII.

53 UN Security Council Resolution 1343 (2001), s/RES/1343 (2001), March 2001.

54 ECOWAS Convention on Small Arms and Light Weapons.

55 Judgment Court of Appeal.

56 Transparency International, *Global Corruption Report 2004* (London: Pluto Press, 2004).

57 "Supersemar Found Guilty, Asked to Pay 'Too Little,'" *Jakarta Post*, March 28, 2008.

58 Tim Daniels, "Repatriation of Looted State Assets: Selected Case Studies and the UN Convention Against Corruption," in *Global Corruption Report 2004*.

59 "Gains Cited in Hunt for Liberian Ex-Warlord's Fortune," *New York Times*, March 9, 2006.

60 Assemblee Nationale Commission Speciale Chargee de l'Examen de la Validite des Conventions a Caractere Economique et Financier Conclues Pendant les Guerres de 1996–1997 et de 1998, Kinshasa, June 26, 2005, www.congonline.com/documents/Rapport_Lutundula_pillage_2006.pdf; and Commission de Revisitation des Contrats Miniers, Kinshasa, November 2007, web.archive.org/web/20080208030750/http://www.mining-congo.cd/.

61 The independence of the commission was questioned, however; see Roger Tangri and Andrew M. Mwenda, "Politics, Donors and the Ineffectiveness of Anti-corruption Institutions in Uganda," *Journal of Modern African Studies* 44, no. 1 (2006): 101–24.

62 This is an argument considered by Priscilla Hayner and Lydiah Bosire in "Should Truth Commissions Address Economic Crimes? Considering the Case of Kenya," ICTJ Memorandum submitted to the Kenya Task Force on the Establishment of a Truth, Justice and Reconciliation Commission, March 26, 2003; and Duthie with de Greiff, "Transitional Justice and Economic Crimes," 6.

63 John Hagan and Patricia Parker, "White-Collar Crime and Punishment: The Class Structure and Legal Sanctioning of Securities Violations," *American Sociological Review* 50, no. 3 (June 1985): 302–16; Kip Schlegel and David Weisburd, eds., *White-Collar Crime Reconsidered* (Boston: Northeastern University Press, 1992); and Duthie with de Greiff, "Transitional Justice and Economic Crimes," 6.

64 Hagan and Parker, "White-Collar Crime and Punishment"; Schlegel and Weisburd,

White-Collar Crime Reconsidered; and David Marcus, "Famine Crimes in International Law," *American Journal of International Law* 97 (April 2003): 245–81.

65 "The single greatest challenge" faced by those actors trying to address corruption, explains Madalene O'Donnell, "is intense opposition from political and economic elites who benefit tremendously from corruption." Madalene O'Donnell, "Corruption: A Rule of Law Agenda," in *Civil War and the Rule of Law: Security, Development, and Human Rights*, ed. Agnes Hurwitz and Reyko Huang (Boulder: Lynne Rienner, 2007), cited in Duthie with de Greiff, "Transitional Justice and Economic Crimes," 8.

66 Laurel Fletcher and Harvey Weinstein, "Violence and Social Repair: Rethinking the Contribution of Justice to Reconciliation," *Human Rights Quarterly* 24, no. 3 (August 2002): 573–639.

67 Piers Pigou, *The Community Reconciliation Process of the Commission for Reception, Truth and Reconciliation* (Dili, Timor-Leste: United Nations Development Program [UNDP], 2004).

68 *The Final Report of the Truth and Reconciliation Commission of Sierra Leone*, vol. 3B, chap. 1, "Mineral Resources, Their Use and Their Impact on the Conflict and the Country" (Freetown: Truth and Reconciliation Commission of Sierra Leone, 2004).

69 Ibid., 2.

70 Kimberley Process, www.kimberleyprocess.com/.

71 *The Final Report of the Truth and Reconciliation Commission of South Africa*, vol. 4, chap. 2, paras. 6–47 (Cape Town: Juta, 2003).

72 Ibid., paras. 48–112.

73 Some 3.5 million people were forcibly displaced between 1960 and 1982 to "homeland" reserves (comprising 8.8 percent of South Africa's total land area) and subjected to strict controls of movement in order to provide cheap labor for mines. Mine workers were housed in squalid, single-sexed hostels, separating families and spreading disease, especially HIV. The imposition of taxes that had to be paid in cash also forced subsistence farmers into the mining industry to obtain cash. The suppression of mine workers' unions and the promulgation of laws, such as the Masters and Servants Act, allowed for strict penalties for miners breaking their "contract" and "deserting" mines and created a captive pool of cheap labor. The economic benefits of these repressive policies went to the largely white elite in the mining industry. *The Final Report of the Truth and Reconciliation Commission of South Africa*, chap. 5, "Reparations and the Business Sector."

74 *Memory of Silence: Report of the Commission for Historical Clarification* (Guatemala, UNOPS, 1999). See Pablo de Greiff, "Articulating the Links Between Transitional Justice and Development," in this volume.

75 *Informe Final de la Comision de la Verdad and Reconciliacion*, Tomo VIII, Segunda Parte: "Los Factores Que Hicieron Possible la Violencia" (Lima, 2003), 90.

76 Ibid., 89.

77 Ibid., 92.

78   Ibid., Tomo IX, Cuarta Parte: "Recomendaciones de la CVR: Hacia la Reconciliacion,"
     84.

79   Following two decades of brutal occupation of East Timor by the Indonesian military
     state and the convulsion of violence that was visited on civilians immediately before and
     after the 1999 independence referendum, the CAVR was established by the UN transi-
     tional authority, and focused primarily on gross violations of killings, forced disappear-
     ances, arbitrary detentions, torture, sexual crimes, and forced displacement. However,
     during the writing phase of the final report, commissioners decided to add research on
     violations of ESCRs, including pillage of Timor's resources by the occupying state:

> As its work in the area of truth-seeking progressed, the Commission increas-
> ingly found evidence of both direct violations of social and economic rights
> and of the close inter-relationship between the violation of those rights and
> the abuses of civil and political rights that had been the chief focus of its
> work. It decided that this reality should be recognised in its Final Report.
> (*Chega! Final Report of the Commission for Reception, Truth and Reconciliation in
> East Timor* [Dili: Commission for Reception, Truth and Reconciliation in East
> Timor, 2005], Chapter 7.9, 47.)

     The research specifically investigated development spending by the occupying Indone-
     sian state that served to strengthen itself but did not benefit the Timorese, and viola-
     tions of the rights to food, education, health, and housing caused by tactics of forced
     displacement and forced labor. However, this added focus did not include an investiga-
     tion of land issues, because although there had been repeated and massive displacement
     of the civilian population, the commission mandate specifically excluded land rights.
     One of the findings of the final report was that the illegal extraction of lucrative natural
     resources and the control of key commodity markets by the Indonesian military and
     civilian state not only violated its obligations as an occupying power to the well-being of
     the Timorese people but amounted to the war crime of pillage, with long-term negative
     effects:

> The plunder of resources such as timber and coffee depleted to precariously
> low levels, assets that are essential to the livelihoods and long-term well-being
> of the population. No less damaging was the social impact of these mea-
> sures. The discriminatory use of resources served to create new divisions and
> to entrench existing ones. The arbitrary use of powers to move the popula-
> tion and evict them forcibly has left an unresolved legacy of uncertain tenure
> and landlessness.... The Commission takes the view that all of these social
> impacts are impediments to reconciliation and need to be addressed within
> that context. (Ibid., 46.)

80   Ibid., 47.

81   Ibid.

82 Massive abuses committed in the run-up to independence and the utter physical and institutional destruction left in the wake of the violence following the 1999 referendum left the weak Timorese judicial system overwhelmed. But, more critically, neither East Timorese nor Indonesian administrations are willing to pursue criminal cases after the conclusion of the Indonesian Ad Hoc Human Rights Court. This reluctance is troubling given that the court was roundly judged to be manifestly inadequate, issuing indictments for none of the top Indonesian commanders, acquitting all the Indonesian defendants, and eventually overturning even the East Timorese defendants' convictions. Although the foreign-supported East Timor Serious Crimes Unit issued further indictments, Indonesia has refused to extradite the accused, and neither the Timorese administration nor the UN seems willing to call for an international tribunal.

83 *Chega!*, chap. 11, "Recommendations," 40–41.

84 This was a common reaction to the final recommendations of the Truth and Reconciliation Commission of Greensboro, North Carolina, in the United States, which investigated the murders of five communist labor organizers by racist Ku Klux Klan members. The commission's recommended initiatives to address economic injustice and improve social services for the poor were felt by some members of the community to be overreaching the mandate and the strength of the findings.

85 An argument considered in Duthie with de Greiff, "Transitional Justice and Economic Crimes," 7.

86 Hayner and Bosire examine this position in "Should Truth Commissions Address Economic Crimes?," 2.

87 Naomi Roht-Arriaza and Katharine Orlovsky, "A Complementary Relationship: Reparations and Development," in this volume.

88 Peruvian, Guatemalan, and Moroccan truth commission reports addressed the problem of structural inequities more generally but did not specifically address the role of natural resources in this marginalization.

89 *Final Report of the Sierra Leone Truth and Reconciliation Commission*, vol. 2, chap. 4, 269.

90 *The Final Report of the Truth and Reconciliation Commission of South Africa*, vol. 6, sec. 2, chap. 5, 155.

91 Hennie van Vuuren, "Apartheid Grand Corruption: Assessing the Scale of Crimes of Profit from 1976–1994" (report prepared by civil society [Institute for Security Studies, Cape Town] in terms of a resolution of the Second Annual Anti-Corruption Summit for presentation at the National Anti-Corruption Forum, May 2006).

92 Terence O'Hara, "Allbrittons, Riggs to Pay Victims of Pinochet: Settlement Ends Case in Spain," *Washington Post*, February 26, 2005.

93 The Peruvian Special Fund for the Administration of Funds Illegally Obtained within State Jurisdiction was established to manage the seized stolen assets from accounts of former president Alberto Fujimori and his close associates, to be used to fund TRCs

and reparations (Decree of Urgency No. 122-2001, arts. 10 [iii] and [iv]). The fund has received US$77 million in confiscated corrupt assets from Swiss banks and US$20.2 million from the U.S. banks.

94   No payment has yet been made on the ICJ case of *DRC v. Uganda* or the Marcos case.

95   Carranza, "Plunder and Pain," 310–30.

96   Ruben Carranza, "Seeking Reparative Justice in the Financing of Reparations Programs" (unpublished manuscript, International Center for Transitional Justice, 12). Carranza notes that after a failed truth-seeking process, the attempts to recover Marcos's assets has revitalized the idea of a commission in order to "ensure that the truth behind all human rights violations is thoroughly documented" (13th Philippine Congress, House of Representatives House Bill No. 3315, Section 8 [B][4]).

97   UN Convention Against Corruption, arts. 60.2, 62.2, www.unodc.org/pdf/crime/convention_corruption/signing/Convention-e.pdf.

98   This condition was reportedly insisted upon by many developing country state parties, who felt earmarks were a violation of their sovereignty. Columbia University Law School workshop "Combating the Financing of Belligerent Groups," New York, March 13–14, 2008. (Chatham House Rules. Attendees included government officials, academics, and NGOs.)

99   Carranza, "Plunder and Pain," 310–30.

100   UN Panel of Experts Report, 35.

101   Alexander Mayer-Rieckh and Pablo de Greiff, eds., *Justice as Prevention: Vetting Public Employees in Transitional Societies* (New York: Social Science Research Council, 2007).

102   Much of the important groundwork for transitional justice and development reforms is laid before the transition even begins, during the tight time constraints of peace negotiations. Having experts on hand to lend expertise on key justice and development issues would help craft peace agreements that help advance these goals and avoid language or compromises that will limit the possibilities for justice and development during the transition. See, e.g., Priscilla Hayner's description of the Liberian peace talks, where there was no one present with expertise on international law or on truth commissions. Priscilla Hayner, "Negotiating Peace in Liberia: Preserving the Possibility for Justice," Henry Dunant Centre for Humanitarian Dialogue, 2007. Additionally, peace agreements are often reached through power sharing of key resource ministries by belligerent parties, which treat the resource as war booty rather than for sound and equitable management. While this may be a strategy for reaching a compromise and bringing an end to atrocities, such wealth sharing is counterproductive to sustained peace. Not only do these arrangements undermine the reform of such sectors so that they will not contribute to further conflict, they also offer an incentive to would-be belligerents that armed conflict is a winning strategy for gaining control over lucrative sectors. See Denis M. Tull and Andreas Mehler, "The Hidden Costs of Power Sharing: Reproducing Insurgent Violence

in Africa," *African Affairs* 104, no. 416 (2005): 375–98; and Roy Licklider, "The Consequences of Negotiated Settlements in Civil Wars—1945–1993," *American Political Science Review* 89, no.3 (1995): 681–90. Matthew Hoddie and Caroline Hartzell, "Power Sharing in Peace Settlements: Initiating the Transition from Civil War," in *Sustainable Peace: Power and Democracy After Civil Wars*, ed. Philip G. Roeder and Donald Rothchild (Ithaca, NY: Cornell University Press, 2005), find that economic power sharing has a negative (but not statistically significant) effect on post-settlement peace duration, suggesting a wide if generally negative range of outcomes. Philippe Le Billon and Eric Nicholls, "Ending 'Resource Wars': Revenue Sharing, Economic Sanction or Military Intervention?" *International Peacekeeping* 14, no. 5 (2007): 613–32, find sharing agreements to be generally implemented and followed by a rapid secession of hostilities, but not by sustained peace. Preliminary results from Helga Malmin Binningsbø and Siri Aas Rustad, "Resource Conflicts, Resource Management and Post-conflict Peace" (unpublished manuscript, 2007), also find that wealth-sharing agreements appear to increase the risk of peace failure.

103 Mary B. Anderson, *Do No Harm: How Aid Can Support Peace—or War* (Boulder: Lynne Rienner, 1999).

104 The KP system still is not foolproof, and diamonds still find their way into the international market with missing or falsified certificates. See, e.g., Partnership for Africa Canada, "Killing Kimberley? Conflict Diamonds and Paper Tigers," Occasional Paper No. 15, Ottawa, 2006, www.pacweb.org/e/images/stories/documents/15_killingkimberley_eng. pdf.

105 See Karen Ballentine and Heiko Nitzschke, eds., *Profiting from Peace: Managing the Resource Dimensions of Civil War* (Boulder: Lynne Rienner, 2005); Ian Bannon and Paul Collier, eds., *Natural Resources and Armed Conflicts: Actions and Options* (Washington, DC: World Bank, 2005); and Philippe Le Billon, *Resources for Peace? Managing Revenues from Extractive Industries in Post-Conflict Environments* (New York: Center for International Cooperation, 2008).

106 For discussion, see Macartan Humphreys, Jeffrey D. Sachs, and Joseph E. Stiglitz, eds., *Escaping the Resource Curse* (New York: Columbia University Press, 2007).

107 An amalgam of columbite and tantalite ore, used in manufacturing electronics.

108 Central Bank of Liberia and IMF reports, cited in Report of UN Panel of Experts to Liberia, para. 25.

109 Despite widespread anecdotal evidence, including in Liberia, there is little systematic empirical evidence linking forests and increased risk and duration of conflict; see Siri Camilla Aas Rustad, Jan Ketil Rød, Wenche Larsen, and Nils Petter Gleditsch, "Foliage and Fighting: Forest Resources and the Onset, Duration, and Location of Civil War" (unpublished manuscript, International Peace Research Institute, Oslo, 2008).

110 A business license, articles of incorporation, a valid contract, and a performance bond.

111 Liberia Extractive Industries Transparency Initiative, www.eitiliberia.org/.

112   The findings were controversial, as the loggers denied the claims, but there were other substantiated findings, such as the exhumations of the bodies from the Youghbor massacre in the MWPI concession, that supported the decision to establish a vetting policy for those winning concessions.

113   Forest Development Authority Regulation No. 103-07: Regulation on Bidder Qualifications, sect. 23.b. This regulation allows individuals to present a defense (sect. 24) and the standard for proof is "clear and convincing evidence" (sect. 23.c).

114   Regulation 103-07, sect. 23.a. For companies, the debarment applies if "significant individuals" in ownership or management meet the criteria. The regulation details precisely who these individuals are (sect. 1.j). This is not a permanent debarment. Individuals may be reinstated after three or more years have passed since listing or a court of competent jurisdiction orders the removal of said person (sect. 25).

115   Individuals must be Liberian, have no conviction for violent offense, and be free of credible allegations of human rights violations, crimes against humanity, or war crimes. National Forestry Reform Law of 2006, sect. 18.16.

CHAPTER 9

Linking Broad Constellations of Ideas: Transitional Justice, Land Tenure Reform, and Development

Chris Huggins

This chapter explores the relationship between transitional justice, land issues, and development. In particular, it looks at ways in which transitional justice initiatives relate to land tenure reform in countries where land tenure remains insecure for the majority of people, and where there have been historical injustices related to land rights.[1] Land tenure reform refers to a process in which the legal, institutional, and regulatory framework for land ownership is altered. It is often used as the main instrument of achieving both more efficient and equitable distribution of land and landed resources. The chapter is intended to introduce the key issues, rather than attempt to raise, let alone answer, all the questions involved in this complex relationship.

Relatively little has been written on the relationship between land issues, broadly defined, and transitional justice.[2] Processes that are conceptualized as transitional justice activities have historically tended to look at only one element of land rights—namely, restitution of property to those deprived of it during a preceding period of conflict or authoritarianism. This preceding period has tended to be defined in fairly limited terms, for a variety of practical and political reasons; historical injustices, such as those stemming from colonialism, have rarely been addressed. At the same time, land tenure reform does not generally involve restitution of specific rights to victims of dispossession, and hence has rarely been linked to the literature on transitional justice and restitution.

In the next section, I use the concept of the rule of law to sketch out how transitional justice, land, and development relate to each other at a very broad, but useful, level of generality. In the two following sections, I examine in more detail how land relates to both development and conflict, particularly in times of transition and with regard to massive human rights abuses. I then look directly at how transitional justice measures, such as truth commissions, restitution, and local informal justice efforts, can address and affect land issues, drawing on the experiences of Timor-Leste, South Africa, and Rwanda. The concluding section makes a number of suggestions concerning how transitional justice measures can be incorporated into a broader and more effective program of land tenure reform in transitional societies.

TRANSITIONAL JUSTICE AND LAND AS ISSUES OF THE RULE OF LAW AND DEVELOPMENT

At a broad level of generality, transitional justice and land relate to each other through the concept of the rule of law—a concept often articulated in terms of its positive impact on development and therefore an explicit goal of development work. According to one UN report, the rule of law "refers to a principle of governance in which all persons, institutions and entities, public and private, including the state itself, are accountable to laws that are publicly promulgated, equally enforced and independently adjudicated, and which are consistent with international human rights norms and standards."[3] For many countries, poor governance has resulted in conflict or authoritarian rule, and the recovery from these states of crisis depends on a radical shift in governance norms. Rule of law programs are justified according to a variety of objectives relating to economic growth, poverty reduction, democratization, and peace.[4]

That there is a relationship between the rule of law and development is generally accepted. Some thinkers contend that legal and judicial reform is, inherently, a form of "development," and also that the interdependent nature of capacities, or development "sectors," means that success in any particular sphere depends on instruments from other instrumental spheres.[5] However, others warn that, while "enhancing the quality of institutions that enact, administer and enforce laws can have positive and significant effects," the weaknesses of the "law and development" movement of the 1960s, which is widely seen to have failed, may be repeated unless legal reforms are situated within a broader agenda of public sector reform.[6] This resonates with warnings that too much attention has historically been paid to the elaboration of laws, and too little to the ways in which those laws are interpreted and implemented.[7]

Within the rule of law field, and particularly in the context of the UN system, progress has recently been made in ensuring that rule of law programs address issues relating to land rights (often conceptualized as part of a larger range of "housing, land and property rights").[8] The increasing awareness of the importance of land issues in the rule of law field is to be welcomed, to the extent that rule of law programming goes beyond law reform and seeks to develop and operationalize an innovative approach to protecting land rights. Land experts have argued that "land reform involves much more than land law reform…it goes to the heart of governance and a failure to focus on that will undermine any good intentions to promote land reform."[9] Land reform is only possible if the "rule of law" can be achieved; however, in countries where statutory laws regulating property rights are outdated, unjust, or contradictory, enforcing those laws will be counterproductive. Typically, legal systems are not easily accessible to the majority of the population and do not adequately protect property rights, particularly customary claims to land and the inheritance rights of women and female children. In many countries, efforts to enhance the rule of law that ignore the need to reexamine and reform land laws will be hollow, as the source of livelihood for the bulk of the population will remain unprotected.

The same UN report cited above defines transitional justice as "the full range of processes and mechanisms associated with a society's attempts to come to terms with a legacy of large-scale human rights abuses, in order to ensure accountability, serve justice and achieve reconciliation."[10] Transitional justice activities typically involve a wide range of international, national, and local-level actors, including state institutions, multilateral initiatives, and civil society. Because of the complexities involved in negotiating outcomes that respect numerous needs (responsibilities under international human rights provisions, national laws, local sociocultural perspectives, and the political equilibrium necessary for the maintenance of peace, to name but a few), transitional justice processes usually involve several discrete elements (with some measure of coordination between them) and a mixture of national and international expertise and support.[11]

There are two defining characteristics of transitional justice. The first is the application of international and domestic laws in order to administer justice for human rights abuses and other crimes. Transitional justice activities have tended to focus on gross human rights abuses, particularly on murder, arbitrary detention, and episodes of torture, including sexual abuse.[12] Even with this limited mandate, it has often proven difficult to satisfactorily address these kinds of abuses, for a variety of political and practical reasons. In recent years, it has been argued that transitional justice processes should seek to address gross violations of social, economic, and cultural rights, in addition to those affecting civil and political rights.[13] Proponents of this view argue that these types of crimes "can be more widespread than civil and political rights violations, involving more perpetrators and affecting more victims. The harms caused by such crimes to individuals and society can be just as serious as those caused by any other crimes."[14]

The second defining characteristic of transitional justice processes is an overt engagement with the processes of transition, in the sense of "a major political transformation, such as regime change from authoritarian or repressive rule to democratic or electoral rule or a transition from conflict to peace or stability."[15] Because of its emphasis on successful transition, other values are also important, including democracy, stability, equity, and fairness to victims and their families.[16] A comprehensive definition of democracy goes beyond the simple process of party-political activity and national and local elections. Particularly when the social fabric of a society has been weakened by war, authoritarian rule, and violence, development and democratization must be essentially restorative, as well as an imaginative practice that also needs to be concerned with the gradual processes of "unmaking" violence and of enabling new nonviolent decision-making practices.[17] Therefore, many development practitioners argue that the task is not simply to seek redress for abuses, but to democratize the decision-making processes at all levels and in all sectors of society.

There are significant overlaps between actors, activities, and concepts within the rule of law sphere and those within the transitional justice realm, with many activities being potentially mutually reinforcing. Indeed, transitional justice is sometimes presented as a subset of rule of law programs.[18] However, for a variety of reasons, specialists operating within rule of law and transitional justice contexts, particularly in relation to land issues, have rarely managed to make manifest the developmental potential of their work, and therefore the advantages of cooperation with development actors.

Rule of law interventions have had some positive effect, but their long-term impacts in transitional contexts, and particularly in postconflict situations, have been disappointing. Insufficient theorization, strategic planning, coordination, and monitoring and evaluation of impacts have typically meant that the instruments of the state undergo some improvements—but the structures and dynamics of decision-making remain the same. A failure to address the political economy of decision-making in the country often means that power structures remain largely intact and changes are only superficial.[19] The approach has often been state-centric, with community institutions and other "informal" institutions often neglected, even though they may be of greater relevance to the lives of the majority than the "formal" sector. Furthermore, there is a constant risk that the gains made in protecting human rights and combating impunity may be undone through an increasing emphasis on "reconciliation" without accountability. Indeed, rule of law activities can potentially be counterproductive, if, for example, they give the impression that "access to justice" prevails in what remains a structurally unjust situation. Some advocates of land reform, therefore, "question the transforming ability of the rule of law, and perceive it as a conservative tool to repress and consolidate."[20]

It is argued here that greater coordination between transitional justice efforts and land tenure reform under the rubric of the rule of law in transitional societies would make for a more effective process of political and economic transition, one that better serves the interests of both justice and development. A first step toward that coordination is to understand the links between land, development, and human rights abuses in times of conflict and transition. I turn to these links in the following two sections.

LAND AND DEVELOPMENT IN TRANSITIONAL CONTEXTS

There is a vast literature on the relationship between secure rights to land and development, which goes well beyond the disciplines of economics or law. It is clear that "land tenure security" is important for development, but in most parts of the world there are bitter ideological and political struggles over what constitutes land tenure security, who should be provided such security, and what constitutes the key threats to such security. The concept of "land rights" is itself highly complex. A multitude of kinds of rights over land can be identified, giving rise to the image of "a bundle of rights" or entitlements, including the rights to possess; to use; to exclude others from using or to allow others to use; to sell; to give away; to dispose of by will; to recover from theft; and to receive compensation for damage.[21] Different kinds of users may be able to claim some, or all, of these rights over particular areas of land. Certain rights may be held in common by members of a group, while others might be exclusive to an individual. Property rights tend to be particularly complex in communities that rely on the utilization of natural resources for a wide variety of subsistence purposes.[22]

Ideally, the state acts as the ultimate guarantor of land tenure security and regulates activities affecting land use in order to ensure that one rights holder does not infringe on the rights of another to an unfair degree. However, the extent to which the state enjoys local legitimacy or has the capacity to effectively ensure that statutory laws are implemented varies widely. In many cases, customary law prevails. The nature and interpretation of customary law tends to vary widely within single nations, and customary law interacts in complex ways with statutory land tenure systems. While this chapter cannot hope to adequately address the issue of the interaction of statutory and customary laws, our definition of "land rights" must remain broad enough to include the use or ownership of land under either, or both, systems.[23] Other kinds of rights pertaining to land and property in postconflict situations, including the right to return, are specifically addressed in the third section of this chapter.[24]

The definition of "development" remains open to debate. The emphasis traditionally placed (especially by international financial institutions) on macro-level economic growth has, to some extent, been tempered by concerns around equity issues, environmental sustainability, and the need for a more "human-centered" paradigm. The use of livelihood frameworks to analyze individual or household-level assets, capacities, and vulnerabilities has placed emphasis on the ways in which household-level survival depends on access to assets, particularly land. To be landless, especially in countries that have undergone political and economic crisis, is often to be among the most vulnerable ranks of the population. People's abilities to use access to land and other assets to generate income and to enhance resiliency against shocks depend on an enabling political and economic environment.[25] The focus on micro-level analysis has arguably helped to draw more attention to the question of how laws are enforced and policies implemented at the local level. The answer to insecure tenure may not necessarily be only "more law" or "better law," but rather improved enforcement and the empowerment of rights holders. This conception generally fits well with a rigorous application of the rule of law model, if power relations and other structural factors can be influenced.

In the development literature, the question of property rights has often been treated with some caution because of its complexity, as well as the political and ideological nature of much discussion around property, particularly in the context of the Cold War and the era of decolonization. While issues relating to property rights are more openly discussed within the mainstream development literature today, there remain wide differences of opinion, even within similar schools of thought. There are major tensions inherent within the development literature as relates to property rights, equity, and development.

In this chapter, I will not attempt to definitively describe what we mean by "development," but will note that development cannot be purely "economic"—it must incorporate improvements in civil, political, cultural, and social freedoms and capacities. Strategies based on the empowerment of local communities are to be preferred to those that rely primarily on "top-down" approaches. From a land tenure perspective, activities that empower local people, especially the poorest, to play a greater role in the local governance of land and natural resources will have ripple effects and hence result in a greater "development" impact than those activities that attempt to secure rights to land, narrowly defined, without increasing local engagement in decision-making processes.

A brief review of some of the key debates and trends related to land and development will be provided next in order to draw attention to the most important concepts and questions.

LAND RIGHTS AND DEVELOPMENT:
CUSTOMARY AND STATUTORY LAND TENURE SYSTEMS

A recent study points out that some three-quarters of conflicts across the globe over the past twenty-five years took place in agrarian states.[26] The author argues that this is not coincidental, drawing attention to the inordinate power of the state over land and natural resources in agrarian contexts, particularly over holders of customary tenure rights. In most developing agrarian states, less than 10 percent of landholdings are registered under a formal system of documentation—the vast majority are held under customary tenure. There are myriad forms of customary tenure, which tend to have elements of flexibility built into them, and the interpretation of custom evolves over time. Most such systems rely on oral tradition, though some form of "informal" documentation is increasingly used, particularly in areas where competition for land is high. Systematic codification of customary forms often results in distortions and misunderstandings.[27] Some specialists prefer to reject the term altogether, preferring "local tenure systems" as a more accurate description.

For decades, the hegemonic discourse or "received wisdom" has been that the customary should and must give way to the modern, usually in the form of an individual title deed.[28] However, customary tenure systems have proven remarkably resilient, even in the face of government hostility and the forces of globalization. This may be because they enjoy more local legitimacy than systems imposed by the government.[29]

Across the developing world, laws based on Western models function in urban areas but have proved to be extremely problematic in rural contexts. In many countries, land laws have been inherited from colonial regimes and remain fundamentally similar to those used by such regimes to ensure the economic dominance of a small colonial elite. Many postcolonial regimes have inherited extremely skewed patterns of land distribution.[30] Independence, in many countries, did not affect colonial property structures, with a new domestic elite sometimes taking the place of the former colonial ruling class.[31]

The tension created by the existence of a tiny title-owning sociopolitical "center" and a vast sociopolitical "periphery" under customary tenure represents a situation of de facto (if not de jure) legal pluralism, where religious, customary, and informal systems compete, interact, and overlap with national laws. Many governments are unable to enforce statutory property rights in rural areas. Because formal land registries often prove difficult to maintain, transfers of registered land may not be recorded, and the registry becomes unreliable and corruption becomes endemic. Eventually, there may be a risk that the "sanctity of title" upon which much of the national economy rests may be completely undermined, leading to economic instability. Legal pluralism is a particularly difficult concept to grapple with after conflict, when the legitimacy of many of the actors involved in lawmaking and norm setting (from local chiefs to heads of state) may be affected by their involvement in fighting or atrocities.[32]

In the aftermath of World War II, and again in the 1960s and 1970s, countries in different parts of the world implemented major state-led land reforms.[33] These have been justified on the grounds of stimulating economic development, as was the case in Taiwan and South Korea; increased agricultural production and economic efficiency, as is the case in the Philippines; or as an attempt to overturn skewed land-ownership patterns inherited from the colonial period, as in Namibia or Zimbabwe.[34] In some countries, notably Japan, Korea, and Taiwan, land reform resulted in greater equity in landholding patterns and sustained production.[35] In others, bureaucratic state structures were insufficiently responsive to local demands, and local-level entities responsible for land administration were unsupported and overwhelmed.[36] Following the mixed results of these large-scale state-led reforms, land reform moved far down the agenda of most governments and international institutions from the 1970s to the early 1990s. But demand from rural people for land reform never stopped.[37]

In the mid-1990s, a market-led model of land tenure reform became the dominant paradigm among land policy experts and the development community, despite significant criticism. Land registration, in order to bring "customary" property into the statutory system, is generally at the heart of this model. Key issues relate to how the market is regulated—for example, through taxes and subsidies on land holdings and land transfers. However, resistance to this model has been fierce, and in recent years even the World Bank has altered its thinking on the role of the market and the centrality of titling to the security of tenure.

Hernando de Soto's *The Mystery of Capital* (2000) renewed attention to the question of formalizing customary tenure in the developing world. While de Soto's arguments were by no means new, they have become extremely influential among policy-makers (though much less so among academics), even inspiring the creation of a global initiative, the Commission on Legal Empowerment of the Poor (CLEP), which is hosted by the United Nations Development Programme (UNDP). De Soto essentially argues that when the assets of the poor—their fields and houses—are not formally registered, they remain "dead capital," unable to generate the extra financial benefits available to those who offer registered property as collateral for loans. It is claimed that establishing the legal framework for secure property rights and asset management would provide a springboard for economic growth in developing countries. De Soto bases his theories on the evolution of property rights in Europe and the United States; the developing world, he argues, is still "trapped in the grubby basement of the precapitalist world."[38]

Many feel this comparison to be unhelpful, given the vast cultural and political differences between the West and the developing world, the history of colonization, and the current context of globalization. De Soto tends to focus only on formal land markets, hence underestimating the vibrant informal markets (rental, sales, and so on) that do not appear as official statistics. The concept of "formalization" is also controversial; the CLEP states that documentation of land rights will allow "informal" rights to take on formal status. The assumption is therefore that "formality" is founded simply on recognition under written law, rather than on "a system of governance based on norms and values accepted as authoritative and binding in society."[39] This ignores the importance of legitimacy, as mentioned above. Customary systems can be "formal" in the sense that they are relatively systematic, have sophisticated regulations, and enjoy the support of the local community. Possession of a formal title may be a *necessary* condition of recognition of binding property rights in "modern" statutory systems, but may not be a *sufficient* condition where the titling system is vulnerable to corruption or otherwise lacks legitimacy.

In particular, de Soto and his adherents have been accused of ignoring the lessons of the many titling programs implemented during the last few decades. Evidence has shown that titling programs result in a loss in tenure security for many who enjoyed user rights under customary systems, even as they may result in increased security for others.[40] The economic benefits of titling are far from clear. Research from South and Central America suggests that land titling disproportionately benefits large-scale farmers and can reinforce existing inequalities.[41] Experts have argued that providing the majority of the population with land tenure security is a matter of long-term political determination and a pluriform set of measures, rather than of a single "silver-bullet" fix, such as systematic registration.[42]

Land experts increasingly acknowledge that customary tenure systems are not necessarily inherently "insecure"; instead, the "so-called insecurity of indigenous property systems is more a function of neglect and sub-ordination in public policy and law than of their essential characteristics."[43] Indeed, in many places the state itself is the primary source of tenure insecurity, through the illegal or legally dubious conversion of customary lands to private or governmental uses.

LAND TENURE REFORM

Land policy experts, and to a lesser extent international development policy-makers, increasingly seek ways to avoid a perpetuation of a harmful dualism — a legally sanctioned minority at the "center" with secure property rights, and a massive majority whose customary rights have been undermined by legislation — through the development of hybrid models. In a number of countries, certain kinds of customary land rights have been given legal validity.[44] New community-based and collective tenure registration practices are being tested, though much remains at the experimental stage. Local dispute resolution mechanisms receive much attention.[45] Many such mechanisms combine elements of statutory law and custom, sometimes embodying a trade-off between justice and local legitimacy. Some of the most challenging issues relate to the property rights of women and the roles of "traditional" leaders in regulating land rights.[46]

Generally speaking, a land policy is formulated or an existing policy is reassessed prior to the elaboration of a land law. In cases where a new land law and land policy must be developed, the process should be based on wide consultation within the government and with other stakeholders, such as community groups, farmers' and pastoralists' associations, and women's rights organizations. Such a process is likely to take many years. In post-genocide Rwanda, for example, it took almost a decade to develop a land policy. The implementation of a land law is often another project altogether, requiring massive funding, government will, donor coordination, and many years of focused attention. Land tenure systems are highly complex and comprise numerous elements. Dozens of regulations determine how land can be allocated, transferred, or used.[47]

Land tenure reform, as a result of all this, is a notoriously slow and difficult process. In most countries, "land reform has not taken place in a uniformly linear fashion. Instead, the pace of change has been uneven, the process often fractured and incoherent."[48] The ways in which land tenure reform interacts with related but separate initiatives, such as judicial or administrative reform, may therefore be difficult to predict or to plan for.

LAND, CONFLICT, AND TRANSITION

This section explains why land issues are particularly important in transitional contexts, with a focus on the transition from violent conflict. It should be noted, however, that while some differentiation may be observed between countries emerging from conflict and those transitioning relatively peacefully from authoritarian rule, there may be many similarities—authoritarianism and civil conflict alike, for example, tend to facilitate the concentration of land in the hands of the powerful, at the expense of the weak.[49]

LAND AS A ROOT CAUSE OF CONFLICT

Land access is often a key cause of conflict. As explained above, land tenure systems in agrarian states across the world represent a continuation of norms and laws established by oppressive colonial regimes, which tended to ignore indigenous land claims as it suited them. This has left many communities, particularly pastoral groups, feeling that land customarily held "in common" by members of their ethnic group was vulnerable to alienation, which they felt was illegitimate. According to Liz Alden Wily, the status of land held under customary land tenure was a key issue in twenty-nine of thirty-two African conflicts since 1990.[50] In these kinds of situations, democratization of the political space has not been accompanied by reforms in the sphere of property rights and what may be termed "environmental governance."

In some cases, inequality in landholdings, illegal or unjust dispossession, and other land-related abuses are overtly articulated as a cause of the conflict by one or more of the warring parties. Land inequality was clearly a conscious cause of grievances in Guatemala, where wealth and political power have been concentrated in the hands of a small privileged minority since the formation of the independent Guatemalan state in 1821. The government there has often refused to recognize the land rights of the indigenous Maya peoples. Some 4 percent of the population controlled 80 percent of the arable land before the war,[51] and land rights were a focal point for unrest. In 1952, President Jacobo Arbenz attempted a land redistribution program in order to alter the semifeudal structure of the rural economy, only to be ousted in a U.S. Central Intelligence Agency (CIA)–backed coup d'état in 1954.[52] An insurgency movement with a strong Mayan component began waging a guerrilla war in 1960, which continued until a cease-fire was declared in 1996. Land rights have been a key issue in peace negotiations and reparations programs.

More often, injustices related to land are a "background" or structural cause of conflict, which may not be cited as a cause by the protagonists. Injustices around land can represent structural causes of conflict in a number of ways. Land scarcity, for example, is closely related to poverty, which forces some to join armed groups as a means of survival. Issues of land access also interact with numerous other economic, political, sociocultural, and environmental problems.[53] The World Bank's 2003 land policy document acknowledges that "deprivation of land rights as a feature of more generalized inequality in access to economic opportunities and low economic growth have caused seemingly minor social or political conflicts to escalate into large-scale conflicts."[54] The expropriation of land rights and population displacement resulting from large-scale infrastructure and energy projects, the establishment of conservation areas, and the razing of informal settlements can create pockets of disenfranchised, impoverished youth who are vulnerable to recruitment by armed groups.[55]

Access to land must be contextualized within the national and the global macroeconomic environment. Tensions induced by a lack of investment by the state in public services, and the streamlining of regulations over natural resources and land in order to facilitate foreign or domestic investment, cause "vertical conflicts," or class conflicts.[56] Typically, the poor benefit little from such policies while bearing the brunt of the negative externalities involved, such as environmental degradation. Awareness of questions of social justice among the general population can increase during times of conflict, making violent resistance likely to spread.

CHANGES TO ACCESS AND CLAIMS TO LAND DURING CONFLICT

Land tenure systems are, in essence, systems of social relations, which "only make sense if the people with whom the property rights holder lives recognise that ownership and vest on that person the rights to impose sanctions against the violation of those rights by anyone else."[57] Social relations can undergo radical changes during conflict and land tenure systems can be profoundly affected. In many parts of the world, customary land tenure is founded upon essentially ethnic or clan-based membership. These systems often accommodate different kinds of access based on different kinds of identities.[58] As communities are affected by the influence of nonstate armed groups demanding support, on the one hand, and government counterinsurgency strategies, on the other, political, family, and ethnic loyalties are tested in new and unexpected ways, putting massive strain on the social fabric. The classification of insiders and outsiders, powerful and weak, friends and enemies can fluctuate rapidly. The effects on land tenure systems are therefore profound and complex. While some of these changes may be classified as "forced eviction," a clear violation of rights, others may be more difficult to classify, particularly those related to customary tenure systems, where decisions over access to land are often undocumented. In general, women and children who lack a "patron" or link to protective institutions during conflict can often suffer reduced access to land in addition to curtailed livelihood options.

In some cases, insurgents or leaders of local communities consciously change local land tenure systems, taking advantage of the inability of state actors to enforce national laws. This was the case in Eritrea (then part of Ethiopia) during the war against the Marxist Derg regime. The Eritrean People's Liberation Front (EPLF) established village assemblies, whose responsibilities included land administration, in areas under its control.[59] In such cases, the avowed aim is a more equitable system of land access. In other conflicts, highly discriminatory land tenure systems may be put in place, in clear violation of fundamental international human rights laws.

Local dispute-management systems, which function in the absence of state systems during conflict, will have an influence on land access, though this may not be a primary objective.[60] The effects of such institutions on land rights, and the local legitimacy of such decisions, should be evaluated early in the transitional phase, as authorities will have to rule on the legality of changes.

In addition to these institutional changes, population displacement is a common result (and indeed also a cause) of conflict. In many cases, land temporarily abandoned by internally displaced persons (IDPs) is opportunistically taken over by others. Fleeing IDPs often congregate in urban or peri-urban areas, for security reasons as well as to benefit from casual labor opportunities. The IDP camps that form can, over time, become well established. At the end of conflict, then, such IDP camps may represent informal but permanent settlements located on prized urban land, which often belongs to an individual or to the state. Forced evictions or inequitable expropriation of informal and spontaneous settlements, which are labeled as "slums" by governments, is a feature of postconflict "development" in such countries as Rwanda and Angola.

Many conflicts have been characterized by the systematic forced displacement of particular communities, including ethnic cleansing. The aim of such displacement may be to allow the takeover of land and property by others. Alternatively, counterinsurgency strategies may involve the forced displacement of communities in order to "drain the sea" of civilian support in which insurgent forces are perceived to be "swimming." Such counterinsurgency operations may have long-term implications:[61] in addition to violations against those actually displaced, they may also violate the rights of other local inhabitants whose land is appropriated for the construction of the new IDP settlements. Protracted IDP crises are found around the world, and raise important questions about the nature of "integration," vulnerability, and return.[62]

In addition, the illegal acquisition of land and other property may be systematically linked to other gross human rights abuses. Perpetrators of human rights abuses can amass huge fortunes from the sale or mortgaging of "grabbed" land; they may use this fortune to finance the structures (such as militia groups) that enable them to commit serious human rights violations. Furthermore, the gains from illegal land acquisition may be utilized to avoid extradition, evade arrest, and defeat prosecution.[63] In some cases, the desire to escape prosecution for the illegal acquisition of land and other land-related crimes may represent a motive for involvement in human rights abuses, where, for example, these have the objective of preventing peaceful regime change.

SECONDARY CONFLICTS OVER LAND AND PROPERTY IN THE EARLY TRANSITIONAL PHASE

The immediate postconflict period is often characterized by rapid change in the political, social, and economic spheres, with major implications for claims to land and property. Action on the part of the government and international actors during this phase is crucial, as problems become more difficult to overcome at a later stage. There are numerous aspects to this, and only the most common and significant are outlined here.[64]

It is during this period that land access changes that occurred during the conflict can become consolidated and compounded by rapid population movements. There may be a postconflict property boom, exacerbated by demands for offices and housing for international agencies engaged in the reconstruction effort. Demobilized combatants and returnees, some born in exile, require access to housing and land but find that the houses and fields that they left behind are occupied by others. Often, their lands may have been sold to a third party. Criminal gangs may occupy property and peasant movements or other groups may organize land invasions. Houses may have been destroyed, leading to a shelter crisis. Women's claims to land have been undermined by changes to sociopolitical institutions and a breakdown of customs, and the large numbers of female- and child-headed households are particularly vulnerable. Documents proving ownership of fields or houses may have been destroyed or lost during the conflict.

In addition, the institutional framework, damaged by violence, population movements, and/or repressive rule, generally finds itself overwhelmed. Particular problems include: weak or divided security agencies that have difficulty in enforcing laws; a political focus on emergency actions (for example, shelter for IDPs) rather than on reestablishing systems; vested interests in maintaining a certain degree of chaos among some key stakeholders engaged in illegal or unethical activities; lack of a relevant land policy; a dysfunctional land administration system; and ambiguous, controversial, or unenforceable laws.

POSTCONFLICT INTERVENTIONS IN THE LAND SECTOR

In order to address the challenges related to land in a postconflict context, a great number of interventions can potentially be designed and implemented by a combination of stakeholders, including the government, peacekeeping forces, international donors, international NGOs, and local civil society organizations, many of whom may also be involved in some aspect of transitional justice. These interventions can be categorized as largely related to the protection of land and property rights, land administration, or dispute resolution.

Key activities related to the *protection of land and property rights* include the physical protection of access to land by peacekeeping forces and the systematic documentation of changes in land access during the final phase of conflict. With a few exceptions, these proactive interventions have been discussed but rarely implemented. Interventions more commonly made manifest include:

- inclusion of land and property rights issues in peace agreements;
- "promotion" of land and property rights (for example, through training and awareness-raising campaigns), especially those of women and other vulnerable groups;
- trial monitoring and assessments of judicial capacity and fairness;
- developing equitable and transparent procedures for evictions;
- assistance from security personnel in the enforcement of eviction orders; and
- assistance to poor and vulnerable groups in obtaining identification documents.

Efforts to *support land administration systems* in transitional societies include:

- capacity building;

- training and development of a national cadre of land rights professionals;
- decentralization and "democratization" of land administration institutions; and
- development or strengthening of land registration systems.

Interventions related to *dispute resolution* (which are becoming more common) include:

- development of formal adjudication systems for land disputes (generally sporadic adjudication systems);
- support to customary and/or local dispute resolution mechanisms;
- training for legal aid organizations; and
- assistance to state-run restitution and compensation programs.

The need for these kinds of postconflict land interventions (along with related interventions dealing with housing and other property rights) gained recognition during the 1990s. The significance of access to and control over land in postconflict states has been acknowledged in numerous UN documents and decisions in recent years.

There have also been suggestions that the enforcement of decisions on land and property rights and the protection of these rights be included in the mandate of peacekeeping forces.[65] Attempts to anchor land-related interventions within rule of law departments in peace operations are slowly gaining ground.[66] While normative frameworks are increasingly well developed, these have yet to be uniformly implemented: "Of the 17 UN peace operations currently in place, few if any have the human and financial resources in place to effectively address land administration concerns in a comprehensive manner."[67] Fewer still have looked into issues of land tenure reform or land restitution. What occurs, therefore, is a process of "cherry-picking," where UN agencies, humanitarian organizations, and bilateral aid agencies engage in land issues on a selective basis. Coordination and sequencing of interventions are frequently problematic.

Because the return of refugees and IDPs is almost always associated with disputes over land, much activity is devoted to addressing the immediate challenges of return. The return of IDPs and refugees often occurs through a combination of assisted return (involving the Office of the UN High Commissioner for Refugees [UNHCR], governments, and other actors) and spontaneous return. Despite the increasing awareness of the legal responsibilities of governments to address return fairly, land and property claims, in particular the thorny issue of secondary occupation of property, are often dealt with through ad hoc measures, which may not be acceptable to all those affected, environmentally sustainable, or compatible with national or international legal standards and norms. Where some citizens are expropriated without compensation or due process in order to accommodate returnees, the result is that land tenure security is undermined and relations between the returnees and their neighbors are endangered.[68] In Burundi, for example, large swathes of valuable land, especially in Burundi Province, were abandoned by Hutu landowners who fled the country following mass state-organized violence in 1972. Upon the return of the refugees and their descendants, the Burundian government has emphasized the importance of "reconciliation" during property disputes, including amicable settlement between two or more parties with claims over the same land parcel (a voluntary so-called land-sharing agreement). Observers in Burundi have already noted that weaker parties in disputes — particularly widows — are liable to lose access to land when disputes arise.[69] The portrayal by authorities of so-called land-sharing as a "local," "voluntary," or "participatory" phenomenon may have blinded some to the inequalities it can involve.

While the right to restitution is firmly supported in normative frameworks and, arguably, in international human rights law, there are debates over the ways in which it can be achieved in practice.[70] Much of the "textbook" restitution work has been achieved in societies where legal and administrative measures can be relatively rapidly implemented at the local level, and where financial and market-based solutions are generally appropriate. In addition, the UN missions to these countries were relatively well funded and received substantial political support from key members of the UN Security Council, in comparison to missions in less strategic parts of the globe. Of course, there are major practical differences between the restitution of the rights of those who have been displaced for a relatively short period and those who have been displaced for decades or generations.

It is also important to note that most discussions of housing, land, and property rights have been characterized by case studies of countries where urban or agricultural livelihoods predominate. More analysis is needed of experiences from those parts of the world where grazing, fishing, hunting, gathering, or a combination of these and other kinds of rights form a vital part of rural livelihoods, and where property rights are highly complex. Occasionally, it seems that land and property experts attempt to apply a "one size fits all" approach, inevitably influenced by Western experiences and models, which tends to be inappropriate to local contexts.

REFORMING THE SYSTEM — BUT TO WHAT EXTENT?

Given the effects of conflict and authoritarian rule on land rights, it is always necessary to restore those property rights that have been lost through abuses. However, in many countries the history of dispossession is long and complex. Two related questions arise: How far should the government "turn back the clock"? and, How fundamental should reform be? These questions have numerous and far-reaching political, human rights, and economic implications.

Timor-Leste is a case in point. The country suffered successive waves of invasion and dispossession, from Portuguese colonization through Japanese occupation to Indonesian invasion. Timorese can claim land on the basis of underlying traditional interests, titles issued during both the Portuguese and Indonesian eras, or through long-term occupation. In the transitional period, the two major political parties, *Uniao Democratica Timorense* (UDT) and *Frente Revolucionara de Timor Leste* (Fretilin), have had different interests. UDT supports restoration of pre-1975 Portuguese titles, as many of its supporters reputedly held property under the Portuguese administration, while Fretilin emphasizes land justice for customary owners and dispossessed groups, with one of its leaders reportedly indicating that bona fide Indonesian titles should be recognized.[71] Customary rights have not been respected by colonial occupiers or adequately protected by law, and alienation of land during the Portuguese and Indonesian periods often represents injustice among customary rights holders.

The question of historical claims to land in Timor-Leste remains largely unresolved.[72] A law on land ownership restitution, with plans for a land claims commission, was expected in 2006 but was delayed, leading to some suspicions that government insiders did not want the issues resolved. In 2006, tensions between Timorese political groups and their supporters resulted in armed violence and widespread acts of arson. There were many aspects to this violence, including differences over the question of property rights.[73]

Clearly, an attempt to turn back the clock by more than a few years can be politically, economically, and technically difficult and risky. In most cases, the strategy advocated is to restore land ownership patterns to those in existence immediately prior to the conflict, through, for example, restoring the condition and integrity of land registers and conducting only as much registration and adjudication is necessary to confirm those titles. Some actors may advocate a systematic land registration exercise, whereby all landholdings in the country will be brought under the statutory system. This is frequently justified on economic grounds, on the basis that it will increase domestic and foreign investment through reducing land tenure insecurity. However, as discussed above, the risks involved are manifold. Injustices and disputes dating from colonial times, as well as more recent abuses related to conflict or authoritarianism, should be evaluated, and if necessary addressed before registration takes place. However, in practice, some actors have been accused of insisting upon registration on ideological grounds, or in order to open rural areas to the forces of globalization, without assessing the risks to community livelihoods.[74]

Critics of the "business as usual" approach point to the fact that in many cases it was precisely these land-ownership patterns that precipitated conflict. Restoring such patterns is therefore likely to lead to an eventual resumption of violence. Instead, it is argued, transitional regimes should "set aside the paradigms of the past and its outputs in the form of nefarious 'legal documents' that hold so little legitimacy and which patently obstruct arrival at compromise and peace."[75] Instead, "fundamental structural change to property norms and political decision-making is required."[76]

For those who favor a radical reevaluation of land tenure patterns, the role of the state as an arbitrator of competing claims becomes a major concern. Can the political system maintain its integrity and overcome the kind of vested interests discussed above in the case of Timor-Leste? Is the role of external actors helpful or divisive? And, how are the interests of different categories of local stakeholders reflected in the positions of civil society organizations or traditional leaders? When questions of property rights are being fundamentally reassessed, the legitimacy of those involved in the eyes of local people is paramount. Social coherence is a vital question, as is the capacity of the government to manage episodes of dissent or unrest. In cases where a negotiated end to authoritarian rule or conflict has resulted in power-sharing agreements, those accused of human rights abuses (including, for example, forced displacement, land-grabbing, and other property crimes) may be powerful members of the government.[77] In short, conflict analysis is critical, and the various centripetal and centrifugal forces acting on society must be assessed.

A second major concern, which is linked to the question of social and political integrity, is the economic situation in the country. A fundamental reevaluation of land rights is bound to affect agricultural and industrial production. In the case of South Africa, leasing arrangements have been utilized to ensure that even after land has been transferred through restitution processes, it remains under large-scale commercial production, at least for the short-to-medium term. The South African government has chosen to limit the extent of expropriation of land during the restitution process in order to avoid undermining perceptions of land tenure security. However, the government's commitment to a business-as-usual agrarian policy has meant that those black farmers who have claimed land and have attempted to start smallholder farm enterprises are struggling to succeed within a wider economic system geared for large-scale production. While the state has provided some support, its "developmental" interventions tend to benefit commercial farmers rather than the smallholder majority. In short, while the multifaceted land reform program was intended to "restore identity and promote reconciliation, whilst redistributing wealth and strengthening the rural economy," some observers have argued that these are competing and possibly irreconcilable objectives.[78]

Every country is unique, and the extent to which macroeconomic struc-tures can be reshaped depends not just on internal and external political rela-tionships but also on the nature of the transition. In many ways, a transition from prolonged conflict during which the infrastructure of the economy has been destroyed offers greater flexibility than a situation in which systems are more functional.

TRANSITIONAL JUSTICE AND LAND TENURE REFORM

Land reform and land tenure reform do not generally involve restitution of specific rights to victims of dispossession, and hence have rarely been linked to the literature on transitional justice and restitution. In a number of countries, there is a strong argument that any attempt to redress injustice over land rights must look not just at individual cases of dispossession but at the entire land tenure system. In many cases, regimes have, through processes of omission or commission, undermined land tenure systems in order to allow key political figures and their supporters to benefit from the resulting land tenure insecu-rity. Maintaining a level of disorder within the system is therefore an instru-mental aspect of the government's strategy to leverage resources to reward cli-ents.[79] This is arguably a form of criminal negligence on the part of the state.

The justifications for land tenure reform are practical as well as legal in nature. If a transitional country has a dysfunctional land tenure system, it is likely that this will have a destabilizing effect on national governance more generally. Even in cases where there is political will within the government to adhere to the rule of law, the temptation represented by an unjust and inse-cure land tenure system will lead to corruption. Over time, those who use this system to enrich themselves will use the proceeds to gain greater influence in government through patronage networks. The result will be increasingly rotten governance at the macro level.

The previous section demonstrated that changes in land access are common during episodes of conflict. Transitional decision-making bodies will, wittingly or unwittingly, support or undermine these changes in land access through a variety of actions and policy decisions. Notwithstanding the legal, conceptual, and practical challenges involved—including difficulties in collecting and analyzing information—it is better that governments in transitional contexts make such decisions on an informed basis. It is argued here that while transitional justice measures are unlikely in themselves to have a significant direct impact on land issues, they can make a useful if modest contribution to achieving the broader aim of reforming land tenure systems in a more just direction.

TRUTH COMMISSIONS

Truth commissions tend to be the centerpiece of transitional justice initiatives and are likely to remain so for some time to come. There are a number of reasons for this.[80] First, truth commissions represent an effective means to "help a society understand and acknowledge a contested or denied history, and in doing so bring the voices and stories of victims, often hidden from public view, to the public at large."[81] Second, truth commissions often enjoy a high degree of credibility (particularly in relation to government-managed entities) because of their mode of operation and their usually broad-based membership. Their recommendations may therefore be seen as independent and legitimate. Third, truth commissions "offer some form of accounting for the past, and have thus been of particular interest in situations where prosecutions for massive crimes are impossible or unlikely—owing to either a lack of capacity of the judicial system or a de facto or de jure amnesty."[82] They have been characterized (and implicitly criticized) by some as "tools of political compromise."[83]

The implications of these features of truth commissions for land issues depend on the particular context. In many countries, the nature of injustices around land has been investigated and is fairly widely known—in Kenya, for example.[84] However, Kenya is a rather extreme case, as it has a very vocal civil society that has pushed for various commissions of enquiry over the years. In such places as Rwanda, commissions on land have been established, but the full details of their findings have not been released. In other countries, assessments of land issues may be framed in technical terms, which means that less attention is paid to identifying those responsible for land-related abuses and that the results may not be very accessible to the average citizen. In general, given the emotive nature of rights to land, and the association with ancestral belonging and sacred areas, the history of control over land may be highly contested in some countries. The role of a truth commission in acknowledging the contested politics of land may often be very valuable, and government endorsement of a truth commission report could represent a legal precedent. An additional dimension to the idea of "contested histories" is very important: whereas the impacts upon victims of abuses related to civil and political rights might be fairly well understood, the repercussions of the loss of land rights tend to be undervalued. Truth commissions therefore represent an opportunity for victims of land-related crimes to describe the full range of these impacts in their own terms, which is likely to increase the level of understanding for the need to redress land-related abuses.

Of course, this depends on the willingness of the commissioners to enquire deeply into these issues. Some observers have argued that "TRCs tend to subordinate truth recovery to reconciliation by seeking non-controversial truth, thereby skirting the root causes of communal tensions."[85] If that is generally the case, there is a real risk that land issues will be only superficially addressed. The history of land use and occupation tends to be highly complex. Truth commissions will therefore have to rely on experts, in addition to the testimony of the local population, in order to enquire deeply into this history. Another relevant question is the historical period that the commission is mandated to investigate. Due to time constraints, financial implications, and political sensitivities, the mandates of truth commissions are sometimes limited to relatively short periods.

The second feature of a truth commission—a perception of independence—may be highly important in any discussion of land issues. By its very nature, customary land tenure is closely associated with community membership, often on an ethnic or clan basis. Some ethnic groups, especially indigenous groups, face systematic discrimination. In addition, the state tends to be involved in disputes as a party as well as an arbitrator. The formation of an independent commission, made up of nationals and nonnationals, is likely to bring a perception of neutrality to discussions of land tenure.

The third feature—some form of accountability for past mass violations—may in some cases be less important for land-related abuses (such as secondary occupation of abandoned land and homes by civilians) than for other issues. However, it is of some relevance, as the aim might be to replace a judicial enquiry (for example, into land-grabbing), by preparing the way for an administrative approach to land issues. An administrative approach, like a judicial process, should lead to those who have grabbed land losing control over that property, but is likely to be less contested by those "land-grabbers" who retain political influence.

In practice, several truth commissions have identified land-related inequality and human rights abuses as a root cause of conflict. Kenya's Truth, Justice and Reconciliation Commission is mandated to look at "the irregular and illegal acquisition of public land and [to] mak[e] recommendations on how the land can be repossessed," though it had not become operational at the time of writing.[86] More commonly, land issues have been left out of the mandates of truth commissions.

RESTITUTION

Transitional justice practitioners often engage with land issues during the design and implementation of restitution programs, which are a form of reparations. Conceptually, reparations are defined as a legal remedy for wrongs perpetrated by a specific wrongdoer to a specific victim. The burden of remedy, however, may not fall on the particular wrongdoer. Under international law, states are legally responsible for remedying the violations perpetrated by past regimes. The right to restitution of property has been included in various international peace agreements, especially since the mid-1990s. Early examples include a 1992 UNHCR-brokered agreement for the repatriation of Guatemalan refugees and the 1995 Dayton Accords for Bosnia and Herzegovina.[87]

Restitution is essentially a legal question. The right to restitution of property that has been illegally seized is established in international law; however, the question of intergenerational restitution—that is, of how a restitution program will treat historical claims, several decades old—is also a political and technical issue. In most cases, the type of dispossession addressed and the historical period involved have tended to be defined in fairly limited terms, usually to minimize the legal problems stemming from overlapping claims from different periods and the financial burden of processing many claims and compensating large numbers of people. In the case of the postcommunist restitution program of the Czech Republic, for example, the "cutoff date" selected for restitution excluded Jewish victims of the Nazis, some three million ethnic Germans expelled from Czech areas shortly before the communist takeover, and thousands of exiles who had defected during the communist period.[88] In other cases, the kinds of properties that may be restituted are narrowly defined.

The case of Kosovo, which is often held up as a restitution success story, is instructive. The Housing and Property Directorate (HPD), established by the United Nations Interim Administration in Kosovo, oversaw the resolution of some 29,000 residential property claims, but was not mandated to address claims over agricultural land or commercial property. These claims were to be addressed by Kosovo's domestic justice system, but the court system has to date lacked the capacity to do so fairly and efficiently. The result has been that many refugees and IDPs have been unwilling to reclaim their homes because their source of income—their fields or businesses—remain out of reach.[89] The implications for economic development, as well as justice, are clear.

In most cases, the political risks involved in addressing "historical" issues are also part of these calculations. The effects of a restitution program on post-conflict stability and "reconciliation" must be considered. Restitution can be a mechanism for addressing tension over land, as "restitution programs channel claims into the legal system that might otherwise destabilize the market by posing a political threat to the security of post-transitional property rights."[90] Restitution programs should be designed in order to complement legal and institutional reforms aimed at reducing conflict, including conflict related to unequal access to land. Most observers agree, however, that restitution programs should not primarily be designed as an instrument for land distribution. Conflation of restitution schemes with land reform undermines their domestic and international legitimacy. Restitution schemes are generally not effective in changing patterns of land access. When property is restituted in situations where the legal architecture is flawed and the overall landholding patterns in the country remain unequal, underlying tensions will continue to be felt. In such cases, restitution could arguably only draw attention to a much more fundamental problem, possibly raising, rather than decreasing, political tensions.

The logical and technical difficulties of providing restitution are especially difficult in countries where land tenure is generally insecure. In many countries, customary rights are not recognized under the law, and land is commonly alienated or "grabbed" by the state or by individuals without the payment of compensation to affected populations. Local people might legitimately ask why restitution programs should address land confiscated during episodes of conflict or authoritarianism, but not land alienated by the state or private individuals at other times. Moreover, in a situation of legal pluralism, the land restituted would be vulnerable to counterclaims pursued through various "informal" arenas. Given the importance of social relationships and principles of reciprocity in most customary land tenure systems, efforts to restitute land under customary tenure will need to emphasize the importance of "reconciliation" as much as legal rights. The UN "Pinheiro Principles" on restitution state that restitution programs should address such land tenure security by taking "measures to ensure registration or demarcation of [restituted] property."[91] But, as discussed above, land registration programs in areas of customary tenure tend to result in both winners and losers, and unintended consequences. It is also doubtful whether a registration program launched on the back of a restitution program would be locally legitimate, sufficiently theorized, or coordinated with land tenure institutions and interventions at the national level. Efforts to improve land tenure security should not depend on land restitution programs for funding or political will.

In conclusion, then, restitution programs are now a necessity under international law in cases where land has been illegally confiscated during periods of conflict or authoritarian rule. In countries where unequal access to land is a root cause of conflict, they can complement but not replace efforts to bring about land tenure reform. I agree with Rhodri Williams that "while restitution should be clearly distinguished from broader reforms, programming in both areas may be necessary to forestall the resumption of conflict over land and property."[92] The capacity and willingness of the international community to implement restitution programs in transitional situations is improving, but experiences of restitution in countries where land tenure is generally insecure or land is primarily held under customary tenure are few, poorly documented, and under-theorized.

LOCAL INFORMAL JUSTICE

In many countries, informal, decentralized, or traditional institutions provide mediation or adjudication services for local people. These institutions are often more legitimate, accessible, and culturally appropriate for many local people than the formal justice system. They are often the most significant form of redress in land disputes for rural populations in developing countries. Following conflict, mass atrocity, or authoritarian rule, the formal justice system may be overwhelmed by the sheer number of cases, and informal systems often represent a vital means to address some accusations, particularly those of a less serious nature. Informal or local justice systems are often incorporated into a transitional justice strategy. In addition, rule of law programs are increasingly engaging with local dispute resolution systems as part of a wider effort to reduce the burden on the formal legal system. However, this is not without its drawbacks. The local cultural norms and customs that govern informal justice systems often diverge from international human rights standards, particularly in terms of due process criteria, and also because of discrimination against some members of the community.[93] In most countries, land disputes represent a significant proportion of all cases heard by local justice systems. The way that transitional justice works with, or "through," local systems, therefore, has great repercussions for land rights.

TRANSITIONAL JUSTICE AND LAND: COUNTRY EXPERIENCES

The examples of Timor-Leste, South Africa, and Rwanda, discussed below, are instructive for thinking about how transitional justice measures relate to land issues.

TIMOR-LESTE

The Commission for Reception, Truth and Reconciliation (known by its Portuguese acronym, CAVR) was established in 2001 and functioned until 2005. The final report of the commission included a chapter on economic and social rights violations, which recognized some of the land-related legacies of occupation and conflict:

> Punishment for those suspected of resisting the [Indonesian] occupation also included burning of their houses, confiscation of land and property for redistribution to political supporters of the occupation.... The arbitrary use of powers to move the population and evict them forcibly has left an unresolved legacy of uncertain tenure and landlessness...the Commission takes the view that all of these social impacts are impediments to reconciliation and need to be addressed within that context.... The Commission finds that repeated displacements, the redrawing of administrative boundaries and *the non-recognition of customary land-ownership* and land-use practices produced a legacy of landlessness and highly complex land disputes.[94] (emphasis added)

The mention of nonrecognition of custom suggests that land tenure reform is necessary, though the commission fell short of recommending such a reform. The commission did, however, recommend that the government institute an inquiry into land disputes that resulted from resettlement programs, with a view to promoting peaceful mediation of these disputes.

The CAVR's report was generally well received, and contributed to the awareness of the importance of land issues in the country, particularly through ongoing dissemination efforts and engagement with government, communities, and schools. However, few of its recommendations regarding land claims have been implemented. One reason for this is that pressure could not be brought to bear because of other problems. The government's decision to provide an amnesty for some crimes and the failure of the Commission of Truth and Friendship (jointly established by Indonesia and Timor-Leste) to address serious crimes against humanity amount to a violation of international human rights law, and the government was criticized by human rights groups and the UN as a result. The efforts of civil society and some UN agencies were therefore focused on advocating for bringing the masterminds of violence to justice. Little attention was paid to the CAVR's calls for reparations for loss of land and property.

Some land claims have been made under a limited claims process established by legislation in 2003. In 2000, a land dispute mediation mechanism was established within the Land and Property Directorate, which has been relatively successful. However, the current system does not deal with cases where one party is the state or a government official, which excludes most claims of dispossession by the Portuguese and Indonesian administrations.[95] Landholdings, particularly in the capital city, have sometimes changed hands multiple times since 1999, without documentation of transfer. Formal legal title therefore cannot be used to accurately establish true "legal" ownership of land.[96] There remains a pressing need for a more comprehensive assessment of land disputes, especially those arising from displacement during the period of Indonesian occupation.

The Community Reconciliation Process (CRP) was an element of the CAVR designed to promote reconciliation in local communities. The objective was to facilitate the social reintegration of perpetrators who had committed "politically-related, 'less serious,' harmful acts during the political conflicts in Timor-Leste."[97] During the CRP, the offender, victims, and other community members were able to make presentations. A panel, formed of local administrative and religious figures (including women) then determined an appropriate "act of reconciliation," which could involve community service, reparation, public apology, and/or other acts of contrition. The offender was then immune from formal prosecution and civil proceedings. There were some concerns that, in an effort to emphasize reconciliation, largely symbolic "acts of reconciliation" had been requested that did not represent the kind of punishment that some victims would demand. Very few compensation payments were made in the CRP.[98] In general, the CRP was conceptualized in terms of reintegration with the local community, and the individual role of the victim was therefore minimized.

The CRP did address some confessions of destruction of houses through arson, which is usually considered a serious crime and which, when committed as part of a widespread, systematic attack, may constitute a crime against humanity.[99] Aside from the question of the legal responsibility of Timor-Leste's government (and the UN) to prosecute arson according to international legal standards, the massive resurgence of arson in the capital, Dili, in 2006 raises questions of a more pragmatic nature. The CRP's treatment of arson cases may in retrospect be viewed as overly lenient. It could be argued that a clearer stigmatization of arson offenses, along with stiffer penalties, may have acted as a deterrent to the use of "house burning" in the 2006 violence.

Despite some CRP rulings on such serious issues as arson, it seems not to have made decisions on related issues of property rights. For example, it has been reported that "some deponents' homes have been taken over as a result of their association with the militias, and little has been done to address this situation, even for those that have submitted themselves to the CRP. Disputes around issues of property and land ownership seem destined to remain a site of contestation for the foreseeable future."[100]

The Timor-Leste case, and the particular forms of violence that occurred in 2006, raises important questions about the relationship between truth commissions, local transitional justice systems, and wider questions of criminal justice. While it would be unrealistic to expect a new land policy or law to be put in place before the CRP started, a process of consultation on land questions would have given a clear signal that the land and property issue was still open to question. It would have avoided an impression of impunity for those who had occupied land or houses.

SOUTH AFRICA

In the case of South Africa, the Truth and Reconciliation Commission (TRC) was intentionally separated from the question of land issues. The Promotion of National Unity and Reconciliation Act limited the activities of the TRC to gross human rights violations,[101] and the only form of suffering that counted as grounds for compensation was that caused by direct physical mistreatment.[102]

Three clauses of the 1993 interim constitution addressed land restitution, which resulted in the promulgation of the Restitution Act. However, land restitution was limited, both in scope—to cases of dispossession of property under racially discriminatory laws—and in time—to cases dating from June 1913 onward.[103] Two official reasons were given for this decision: first, that land transfers predating 1913 were largely undocumented, and hence difficult to address; and second, that looking earlier than 1913 would have far-reaching and potentially explosive implications for ethnic relations.[104] It would be opening a Pandora's box.

A more significant issue, though one that was not publicly announced by the African National Congress (ANC), was that maintaining the broad parameters of the postapartheid property rights regime was deemed to be essential to the stability of the economic order.[105] In other words, the ANC thought that continued economic development depended on essentially maintaining the post-1913 property rights regime. The South African experience is therefore somewhat paradoxical, in that it is in some ways one of the most comprehensive and ambitious land reforms in the sub-Saharan region, but is being implemented within a firmly neoliberal framework by a government that is determined to maintain the existence of a highly commercialized farming sector.[106] In the words of a former "insider" to the transitional process, the result of political negotiations was, therefore, that

> the historically received distribution of property rights should be protected, except where the legitimacy of a particular holding was undermined by its dependence on a prior unjust transfer . . . land restitution was conceived primarily as an exercise aimed at doing particular justice to victims of apartheid forced removals. The contribution of land restitution to reconciliation between black and white South Africans was a desired side-effect, rather than a central policy goal of the process. When coupled with the primacy given to the constitutional protection of property rights, this policy choice produced a scheme that made the achievement of land restitution independent of the need to repair the moral and psychological damage done by apartheid land law.[107]

The TRC was seen by many international observers as an instrumental part of the country's peaceful transition out of apartheid. However, particularly within the country, it has since been reevaluated. Given the failure of successive governments to significantly change the economic superstructures that underpinned the apartheid, "in the absence of this broader agenda to deal with the deprived of apartheid, the catharsis afforded by the SATRC was short-lived for the majority who remain underprivileged. Personal and national reconciliation were unachieved and the re-invention of South Africa postponed."[108]

While we should be wary of pinning unrealistic expectations on any truth commission, we should note that this brief discussion raises two important questions.

First, regarding the relationship between land restitution and "reconciliation," we may ask to what extent reconciliation relies on direct relations, or negotiations, between the dispossessed and those who are expropriated in order for land to be restituted. In the South African case:

> the statutory scheme for land restitution precludes the need for reconciliation between black and white South Africans over the land issue. Rather than facilitating a process of national reconciliation, the state's appointed role in relation to land restitution is to smooth over any possible conflict between the race groups by making payments from general revenue, either to compensate current landowners in the event that their land is successfully claimed, or to fund the costs of equitable redress where the actual land claimed cannot be restored.[109]

Second, at a more general level, it often appears that the issue of "land reform for redress of historical injustices" has been rather too narrowly defined by the government as "restitution for victims of apartheid forced removals." Reform of the system of communal tenure prevailing in the former homelands has been the most neglected area of land reform. Land in the former homelands is under the control of a variety of state institutions, most of which are unable to adequately document and administer land use. Systems for transfer of land are in crisis, leading to widespread land tenure insecurity and lack of investment. However, because most people living in the former homelands cannot trace their presence there to a specific instance of forced eviction by the apartheid regime, "Reform of the system of communal tenure in the former homelands...while also addressing the historical legacy of inferior rights for black people, does not fit neatly into the pattern of historical redress."[110]

RWANDA

In Rwanda, the question of land has been linked to reconciliation, but within very narrow limits, and entirely on the government's own terms. Citizens have been required to "share" land with returning refugees—in the name of reconciliation—in a process often marred by corruption and nepotism. The wider question of the relationship between control over land and social conflict has not been openly addressed. Dissatisfaction with the "land-sharing" policy has been dismissed by government officials as being "engineered" by antigovernment elements.[111] The National Unity and Reconciliation Commission, a government body, was established to find ways of promoting reconciliation. While it has organized debates, it has arguably remained too close to official government rhetoric to present a real neutral space for dialogue. The National Unity and Reconciliation Commission produced a report on reconciliation and land in 2006, but this did not offer many concrete recommendations and did not result in any operational linkages between transitional justice initiatives and ongoing land reform activities.

The modern gacaca system in Rwanda differs greatly from the traditional model, and is an official government institution intimately linked to the state apparatus of prosecutions and incarceration, and applying codified, rather than customary, law. Gacaca judges are not community elders, as in the past, but rather elected and often comparatively young. Crimes committed during the genocide that are related to property—such as looting of clothes and household goods—can by law be resolved privately between the parties, or are dealt with at the most local level of the gacaca system. Issues relating to land generally date from before the genocide—particularly the flight of many Tutsi from the country during the "social revolution" in 1959—or from the return of refugees after the genocide. The majority of land disputes do not fall within the mandate of the gacaca system.[112]

However, some accusations of participation in genocide are linked to land disputes. A recent opinion survey in a Kigali neighborhood found that more than two-thirds of respondents knew of cases of false accusations of criminal behavior, including participation in genocide, due to property disputes in the neighborhood.[113] Independent researchers have also reported many such cases.[114] It is possible that these will multiply if the gacaca process continues and overlaps with the planned national land registration process. It is well documented that land disputes tend to increase in frequency prior to, and during, registration processes.

Another issue is the relationship between damages claimed by victims of genocide crimes and the landholdings of the perpetrators. A definitive reparations policy has yet to be decided upon. At times, official statements have suggested that the possessions of those found guilty of genocide crimes would be seized to pay for reparations. Such a policy, if it included family fields in the goods to be seized, would leave hundreds of thousands of families landless. However, this has yet to be implemented and it is not clear whether such steps will ever be taken. In cases where the landholdings belonging to the families of genocide defendants are being expropriated by the state, such as in Kigali city, expropriation fees have been withheld until compensation payments have been decided upon in gacaca. This policy affects the ability of the expropriated households to purchase alternative land and shelter.[115]

The Rwanda case demonstrates that even when there is no formal link between the treatment of land tenure issues and transitional justice initiatives, there are unexpected (and sometimes underreported) links in practice. Land and property rights are central to the lives of those living in developing countries, and land disputes are part of everyday life. Conflict and transition exacerbate that trend. Making accusations in transitional justice mechanisms, such as gacaca, may represent just another form of "forum shopping." Addressing land issues in more systematic ways, and raising awareness of these risks early on in the transitional justice process, may reduce the impacts of this.

CONCLUSIONS

Transitional justice and land reform are broad "constellations" of ideas, understood differently by different actors. In countries where the land tenure system is dysfunctional, transitional justice mechanisms could play a role in bringing local and international attention to the need for land tenure reform. However, the relationship between transitional justice and land tenure reform has rarely been very direct or well coordinated. The process of negotiating and implementing programs on such crucial issues is usually long, complex, and messy. This does not fit well with the agendas of domestic and international actors, who often want a defined timeline for the key steps in the transition process. For this reason, "land and other economic rights are usually left to the post-transition period of constitutional and legal reform. However, without the presence of an external oversight body and with the problematic historical origins of the land question, politicians rarely have the energy or interest to address them later."[116]

While this chapter has generally argued that transitional justice programs should look at land issues from a broad perspective, which includes a possible need for tenure reform, there are risks involved in looking at land issues. There is a risk, for example, that by bringing questions of systematic tenure security, concrete cases of dispossession will be conflated with more general questions of inequality. Redress for specific violations of land and property rights may become confused with questions of socioeconomic entitlement.[117] Nevertheless, as a former member of the Peruvian truth commission advises, while structural consequences and causes are difficult to address within a reparations program, truth commissions can still address land issues by presenting "agendas of institutional reform, reporting the truth about the nature and dimension of the harm done, and even formulating recommendations for changes in State policy on economic and social justice issues identified to be at the root of the violence."[118]

The cases briefly discussed in this chapter demonstrate that the situation in each country is unique, and the complexities of reality defy attempts to identify universal recommendations. The unique aspects of every country and of every historical "moment" require unique responses, as other studies have found.[119] The following are hence offered as points for discussion.

- Truth commissions, which are usually the keystones of transitional justice processes, provide the first platform for discussion of land issues within transitional justice processes. The primary focus should be on full disclosure of all property-related abuses and grievances.

- Transitional justice mechanisms should not perceive land only as a commodity to be reallocated as part of a reparations program. In countries where land access has been a root cause of conflict, it is important that the land tenure system, the land administration structures, and other regulatory aspects are examined. Where the fundamental architecture of the land tenure system is flawed, reallocating or redistributing land will not solve the problem if the system itself remains dysfunctional. While it is unlikely that transitional justice measures could complete this task on their own, they can still make a contribution to it, at least by placing the issue solidly in the public agenda.

- In some cases, informal justice mechanisms may be supported and altered as the result of the work of transitional justice mechanisms. Informal institutions will likely continue to resolve disputes over land long after the end of the transitional justice program. The influence of the principles, instruments, and vocabulary of transitional justice initiatives are therefore likely to have a lasting impact on the treatment of land issues in the country.

- Capacity-building activities of local government and nongovernmental actors should include training in ways in which local, spontaneous agreements on access to land and housing (such as local discussions on the return of IDPs to specific neighborhoods) can be supported by government. While transitional justice initiatives must be time-bound, efforts at reconciliation and dispute resolution may take decades to produce lasting results, and require sustained political commitment.

- In many cases, land issues will have an unintended impact on transitional justice initiatives. Transitional justice mechanisms may be abused by those involved in land disputes for the purpose of score settling. This experience suggests that adequate and legitimate mechanisms for the resolution of land disputes should be put in place, and that information should be shared between these mechanisms and the transitional justice initiatives in order to facilitate the detection of such score settling.

- In countries where productive land is scarce, strategies to promote "off-farm" livelihoods are an essential part of dealing with competition for land. Transitional justice mechanisms can address this, particularly where access to employment has been blocked due to systematic discrimination. Restitution of employment is a neglected opportunity in some cases.[120]

NOTES

1   See James Riddell, "Contemporary Thinking on Land Reform," Sustainable Development Department, Food and Agriculture Organization, Rome, 2000.

2   A broad definition of land issues considers such issues as social justice, economic development, and poverty reduction, as well as legal rights to land. For one example of a broad approach to the issues, see G. Dolan, "No Transformation in Kenya without Addressing the Land Question" (LL.M. dissertation, Transitional Justice Institute/The Law School, University of Ulster, Jordanstown, 2007). Property restitution in transitional contexts is one land-related question that has received critical attention to date (see, e.g., Rhodri C. Williams, "The Contemporary Right to Property Restitution in the Context of Transitional Justice," ICTJ Occasional Paper, May 2007; Rhodri Williams, "Post-Conflict Property Restitution and Refugee Return in Bosnia and Herzegovina: Implications for International Standard-Setting and Practice," *Journal of International Law and Politics* 37, no. 3 [2005]: 441–553; and Scott Leckie, ed., *Returning Home: Housing and Property Restitution Rights of Refugees and Displaced Persons* [Ardsley: Transnational Publishers, 2003]) and it is likely to be a central element of any transitional justice initiative that is sensitive to land and property rights issues. Given the existing studies of restitution programs, and the neglect of potential links to other activities, this chapter attempts to identify other elements and pays somewhat less attention to restitution than is usually the case.

3   United Nations Secretary-General, *The Rule of Law and Transitional Justice in Conflict and*

Post-Conflict Societies, S/2004/616, August 3, 2004.

4   Kirsti Samuels, "Rule of Law Reform in Post-Conflict Countries: Operational Initiatives and Lessons Learnt," Social Development Paper No. 37, Conflict Prevention and Reconstruction Division, World Bank, 2006.

5   Amartya Sen, "What Is the Role of Legal and Judicial Reform in the Development Process?" (paper presented at the World Bank Legal Conference on the Role of Legal and Judicial Reform in Development, Washington, DC, June 5, 2000).

6   Kevin E. Davis and Michael J. Trebilcock, "Legal Reforms and Development," *Third World Quarterly* 22, no. 1 (2001): 21–36.

7   See, e.g., Johan Pottier, *Re-Imagining Rwanda: Conflict, Survival and Disinformation in the Late Twentieth Century* (Cambridge: Cambridge University Press, 2002); and Ambreena Manji, *The Politics of Land Reform in Africa: From Communal Tenure to Free Markets* (London and New York: Zed Books, 2006).

8   Dolan, "No Transformation in Kenya."

9   Patrick McAuslen, *Bringing the Law Back In: Essays in Land, Law and Development* (Aldershot: Ashgate, 2003).

10 Ibid.

11 Support may come in numerous forms, including financial, technical, and diplomatic, and may be provided directly to government, through partnerships with government agencies, or indirectly through civil society.

12 Louise Arbour, "Economic and Social Justice for Societies in Transition" (Second Annual Transitional Justice Lecture, New York University School of Law Center for Human Rights and Global Justice and the International Center for Transitional Justice, New York, October 25, 2006).

13 Ibid.

14 Roger Duthie, "Toward a Development-Sensitive Approach to Transitional Justice," *International Journal of Transitional Justice* 2, no. 3 (2008): 292–309.

15 Louis Bickford, "Transitional Justice," in *The Encyclopedia of Genocide and Crimes Against Humanity*, vol. 3, ed. Dinah Shelton (Farmington Hills, MI: Macmillan, 2004), 1045–47.

16 Ibid.

17 Based on comments on an earlier draft of this chapter by Undine Whande.

18 Samuels, "Rule of Law Reform in Post-Conflict Countries."

19 Ibid.

20 Dolan, "No Transformation in Kenya."

21 See, e.g., Theo R. G. van Banning, *The Human Right to Property* (Antwerp, Oxford, and New York: Intersentia, 2002); and Patricia Kameri-Mbote and Migai Aketch, "Ownership and Regulation of Land Rights in Kenya: Balancing Entitlements with the Public Trust" (paper presented at KIPPRA workshop on land issues in Kenya, KICC, July 31, 2008).

22 For example, some members of the community might have the right to the fruit of a particular tree, while others have the right to graze their goats on the fallen leaves from the tree, and a third category could collect fallen branches for firewood. Such complex tenure systems are discussed in Edmund G. C. Barrow, "Usufruct Rights to Trees: The Role of *Ekwar* in Dryland Central Turkana, Kenya," *Human Ecology* 18, no. 2 (1990): 163–76.

23 For more on this huge topic, see, e.g., John Bruce and Shem Migot-Adholla, eds., *Searching for Land Tenure Security in Africa* (Iowa: Kendall/Hunt, 1994); van Banning, *The Human Right to Property*; H. W. O. Okoth-Ogendo, "Formalizing 'Informal' Property Systems: The Problem of Land Rights Reform in Africa" (background paper prepared for the Commission for the Legal Empowerment of the Poor, 2006); and Kameri-Mbote and Aketch, "Ownership and Regulation of Land Rights in Kenya."

24 These include the voluntary right to return to a place of origin (most recently examined in the "Pinheiro Principles" discussed below), the right to have stolen property restored or to receive compensation for destroyed property, and the rights to adequate housing and secure tenure. See, e.g., UN Committee on the Elimination of Racial Discrimination, General Recommendation no. 22 (1997), art. 5; Article 25(1) of the Universal Declaration of Human Rights (1948); and Article 11(1) of the International Covenant on Economic, Social and Cultural Rights.

25 Jon D. Unruh, "Post-Conflict Land Tenure: Using a Sustainable Livelihoods Approach," Food and Agriculture Organization, Rome, 2004.

26 Liz Alden Wily, " 'It's More Than About Going Home.' Land in Emergency to Development Transitions in Conflict States: Who Should Do What?" (paper presented at Humanitarian Policy Group [HPG]–Overseas Development Institute [ODI] conference "Uncharted Territory: Land, Conflict and Humanitarian Action," London, February 2008).

27 See, e.g., Johan Pottier, " 'Customary Tenure' in Sub-Saharan Africa Today: Meanings and Contexts," in *From the Ground Up: Land Rights, Conflict and Peace in Sub-Saharan Africa*, ed. Chris Huggins and Jenny Clover (Pretoria: African Centre for Technology Studies / Institute for Security Studies, 2005).

28 Robin Palmer, "Literature Review of Governance and Secure Access to Land" (report prepared for the UK Department for International Development [DFID], March 2007).

29 According to Weber's theory of property rights, "property arrangements are considered legitimate so long as a substantial portion of society believes so and is willing to respect and accept the disciplines and burdens of maintaining the property status quo." Cited in Bernadette Atuahene, "From Reparation to Restoration: Moving Beyond Property Rights to Restoring Political and Economic Visibility," *Southern Methodist University Law Review* 60, no. 4 (2007): 1419–70.

30 Obvious examples include South Africa, Zimbabwe, and Guatemala.

31 While ad hoc measures are often taken to reduce tensions around land, the overarching architecture of property distribution has tended to remain the same. In Kenya, e.g., "various settlement schemes, most notably the 'million acre' scheme, were devised to defuse the situation and thereby ensure that the rest of the colonial economic structure could be preserved intact." David Maughan-Brown, *Land, Freedom and Fiction: History and Ideology in Kenya* (London: Zed Books, 1985), 188.

32 Unruh, "Post-Conflict Land Tenure." See also the case of customary chiefs in North Kivu in Koen Vlassenroot and Chris Huggins, "Land, Migration and Conflict in Eastern DRC," in *From the Ground Up*.

33 At the risk of oversimplifying, land reform generally refers to a reform of landholding patterns, in which some redistribution of land takes place. This should be differentiated from *land tenure reform*, in which the legal and regulatory framework for land ownership is altered, and *agrarian reform*, in which land reform is paralleled by major changes in the economic, institutional, and technical structures of agricultural production and rural life.

34 Batty Fodei, "Pressure from Above, Below and Both Directions: The Politics of Land Reform in South Africa, Brazil and Zimbabwe" (paper presented at the annual meeting of the Southern Political Science Association, New Orleans, January 6, 2005).

35 Sen, "What Is the Role of Legal and Judicial Reform?"

36 Lionel Cliffe, "Policy Options for Land Reform in South Africa: New Institutional Mechanisms?" Institute for Poverty, Land and Agrarian Studies (PLAAS) Policy Brief No. 27, October 2007; and van Banning, *The Human Right to Property*.

37 Riddell, "Contemporary Thinking on Land Reform."

38 Hernando de Soto, *The Mystery of Capital: Why Capitalism Triumphs in the West and Fails Everywhere Else* (New York: Basic Books, 2000).

39 Okoth-Ogendo, "Formalizing 'Informal' Property Systems."

40 Van Banning, *The Human Right to Poverty*, 345, cites the well-known example of Kenya, where formalization of land tenure has become "an instrument for the rich to encroach on untitled land."

41 Stephen Baranyi, Carmen Deere, and Manuel Morales, *Land and Development in Latin America* (Ottawa: North-South Institute / International Development Research Centre [IDRC], 2004).

42 Van Banning, *The Human Right to Poverty*, 346. This is not to deny the relevance of registration as part of wider measures, depending on the economic, political, and legal context.

43 Okoth-Ogendo, "Formalizing 'Informal' Property Systems."

44 In Mozambique, e.g., the legal status of customary tenure is established not only through the land law but through the constitution, which means that a great variety of customary rights—individual and communal, rural and urban—are recognized. Edward Lahiff,

"The Politics of Land Reform in Southern Africa," Institute for Development Studies, Sustainable Livelihoods in Southern Africa Programme Research Report 19, 2003.

45   Customary systems alter over time. In some cases, community-owned land and other customary safety nets for vulnerable categories (such as separated or divorced women) have been squeezed out of existence due to land alienation, population growth, and sociopolitical changes.

46   In such places as South Africa, some traditional authorities have been associated with abuses of their powers over land since their co-optation and collaboration with the apartheid government. The South African land reform process therefore generated debates around the division of rights over land to be given to groups of local land users and the chiefs.

47   In Rwanda, e.g., some twenty-eight pieces of secondary legislation, ministerial orders, or other subsidiary regulations are being written in order to make the land law operational—a process that is still incomplete.

48   Manji, The Politics of Land Reform in Africa.

49   See Tony Addison, "The Political Economy of the Transition from Authoritarianism," in this volume.

50   Alden Wily, " 'It's More Than About Going Home.' "

51   Alvaro Del Carpio Leon, "Analysis and Improvements of the Land Restitution Process in Guatemala" (master's thesis, International Institute for Geo-Information Science and Earth Observation, the Netherlands, March 2005).

52   Craig Kauffman, "Transitional Justice in Guatemala: Linking the Past and Future" (paper prepared for the ISA-South Conference, Miami, November 3–5, 2005).

53   Access to markets is important. As Pottier has noted for Ituri, northeastern Democratic Republic of Congo (DRC), "warlords have loyal militias because they control the unfree labour of the unprotected. He who can claim a piece of land, or an entire region, can claim its people." Johan Pottier, "Emergency in Ituri, DRC: Political Complexity, Land and Other Challenges in Restoring Food Security" (paper presented at the FAO international workshop "Food Security in Complex Emergencies: Building Policy Frameworks to Address Longer-term Programming Challenges," Tivoli, September 23–25, 2003, 9–10).

54   Klaus Deininger, Land Policies for Growth and Poverty Reduction (Washington, DC: World Bank; and Oxford: Oxford University Press, 2003), 157.

55   In Sudan during the 1980s, e.g., anger at the expansion of mechanized agriculture into parts of the Southern Blue Nile and Nuba Mountains regions caused many local people to join the Sudan People's Liberation Army against the government. Chris Huggins and Benson Ochieng, "Paradigms, Processes and Practicalities of Land Reform in Post-Conflict Sub-Saharan Africa," in From the Ground Up.

56   Stephen Baranyi and Viviane Weitzner, "Transforming Land-Related Conflict: Policy, Practice, and Possibilities," Policy Brief, International Land Coalition, Rome / North-

South Institute, Ottawa, 2006.

57 Patricia Kameri-Mbote, "Righting Wrongs: Confronting Dispossession in Post-Colonial Contexts" (keynote presentation at the conference "Land, Memory, Reconstruction and Justice: Perspectives on Land Restitution in South Africa," Cape Town, September 2006). In statutory systems, it is the state that imposes the sanctions, though the property rights holder initiates the process by making a complaint to the state.

58 For agro-pastoralist and pastoralist contexts, e.g., Ben Cousins identifies several categories of users: "individuals, households, kinship groups, corporate groups, villages, communities, tribes, ethnic groups"; as well as users of different status: "owners, co-owners, primary, secondary and tertiary users, lessors and lessees, unrecognised or 'illegal' users." Ben Cousins, "Conflict Management for Multiple Resource Users in Pastoralist and Agro-Pastoralist Contexts," in *War and Rural Development in Africa*, ed. Jeremy Swift, *IDS Bulletin* 27, no. 3 (1996): 41–54.

59 Huggins and Ochieng, "Paradigms, Processes and Practicalities."

60 In the absence of effective administration by a central government in Somalia, customary institutions, local authorities, and Islamic courts have been dealing with land issues, though this has been little documented to date. Mark Bradbury, personal communication with the author, April 2008.

61 Internal Displacement Monitoring Centre, "Ensuring Durable Solutions for Rwanda's Displaced: A Chapter Closed Too Early," Global IDP Project / Norwegian People's Aid, 2005.

62 Brookings Institution/University of Bern, "Expert Seminar on Protracted IDP Situations," Geneva, June 21–22, 2007.

63 Duthie, "Toward a Development-Sensitive Approach to Transitional Justice."

64 For a wider discussion, see UN-Habitat, *Handbook on Post-Conflict Land Administration and Peacebuilding, Volume 1: Countries with Land Records* (Nairobi: UN-Habitat, 2007); Chris Huggins, "Land in Return, Reintegration and Recovery Processes: Some Lessons from the Great Lakes Region of Africa," in *Uncharted Territory: Land, Conflict and Humanitarian Action* (Humanitarian Policy Group of the Overseas Development Institute; forthcoming); Leckie, ed., *Returning Home*; African Centre for Technology Studies (ACTS), "Report of the Conference on Land Tenure and Conflict in Africa: Prevention, Mitigation and Reconstruction," ACTS, Nairobi, 2004; and Clarissa Augustinus and Michael Barry, "Strategic Action Planning in Post-Conflict Societies" (paper presented at the International Symposium on Land Administration in Post-Conflict Areas, Geneva, April 2004).

65 UN-Habitat/UN High Commissioner for Refugees, "Housing, Land and Property Rights in Post-Conflict Societies: Proposals for Their Integration into UN Policy and Operational Frameworks," Report of the Expert Meeting, Geneva, November 2004.

66 Particularly following the 2000 "Brahimi Report," which stressed the need for adequate

resources to be allocated for rule of law and human rights work both within the UN Department of Peacekeeping Operations (DPKO) headquarters and in peacekeeping operations. UN General Assembly/UN Security Council, *Comprehensive Review of the Whole Question of Peacekeeping Operations in all Their Aspects,* A/55/305-S/2000/809, August 21, 2000, cited in Scott Carlson, "Legal and Judicial Rule of Law Work in Multi-Dimensional Peacekeeping Operations: Lessons-Learned Study," UNDPKO, New York, 2006.

67 UN-Habitat, *Handbook on Post-Conflict Land Administration and Peacebuilding.*

68 John Bruce, "Drawing a Line under Crisis: Reconciling Returnee Land Access and Security of Tenure in Post-Conflict Rwanda," ODI-HPG Working Paper, June 2007.

69 International observer, Burundi, personal communication with the author, January 2008.

70 Originally framed as a right to return to one's country, the "right to return," which is enshrined in many international human rights and refugee law instruments, has in recent years been reinterpreted as an individual right to return to one's home, with compensation in lieu of return seen as a less effective remedy to be pursued only under certain conditions. See UN Commission on Human Rights, *Principles on Housing and Property Restitution for Refugees and Internally Displaced Persons,* E/CN.4/Sub.2/2005/17, June 28, 2005, commonly known as the "Pinheiro Principles."

71 Daniel Fitzpatrick, "Land Policy in Post-Conflict Circumstances: Some Lessons from East Timor," *Journal of Humanitarian Assistance* (November 2001), jha.ac/articles/a074.htm.

72 More details on claims and dispute resolution mechanisms are presented in the following section.

73 Andrew Harrington, "Ethnicity, Violence and Land and Property Disputes in Timor-Leste," *East Timor Law Journal* 2 (2006).

74 Robin Palmer, "Oxfam and Land in Post-Conflict Situations in Africa," in ACTS, "Report of the Conference on Land Tenure and Conflict in Africa."

75 Dolan, "No Transformation in Kenya."

76 Alden Wily, " 'It's More Than About Going Home.' "

77 Such is the case in Liberia, for example. See Abdul Rahman Lamin, "Truth, Justice and Reconciliation: Analysis of the Prospects and Challenges of the Truth and Reconciliation Commission in Liberia," in *A Tortuous Road to Peace: The Dynamics of Regional, UN and International Humanitarian Interventions in Liberia,* ed. Alhaji Mohamed Sirjoh Bah and Festus Boahen Aboagye (Pretoria: Institute for Security Studies, 2005).

78 Ruth Hall, "Land Restitution in South Africa: Rights, Development, and the Restrained State," *Canadian Journal of African Studies* 38, no. 3 (2004): 654–71.

79 Patrick Chabal and Jean-Pascal Daloz, *Africa Works: Disorder as Political Instrument* (Bloomington, IN: Indiana University Press, 1999).

80 UN Office of the High Commissioner for Human Rights, *Rule-of-Law Tools for Post-Conflict States: Truth Commissions* (New York and Geneva: OHCHR, 2006).

81 Ibid.

82 Ibid.

83 George Wachira and Prisca Kamungi, "Truth and Reconciliation Commissions and Transitional Justice in Africa: Lessons and Implications for Kenya," Nairobi Peace Initiative, April 2008.

84 Ibid.

85 Ibid.

86 The Truth, Justice and Reconciliation Bill, 2008 (Third Draft).

87 Rhodri Williams, "Stability, Justice and Rights in the Wake of the Cold War," in *Housing, Land, and Property Rights in Post-Conflict United Nations and Other Peace Operations*, ed. Scott Leckie (New York: Cambridge University Press, 2009).

88 These restrictive limitations on restitution claims were slightly altered following legal challenges, including from the European Court of Human Rights. Williams, "The Contemporary Right to Property Restitution."

89 Margaret Cordial and Knut Rosandhaug, "The Response of the United Nations Interim Administration Mission in Kosovo to Address Property Rights Challenges," in Leckie, ed., *Housing, Land, and Property Rights.*

90 Eric A. Posner and Adrian Vermeule, "Reparations for Slavery and Other Historical Injustices," *Columbia Law Review* 103, no. 3 (2003): 689, 691, cited in Atuahene, "From Reparation to Restoration."

91 UN Commission on Human Rights, Principle 15.

92 Williams, "The Contemporary Right to Property Restitution."

93 In particular, the opinions of women, young males, the very poor, and ethnic minorities may be undervalued.

94 Commission for Reception, Truth and Reconciliation of Timor-Leste (CAVR), *Chega! The Report of the Commission for Reception, Truth and Reconciliation of Timor-Leste* (Dili: CAVR, 2005), Executive Summary, 108–44.

95 Daniel Fitzpatrick, "Mediating Land Conflict in East Timor," in *Making Land Work, Volume II: Case Studies* (Canberra: Australia Agency for International Development, 2008).

96 Harrington, "Ethnicity, Violence and Land and Property Disputes."

97 www.cavr-timorleste.org/en/reconciliation.htm.

98 Piers Pigou, "The Community Reconciliation Process of the Commission for Reception, Truth and Reconciliation," UNDP, Dili, Timor-Leste, April 2004.

99 Jane Alexander, "A Scoping Study of Transitional Justice and Poverty Reduction," UK Department for International Development, London, January 2003.

100 Pigou, "The Community Reconciliation Process."

101 Promotion of National Unity and Reconciliation Act, Act 95-34, July 26, 1995.

102 Jon Elster, "Introduction," in *Retribution and Reparation in the Transition to Democracy*, ed. Jon Elster (Cambridge: Cambridge University Press, 2006).

103 The date of June 1913 marks the promulgation of the Native Land Act, which established racial "zones" and hence sought to legalize the dispossession of vast areas of land by the colonial government for use by white settlers.

104 Department of Land Affairs, *The Green Paper on South African Land Policy* (1996).

105 Theunis Roux, "Land Restitution and Reconciliation in South Africa" (paper presented at Special Event on Transitional Justice in South Africa, University of Cambridge, Cambridge, November 2006).

106 Lahiff, "The Politics of Land Reform."

107 Roux, "Land Restitution and Reconciliation."

108 Wachira and Kamungi, "Truth and Reconciliation Commissions."

109 Roux, "Land Restitution and Reconciliation."

110 Lahiff, "The Politics of Land Reform."

111 National Unity and Reconciliation Commission (NURC), "NURC-GTZ Conference on the Presentation of the Grassroots Consultation and Evaluation Report," Conference Report, Kigali, Rwanda, July 25, 2002.

112 In some cases, gacaca tribunals have punished those who cultivated the fields of Tutsi during the genocide, even if they did not participate in the genocide. Penal Reform International, "Le jugement des infractions contre les biens commises pendant le génocide: Le contraste entre la théorie de la réparation et la réalité socio-économique du Rwanda," rapport de monitoring et de recherche sur la Gacaca, Kigali, July 2007.

113 Confidential NGO report, Kigali, 2007. The questionnaire conflated accusations of genocide crimes with regular crimes, but it is likely, given the frequency of gacaca hearings, that genocide accusations form the majority of these cases.

114 Ph.D. candidate, personal communication with the author, August 28, 2008.

115 Independent land expert, interview with the author, Kigali, May 2008.

116 Dolan, "No Transformation in Kenya."

117 Lisa Magarrell, "Reparations for Massive or Widespread Human Rights Violations: Sorting Out Claims for Reparations and the Struggle for Social Justice," *Windsor Yearbook of Access to Justice* 22 (2003): 85–98.

118 Ibid.

119 Anga Timilsina, "Getting the Policies Right: The Prioritization and Sequencing of Policies in Post-Conflict Countries," Pardee Rand Graduate School, 2007.

120 Alexander, "A Scoping Study of Transitional Justice."